DICTIONARY OF CRYPTOZOOLOGY

by

Ronan Coghlan

Foreword by Jonathan Downes

BANGOR:
XIPHOS BOOKS
2004

ISBN: 0-9544936-1-3

Cover Design by Mark North.

I must express my thanks for help rendered to Jonathan Downes, Richard Freeman, Gary Cunningham, Neil Arnold and Tim the Yowie Man; also to my wife Mourna Lee for technical help and to my daughter Ivona for advertising input.

Published by

Xiphos Books,
1, Hillside Gardens,
BANGOR,
BT19 6SJ,
Northern Ireland.

First Edition.

Foreword

by Jonathan Downes

I have been obsessed by cryptozoology – the study of hidden animals – since I was seven years old. As a child, I had always been interested in the natural world and nature study was my favourite class in school. I was lucky enough to be brought up in Hong Kong which had – and still has – a rich and varied fauna. However, one day in 1967, my mother brought me a library book. It was essentially a children's version of Bernard Heuvelmans' seminal work *On the Track of Unknown Animals,* but it changed my life forever. The idea that there could be creatures such as the Loch Ness Monster, the yeti, Bigfoot and the giant mystery cats of Africa was fantastic; but even better was the idea that dragons and other creatures which I had read about in storybooks had some sort of corporeal reality. At the age of seven, torn between the wondrous vistas which the new book had opened up for me and obsession with the rich and curious world of C.S. Lewis's Narnia books with dragons, unicorns, satyrs and centaurs, I knew exactly what I was going to do with my life: I was going to be a monster hunter.

In 1992, I founded the Centre for Fortean Zoology, the world's only truly global cryptozoological organisation. Since then we have published nearly 40 issues of our journal, seven annual yearbooks and a large number of other books – some by me, some not. We have funded research and expeditions all over the world and I have – mostly – realised my childhood ambitions.

At the Centre for Fortean Zoology we have a large and ever growing library of cryptozoological material. We have books covering every esoteric zoological subject imaginable, but, until now, there has always been one missing. There had always –we believed – been a gap in the market for a low-priced cryptozoological dictionary which would provide an invaluable tool for researchers at all levels. We had always planned to write something of the sort ourselves. I must admit to having been mildly annoyed when my good friend Ronan Coghlan telephoned me to say he was embarking on this project. After all, I had always wanted to do it. However, when I finally read the manuscript which makes up this volume, I was both overawed and amazed. Ronan has done a far better job than I would have done. This book is not just a useful tool for the researcher, it is a major work of scholarship. Even though I have been working now as a cryptozoologist for many years, it includes cryptids that even I had not heard of. Because of this I am overjoyed – even a little humble – to have been asked to write the foreword to this book. I believe that it is going to be seen as one of the major cryptozoological texts of the early 21st Century and I am very pleased to have been involved with its inception.

Jonathan Downes,
Director, Centre for Fortean Zoology.

Introduction

By cryptozoology – a word coined by Bernard Heuvelmans (1916-2001) – is meant the study of animals known only from reports, legends and folklore and not yet recognised by the official scientific establishment. In the widest sense, cryptozoology also includes zoomythology (the study of beasts of mythology) and zooform phenomena (see glossary), not to mention animals thought extinct but which may still survive. This small dictionary endeavours to include creatures from the entire spectrum of cryptozoology. It does not, however, include legendary beasts of the dwarf or goblin kind, such as the alux and tokoloshe, accounts of which may be found in the present writer's *Handbook of Fairies* (1998).

When many people hear of animals such as the Loch Ness Monster or Bigfoot, their immediate reaction is to scoff. They are perhaps not aware that many animals have been discovered which were once thought to be mere legends until their existence was proven. These include the okapi, mountain gorilla and giant forest hog, all as legendary as the yeti today before their existence was verified. In the late 20th Century a number of large new animals emerged from the forests of Vietnam, their existence hitherto unsuspected. These included the Vu Quang ox or saola and two varieties of muntjac. If animals of that size can thrive unknown in a jungle that was crisscrossed by fighting soldiers, there is no reason to suppose that nature hides no other large creatures as yet beyond our ken. Even the most orthodox of scientists will admit that many smaller creatures await discovery. Goodness knows what the vasty deeps of the Ocean conceal. One thinks in this connection of the coelecanth, supposedly extinct for 65 million years, but discovered in modern times to be alive and well.

A work like this is reliant on its sources and the present writer cannot vouch for the accuracy of every report mentioned.

The International Society of Cryptozoology, founded in 1992, now appears sadly moribund. However, there remain sundry organisations dealing with the subject. In particular, a flourishing body which the present writer can recommend heartily is:

Centre for Cryptozoology,
15, Holne Court,
Exwick,
EXETER,
EX4 2NA,
England.
telephone/fax: 001392 424811
e-mail: cfz@eclipse.co.uk
website: http://www.cfz.org.uk

Its tireless founder, Jonathan Downes, despite a plethora of health problems, has built it into a vigorous and truly international organisation.

GLOSSARY

ape In English, this term is confined to large, tailless monkeys: the gorilla, orang-utan, gibbon, siamang, chimpanzee and bonobo. However, the word was originally synonymous with *monkey* and this is reflected in the term Barbary ape, which in fact designates a species of monkey.

cryptid A supposed animal studied in cryptozoology.

felid In everyday English *feline* is used as both a noun and an adjective; but technically zoologists insist on using *felid* for the noun; likewise **canid**, **equid**, etc.

lagomorph A hare or rabbit.

melanistic Black in colour, as the result of too much eumelanin.

monotreme An egg-laying mammal.

octopuses Correct plural of *octopus*. The use of *octopi* is wrong, but the somewhat archaic *octopodes* is permissible.

orang Malay, "man", used as the first part of the names of cryptids in Malaysia.

orang-utan This ape is also known in the forms *orang-utang, orang-outang*, but *orang-utan* is far preferable, the others being based on mishearings of the original Malay term.

oviparous Egg-laying.

panther A rather confusing term. These days, in Europe, it is applied to the leopard, especially the black (melanistic) one. Thus the term *black panther* would signify a black leopard. However, in the United States panther is used to signify a puma and many of those who speak of "black panthers" mean black pumas – though black pumas are virtually unknown.

tulpa In Tibetan lore, a sort of mental projection of a creature which takes on an actual form.

viviparous Bringing forth young alive.

zooform phenomenon A preternatural phenomenon in animal shape.

Animal related adjectives (The name of the animal concerned follows the adjective)

bovine cow	**pithecoid** ape
caprine goat	**porcine** pig
cervine deer	**simian** ape or monkey
cetacean whale	**struthious** ostrich
corvine crow	**ursine** bear
equine horse	**vespertilian** bat
gallinaceous hen	**vulpine** fox
hircine goat	
ichthyous fish	
lupine wolf	

Abbreviations in text

ABC Alien Big Cat, i.e., a large felid roaming where, according to usually received wisdom, such cats are not to be found.

BHM Big Hairy Monster, i.e., a large humanoid beast such as bigfoot, covered in hair.

The two countries today called the Congo are distinguished by their capitals – Kinshasa and Brazzaville.

A

AARE SERPENT A large serpentine monster with four feet was alleged to have emerged from this Swiss river in 1480 and it was regarded as a portent of the floods which followed.   [M7]

AAURATA In medieval belief, a fish whose head shone like gold.   [151]

ABANAUAYU A term, meaning 'man of the forest', applied to wildmen in the Caucasus. The most famous member of this species was no wildman but a wild woman called Zana, who was captured in the 19th Century. She had previously been owned by other individuals before she became the prisoner of Edgi Geneba, a farmer, who initially kept her in an enclosure, though she was later permitted to wander freely. Her body was covered in hair and her face singularly intimidating, while her expression was definitely animal rather than human. She started giving birth to half-human children. At first she would bathe them in the cold river and the human element in their nature was unable to withstand this and they would die. This led the villagers to take further babies from her. She had two sons and two daughters, who seemed completely human, though perhaps a little odd. The youngest died in 1954 and all had descendants. There seem to have been dark, almost negroid, features amongst their offspring. G. Krantz examined the skull of one of the grandsons and asserted that it lacked neanderthaloid features. One suggestion is that Zana was a primitive *Homo sapiens* belonging to a group of hidden Mesolithic humans.

   In this region there are various stories of humans keeping BHMs as pets. Khabas Kardanov encountered a BHM who had apparently been tamed and she eventually moved into his house after he had been feeding her. She developed the embarrassing habit of stealing tomatoes for Kardanov.

   It was probably a member of this race that was examined by Russian military doctor V.S. Karapetian in the Caucasus in 1941. The creature had the vacant stare of an animal, seemed incapable of speech and was covered in fur like a bear's. The lice crawling on it were unlike those which favour humans with their presence.   [B3]

ABADAN SEA SERPENT This beast was reported from Abadan on the Persian Gulf in 1939 by the captain of the *British Power.* Its head was described as horselike and it topped a long neck.   [H12*]

6

ABASAMBO A legendary big cat in Ethiopian folklore, perhaps identical with mystery big cats reported from other African countries.   [61]

ABATH A one-horned beast, thought by some to be a female unicorn, said to come from Malaysia.

ABOMINABLE SNOWMAN A term used initially for the yeti and subsequently extended to other unidentified creatures of a similar nature. We owe this term to one Henry Newman writing in the *Calcutta Statesman* in 1921. *See* **Yeti.**

ABREMON A fish in the lore of the Middle Ages which gave birth parthenogenuously and sheltered her young in her abdomen in stormy weather.   [151]

ABU SOTAN A wild member of the cat family with stripes or blotches, said to live near the River Rahad in Sudan. K. Shuker considers it to be identical with the wobo of Ethiopia.   [A7]

ACHI Term for a hominid used in Venezuela. [#4]

ACHILL WOLF After the extinction of the wolf in Ireland in the 18th Century, a vague legend grew up that a population of small wolves persisted on Achill Island off the west coast.

ACHIYALABOPA In the legends of the Pueblo Indians, a huge bird with sharp wings.
                    [B7]

ACIPENSER Zoologists of yore believed in this fish. Its scales were reversed and it swam against the stream.   [H12]

ADAM-JAPAIS A local name for a wildman in the Pamir region. [T1]

ADARO A horned merman of Melanesian lore. The horn resembles a shark's fin and it has fins on its feet. It has a prong on its head and gills. The adaro is thought to be hostile to men; it will shoot at them, using flying fish as missiles. Although a sea creature, local lore makes the home of the adaro the sun, whence they travel to earth on rainbows. [C12]

ADLET *see* **Human-Dog Hybrid.**

ADNE SADEH In Jewish lore, this extraordinary beast looks just like a man, but he is no man, but an animal. He is fastened to the ground by an umbilical cord. Should this be severed, he will die. He eats anything that comes within snatching distance and anything he can reach on the ground.   [G4]

AFA A legendary creature said to inhabit the marshes of southern Iraq. It was supposed to have legs and to be dangerous.   [C25]

AFANC A water dwelling creature in Welsh lore. The original form of the word was *avac*, corresponding to Irish *abhac*, 'dwarf', originally a water-dwelling dwarf connected with *abha*, 'river'. The word *avac* was changed to *afanc*, meaning a beaver. The afanc seems to have been humanoid, as it was able to throw a spear. An afanc was said to dwell on the River Conwy. It was captured, enchained and placed in a pool, probably Glaslyn in Snowdonia. An afanc in Llyn Barfog was said to have fought with King Arthur. Some confusion exists concerning a story about an afanc and a hero called Hu Gadarn. This is a late and artificial tale and Hu Gadarn is not a genuine character of early Welsh tradition.   There is supposed to be an afanc buried near the village of Brynberian, according to T. Roberts *Myths and Legends of Wales* (1984). The suggestion that the afanc was originally conceived as a monster of the Loch Ness kind seems mistaken. [U2]

AGATCH-KISHI Karachai term for a wildman.

AGOGWE Small hairy manlike beasts reported to live in Tanzania. A Captain Hichens, writing in 1937, claimed to have seen them. According to native lore, if you leave beer and food out for them, they will do gardening work for you in return. They may be identical with the "little red men" of which S.V. Cook had written in 1924 or the "little brown men" observed by C. Burgoyne amongst a group of baboons in Mozambique in 1927. The symbiosis that obtained between them and the baboons is certainly interesting. B. Heuvelmans has suggested they might be surviving australopithecines..   [H9]

AGOPOGO Name given by a journalist to the South Saskatchewan River Monster.

AGRIOGOUROUNO A were-boar in Greek folklore. [S17]

AGROPELTER A humanoid in North American folklore, which seems to have been particularly well-known to loggers. They are said to live about the Great Lakes and will attack humans and other animals by throwing wood at them.   [R7]

AGTA A race in Filipino belief, consisting of huge arboreal black men. [4]

AHAMAGACHKTIAT A legendary animal in the traditions of the Mohegan Indians. It is probably the same as the Unami *amangachktiat*. Both signify a large-rumped animal and we may be dealing here with the memory of some extinct American mammal such as the mammoth or short-faced bear.

AHIFATUMOANA Tahitian term for the sea serpent.

AHLUS An alternative name for duendes in Belize.   [R7]

AHO-AHO An unidentified creature looking something like a sheep in Guarani lore. [#12]

AHOOL *see* **Athol.**

A HOO LA HUL Yupik Indian name for BHM.

AHUIZOTL A strange water creature in Aztec lore, having features reminiscent of both monkey and dog, with a hand on the end of its tail. It uses this tail to capture people and pull them into the water, for it wishes to take their eyes, teeth and nails. If this creature has a basis in reality, the hand on the tail is perhaps a fictional addition because said tail is used by the ahuizotl to drag people to their watery doom.   [B10]

AIDAKAR A monster reported from Lake Kol-Kol in Kazakhstan. It is said to be 48'/15m long. [C1]

AIGAMUXO A monstrous race in the legends of the Khoi-khoi (Hottentots). They seem to be humanoid and they have long teeth with which they eat people. They are said to have eyes in their heels.   [B10]

AIGULA Mystery beast of France which had been killing people with its teeth until killed itself in 1766. It was said to have eyes at the end of its snout. Locals averred it was an ape. Apes, however, lack snouts and, even if they didn't, they would hardly have eyes on the end of them.   [#8]

AIKORA LIZARD In 1906 near the Aikora River in New Guinea, some miners discovered caves and averred they contained hairy or furry lizards of large size. [S5]

AJATAR A kind of dragon from Finnish legend, notable for spreading disease. [26]

AKAWAI A hominoid in the lore of the Arawak Indians of South America and Cuba, also called the *araidai.*   [R7]

AKHLUT The Eskimo believe that this is a killer whale that comes ashore and assumes the form of a wolf. Its lupine tracks can be traced from the coast. [4]

AKRON CREATURE Two witnesses in 1960 in Akron (Ohio) claimed to have seen a large creature with bat-like wings walking, with apparent unconcern, up the road. Various rumours have credited similar creatures with living in an area called The Gorge near here.   [144]

AKWE'TIYI A legendary beast of the Cherokee that once dwelt in the Tuckasegee River (North Carolina).   [119]

AL In early times the Persians believed in the *al*, which they regarded as a humanoid with huge tusks and fiery eyes. In modern times the term remains in use amongst the Afghans, but is now applied to necrophagous female creatures.   [120]

ALABAMA APE-MAN This creature resembles a chimpanzee, but has the upright stance of a human. It is said to inhabit the north-eastern area of the state, which contains woods.   [148]

ALABAMA TROGLODYTES These 4'/1.2m tall hair-covered creatures seem to have emerged from caves near Huntsville (Alabama) and aroused the chagrin of the local farmers by killing cattle. A sheriff and deputies chased them back into the caves. Unfortunately, the account is completely lacking in names and dates. [D9]

ALAKWIS Amongst the Bella Coola Indians, a term for humans who, over the generations, have lost their humanity and become hairy. [M6]

ALASKAN TAILED MAN According to an article that appeared in *Alaska Life* in 1944, one Frank Read found, attacking a fish trap on the Alaskan coast, a creature with a human-sized head, a neck, narrow shoulders, strong arms ending in long claws and a body which tapered into a tail reminiscent of a snake's. The creature swam away in human fashion.   [F3]

ALASTYN A form of the Manx *cabyll uisce* or water horse which can assume human form, but which retains its horse's ears.   [4]

ALBAWITCH A term used around Columbia (Pa.) for a bigfoot-type creature. [90]

ALDINE CREATURE A creature that has been reported in Aldine (Texas) for over twenty years. One observer said it was furry, about 3'/1m tall and bore some resemblance to a goat. It proceeded with a wobbling gait and may have been injured.   [145]

AL-FANTAS MONSTER The body of an unidentified creature was washed up on the shores of Kuwait in 1997 and was given this name. It bore a strange resemblance to a human and was at first mistaken for a dead person. [32 35]

ALICANTO A bird in Chilean legend that comes in two varieties – the gold and the silver. Alicantos eat gold or silver, depending on their variety. They cannot fly because of their heavy metal diet. A prospector following an alicanto in the hope that it will lead him to the source of its provender should tread carefully, for, if it realises it is being followed, it may lead its pursuer into a chasm.   [B10]

ALIEN BIG CAT A general term used to cover large felids seen roaming where they are not supposed to be. The majority of the sightings seem to be of the puma (*Panthera concolor*) or the black panther (*Panthera pardus*). The use of the term panther has caused some confusion in the United States, where it is used to mean a puma. A black panther is not a black puma, but a panther (leopard) affected with melanism (the black equivalent of albinism).
  In Britain such sightings really began with those of the famous Surrey Puma, reported but unapprehended in 1964. Since then many large cats have been reported; *see* **Beast of Exmoor; Beast of Bodmin; Beast of Gloucester**. Two acts of Parliament, the

Dangerous Wild Animals Act (1976) and the Wildlife and Countryside Act (1981) made it much more difficult to keep exotic felids and it is likely that some were released and even bred. D. Francis maintains that there is an unknown species of big cat which is native to Britain, but it is difficult to argue from such a standpoint. Another theory is that a race of large feral domestic cats has developed. Some of the animals noted may be the Jungle cat (*Felis chaus*) which can interbreed with domestics. It is possible that some of the sightings are of leopard-cats (*Felis bengalensis*), originally imported to interbreed with domestics to produce the domestic breed known as the Bengal cat. The situation in Britain has been somewhat complicated by allegations that lynxes are purposely being let loose in the countryside for hunting purposes.

In the United States, some of the large mystery cats reported may be relict pumas or pumas returning to areas whence man had once driven them. The black cats seen may be a different matter, as black pumas seem virtually unknown. Indian traditions speak of black cats the size of pumas but distinct from them; *see* **Devil Cat**; *see also* **Wooleneag**. In a country the size of America, relict populations might have thriven in remote places and now be extending their range.

Puma and black panther-type cats have also been reported from Australia. From about 1978 the Cordering cougar was the subject of much discussion in Western Australia. Earlier, in 1972, black panthers had been reported from the same state. Rare Fauna Research of Victoria has collected about 3000 reports of puma-like animals. In New South Wales, considerable attention was drawn to the Emmaville Panther between 1958-62 and again from 1969-72. M. Smith reckons there is one kind of cat only and the "black panthers" are melanistic pumas, but melanistis pumas are virtually or completely unknown. Healy and Cropper point out that these animals do not exist in Aboriginal lore. The implication is that they have been introduced. According to the *Sydney Sun-Herald* (2nd November, 2003) an inquiry has established that it is more likely than not that there is a colony of big cats outside Sydney.

There have also been alien big cat reports in a number of European countries, notably France and Germany. New Zealand has had reports of black panther type cats in Mid-Canterbury. [B4 F8 F9 H6 S11]

ALKALI LAKE MONSTER A large monster said to dwell in this Nebraska lake (now known as Lake Walgren). It comes ashore at times to sample the local cattle. It has a stink about it – possibly something to do with halitosis – which can actually kill people. Its mouth is huge and it once swallowed an island in the lake where Indians took refuge from it. It has not been reported since the 1920s. [B7]

ALKLAHA A huge monster, according to dwellers in Siberia. Winged, it seems to be darkness personified, for it swallows the moon each month and the sun whenever possible. [134]

ALKONOST A bird with a human face in Russian legend. It lays its eggs in the water and calm follows, but, when the eggs hatch, a storm occurs. [4]

AL-KUBARA A possible Algerian hominoid sighted by Tim Cash and others in 1972. The creature was known to the locals and regarded as harmless. [70]

ALLIER MONSTER A black monster with three heads was reported from this river in France about 1934.   [E]

ALLIGATOR MAN A giant creature combining features of both man and alligator was reported in New Jersey in 1973. [C18]

ALLOPECOPITHICUM Athanasius Kircher in his *Arca Noe* (1675) considered this creature not alone to exist, but to be the hybrid of a wolf and an ape. Maybe some report of a baboon lies behind the creature.

ALMAS The wildman or BHM of Mongolia. The term has been extended to apply to such creatures elsewhere in Asia. Amongst the Kazakhs, the term *almast* is used. Around 1906 an almas was spotted by a Russian caravan led by B.B. Baradiyn. Amongst the Mongols almas were regarded as evil-smelling and shaggy. Old females tended to be left to themselves and to dwell in thickets of saxaul bushes. Mongolian soldiers claimed they had shot almas on the Chinese-Mongolian border in 1940.   Nagnit, a pharmacy manager in Ulan Bator, told the respected Professor Rinchen that he had once had a clear view of an almas. Almas tend to be speedy, able to outrun camels. They are not generally considered aggressive.   [T1]

ALMASTY The Kabarindian term for the wildman. It is probably of the same species as other wildmen reported from the Caucasus and its name was probably influenced by the Mongolian term *almas*, but that does not necessarily mean they are identical. An illustration taken from descriptions of almasty shows a protruberant face that is comparatively hairless. The almasty seems to have an appetite for carrion and the placenta of animals that have given birth. They will also consume small animals and vegetable   and   mineral   matter.   They   will   purloin   human   edibles. [B3 M6]

ALOR-SOLOR CAT A creature reported from the islands of Alor and Solor in Indonesia. It is the size of a domestic cat, but it is said to have two little knobs, somewhat like horns, on its head.   [S8]

ALTAMAHA-HA The Tama Indians, before ever the paleface trod the banks of the River Altamaha in Georgia, claimed it boasted a serpentine monster. In the 1920s, white men started reporting this too. A witness in 1959 estimated it at 35'/10.5m. Around 1970 two witnesses stated its face was protruberant, it had a triangular ridge on the top of its body, a dorsal fin and was 10-12'/3.5m long. In 1980 witnesses saw the creature trying to free itself from some mud. The men could make out about 20'/6m of it and again its back's triangularity is mentioned. A couple on one occasion saw what they thought to be a young of the monster on the riverbank. The animal has also been reported from the river's tributaries.

In all, there have been at least 350 reports of the creatures, indicating a population rather than a single animal, which would account for diversities in description. [M8]

ALULA WHALE A brown killer whale with white speckles and some singularity of shape, which has been observed in the Gulf of Aden. [B6]

AMAJUNGI *see* **Kakundari.**

AMALI A mystery African animal mentioned by A.A. Smith (better known as "Trader Horn"). He took it to be identical with the jago-nini. He claimed to have seen its footprints, which were five-clawed and the size of a good frying pan. It is perhaps identical with mokele-mbembe. [C10]

AMAM A huge snake in the sea in Micronesian mythology, so big, it is said, you can sail into it, only realising what you have done when you can no longer see the stars. [4]

AMAROK A huge wolf in the legends of the Eskimo of Greenland. One actually seems to have been killed and its skin now reposes in Copenhagen Museum. It may be identical with the *waheela* of northern Canada. [S4]

AMARTOQ Man-eating headless giants in whom the Eskimo believe. If there is any real creature behind this legend, it may be one that holds its head below the level of its shoulders, making it difficult to discern. [B7]

AMBIZE A 500 pound legendary fish, sought after by those of piscatorial bent in central Africa. It is said to taste of pork. [H*]

AMERICAN LION In the United States and occasionally in Canada, lions looking like African lions – males, females and cubs – have been reported. In the 18th Century maned lions were reported from New York state and Pennsylvania. Indians told the Dutch settlers on Manhattan Island of maned male cats. In 1836 one was observed in West Virginia. A more recent example to be found was Nellie the lioness in Illinois in 1917. A male lion was reported from the same region at the same time. Neither cat was captured.

A lion was seen at Elkhorn Falls (Indiana) in 1948. He was similar to a maned beast seen later on a couple of occasions with what appeared to be a black panther. A maned lion was seen in Ontario in 1960, one surfaced in Florida in 1978, one showed up in Ohio in 1984, one in Texas in 1985 and another in Ohio in 1992. Other Ohio sightings were in 1959, 1971, 1977 and 2002 (the latter, resembling a lioness, might have been a puma). Surprisingly, maned lions with stripes were reported in California in 1868, in Mexico in 1940 and in Pennsylvania in 1986. These are not features of the usual African and Asian lions.

Loren Coleman thinks these sightings may be due to the survival of the American lion (*Panthera leo atrox*), a considerably larger species than its Old World counterparts. It is supposed to have become extinct 10,000 years ago. Although Old World lions live in prides, the American lion was a less gregarious animal.

Loren Coleman, because of a sighting of a male lion with a black felid, has thought the "black panthers" sometimes seen in the US might be females of the species.

However, such extreme sexual dimorphism is unlikely. Moreover, animals described as lionesses, but of a tan colour, have also been observed.   [C19]

AMERICAN PTEROSAUR Various reports indicate that there may be surviving pterosaurs in the United States. One of the best-known ones is centred in Arizona. Here in 1890 the *Tombstone Epitaph* published a story saying ranchers encountered a pterosaur on the ground. It seemed infirm and unwell, for it was trying to take off and not succeeding. It had leathery wings, a beakful of teeth, was 92' long and had a wingspan of 160'. The ranchers shot it to death. However, H. McClure, who had known the ranchers concerned, said the story was inaccurate: the beast's wingspan was much smaller and the ranchers had not managed to kill it.

An encounter with a pair of apparently featherless winged creatures took place in Pennsylvania in 1981 and it is suggested that they were pterosaurs.

A creature of this nature was once supposed to dwell in Lake Elizabeth (California). Major H. Bell described it in 1855. It gave a hissing, screaming roar and had huge batlike wings. It didn't smell too enticingly, either. Don Felipe Rivera some time later shot at it fruitlessly with his revolver. Later, Rivera claimed to have observed it flying towards Arizona and it was seen no more.

However, it is in Texas, around Raymondville and Brownsville, that we must look for most pterosaur reports. In February, 1976, a creature with pterosaur-like features was seen by two witnesses near Brownsville. A few days later a similar creature was seen near San Antonio by three teachers. They estimated its wingspan at 15-20'/5m. Imagine the shock of A. Guajatdo (of Brownsville) when he turned on the lights of his station wagon to see a horrid creature with bat-like wings and a beak 2-4'/60cm-1.2m long. In 1983, between Raymondville and Brownville, J. Thompson saw a flying creature with featherless wings and a 5-6'/1.5-1.83m wingspan. Earlier, in 1976, a beakless creature, its face reminiscent of a bat's or monkey's, had flown at A. Grimaldo of Raymondville and tried to carry him off. Is this a different creature or had it lost its beak in a mishap? Or did the other creatures in this area really have beaks and could they have been some kind of bat? It is possible that these Texan creatures have their home across the border in Mexico's little-explored Sierra Madre Oriental. [S6 K9]

Supplementary note: There is a common belief that there once appeared in the *Tombstone Epitaph* a photograph of a pterosaur's cadaver nailed to a door with sundry cowboys standing around. Although quite a number of people seem to remember seeing this photograph, no one has been able to produce a copy. There is no copy in the *Tombstone Epitaph's* archives.

AMERICAN TIGER There have been various reports of tigers in America. For those in the Okefenokee Swamp, *see* **Okefenokee Tiger.** Other reports include a sighting in 1767 when J. Carver saw what he called the "tiger of America" on an island in the Chippewa River, Wisconsin. In 1823 there was a report of a brindled animal described as a tiger from Russelville (Kentucky). A large striped cat was reported in Kentucky in the 1970s. A big cat with brown stripes was seen near Marlington, West Virginia, in 1977. In 1986 tiger-like animals were reported from Pennsylvania and there were similar reports from Ohio in 1994. In all of this, it is important to remember that, at least sometimes, santer cats were described as striped.   [C19]

AMHULUK A monster said to be found in Forked Mountain Lake (Oregon). [C/H]

A-MI-KUK A long-armed leathery sea animal which supposedly haunts the Bering Straits according to the Eskimo. It will chase you to the shore and, should it fail to catch you, it can swim through land as well.   [M7]

AMORPHOUS CREATURE A strange creature observed by a diver in the South Pacific in the 1950s. He was watching a shark when a slowly pulsating brown mass arose from the depths and, coming up underneath the shark, absorbed it into its ill-defined shape and then sank once more into the waters whence it had come. What this creature was none can say, but K.P.N. Shuker plausibly suggests a huge jellyfish of unknown species.   [S13]

AMPHIPTERE This creature had a head like a dragon's, a snake's body and small wings. It had two tongues, one shaped like an arrow. One was supposed to have been in the vicinity of Hensham (Essex) in 1669, but it was of a timid disposition. [S3]

AMPHISBAENA A snake with a head at each end. The name was first used by Nicander. It is mentioned by the writer Lucan in his *De Bello Civilis* (popularly known as *Pharsalia*), a work of mixed fact and fiction. People certainly believed in this creature, but Sir Thomas Browne hotly denied the possibility of its existence. In Puritan North America, however, a snake with heads at both ends was discovered in the time of Cotton Mather at Newbury, Massachussetts.

A'NASA An animal reported from Sudan in the 19th Century. It had a single horn like an unicorn, a thick body, coarse hair and a tail like a boar's. It was the size of a small donkey and supposed to be edible. C. Gould says it was also called *nillekma* or *arase*. [G5]

ANCIENT ONE A creature of the Black Lake in Estonia. This lake, so runs the tale, had no fish in it. Then one day it was dragged and a creature resembling a hairy, yellow fish was discovered. The fishermen took it ashore, but the waters of the lake rose up to overwhelm them, so they hastily returned their catch to its depths.   [M7]

ANDEAN WOLF This creature, probably an unidentified member of the dog family, has been reported from Chile.   [30]

ANFISH A hairy and dangerous creature reported from the marshes of southern Iraq. [C25]

ANGEOA A huge monster in Eskimo legend, said to reside in Dubawnt Lake in northern Canada.   [K4]

ANGOUB In Huron lore, a term applied both to sea-monsters and lake monsters. [B15]

ANGULO According to Purchas (died 1626), a fish found in the River Congo. It doesn't taste like fish, but like pork, and devours the herbage of the river bank. [H12]

ANHANGA Preternatural deer with fiery eyes in the lore of the Amazon. It is regarded as a protector of nature. [4]

ANI-ANI An 18'/5.5m hairy humanoid with a rank smell in the folklore of the Zambalo of the Philippines. He is said to be able to change from beast to man and from man to beast. [R1]

ANKA A huge bird in Arabian lore, now believed extinct. It ate children and anything else it could carry off. [120]

ANKERDINE BEAST *see* **Worcestershire Mystery Animal**.

ANTARCTIC KILLER WHALE This creature, whose scientific status remains unknown, was seen in Prydz Bay (Antarctica) in 1980. [E]

ANTARCTIC NARWHAL There aren't supposed to be narwhals in the Antarctic, but some were allegedly espied there during the Dundee Expedition of 1892-3. [S5]

ANTARCTIC WHALE A whale, unknown to science, in length 20-30'/6-9m with a slender dorsal fin, has been described on a number of occasions in southerly waters. A sketch was made in 1902. It may range as far north as Chile. [B6]

ANTHIAS A kind of fish described by Aelian. If one of their number succumbed to the angler's hook, the others would come to its rescue.

APALALA A water-monster, perhaps serpentine, in Buddhist legend. He lived in the River Swat. [K5]

APAMANDI Bakunu name for the kikomba. [H7].

APEMAN Creatures called apemen appear in the folklore of Belize. They look like humans, but their footprints are simian. [R7]

APOTAMKIN A monstrous hairy fanged creature in the beliefs of the Passamaquoddy and other Indians. It is used as a bogeyman figure. [4]

APOTHARNUS A combination of horse and man, mentioned by C. Wolfhart in *Chronicles of Prodigies and Apparitions* (1557). Females of this species are bald and bearded. They favour a watery habitat.

ARABIAN OSTRICH   This struthious bird was regarded as extinct from the 1940s. However, a dead one was discovered in 1962, so it may still exist.   This bird was also known as the Syrian ostrich.   [B6]

ARAIDAI *see* **Akawai.**

ARASSAS Alternative name for the tatzelwurm.

ARENOTELICON A creature with a serrated ridge down its back, looking somewhat like an hyena or tiger and once supposed to live in Europe's forests. It was said one was captured in Germany about 1530.   [65]

ARGALAN-ZAN Amongst the Buryats of Siberia, this creature was held to be the Prince of Animals in the olden times. It was possibly the mammoth. Informed of the oncoming Flood, he declined to board the boat on which the animals were to be saved, thinking himself too large to drown. He wasn't.   [137]

ARGENTINE HOMINOID An apelike creature blamed for attacks on people and livestock near Arroyo Salado not far from Rosario de la Frontera, Argentina, in 2003. It was described by one Demetrio Villabo as huge, bipedal, covered in hair and with hands that ended in claws. A hunt in February 2003 appeared to disturb the creature, which was vaguely made out amidst the trees. It seems to have killed a pursuing dog. We may actually be dealing here with a ground sloth rather than an hominoid.[54 #9]

ARIMASPIAN In ancient Greek lore, the Arimaspians were a one-eyed race who stole gold from the griffins. They may be the same as the Erh Fu of Chinese lore. It has been suggested that they were miners and the single eyes were lamps carried on the head. Aeschylus speaks of them as horsemen. They have been depicted as hairy wildmen, leading to the suggestion that they were of the almas type.   [C26]

ARIZONA CREATURE A sighting of this creature was reported in the *Arizona Champion* in 1888. Its head resembled a fox's, its body and tail were canine and its neck was like a deer's. Local Mexicans were said to be familiar with the animal.

ARKANSAS CREATURE A man-like creature (or, as some suggested, a very strange man) reported from Arkansas in 1972. It was observed in the neighbourhood of Springdale and was of such an alarming appearance that one P. Ragland actually took a pot shot at it. On 20th July a Mrs Humphrey encountered what she claimed was the biggest thing she had ever clapped eyes on, which walked sometimes on two legs, sometimes on all fours. Bill Hurst saw it and was particularly impressed by its large eyes.

ARLINGTON ANIMAL This unidentified creature was on the loose in Arlington (Virginia) in 1974. It lacked hair and a tail and had big teeth. It killed a number of pets. [B9]

ARRAN SEA-CREATURE This beast was seen in 1931, taking its ease on rocks on the shore of the Scottish island of Arran. It looked like a seal, but had a beak like a parrot. Perhaps it was an elephant seal (*Mirounga*).   [146]

ARRANCALRNGUAS A creature said to look like a winged dog in the folklore of Honduras. Its name signifies 'ripper of tongues'. It is said to pull out the tongues of its victims with its tail.   [A]

ARTRELLIA Artrellias are large lizards reported by the natives of Papua-New Guinea. They are said to be 30'/9m long and to lurk in trees with a view to dropping on unexpecting prey. J. Blashford-Snell obtained what was supposedly a young artrellia, which was identified as a Salvadori's monitor (*Varanus salvadori*), but these animals do not reach the length ascribed to the artrellia. This leaves us with three possibilities: the natives were wrong about the length of the artrellia, the artrellia is a new subspecies of Salvadori's monitor or the lizard obtained by Blashford-Snell was not, in fact, an artrellia. [35]

ARULATAQ Huge, long-haired hominoids of Alaska.   [30]

ARWE A monstrous serpent of Ethiopian legend. A young girl had to be sacrificed to it each year, until the hero Angabo slew it. It was also called Waynata. [M10]

ASPIDOCHELONE In the *Physiologus*, a creature which combines elements of snake and turtle.   [H8]

ASTOMI A peculiar species of human of which Pliny speaks. They had no mouths and derived nutriment from smells, but strong smells caused them to perish. They were to be found at the source of the Ganges.

ATAHSAIA Zuni Indian name for BHM.

ATHOL A large bat-like creature said to have a wingspan of 12'/3.66m. Its face has been compared with a monkey's. Very rare, it lives in caves and is mainly a fish-eater. Its feet are said to be back to front, which is consistent with a bat's habit of hanging upside down. While it isn't certain the creature is a bat, most evidence, apart from the fact that it is much larger than any known bat, points in that direction. The athol, if it exists, is indigenous to Java. Its cry was supposedly heard by E. Bartels in 1927. [C13]

ATHOL MONSTER A monster seen in Lake Ontario off Athol Township according to a report in the *Prince Edward Gazette* in 1842. Its head was about 4' out of the water, it had a distinctive ring around its neck and it was estimated at 30-40'/9-12m long.

A 'TIX? A huge animal in the folklore of the Kaska Indians of British Columbia. It was hairy, had tusks and resembled pictures of an elephant. It was supposed to eat people. It sounds like a reminiscence of a mammoth.   [130]

ATLAS BEAR A subspecies of brown bear (*Ursus arctos crowtheri*) which may still exist in the Atlas Mountains of North Africa.

ATSHEN *see* **Windigo.**

ATURKI A monster supposed to inhabit the Williamette River in Oregon, according to the lore of the Kalapuya Indians.   [F1]

AU ANGI-ANGI A bipedal reptile, 20'/6m in length. It has large eyes. Its tail is long and slim. Its skin is reminiscent of a crocodile's. The forelegs are small, the hind legs thick. It is said to be found in Lake Murray, Papua-New Guinea.   It may be identical with the artrellia.   [#4]

AUL A large unidentified bat, said to inhabit Java.   [#4]

AULLAY A huge creature which resembled a horse with a trunk. It was said to be as much bigger than an elephant as an elephant was bigger than a sheep. This mighty beast comes from Indian mythology and was ridden by a giant named Baly. Readers of T.H. White's *The Sword in the Stone* (1938) may remember thet Madam Mim turns herself into one of these creatures.   [B13]

AUSTRALIAN GIANT According to Rex Gilroy, the Aborigines once believed in giant hominoids that lived in Australia. Around Townsville they were called *Narragun*, elsewhere the names *Illenkanpaska* and *Bullo* were used. A different type of giant was the *Goolagah*, which Gilroy thinks may have been like a gigantopithecus. [G3]

AUSTRALIAN PTEROSAUR Pterodactyl-like creatures are said to figure in the legends of the Aborigines. One of these was said to have lived in the area of the Murray River and to have attacked a village, killing two tribesmen, in retaliation for the stealing of its baby. A sighting is said to have taken place in 1994 when a couple saw something with a 30-50'/9-15m wingspan flying over Perth. It was larger than any bird. It had a reddish-brown leathery skin and a long tail. [G3 2]

AYPA An animal reported from Brazil in the 18th Century. It was described as looking like a tiger with large teeth. Its body was covered with scales.   [S7]

AZEMAN Female werewolf in the lore of Suriname.   [4]

AZHI DAHAKA In the Zoroastrian religion, a dragon created by the evil god Ahriman and chained up by the hero Atar, who will finally kill it when it breaks free. This dragon was depicted with three heads and huge wings which obscured the stars.   [134]

AZ-I-WU-GUM-KI-MUKH-'TI According to Eskimo tradition, a scaly animal of slender build, whose head is somewhat canine and whose tail lands a lethal blow. It is found among herds of walrus.   [M7]

B

BADAK TANGGILING *see* **Scaled Rhinoceros**.

BADAVA A curious creature of Indian myth, composed of flame, with a horse's head. [D1]

BADGER-LIKE ANIMAL In May, 2003, a couple near Minersville (Pa.) struck a badger-like but unidentified animal as long as their car. It seemed uninjured and made off into the woods. In describing the animal as "badger-like", the witnesses were probably thinking of the American badger (*Taxidea taxus*) rather than the European badger (*Meles meles*). [28]

BADIGUY This is supposed to be a large snake of central Africa that kills hippopotamuses and stretches up to reach high vegetation. This invites the suspicion that it is not snake but saurian with a body beneath the water, the neck only being visible. However, its tracks on shore, where it sometimes ventures, are serpentine. [H9]

BADMINTON BLOODSUCKER A never-identified beast which killed sheep, sucked their blood, but hardly nibbled their flesh, was reported from Badminton, England, in 1905.

BADOONGI Huge birds believed by the Abenaki Indians to have flourished in days agone.

BAETYL In ancient Greek belief, a stone that was actually alive. Damasios (5th-6th Century AD) tells us of a particularly lively baetyl of globular shape that could actually talk and change size. [#9]

BAGGE'S BLACK BIRD Huge sheep-sized birds (black, need I add?), bellowing like bulls, observed above Lake Bujuku, Uganda. Where does the *Bagge* part of their name come in? I hear you wonder. The only person to see these avian titans was the native guide of one Stephen Bagge, so if all were fair they should really be called Bagge's Guide's Black Birds after this anonymous cicerone. [E]

BAGHEERA The name (taken from *The Jungle Book*) given to an ABC, allegedly seen in Rome and said to have been a black panther, in 1990. [#6]

BAGINI In Australian aboriginal lore, these creatures are half woman and half animal. They look like beautiful females, but have clawed fingers and toes. They have a tendency to rape men. [J1]

BAGRADA SERPENT According to Pliny, the Roman commander Regulus (died *ca.* 250 BC) and his army encountered a serpent 150'/45.7m long in the River Bagrada in

North Africa and the only way they could overcome it was with ballistas and other engines.

BAI MA A strange equid in Chinese legend. It is coloured white, has a bovine tail and roars like a tiger.   [97]

BAI-XIONG A white-coloured bear found in China. Its existence is not in doubt – some have been exhibited in zoos – but its biological status in the bear family is unknown as yet.

BAKANGA A beast supposed to dwell in the Central African Republic. It looks like a lion without a mane and possibly has spots like a leopard. Strangely, it makes a barking noise, like a dog's. It may be identical with the marozi of Kenya.   [S7]

BAKU A dream-eating creature of Japanese legend. It is supposed to bear some resemblance to a tapir.

BAKUNAWA A winged fish of gigantic proportions, which was believed in by the West Visayans of the Philippines. To this creature they ascribed the eclipse, saying it would swallow the sun or the moon on occasion.   [R1]

BALD MOUNTAIN CREATURE In 1974 witnesses claimed to have seen an amazing creature at Bald Mountain, Washington state. It was the size of a horse, its head was the shape of a football and graced with antennae, it was covered with scales and its legs were rubbery with suckers on the ends. It gave off a green light. Ernest Smith, grocer, saw it first and it was later seen by a married couple. NASA is said to have sent in investigators.   [B11]

BALI LEOPARD No leopard has ever been reported from the island of Bali, yet certain clawmarks imply the existence of a population of such animals.   [B6]

BALI TIGER An animal supposedly extinct since 1937, yet clawmarks indicate it may still survive.   [B6]

BALLON MONSTER In this region of Alsace, a flood was recorded in 1304. During this, a monster described as a dragon was reported in the waters. When the flood subsided, it came ashore, attacking man and beast.   [M7]

BALLS OF LIGHT When the celebrated *Kon-Tiki* was making its voyage in 1947, those aboard saw mysterious balls of light, apparently submarine creatures, flashing on and off below them.   [B6]

BALLYFERRITER FLYING CREATURE A large black animal resembling a bat which frightened Kathleen O'Shea in Kerry, Ireland, in 1980.   [S2/B]

BALLYVOURNEY CREATURE This unidentified animal, 2.5'/1m in length, was seen crossing a road at this Irish location. It had a face like a cat. The Bords suggest it was a lynx.   [B9]

BALONG BIDAI A monster that looks like a mat and lives in the water (into which it will pull the unwary passer-by) in Malaysia.   [E]

BALVAIG BEAST A humanoid monster reported from Scotland. It is said to have clawed the flesh off a man who approached it too closely.   [146]

BAN MANCCHE A hominoid of Nepal. It is smaller than men and hairy, with two eyes in the front of the head and two in the back. Its feet are big, its heels small. [L1]

BANDON SEA MONSTER This creature had a body like that of a hairy cow and a nose described as bulbous. It was estimated at 12'6"/3.8m long and was observed from Bandon (Oregon).   [101]

BANIB-BA-GUNWUWAR A creature reported from Lake Albacytya in Victoria (Australia). It means literally 'bunyip and swan' and seems to combine features of both, having a bunyip's body and a long neck. [S11]

BANNOG A gigantic bird in the folklore of the Ilokanos and Tinguians of the Philippines, capable of carrying off men and cattle for its nestlings.   [R1]

BARDIN BOOGER A hairy hominid, noted for its strength, reported from the vicinity of Bardin, Florida. It is supposed to have once attacked and shaken a truck. [50]

BARMANU A primitive humanoid said to dwell in the Shisi Kuh Valley in Pakistan. Its name indicates it is hairy. It utters cries like those of both a human and a jackal. [33]

BARMBORO WILDCAT A mysterious wild felid that figures in English legend. Barmboro is now called Barnborough (Yorkshire). A large ferocious cat is supposed to have fought with Percival Cresacre here in 1456. Both were killed and the cat was incorporated into the Cresacre coat-of-arms.   [L3]

BARMOUTH BEACH MONSTER A 10'/3m sea monster espied from this Welsh locale in 1975. [12]

BASAJUAN A 5-6'/1.5m foot hominid, reported from the Basque Country in Spain. It is hostile to humans. The basajuans are supposed to be strong, hairy creatures, which lived in the land before the Basques. They are still supposed to be there and, when shepherds hear their cry, they know a storm is coming.   In Basque legend, this creature is sometimes depicted as a single person with vampiric tendencies who was killed by three brothers whose sister's blood he had been sucking. He was credited with a wife called Basa-Andre, a wild woman. A female equivalent to Basa-Juan, but distinct from Basa-Andre, is Zuberoa. [30 B13 98]

BASILISK A creature first mentioned by ancient writers, who described it as a snake with the mark of a crown on its head (amongst earlier writers, a crown resembling a crest). Its glance was supposedly deadly and to kill it you had to show it its reflection in a mirror. In the 12th Century appeared the legend that it was hatched from the egg of a geriatric rooster. A new name now arose for it: *cockatrice*. A toad with neighbourly instinct would hatch the cock's egg. A snake could also perform this helpful task. The basilisk in its final form had a snake's head, a cock's body and wings. The only animal that could successfully fight a basilisk was a weasel. The only plant that its glance did not wither was rue.

In 1202 a well in Vienna was exuding horrid fumes and at length a basilisk was pulled out of it, or so the legend goes. In 1587 a beast that looked like a snake, but was identified as a basilisk, was killed in a cellar in Warsaw.

A cockatrice's egg was said to have been hatched under some peat at Dale in the Shetland Islands. The peat was burned and the cockatrice died. At Saffron Walden (Essex) a knight in reflective crystal armour slew such a beast. A cockatrice was said to have a den in Wharvell (Hampshire). A man lowered a mirror into it and it fought its reflection until it died of exhaustion.

When Leo X was pope (1513-22), a basilisk was said to have started a plague at Rome.

The ultimate original of this animal may have been a cobra. [C26 S9 L4]

BASKET MONSTER In Zulu lore, a monster that looks just like a basket, but can then spring up on its legs and run off. It possibly has a taste for human flesh, but it is doubtful if it could tackle a grown adult. [K5]

BASTOS' MONSTER A guide named Sebastian Bastos in the Amazon region claimed that once his beached canoe was destroyed by a monster that emerged from the water. Beasts of this kind, about 18'/4.56m long, turned out to be well-known to the Indians. [S6]

BATSQUATCH In 1994 Brian Carsfield, an 18-year old whose probity was unquestioned locally, was driving home in the vicinity of Mount Rainier (Washington) when his truck stopped inexplicably and an incredible winged figure landed in front of him. It had gigantic wings, a face reminiscent of a wolf's, hands with fingers and feet like a bird's. It stood at 9'/3m tall. Although its teeth looked sharp, it did not have fangs. Eventually, it flew away in the direction of Mount Rainier.

An anonymous individual e-mailing a website later claimed to have seen the creature. He said it was coloured purple and had a 40' wingspan. [S8]

BATTLE RIVER MONSTER A serpentine monster, said to be impervious to bullets (though this may simply indicate the witness concerned was not the shot he thought himself to be) and an estimated 30'/9.15m in length, was reported by four witnesses on separate occasions in this Alberta river in 1934.   [C1]

BATUTUT A mystery primate of Sabah, a Malaysian state on the island of Borneo. Supposed footprints of this beast were found in 1970.   [C20]

BAUANG SEA SERPENT A serpentine creature seen from the Philippine coast by a film crew in 1966.   [B9]

BA'WAS A simian creature of which the Tshimshan Indians of Canada make masks. Modern Tshimshan identify the ba'was with the sasquatch, but whether this is due to the intrusion of white cultural influences cannot be determined.   [W]

BEACH BEAST A strange creature reported by Raphael Kickens on the beach at Llanca on the Costa Brava (Spain). There were strange flashes of light and a black figure jumped a considerable height onto a rock. In the vicinity was a red light which seemed to pulsate. The creature, which was lithe, jumped to the other side of the rock. A white light came bounding towards the witness, who then, very understandably, fled. [#9]

BEAR LAKE MONSTER Bear Lake, which straddles Utah and Idaho, is supposedly home to a monster. The Indians say it is like a snake, except that it has 18"/45cm legs. It sometimes hauls itself ashore and covers small distances. According to one report a specimen was actually captured in 1876. In 1881 the *Deseret Evening News* said the beast in the lake had a long, undulating body of a light cream colour. The monster was spotted in 1937 by a boy who had been swept into the lake, but was subsequently rescued. He said it had a long head, reminiscent of a snake's. The *Salt Lake Tribune* reports an encounter with the monster in 2002. [B11]

BEAR-DRAGON A beast, a combination of bear and dragon, nearly 50'/15m long, mentioned in the *Nihon-gi*, a Japanese work compiled about AD 720. [J2]

BEARLIKE CREATURE A bipedal creature which in other respects resembled a bear, about 3'/1m high, was seen near Gayndeh (Queensland) in 1999.   [#9]

BEARLIKE MONSTER A creature reported outside the Office of Tibet in New York City.   [B11]

BEARMAN 1 Mystery creature blamed for attacks in Nalbari, Assam, India, in 2003. It is said to become invisible before it attacks people and to vanish if light is pointed at it. At least twenty people are supposed to have suffered from the creature's claws.   [12]
2 A creature called a bearman was captured in Lithuania in 1661 and sent as a present to the king of Poland, Jan II.

BEAST OF AUXERRE A mystery animal, variously said to be a wolf, tiger or hyena, reported from this area of France in 1732-4.   [#8]

BEAST OF BALLYMENA A bipedal furred creature which has been reported from the vicinity of Ballymena, Ireland.   [D3]

BEAST OF BARRISDALE A Scottish loch monster, which, unlike many such, was credited with the ability to fly. Loch Hourn seems to have been its haunt. It was said to have pursued a terrified crofter to his very door in the 19th Century.   The *Scots Magazine* in 1975 asserted that the beast lived in the hills of Knoydart and compared it with a pterodactyl.   [F4]

BEAST OF BENBECULA A creature whose remains were discovered on an Hebridean beach by Louise Whitts in 1990. She photographed the remains, but, when she later showed the photograph to biologists, they were unable to identify the animal. [#9]

BEAST OF BODALOG A creature never seen. It apparently lived in a river near Rhayader (Wales), from which it would emerge onto a farm called Bodalog, where it killed sheep.   That the sheep had been indeed killed was implied by the fact that each had received a single bite, which may have been poisonous (but this is not established). That the beast lived in the river was inferred from the fact that foxhounds on its trail stopped there. There have not been any recent reports of its activity.   [S5]

BEAST OF BODMIN A beast (or beasts) on Bodmin Moor in Cornwall, in appearance like a black panther. Video footage suggests the animal in question might be some kind of wildcat. A large skull found on the moor was examined by the British Museum (Natural History) and proved to be that of a leopard. It must be remembered that a black panther is in reality a black-coloured leopard.   [103 104]

BEAST OF BOLAM A large hominoid reported from the vicinity of Bolam Lake (Northumberland). The earliest encounter reported took place around 1998. . Perhaps about 2001 a young woman saw a monkey-like creature. Later witnesses included a party of anglers who said they had met the creature at night time. It had sparkling eyes and was 7-8'/2m tall. The Centre for Fortean Zoology placed a stakeout on the lake in 2003. For some reason its electronic equipment failed. Then its doughty director, Jonathan Downes, together with five members of his entourage, observed a huge man-shaped figure. Tree formations nearby were reminiscent of the so-called "bigfoot beds" found in North America. [#1]

BEAST OF BRASSKNOCKER HILL A creature reported from this wooded area of Bath, England, in 1980. According to one report it wore spectacles, but this seems to have been due to white rings around its eyes. Some thought it an ape or monkey, some a rodent. Reporter Terry Hooper said there was a smell of monkey urine around a tree where it was supposed to have been. He was closely familiar with this smell, having once been urinated on by a chimpanzee.   [#1]

BEAST OF BUNGOMA A fierce creature in Kenya, said to have left hundreds of animals dead in its wake. It may have been a leopard which was eventually trapped by rangers and then again it may not.   [A7]

BEAST OF 'BUSCO This creature is a massive turtle of unknown species which inhabits Fulks Lake near Chorobusco (Indiana). Witnesses attest to the Beast's size, one likening it to a pickup truck. It was given the name Oscar. An attempt to pull him out in 1949 failed.   Some thought Oscar died after this, but there have been a number of subsequent reports. In Chorobusco there is an annual festival called Turtle Days. [B7]

BEAST OF CHISWICK   Chiswick, a part of London, was in 1994 home to a mysterious beast. Its body was compared with a dog's, fur to a grey squirrel's, face to a kangaroo's and some said it had white spots. Its build is described as scrawny. It was said to tear open rubbish bags and attack pigeons.   [#1]

BEAST OF EXMOOR Probably the most famous of Britain's ABCs, there may in fact be more than one animal to which the name applies. Although there have been sightings from the 1970s, a shocking amount of killings on the moor led the marines to be sent in to destroy the beast in 1983. A number of dogs were shot in the course of their operation and afterwards the killings died down. In June of that year, reports of a large black felid started coming in.   It crossed the road in front of a motorist, who averred it looked just like a large cat with a long tail. One cat observed was described as fawn-coloured with a black head and tail, which made it look like a gigantic Siamese cat. A grey cat was also reported. On one occasion, two animals were seen in a field together, one black and one brown. In 1983 a black cat was observed with a white front and neck. In 1987 a black cat with a white front and white leg was seen.

   An examination of the evidence suggests there are at least two large cats on the loose. A poll taken from witnesses showed that 80% claimed to have seen a black cat and 20% a brown. It occurs to the present writer that there may have been two cats initially – a black panther and a puma. These may have crossbred producing a number of other specimens, which are likely to be infertile. It has also been suggested the large cats are the evolved and possibly mutated descendants of feral cats. As to the killings, these are consistent with those of a large felid, though a local woman, Anne De Ville, made the interesting suggestion that they may have been perpetrated by an eagle. A golden eagle has been seen in the Devon area.   [B4 B14 F8]

BEAST OF GLOUCESTER Large black ABC seen in the area of Gloucester. It has even been reported from Robinswood Hill, a conserved wilderness area within the town itself. In 1994 a couple of possible lynx sightings were also made in the Gloucester area.

BEAST OF HACKNEY MARSHES A beast of undetermined nature reported from this area of London in the 1970s. It was compared with a bear.

BEAST OF LAGRAULAS The sighting of this curious and mystery animal was reported from the department of Gers (France) in 1982. Its head was catlike and it had long ears, broken at the ends. It had a long tail ending in a curl and a yellow spot on its abdomen.   [#8]

BEAST OF LE GEVAUDAN   A mystery beast which attacked shepherds and shepherdesses in France between 1764 and 1767. In that year a beast was shot by a hunter named Chastel. It was said he used a silver bullet, as though he suspected his adversary were a werewolf. The slain animal much resembled a wolf, but appeared to display some anomalous characteristics. According to one version, its feet resembled hooves. It was stuffed and taken to King Louis XV, but the taxidermy had been ineffective, the specimen stank and it was buried before it could be examined scientifically.

Because of this lack of examination, much speculation has arisen as to what the beast actually was. An hyena was mentioned, as was a cross between a wolf and a she-bear. It has been suggested in modern times that the killings were carried out by a society of Wolf Men, analogous to the Leopard Men of Africa. Chastel was supposed to be the leader of this, but such a role is not consistent with what we know of Chastel's character. A most peculiar sighting had been reported in 1774. An animal standing on its hind legs, the size of a donkey, with reddish hair and a long tail, short ears and a porcine snout, had been seen going towards some cattle. The cattle had understandable reservations about this figure, so they lowered their horns to discourage its further approach. It took the hint.

A rumour which grew up around 1996 that the Beast's skin had been found and shown to be an hyena's was no more than that. The identity of the creature remains a mystery. [#8]

BEAST OF LETTIR DALLAN   A creature mentioned in the early medieval Irish *Triads*. It was the offspring of a lake monster and the daughter of a priest. It had a human head and its body was like the bellows of a smith.   [M7]

BEAST OF MARGAM   An ABC, perhaps a puma, reported from this location in Wales, notably in 1985 and 1990. This area contains a 25,000 acre forest. [#6]

BEAST OF REAUVILLE-TRICASTIN   This mystery animal (dubbed *Felix* by the Press) was reported from the department of Drome (France) in 1988. It was identified with various different animals.   [#8]

BEAST OF ST MICHAEL'S   Legend has it that, in days agone, St Michael's Church, Cornhill (London) was visited, during a storm, by a creature that entered through the south window. Its claw marks were found on the stone.   [146]

BEAST OF SKIDDAW VIEW   This creature is known from its breathing alone. According to a report made in October 2000, a camping family in this part of Cumbria heard heavy breathing in some bushes. There was evidently some kind of creature in there. The noises were heard for three nights in a row, but the breathing creature was never identified. It could have been anything from an unknown animal to a hedgehog with emphysema.   [96]

BEAST OF VIENNA For a time animals in Vienna (North Carolina) were being carried off by this mystery predator, a yellowish felid.   [119]

BEAST-BIRD A New Jersey newspaper, the *Ashbury Park Evening Press* (22nd January, 1909) stated that an 18'/5.5m tall beast-bird was encountered by Dan Possack, whom it addressed with surprising fluency in the English language. Possack was scared by such an unexpected encounter and ran like blazes, the beast-bird in pursuit. It grabbed him and they fought, Possack plying a hatchet. He at length knocked out one of the creature's eyes. It screamed, inflated its body and floated off.

BEATHACH MOR LOCH ABHA *see* **Big Beast of Loch Awe**.

BEATHACH MOR LOCH ANASLAIGH This Scottish Gaelic name (meaning 'the Great Beast of Lake Ainslie') was given by Scottish settlers to a beast with a head like a horse's said to occupy this lake in Nova Scotia.   [K4]

BEAVER WOMAN The Blackfoot Indians were quite positive that you should give beaver women a wide berth. They dwelt in lakes, their backs and lower parts covered with beaver-like fur, while the rest of them had a human appearance. They would, by hiding their castorine features, lure hapless young men to their doom. They also attacked women, but children were safe from them.   [B7]

BEDFORD CREATURE At Bedford (Kentucky) a creature that walked on its hind legs and seemed to have features like a dog, puma or bear, but was not identical with any of these creatures, was the centre of attention in 1962. Its arms reached its knees and it had black hair. In 1975, several creatures which made noises like pigs were heard (and perhaps vaguely seen) in a nearby wood along the banks of the Ohio. There was also some evidence of unknown creatures in cornfields.   [B11]

BEEBE'S FISHES William Beebe (1877-1962) descended into the depths of the ocean in a bathysphere and observed a number of fishes, unclassified by science, to which they had until then been unknown. These included varieties of gar, anglerfish, sailfish, the *bathysphaera intacta*, which boasted blue lights along its sides and tentacles depending from its belly, and the five-lined constellation fish. A non-deep sea fish, Beebe's manta, was seen by him in 1923, but it has not yet been classified properly by scientists.

BEHEMOTH A huge terrestrial monster in Jewish lore. Because he imbibes so much water, he has been given a special stream, the Yubal, to quench his thirst. The produce of a thousand mountains is needed to satisfy his hunger each day. Eventually, he and leviathan will engage in a mighty combat.   [G4]

BEHEMOTH BANNOCK BIRD A legendary bird amongst several Native American tribes, including the Bannocks and Shoshone. It was supposed to be five times the size of an eagle and could carry off deer, pronghorn and mountain sheep. It may be identical with the nunyenunc.   [H]

BEIGORRI Preternatural red cow in Basque lore which guards caves and gorges. [4]

BEIRUT GIANT LIZARD A large lizard said to be roaming round Beirut in 2003. At first reports of the animal were not taken seriously, but, with mounting evidence, the civil defence authorities started to take steps. There is speculation that the creature is a Komodo dragon (*Varanus komodoensis*) and rumour has it that it was released by a German.

BEITHIR A creature in Scottish Gaelic folklore, possibly of the serpent kind. The term is also used for a monster generally and possibly for a large skate. In these senses it may come from an early Celtic *betrix*. (In modern Gaelic it means a bear, but this is clearly from English, as *th* in Gaelic is pronounced like English *h*). However, in folklore it often means a giant water-snake, capable also of travelling on land. One such was supposedly seen above the Falls of Kilmorack in 1975. In 1965, Maureen Ford saw a body with caterpillar-like humps on the roadside. It was 20'/6m long and of a grey hue. It made a noise like someone dragging weight. For some reason she or later commentators thought it might be identical with the legendary *beithir* [6]

BEKK-BOK *see* **Kra-dhan**.

BENIN RHINOCEROS It is possible that in Benin (formerly Dahomey) there exist undiscovered rhinoceroses, maybe even an undiscovered species. This is because rhinoceros-horn clubs have been discovered in this country, even though it is outside the range of known rhinoceroses. Benin here should not be confused with the historical kingdom of Benin, which lay in modern Nigeria.   [S4]

BERGSTUTZ Alternative name for the tatzelwurm.

BERMUDA GIANT JELLYFISH In 1969 skin divers were pursued by a huge unknown species of jellyfish off Bermuda. [S5]

BERREADOR A curious creature reported from the banks of the Uruguay River, which separates Uruguay from Argentina. Only its mouth has been made out amongst the foliage on the banks.   [#12]

BERUANG API A term used to denote the Malay sun bear (*Helarctos malaysos*), but it may refer to a distinct subspecies. This is suggested by descriptions of its behaviour. [115]

BERUANG RAMBI This term is used to designate the Malay sun bear (*Helarctos malaysos*), but to make matters confusing, in Borneo it seems to mean another kind of creature as well. The natives say this creature is neither bear nor orang utan. The Earl of Cranbrook felt it was some kind of primate.   [94]

BERWICK SEA MONSTER A lighthouse keeper of Berwick, on the English-Scottish border, reported a 40'/12m monster proceeding speedily.   [C3*]

BHANJAKRIS A term used in India to refer to some kind of BHM. [41]

BHUTANESE LAKE MONSTER King Jigme Dorji Wangchuck of Bhutan (reigned 1952-1972) saw an unidentified animal in a lake in his country. It was coloured white and proceeded speedily.

BIASD NA SROGAIG A clumsy lake beast with a single horn, believed to live on the Isle of Skye (Scotland). It was bulky and its legs were ungainly.

BICHO-PAPACIRCO A man-beast which features mainly in Brazilian nursery lore, where it is used by parents as a bogeyman to frighten children.   [4]

BIG BEAST OF LOCH AWE A Scottish lake monster with twelve legs, sturdy of build. It has been compared to a large horse, but it is a long time since anyone has claimed to have clapped eyes on it. Timothy Pont (16th Century) says that people would not fish in this lake because of the giant eels, big as a horse, which it contained. [F4 C25]

BIG BIRD Many large avians have been reported from places in the United States. I feel that in a good number of cases they may be birds known to science which the observer failed to identify. However, a particular instance at Lowndale (Illinois) in 1977 involved a bird picking up a child and carrying him for a few feet. Certainly this seemed beyond the capability of any local bird. A second huge bird was also seen. A number of other large birds which witnesses could not identify were seen in Illinois that year. This was not the first time such creatures had been seen in the state. Back in 1948 R. Price and V. Babb had reported seeing a bird the size of an aeroplane. Scientists were dismissive, saying no bird could pick up a weight as great as the child's. *See* **Thunderbird.** Birds of a huger size than any known to science are not, however, confined to America. In 1838 Marie Delex, a five year old girl, was carried off by an avian colossus in Switzerland. Her body was found two months later. A mystery big bird was reported a number of times near Bradford (Yorkshire) in 1982-3. It was dimly photographed by journalist Mike Priestley. Some have suggested the creature was a pterodactyl. [H B8 141]

BIG CHAPMAN'S LAKE MONSTER A creature seen in this Indiana lake in 1934. Only the head appeared. Its eyes were large and cow-like. [C/H]

BIG FIN A name applied to a species of squid. Paralarval forms have been described, but its adult form is unknown.   [S8/A]

BIG GREY MAN This creature (in Gaelic, *Fear Liath Mor*) is reputed to haunt Ben MacDui (often misspelled Ben MacDhui) in the Scottish Cairngorms.   In 1890 mountaineer Norman Collie heard crunching sounds behind him as though something with extremely long legs were walking after him. He took to his heels. A.M. Kellas and his brother saw a giant coming towards them on the mountain, so they departed instanter and were sure it was following them. P. Densham in 1945 heard footsteps on the mountain and was seized by a compulsion to throw himself over a cliff. This he resisted with difficulty. A great brown creature, estimated at 20'/6m tall, was seen on the mountain by an anonymous witness. Yeti-like tracks have been reported.

The Big Grey Man has also been reported from the islands of Skye and Canna. It has further been reported in Ireland, garbed in misty apparel. In addition, a wildman was supposedly captured in Scotland in the 17th Century by one of the Munro clan.   [G6 H1]

BIG HEAD A longhaired, disembodied creature in the legends of the Tuscarora nad Huron Indians. Big heads had an evil reputation. M. Hall has opined they were giant owls.

BIG JIM Name given to a giant rattlesnake said to have thriven in Indiana. It was supposed to have killed a logger in 1881 and thereafter it was blamed for many livestock deaths. This or a similar snake, said to have been one of Big Jim's offspring, was killed in 1908 and when stretched the skin measured 12'/3.66m. Rattlesnakes are not supposed to exceed 9'/2.74m. *See* **Giant Rattlesnake**.   [#11]

BIG MO Name given to a bigfoot-type creature, dirty white in colour, seen at Aurora (Illinois) in 1974.   [R2]

BIG MUDDY MONSTER A hominoid sighted in the vicinity of the Big Muddy River in Illinois in 1973. It was white in colour. One sighting was by a couple parked on a boat ramp. The creature was described as making loud but inhuman noises. It was also reported in 1974 and 1975. Toby Berger, a local police chief, proved very broadminded about the matter, attesting to the reliability of witnesses.   [C11]

BIG OWL A huge owl in the legends of the Cree. It drives away the game, causing starvation. It will then attack people themselves to feed its hungry young. [A]

BIG YELLOW A strange creature seen by American soldiers during the Vietnam War. It was 7-8' tall, had clawed hands, was yellow and gave off a yellowish glow. It seemed impervious to armour-piercing ammunition.   [#7]

BIGFOOT Although this name is of comparatively recent origin, it was long preceded by reports and traditions of hairy manlike or apelike creatures to which different names were given. The term *Sasquatch* (an anglicised version of an Indian word) is perhaps the best known of these. There are over six hundred places in the United States and Canada whose names make reference to such creatures. In the 18th and 19th Centuries there were widespread reports of such animals. Unfortunately, one of the most widely known of these reports, which concerned the capture of a young sasquatch named Jacko, seems to be totally fraudulent. In 1882 many sightings of a bigfoot-type creature occurred in Round Valley (California). One was seen in the Cascade Mountains (Oregon) in 1885.

In 1893 a "wild man" was recorded as far east as Long Island, while in 1894 reports came in from New Jersey and Kentucky.

In 1924 a number of miners claimed to have been besieged by sasquatches in their log cabin at Ape Canyon (Oregon). The creatures jumped on the roof and flung rocks at the walls one night. There was another report from Long Island in 1931, while one came in from Pennsylvania in 1932.

A sasquatch was seen by members of the Chapman family in 1941 in British Columbia. This is regarded as the first of the modern sightings.

Although sasquatch-like creatures had long featured in Indian lore and white media, the story which catapulted the creature into public consciousness was based on a hoax, when a man named Wallace left fake footprints around a construction site in California where he had a team working. One Jerry Crew, discovering them, took plaster casts and, when the story reached the papers Andrew Genzoli, editor of the *Humboldt Times* coined the word 'bigfoot' to designate the creature.

In 1967 two men named Patterson and Gimlin supposedly sighted a bigfoot and filmed it. Opinion remains divided on whether the film is a hoax and the bigfoot in it a costumed human. It has been suggested that John Chambers who made, *inter alia*, the costumes for *Planet of the Apes* may have designed that of the bigfoot in the film. This notion seems to be based on rumour and inference – Chambers was the only one known to be able to make such a costume, *ergo* he did so. This sort of reasoning is unsound and Chambers vehemently denied involvement. An assertion that one Jerry Romney wore the suit as part of a film made for American National Enterprise has been denied by Romney.

Even if there has been hoaxing in bigfootery, this does not invalidate other reports of bigfoot sightings. It is important to remember the creature was being seen long before Wallace wore his first diaper.

Coleman and Huyghe argue that there is more than one kind of bigfoot and have split the BHM brigade into a set of classes. The sasquatch properly so-called ranges from 6-9' tall and is placed in the category of *neo-giant*; a taller bigfoot ranging from 10-20' they label a *true giant*; *marked hominids* are about 7' tall and can be of more than one colour; *neandertaloids* are surviving populations of Neanderthal man; *erectus hominids* are found only in Asia and Australia; *proto-pygmies* are small hairy hominids; *unknown pongids* are apes which are a complete mystery; and *giant monkeys* are giant monkeys. They include another category, *merbeings*, but I feel they are mistaken to do so. Numerous hominid monsters are given separate articles in this work and I leave it to the reader to work out into which category, if any, each fits. It should be noted, however, that veteran researcher John Green thinks there is only a single kind of bigfoot.

Some would argue that the neo-giant sasquatch occurs only in western America and Canada and more easterly versions are all marked hominids. The sasquatch population is put by G. Krantz at 2000+. The hair colour varies from brown to black. White specimens are not unknown. The hair of the lower leg can be of a different shade from that above. It is generally reported as having a human gait, though it is sometimes said to shuffle. It seems to have a cone-shaped head like a gorilla or orang-utan which would imply a protrubrant abdomen. The face is on the flat side with a prominent nose but an otherwise pithecoid appearance. It probably does not use tools, but there may be exceptions to this. Sasquatches do not have the power of speech. They tend to stand dead still when observed. Some complain of a noxious smell in their presence. While the jury is still out as to what their proper niche in the animal kingdom may be, some feel they are gigantopithecuses, huge and supposedly extinct apes known from fossils in Asia. This presupposes that at some stage they travelled across Beringia into the New World. One of the objections to the existence of bigfoot is lack of appropriate foodstuffs. This could be remedied by partial hibernation, although primates do not usually hibernate. This could, however, be the exception to prove the rule. It is also possible that they store meat in the snow where it freezes and remains accessible to them in the winter season. Wolverines behave in this manner. Reports of bigfoots wandering at night suggest they are partially nocturnal. Again, this is not generally consistent with primate behaviour, but it would be rash to infer from this that bigfoot reports do not refer to primates. They are also said to be able to swim swiftly under water, which no recognised great ape is thought able to do. They are apparently carnivorous: one was espied eating venison. A Dakota Sioux belief seems to be that they can walk in and out of another dimension. Some have argued for a connection between UFOs and bigfoot.

Tracks and their casts have generally failed to convince scientists of bigfoot's existence. However, one cast, the Skookum Cast, bears the impression, not merely of a footprint, but of a possible bigfoot lying on its side. It was taken in 2000 in Gifford Pinchot National Forest, Washington state. J. Meldrum, anatomy and anthropology professor at Idaho State University in Pocatello, regards this as evidence for the animal's existence. Alleged bigfoot footprints have as a general rule five toes, but four-toed and three-toed ones have been reported.

In 2003 J. Chilcutt of the Conroe Police Department in Texas claimed to have found six footprints that proved the existence of bigfoot.

Bigfoot is protected in Skamania County (Washington), which has been declared a sasquatch refuge. [N1 H3 S1 C21 C16 G7 K8/A B8* C3*]

BIGHEAD A 7'/2.13m tall bipedal creature with a head much larger than its body (=? with a head unduly large in proportion to its body) and with no visible hands or feet, reported from Butler (Ohio) in 1978. The creature was seen on a number of occasions after nightfall.

BILI APE There have been stories of unknown apes in the Congo (Kinshasa) and the finding of a large skull has indicated the possible presence of a new kind of ape. The skull appears to be flatter in front than a chimpanzee's. Many argue it is a chimpanzee, but, if so, it may be a new species. The creature has been captured on film. Some locals refer to these apes as "lion-eaters" because they are so tall. A 6'/1.8m tall Norwegian missionary claimed she once saw one that was taller than she. E. Louis, geneticist, says the mitochondrial DNA taken from faecal samples is chimpanzee-like.

BILLIWACK MONSTER A monster said to lurk about the abandoned Billiwack Dairy of Aliso Canyon (California). The creature is described as large and muscular with grey hair and a ram's horns. It stands upright and tends to be seen at night. It made a notable appearance in 1964 when it was encountered by boy hikers.   [M5]

BILUNGI An ape or hairy hominoid supposed to be found in the Congo (Kinshasa), according to evidence passed on to Heuvelmans by an old settler. The creatures are supposed to be found near Lake Tumba. Natives describing one that had been killed said it had brown, hairy arms and a well developed thorax. [F8]

BIPEDAL MYSTERY CATS There have been a number of reports of felids which, strange as it may seem, walk on their hind legs. Examples come from White Oak Swamp (South Carolina) in 1948 and New Brunswick in 1951. One attacked a man in Decatur in 1970. In California such creatures have been reported in the region of Mount Tamalpais. They are black in colour. One description gives the height of the beast as five feet. The animal is credited with chasing and attacking humans. While it is possible for a puma to stand on its hind legs, most of the animals described seem to be black and pumas are hardly ever that colour. *See also* **Wampus Cat**. B. Steiger maintains that such bipedal felids are were-creatures. [M5 S7]

BIPEDAL SHELLED CREATURE A clawed creature that walked upright like a human and had a shell like a turtle's, reported crossing the road on the way to Athena (Oregon) in 2000. [99]

BIRD WOMAN One of a race of flying women, known for their beauty, said to inhabit the Rocky Mountains; *see also* **Flying Woman**. [B7]

BIRDMAN Two flying manlike creatures with wings were seen at Pelotas (Rio Grande do Sul), Brazil, in the 1950s. [B9]

BIRDMAN (JAPANESE) A Japanese soldier opened fire on what appeared to be a 7'/2.13m winged man near Kyoto in 1952. A sergeant told him he had had a similar sighting a week before. [B9]

BIR-SINDIC A mystery ape reported from Assam, perhaps identical with the olo-banda. Both terms may refer to a relict population of orang-utans in the area. [#4]

BIS-COBRA This poisonous creature is the subject of belief in India. It may be a lizard. Its poison is said to be very virulent, many cases having been reported. The Indians said it had eight legs and was a snake/lizard hybrid. It is said to spread its venom by spitting. The trouble with identifying this animal is that the name has been applied to various different lizards. A paper read at a meeting of the Bombay Natural History Society in May, 1888, suggested that the bis-cobra was an actual animal no longer called by that name. [#11]

BISHOPSVILLE LIZARD In 1988 in Bishopsville (South Carolina), a motorist claimed he had been pursued by a reptile which had red eyes and which was 7'/2.13m tall. The beast appeared able to run at 40 m.p.h. [93]

BLACK ALLIGATOR *see* **Sil:quey**.

BLACK BIRD-OF-PARADISE An unidentified bird reported from Goodenough Island, off the coast of Papua-New Guinea. [30]

BLACK COUGAR This animal was reported from Arizona in 2003 and 2004. There is some possibility it was also seen with a cub. However, melanistic cougars (*Panthera concolor*) are virtually unknown. But the jaguar (*Panthera onca*) was by no means unknown in Arizona in days agone and has been rumoured to be making a comeback in that state. Black jaguars have been recorded from time to time.

BLACK DOG A preternatural black animal found in the folklore of Britain and elsewhere. It is large – about the size of a calf. Its coat is often as shaggy as a sheep's fleece. It is blacker than night itself. It has huge eyes, glowing and blazing. Sometimes it is headless; sometimes it screams; sometimes it has a chain. Black dogs seem to lack substance on the earthly plane. Beliefs surprisingly similar to British ones about this animal seem to have obtained amongst 19th Century American blacks.

A celebrated instance of a black dog's appearance was in a Suffolk church. This was in Blythburgh in 1577. The dog entered the church during a storm. Two people died (though unattacked) and the dog injured another,

The black dog is sometimes hostile, but by no means universally so. One of them, the Gurt Dog, was especially regarded as protecting children. They have also guided travellers. The Black Dog of Cottingham (Northamptonshire) is friendly, walking along as the wayfarer's companion. The appearance of a black dog could presage death, but not necessarily the death of a witness.

The terms *shuck, shag, trash, striker, barguest, padfoot* and *guytrash* have been applied to the animal. Charlotte Bronte described the Guytrash as a lion-like creature, with long hair and a huge head. Black Shuck of Norfolk seems to be hostile. The barguest is generally regarded as protective.   [B8 L2 L3 C4]

BLACK DWARF A diminutive hairy humanoid reported from the region of Casilda, Argentina.   [28]

BLACK FISH Poisonous piscid reported from the Shatt-el-Arab (Iraq); many deaths have been ascribed to it.   [E]

BLACK HOWLER A wild feline animal, about the size of a bobcat. It featured in Ozark folklore and there have been a number of modern sightings.   [30]

BLACK HYENA This astonishingly coloured creature was seen by Dikembe Zgaur of Kenya with an hyena group, in company with a white hyena. These colours seem unique amongst the species. At first he thought it might be an aardwolf (*Proteles cristatus*), then realised that hyenas would not let aardwolves join in with them.   [2]

BLACK LAKE MONSTER A serpentine monster, perhaps as long as 30'/9m, reported from this lake in Quebec in 1894 and 1896.   [G2]

BLACK LION Such animals have occasionally been reported – a whole pride of them in Kruger National Park, South Africa – but their existence has not yet been accepted scientifically.   [S7]

BLACK OAK TURTLE A giant turtle observed in swamps at Black Oak (Illinois) by a surveyor and a farmer in 1950.   [C/H]

BLACK RIVER MONSTER A monster reported from the Black River, New York. Its appearance sometimes coincides with electrical storms. It is said to be uncatchable with nets. A witness in 1951 claimed it was 15'/4.5m long, dark brown and with eyes that reminded him of silver dollars.

BLACK SEA SNAKE Not a sea snake of black colouring, but one discerned in the Black Sea in 1952. It was estimated to be 80-100'/24-30.5m long. Its upper parts were dark brown, its underparts white.   [E]

BLACK TIGER There have been a number of reports of black tigers, but some of these may simply have been black panthers. 18th Century artist James Forbes painted an undoubtedly black tiger which had been shot around 1772. However, no black tiger is known from scientific examination.   [S7]

BLOB Unusual blobs which may be unidentified living creatures are reported from time to time. A number of these appeared in a pond in Independence (Louisiana) in 1993 after Hurricane Andrew. In time, the biggest one shrank a little. No one could tell if they were animal, vegetable or mineral. In the same year a blob was seen in a pond near Shrewsbury (Ontario). The Bermuda Blob was said to have had appendages which may have been limbs. A blob that turned up on the beach at Tasmania, called the Tasmanian Globster, seems to have had a small mouth. The Newfoundland Blobster of 2001 seemed to have a skeleton, but was unidentifiable. In July 2003 two strange blobs were found in Fallen Lead Lake (Nevada). They may be jellyfish. In August 2003 a blob appeared in the water off Little Egg Harbor Township (NJ). Though biological, its nature could not be determined. A local said it smelt like a dead horse. I am not personally familiar with such an aroma, but would guess it is not enticing.   [#9 15]

BLOCK ISLAND CREATURE In 1996 a sea creature was captured near Shoreham (Rhode Island). It was 10'/3m long and had feelers. Locals were unable to identify it. [78]

BLOODSUCKER This creature is supposed to have attacked two poachers and sucked blood from one in Glen Tilt, near Blair Atholl, Scotland. The incident is an undatable legend. There does not seem to be an actual description of the creature.   [146]

BLOOP MAKERS Scientific listening stations have picked up noises from under the sea to which they give the name of *bloops*. They are perhaps coming from living organisms, but, as they are louder than those made by any creature known to science, they may consequently issue from some amazingly huge creatures.   [90]

BLUE BEN A creature reported to live in a tunnel beneath Kilve and Potsham in Somerset, England. The monster built himself a causeway across the mud to his habitation, but one day he fell in and drowned. A fossilised ichthyosaur was found near the spot where he was supposed to have met his fate and some maintained it was Blue Ben's remains. Although Graham MacEwan mentions this as a genuine tradition, Ralph Whitlock thinks it may be a modern synthetic one.   [H5]

BLUE LAKE MONSTER   Blue Lake in California was the scene in 1870 of the appearance of a monster which startled a shoreside picnic. One onlooker compared it with a Chinese dragon, while it was also said to have a long neck. There have been no reports since 1871.   [M5]

BLUE-SEA LAKE MONSTER The monster of this Canadian lake is supposed to have a head like a horse's. It is said to be 6-7'/2m long. There was a sighting about 1913 and there have been many others. It is reported to come ashore and slither on its stomach. Indeed, there is a tradition that such a monster was killed by Indians as it made its way from Blue-Sea Lake to Cedar lake.   [M7]

BLUE SWAN   In about 1995, blue swans were reported over the River Wesnum at Norwich. No explanation of their colour was forthcoming.   [#5]

BLUE THING The description of this is such that *thing* seems the best word to denote it. It was reported by a hiker on the Ice Age Trail outside Lodi (Wisconsin) in 1999. At first she thought it was someone dressed in blue on a bicycle. Then she realised there was no bicycle and the Blue Thing was just gliding along the path. There was a plume of something behind its head. The report lacks any further description.   [104]

BLUE TIGER A tiger with a blue pelage marked with black tigrine stripes, reported from China and Korea. A notable, though not the only, sighting was made by H.R. Caldwell in 1910.   [S7]

BLUTSCHINCK A bearlike monster supposed to live in a lake in the Tyrol (Austria). It will emerge and seize victims.   [130]

BMONA A huge bird, responsible for wind, in the myths of the Abanaki Indians. [4]

BO In Chinese lore, a creature with features generally reminiscent of a unicorn. It has, however, the claws and teeth of a white tiger. Weapons will not harm it. [120]

BO CREATURE This creature was said to be on the loose in Sierra Leone in the 1990s. Report had it that it resembled a cross between a baboon and a human and wore boots. It would drag off hapless victims and there is some evidence it was regarded as part of a population of "human baboons".   [A]

BOBO A sea creature seen off the west coast of the USA from about 1936-46. It had a face like a gorilla's.   [E]

BOCKMANN A creature half man, half goat, in German folklore. It is said to be of unpleasant disposition. [C12]

BOITATA In Brazilian tradition, a fiery serpent that preys on other animals. The reason for this is that it dwells in the water and needs their energy and light to keep its fire aglow and unextinguished. The term is also applied to a fire-spitting creature resembling a bull. [4]

BOIUBA A large snake believed to live in the Amazon region.   [#12]

BOKYBOKY A mystery animal, perhaps some kind of civet or mongoose, reported from Madagascar.   [E]

BOLLA A serpentine or dragonlike creature in Albanian lore which, after twelve years, changes into a fire-breathing dragon with nine tongues or a huge hairy woman. This creature causes drought and the Albanians were wont to propitiate it with human sacrifice. It is also called the *kulshedra.* It sounds as though the beast is in fact no more than a personification of drought or some deity in origin whom the Albanians considered responsible for drying up the land.[4]

BONNACON A quadruped with curled and therefore ineffectual horns, it bore some resemblance to a bull, but had a horse's mane, according to Pliny. It could release a stink to ward off its enemies.   [9]

BOOAA A large beast, resembling an hyena, reported from West Africa   [#1]

BOOBOOSHAW A strange, black creature, apparently very thin, which was said to be in the vicinity of Port Washington (Wisconsin) in the 1960s.   [A1]

BOOBRIE A gigantic bird reported from Scotland. It lived in the waters of both lake and sea, its beak was fierce like an eagle's or hawk's, its feet were webbed and taloned. It had a taste for mutton, so sheep in its vicinity were indeed imperilled. It was said to resemble a diver (the bird). A witness described this creature to J.F. Campbell. He said it had a white streak on its neck and breast. The feet were webbed, but also clawed. The legs were short and powerful. Lambs and otters formed its diet. P. Costello thinks what was being described was no bird but a long-necked lake monster. [F4 C25]

BOOGER A general term used in the United States for a bogeyman, first recorded as such in 1866. However, in cryptozoology, it has been used to signify a hairy humanoid that disports itself in the vicinity of Clanton (Alabama). It is also used for other bigfoot-like creatures in the Deep South.   [B7]

BOOGIE MAN Alternative name for the Bardin Booger.

BOQS A humanoid being in the folklore of the Bella Coola Indians of coastal British Columbia. The face of the boqs is hairless, but the rest of the body is completely hirsute. The eyes are human-like. Boqses are credited with supernatural powers. [G7]

BORBOTHA Fish of medieval legend, resembling a large eel. [151]

BORNEAN TIGER There have been alleged sightings of tigers in Borneo in recent times. Whether they are native to the island or have been introduced by local rulers is uncertain, as is their very existence.   [E]

BOTO In Brazil it is believed that there is a kind of dolphin that can transform itself into a boy. This they call the boto.   [122]

BOUDAS A were-hyena, believed in in certain parts of Africa. [122]

BÖXENWOLF An alternative term for a werewolf, used in Germany.

BRACKFONTEIN RIDGE ANIMALS Cave paintings of two unidentified animals at this location in the Orange Free State, South Africa. One has been tentatively identified as an hippopotamus, but appears to have bristles inconsistent with such a beast. It has been suggested that the other is a water-dwelling sabretooth, but to me it looks more like a walrus that has been to Weight Watchers. [#1]

BRAEMAR MONSTER A creature which, according to legend, King Malcolm III of Scots (reigned 1058-1099) kept on an island in the River Dee. It was described as being like a crocodile and may conceivably have been one.   [F4]

BRAN A monster which was and perhaps still is to be found in Lough Brin, Kerry (Ireland). It was certainly known in the 19th Century and sightings have been reported in the second half of the 20th, even though the lake is supposedly bereft of fish. It is supposed to have both phocine and draconic characteristics. [C25 M7]

BRAXTON MONSTER A creature reported in 1952 from the vicinity of Charleston (West Virginia). Its head was said to resemble the ace of spades, whatever that is supposed to mean. It had a fiery red face, a green body and was 10'/3m tall. In 1960 a bigfoot-like creature was seen near Hickory Flats in the same area.

BRAY ROAD BEAST A creature of Walworth County (Wisconsin) which many suspect is a werewolf. It has been reported since around 1991. It seems to have been first observed by a motorist on the road from which it took its name. It was kneeling by the roadside eating roadkill. It had large ears, claws and fangs. Its hair was brownish-grey. Its eyes glowed. In Autumn, 1991, a woman who had disembarked from her car re-embaeked rather quickly when she saw the beast coming towards her. Reports continued to come in. After early 1992, however, they ceased for the time being. Then, in 1999, it was seen once more. Roars attributed to the beast tended to be heard until at least 2001. [A1 R4]

BRAZOS RIVER MONSTER This creature, with a head reminiscent of an alligator's and a long serpentine body, was reported in this Texas river in 1853. [E]

BRENIN LLWYD A strange creature reported to live amongst the mountains of Snowdonia in Wales. He was regarded as the lord of the mist and, while descriptions of him seem to be non-existent in early times, he was reputed to seize victims who wandered into his domain and could not hear his approach. He seems to have been at first ap ersonification of the mist.

However, in more recent times, it has been suggested that there is some sort of animal up there which has given rise to the legend and witnesses have claimed to have seen such a creature. One said it stood on two legs, but looked more like a bear than an ape. It appeared fearful rather than aggressive, though this fear prompted it to attack a campsite. [T3 R4*]

BRENTFORD GRIFFIN There is a brewery near Brentford so called and a public house of the name in Brentford itself. In 1984 one Kevin Chippendale claimed to have seen something like a dog with wings near an apartment building called the Green Dragon. He said he had had another sighting in 1985 and thought the creature was similar to a griffin. Angela Kehoe claimed a sighting of a birdlike black creature. The griffin is also supposed to have been seen by a psychologist named Olssen.

A legend has appeared about the Brentford Griffin, though I cannot vouch for its age or antiquity. It claims Charles II procured a griffin for Nell Gwynn (died 1687) and it fell into the river. It made its way to an island, where in the 1800s it was joined by another escaped beast of the same kind, brought back by one of Captain Cook's expeditions. They reproduced, giving Brentford its griffin population.

Writer Robert Rankin says that while he did not believe in the griffin, he did his best to encourage the story. It has been alleged he invented the whole thing, which was nothing more than a downright hoax. People started telephoning a Griffin Hotline Rankin had set up and reported previous sightings by themselves or others. *See also* **Griffin.** [C21/A]

BRIAOU Mystery primate of Vietnam, probably the same as the Ngoui Rung.

BRIBIE ISLAND SEA MONSTER A whitish-grey monster seen off this Australian island on two occasions in 1962. Its neck was long, its body resembled a whale's and it had a tail and fins like those of a fish. [E]

BRIDGEPORT ANIMAL In 1927 this peculiar creature was espied by huckleberry pickers who chased it. This occurred near Bridgeport (New Jersey). It had feathers and four legs and the sound it made seemed to combine features of an owl hoot and a bark. [C19]

BRIGDI A sea monster in Shetland lore which would pursue and smash boats. [W3]

BRITISH BEECH MARTIN   While the pine marten (*Martes martes*) is a recognised British animal, the beech or stone marten (*Martes foina*) is supposed to have become extinct there at the end of the last Ice Age.   However, there is some evidence of the creature's survival, perhaps even to the present day.   In modern times, one was killed by a motorist on the road in Devon.   A paper published in 1877 averred that the beech martin formed part of Devon's fauna, where it was known as the marten-cat, but it was much threatened by gamekeepers.   It was also said to be found in Dorset and Somerset.   The pine marten referred to above should not be confused with the American animal so called (*Martes americana*). [D7]

BRITISH HOMINOID   Reports of hominoids not unlike bigfoot have come in from parts of Britain over the years.   In 1991 an enormous pithecoid creature was seen on the road between Manchester and Sheffield.   It was brown-haired and 8' tall.   An apelike creature with glowing eyes was seen near Torphins (Scotland) in 1994.   Its coat was black and hairy.   The same or a similar creature was seen watching a house.   A humanoid around 6'8"/2m tall with a black/brown coat was seen near Cannock Chase (Staffordshire) in 1998.   In 2002 on the Stafford-Penbridge Road an apelike creature pursued a car and looked in the window.   Near Friston Park (Surrey) an 8' hominid has been reported.   A "brown man" seen on Simonside Ridge near Rothbury (Northumberland) may also fall into the hominoid class.   Certain other hominids have been given articles of their own. *See* **Big Grey Man, Falkland Hominid, Quickfoot, Sherwood Forest Thing, Smitham Hill Beast, Beast of Bolam.** [31]

BRITISH LION   Occasional intriguing references to lions in Britain turn up in historical sources.   Holinshed's *Chronicles* (16th Century) mention lions in Scotland with manes that could vie with those of northern Africa, but extinct in the writer's time.   The Welsh poem *Pa gur* (?11th Century) says Kay (*Cei*), King Arthur's companion, went to Anglesey to destroy lions (*lleuon*), but these may have been creatures of a vague supernatural and monstrous nature.   The cave lion (*Panthera leo spelaea*) was to be found in England in prehistoric times, but the fossil record does not indicate its survival later than 40,000 years ago.

BRITISH WOLVERINE   Reports of the wolverine (*Gulo gulo*), otherwise known as the glutton or carcajou, have been made from various parts of Britain – Devon, the Highlands of Scotland, Wales – but it seems unlikely a population of these ferocious animals has been introduced.   It is more probable that sightings have been of badgers – perhaps muddy albino badgers – or even cats or dogs.   It is not impossible of course that the odd single specimen ranges loose in the British countryside.   [#1]

BROWN AND WHITE DOLPHIN   A kind of dolphin reported off Senegal.   It resembles the Atlantic spotted dolphin, except that it has no spots.   [B6]

BROWN JACK   An anglicised term for a small hairy hominoid of Australian Aboriginal folklore.

BROWN TIGER A form of tiger reported from Bengal, a region divided between India and Bangla Desh. [S7]

BROXA In Jewish lore, this bird comes in the night and imbibes the milk of goats. [4]

BRUCKEE A lake monster with plantigrade feet reported from Lake Shandagan, Ireland. [M7]

BRUSHMAN Term used for a BHM.

BRUYUNS' DOLPHIN A creature said to be like the striped dolphin in appearance, except that it doesn't have stripes. [B6]

BUATA The natives of New Britain believe in the existence of this creature, which they say looks like a wild boar, but is bigger. Human beings feature in its diet and it is credited with the power of speech. [K7]

BUBBLE GUM DOLPHIN A dolphin seen off the coast of Hong Kong. Though its existence is not in doubt, no one can be sure of its classification. Its colour would remind one of … guess what? … bubble gum. [S5]

BUCKLEY'S CREATURE William Buckley was an escaped convict who lived among the Aborigines of Australia. He relates that he once saw a large-bodied, scaly, four-legged, long-tailed animal that lived in the swamps. A biography of Buckley was published in 1852. [G3]

BUDE SEA SERPENT A passing clergyman saw this animal off the Cornish coast in 1911. [146]

BUGGER Term for a BHM used by commercial fishermen in Florida. [G7]

BUFFALO FISH A creature reported in the 1880s from Okauchee Lake, Wisconsin. [C1]

BUFFALO LION A possible variant race or species of lion, in which the males have no manes, found in Kenya. The individuals involved, however, may be ordinary African lions with hormonal imbalances. [E]

BULGARIAN LYNX The lynx is supposedly extinct in Bulgaria, but there is evidence that this is not the case. [#4]

BULL LAKE MONSTER A monster, reported to look like a large dinosaur 40-50'/12-15m long, swimming with its head out of the water, was allegedly seen in this Wyoming lake in 1906.

BULL-HEADED MONSTER An animal with a bull's head, camel-like forefeet and horse-like hind legs, very heavy, was allegedly killed in Scotland in 1811.   [C3*]

BUNG BUNG A legendary cat of Cameroon, perhaps identical with mystery cats reported from other parts of Africa.   [67]

BUNNY MAN This is supposed to be either a humanoid with rabbit-like features or else someone in a rabbit costume. It has been reported from 1970 around Washington (DC). Angie Proffitt around this time saw what she was sure were the ghosts of children Bunny Man had killed. In one version of the legend, Bunny Man is an escapee from a lunatic asylum in Fairfax County, but in fact this institution never existed.   [1]

BUNNYAR Mystery creature of Western Australia, perhaps the same as the bunyip.

BUNYIP A creature in the legends of the Australian Aborigines. Its name may come from Wergaia *banib* and the earliest version of the word in English may be *bahnyip* which appears in 1812 in the *Sydney Gazette,* where the animal is described as "seal-like". The term, however, has been used somewhat vaguely and even applied to Indian cattle and perhaps crocodiles. Generally, though, it was regarded as a water creature, inhabiting rivers, lakes and lagoons, though some said bunyips lived in burrows. It was claimed they were oviparous. They are associated with a booming sound that some assert is the cry of the Murray bittern (*Botaurus poiciloptilus*). G. Taplin, who was familiar with both, discounted this.

Aboriginal drawings of the bunyip exist. One drawing made in 1848 could be reconciled with the shape of the diprotodon, a large and supposedly extinct Australian animal. Another looked like an emu, but was done under the supervision of a "learned doctor", who may have influenced the artist.

Another depiction was made, perhaps in the early 19th Century. The Aborigines of Ararat (Victoria) killed some huge creature (or else it died) at Fiery Creek. The natives stuck spears in the turf around the dead body to form an outline. The outline was renewed from time to time and was still to be seen in 1840. A drawing exists of it, but it is hard to work out from it just what kind of animal it illustrates.

Numerous accounts exist of bunyips and Victoria seems to be a particular centre of their activities. Over the border in New South Wales, the *Wagga Wagga Advertiser* of 1875 reported a strange beast like a retriever in Midgen Lagoon. In Coral Lake, the head of a strange animal that some said looked like an old Aborigine was seen. A population of strange animals was supposed to be found in Lake George. Morgan's *Life and Adventures of William Buckley* (1852) said the bunyip was believed to be found in lakes in Tasmania and that a woman had actually been killed by one. The Great Lake in that state was supposed to house a resident bunyip. Charles Headlen reported an encounter with a strange animal like a sheepdog when he was boating on this lake. It had appendages which he described as "flippers or wings".

A possible bunyip skull was pronounced by Professor Owen of London (who hadn't examined it) to be that of a calf. Scientists after this became sceptical of the bunyip's existence.

Reports of the bunyip continue to come in, however. Many modern reports come from the Macquarie River in New South Wales. In the Little Murray River in 1947 a strange unidentified black creature which spouted and whistled was discerned. The whistling was supposed to have reached an astonishingly high volume. A whining monster with a taste for swans was reported from a lagoon near Lismore (New South Wales) in 1971. What, however, are we to make of the two-headed bunyip of Tuckerbill Swamp in the same state, of which reports continued until about 1930?

Some commentators have suggested that bunyips are seals. Aborigines who are familiar with seals have denied this. Whites claim they resemble, but are distinct from, seals.

Healy and Cropper have concluded there are two kinds of bunyip and, indeed, E.S. Hall claimed to have seen both varieties, one in 1821, the other in 1822. These are:

(a) a seal- or doglike bunyip;
(b) a four-legged calf-sized bunyip with a maned neck not unlike an emu's, small tusks, a horselike tail and fur or feathers.

Australia boasts about 150 Aboriginal languages. It is possible that some words in those which denote monstrous animals are actually referring to the bunyip.
[H9 H6 S11 B2]

BURES MONSTER A chronicle of 1405 speaks of this creature which appeared in Suffolk. Large, with a crest on its head, it slew sheep and was said to have devoured a shepherd. It was impervious to arrows and was at last chased into a marsh, from which there is no record of its emergence. It had a long tail and teeth reminiscent of a saw. Apart from the crest, it would tend to remind one of a crocodile.   [#1]

BU-RIN A huge snake reported from Myanmar. It is water-dwelling. It has been said to live in the vicinity of Putoo, in the north of the country. Its length has been estimated at 40-50'.   [S8/A]

BURRONJOR A large monster in the folklore of the Australian Aborigines, which took its name from Burrunjor, the region of Arnhem Land where it was supposed to have its home. It is supposed to look like a dinosaur. Tribesmen believe in it to this day and it is said to be heard crashing through the jungle.   [G3]

BURROWING VIETNAMESE SHARP-NOSED SNAKE Animal suspected to exist in Vietnam. [C20]

BURRUM MONSTER Burrum, a lake near Childers (Queensland), was the scene of a sighting of a long-necked monster about 1900.   [C1]

BURU These animals, which appear to have been saurids, were said to have lived in a valley in the Himalayas. As described by the Apa Tani tribesmen, the buru was a heavy animal, its neck and tail about the length of a man's arm. The head was broad and bore three plates, one on top and one on each side. It had feet like a mole's, short legs (an aged priest said they weren't legs properly speaking) and blunt spines in three rows, one along its back, one on each side. In colour, its upper parts were blue-black, its underparts whitish. The skin was reminiscent of a fish's.

Burus lived in water and apparently hibernated, for they would sink into the mud in winter. The Apa Tani at some time past drained the lake and wiped out the remaining population.

Inspired by rumours of still-living burus in a valley called Rilo, an expedition was launched thither. The locals said that, for the burus to appear, it was necessary for rainfall to turn the swamp into a lake. This did not happen while the expedition was there, leading its members to the unwarranted conclusion that the burus were extinct.

R.P. Mackal thinks the burus may have been monitors, but, bearing in mind how fierce that giant monitor, the Komodo dragon, can be and also that the Apa Tani did not regard the buru as dangerous, such a conclusion requires caution. On the other hand, K. Shuker argues that they may be lungfish, while R. Freeman suggests the possibility of a giant salamander.   [I M2 S4]

BUSH BEAST A creature seen in 1966 near Fontana (California). It seems to have been bipedal. It was covered with moss and slime, had brown hair and was over 7' tall. [K2]

BUSHMAN Term used for a BHM.

BUSSE If anciently you ventured into Scythia, you might have encountered the busse. Its head was like that of a hart, its body bovine or taurine. It was coloured like an ass. It was no part of the folklore of this animal that you might wait a long time for a busse and then three would come along together.

BUTATSCH-CUN-LIGS A Swiss monster of a dangerous nature. Its general shape was that of a cow's stomach. It spat fire and it was covered with eyes. It lived in the Luschersee.   [M7]

BYTHIAE Females of Scythia with two pupils in each eye, according to Apollonides. [A2]

C

CAA-PORA A South American hominoid reported from the Parana River which divides Paraguay from Brazil. It is also found in the more northerly Brazilian state of Goias. [#12]

CABBIT The supposed hybrid of a cat and a rabbit, decried by science as genetically impossible. The term *racat* is also used for such a creature. A creature found in El Salvador in the 1980s was held locally to be a cabbit and there is a population of these creatures in the country. Claims made for the existence of cabbits have not been validated. Sometimes, owing to a genetic quirk, a cat can be born with hindquarters that look rabbit-like and in this we probably have the origin of the myth of the cabbit. [23]

CABYLL UISGE A kind of lake monster in the folklore of the Isle of Man. Its name in Manx signifies 'water horse'.

CADBOROSAURUS A creature nicknamed "Caddy" which has been reported from the west coast of Canada. There have been many alleged sightings. A description and drawings provided by O. Ferguson, who claimed a sighting in 1897, furnished details of a serpentine yet vertically undulating creature, about 25'/7.6m long. Other supposed sightings produced varying lengths – one claimed to have seen a specimen of 90'/27m. In 1937 a decomposed carcass, suspected to be that of a cadborosaurus, was found in the stomach of a sperm whale. It was 10-12'/3.5m long. Captain W. Hagelund, fishing in a place called Pirate's Cove, claimed to have captured a baby specimen, which he kept on his boat in a bucket of water. He said it had scales and, on the underparts, a soft yellow fuzz. In the shoulder area were two flipper-like feet, while the tail was composed of two overlapping flippers. Moved by sympathy for his captive, Captain Hagelund returned it to the water, for which act of compassion who can scorn him? It seems the creature comes ashore occasionally. In 1991 Terry Osland heard one jumping back into the sea just before she arrived on the scene.   [S6 L*]

CADEJO In the folklore of Nicaragua and Costa Rica, it is said that each of us has a pair of spectral hounds called cadejos attached to him, a benign white one and a malign black one. Sometimes, if you are menaced by the black cadejo, the white one will fight it to give you a chance to escape.   [A]

CAI-CAI-FILU A South American monster with characteristics of both horse and serpent in which the Araucanian Indians believe.   [#12]

CAITETO-MUNDE A mystery animal reported from South America, perhaps a form of peccary.   [E]

CALADRIUS A white bird with a yellow beak. It would turn its head away from someone who was dying, but look at someone who was going to live. In this case, it would absorb the person's sickness.   [S12]

CALCHONA This seems to be a kind of large, woolly and bearded dog in Chilean and Argentine folklore. Horses are afraid of it and it steals lunch boxes from travellers. [B10 #12]

CALLER A snake in the legends of China and Vietnam. It will call out in human speech to a wayfarer asking whither he is bound. Having ascertained this, he will follow him with murderous intent. Hoteliers in days agone knew the antidote to this creature was a kind of insect whose bite was death to the caller. The bodies of callers that lived a full life span could be used to make lamp oil, which the wind could not put out. [#11]

CALUMET BEAST An animal spotted in Calumet (Oklahoma) which was described as looking like a cross between a wolf and a deer. Body, legs and head, said Mrs L. Laub who saw it in 1951, were reminiscent of a deer, but it had long hair and a bushy tail. The ears were small and pointed. For feet it had large pads. Her husband had seen a similar animal in 1949.   [B9]

CAMAHUETO A horned monster reported off the coast of Chile. It has a tendency to eat humans.   [E]

CAMAZOTZ   A large bat or batlike creature in the lore of the Zapotecs and Mayas. It may lie behind supposed pterosaur traditions in Mexico. It may be based on *Desmodus draculas*, a relative of the vampire bat known only from fossils.   [2]

CAMDEN COUNTY SEA SERPENT We have a misnomer here, because the creature in question was not reported from the sea, but from the Lake of the Ozarks in the inland state of Missouri. In 1935 it was said that this beast with a green scaly head, a serpentine neck, a long, red tongue, a single green eye and a row of knobs along its back was observed in this body of water. There are miles of caves around and perhaps under the lake: here perchance the beast lurks. [B11]

CAMEL-FISH A fish like a camel in shape, whose existence is attested by the Persian writer Kazvini (12th Century).   [H9]

CAMELOPS A native American camel, long thought to have become extinct by the end of the Pleistocene. In 1928 a skull was discovered of this beast in an unfossilised state, which indicates the species had persisted much later than had been believed, unless freak circumstances had caused its preservation.   [S6]

CAMPBELTOWN LOCH MONSTER In 1934 two witnesses observed this creature in this loch in Kintyre, Scotland. It was very large, raising itself to a twelve foot height, then crashing down into the water. It was coloured silver with slender, dark bands. The front part of its body resembled a giraffe.   [H5]

CAMPCHURCH A one-horned animal the height of a stag, with a single mobile horn and the forefeet of a stag and hindfeet webbed like a duck's, reported near the Straits of Malacca by A. Thevet in 1675. [S/2A]

CAMROS In Persian mythology, a bird which dwelt in the Tree of Life. [4]

CANAVAR *see* **Lake Van Monster.**

CANBERRA LAKE MONSTER Strange turbulence on Lake Burley Griffin in Canberra was witnessed by a couple of passers-by in August, 2000. Speculation has arisen, especially from cryptozoologist Tim the Yowie-Man, that some kind of unknown animal was responsible. Lake Burley Griffin is an artificial lake, created in 1963 by the damming of the Molongo, in which any monster currently in the lake would previously have lurked. In 1886 a strange animal, whitish in colour, the size of a dog, was seen in the Molongo. [84]

CANVEY ISLAND MONSTER A strange creature, in a state of rotting decay, but possibly bipedal, was washed up on Canvey Island (Essex) in 1954. It was 2.5'/75cm. long. In 1955 another such creature was found in a better state of preservation, with skin tough like a pig's, noticeable gills, large eyes and sharp teeth. The only authority for this version of the story seems to be F. Edwards *Stranger Than Science* (1959). Although an account of the creature appears on the Canvey Island website, it seems taken entirely from that of Edwards. However, M. Goss has examined contemporary sources and photographs and suggested, with much plausibility, that the creatures were decomposing angler fish.

CAPE BRETON SEA SERPENT A creature with a head like a turtle's and a thick, serpentine body, about 30'/ 8m long, was observed by W. Cartwright off Cape Breton Island, Canada, in June, 2003. [#1]

CAPE SABLE ISLAND MONSTER A huge sea monster seen off Cape Sable Island (Nova Scotia) in 1976. It was observed by Eisner Penny, who said it was 70-80'/21-24m long and looked like a whale, though it was bigger than any creature he had ever seen. It had a "peaked" head and a mouth like an alligator's. A couple of days later, Keith and Rodney Ross saw it and reported it had a brace of tusks as well as teeth, a "brown mass of flesh" which extended from its head to its neck, and protruberant eyes. It had a vertical fishy tail.

In the same area two days later, a creature rising from the depths so scared a man named Wickerson that he turned on the motor of his boat and shot off – even though the boat was anchored to a railing. Wickerson described the creature as horrible. [C22]

CAPE YORK DINOSAUR A creature supposed to inhabit Cape York (Queensland), Australia. There seem to have been traditions about this animal, its trails have been discovered and, above all, its stentorian cries of astonishing volume have been reported. Early colonists appear to have seen the creature and averred it was quadrupedal. [G3]

CAPPY The name of a monster supposedly to be found in Capitol Lake, Washington state. [34]

CARBUNCLE A mystery animal with a mirror in its head, reported from Paraguay and Peru. Small in size, it is also known as the *anagpitan* and *teyu yagua*. An early reference to the creature was by Martin Barco de Centenario in 1602. *See* **Carrabuncle.** [#12]

CARCHAROCLES MEGALODON Twice as long as the great white shark, this creature of the seas is supposedly extinct, but there have been reports of huge sharks whose descriptions are consistent with it. Polynesians speak of a fish called "lord of the deep" which may be this mighty piscid. A shark perhaps as long as 300'/91m was reported in 1918, another was seen by Wild West novelist Zane Gray, which he calculated might have been 40'/12m in length, in 1927. His son saw a similar beastie in

1933. All these sightings took place in the Pacific. However, the Greys' sightinge can be reconciled with those of a whale shark (*Rhinocodon typus*). [#1]

CARIBBEAN MONK SEAL This seal (*Monachus tropicalis*) is supposed to have been extinct since 1952, but reports of sightings still come in.   [E]

CAROLINA PARAKEET A bird (*Cornuropsis carolinensis*) supposedly extinct since 1918. However, there is some evidence that members of the species survived this date. Still existing populations may be awaiting discovery.   [S4]

CARRABUNCLE A strange water creature said in the 19th Century to be found in Lough Geal, on the slopes of Mount Brandon, Co Kerry, Ireland. It was variously described as a snake which made the light shine after nightfall or a huge animal which had gold and jewels hanging from its skin. The wife of the local publican opined it was some kind of fish. The postman said it lit up the lake. It is interesting to note that the lake's name means the bright (or silver) lake.

It has been suggested that the creature may be somehow linked with the *carbuncle*, a mysterious creature reported in South America by the Spaniards. Martin Barco del Centenara identified this with a creature he had seen in Paraguay, small, with a shining mirror in its head. He wrote about 1602. The Irish creature is first mentioned in 1756. [C26]

CARROG A creature of Welsh legend. A piece in the journal *Bye-Gones*, dated 1896, said it was like a dragon. Another correspondent claimed, however, that it was a huge wild boar.

CARTER LAKE MONSTER A monster like a giant snake has been reported in this lake in Michigan.   [C/H]

CARTRON CREATURE The village of Cartron lies in Mayo, Ireland. A most curious creature appeared here in 1968. It was grey or brown or generally dark in colour, with four legs, but when it stood upright it had a lizardlike appearance. Dogs reacted to it with many a hostile bark. When it moved forward, its back became humped. Its head was somewhat feline. Someone struck it on the head with a stick, it then attacked a dog, was attacked by two other dogs, made it to the beach and expired. An attempt to burn it proved unsuccessful. It was left on the strand and did not rot, but was eventually washed out to sea.   [D3]

CARUGUA A hominoid reported from Paraguay. It is said to tear out the tongues of cattle, thereby killing them. These killings were said to have taken place in the 1940s and 1950s. [#4]

CASCO BAY SEA SERPENT A sea serpent exceeding 10'/3m in length seen near Cape Elizabeth (Maine) in 1958. [B9]

CASPIAN TIGER It has been thought likely that this subspecies of tiger is extinct, but local hunters deny this.

CASTLE OF VAYNE BEAST This ruined castle in Scotland is said to be tenanted by some monster that guards treasure there.   [146]

CAT DESTROYER A strange animal which preyed upon cats in Sciotoville (Ohio) in 1888. There seems to have been only one witness, a Dr Bing, who said it belonged to no known species. The head was somewhat vulpine, the colour dark brown.   [#11]

CAT SITH The fairy cat of Highland mythology. It is black except for a white spot on its breast. The spelling *cait* which is sometimes used is in fact the plural form.

CATH PALUG A monstrous and apparently supernatural felid in Welsh legend. It is mentioned in the poem *Pa gur*, couched in very obscure early Welsh, in which it seems King Arthur's lieutenant Kay (*Cei*) killed it. It gave its name to an herb, *palf y Gath Baluc*, in English silverweed (*Potentilla anserine*). It entered continental Arthurian romance, probably via Brittany, where it was called Chapalu. In one romance Arthur killed it; in another, it killed Arthur. [B2/A]

CAT-HEADED CREATURE A sea-beast seen by T. Helm in the Gulf of Mexico in 1943. It was also seen by his wife. It seems to have been quite large and the head was like a cat's, except that no ears were visible. The eyes were to the front like a cat's, rather than to the side, like a seal's. The animal's colour was chocolate brown. [H9]

CAT-HEADED LIZARD Such beasts have been reported in the Alps for centuries. One is said to have been shot by Jean Tinner about 1711. It was 7'/2m long.   These animals are quite possibly identical with the tatzelwurm, *which see.*   [S5]

CATOBLEPAS Whosoever stared the catoblepas in the eyes would die at once, so Pliny informs us. Its head, he tells us, is so heavy it is always bowed down. The animal which inspired this legendary creature is thought to be the wildebeeste or gnu (*Connachaetes*).   [C26]

CAT-THING An animal described as "cat-like" with glowing eyes killed sixteen people in Bulgaria in 1993.   [65]

CAUCIUS In medieval lore, a fish that could not be caught with a hook, even when it took the bait.   [151]

CAULDSHIELDS LOCH MONSTER A monster reported from this Scottish loch in 1815. Sir Walter Scott asked a witness if what he had seen might have been an otter, but he replied that it was more like a cow or a horse.   [C25]

CAVAN BLOODSUCKER In 1874 a mystery animal in Cavan, Ireland, killed over forty sheep and drank their blood, but hardly touched their flesh. The *Cavan Weekly News* said it had attacked people. [65 C3*]

CAX-VINIC Alternative name for the salvaje.

CCOA A huge cat in the myths of the Kauri Indians of Peru. It has a tendency to rain hail and lightning on crops. [C]

CEFFYL Y DWR A monster of Welsh tradition, said to live in lakes. Its name, like the Gaelic *each uisce,* means 'water horse'. This does not mean there is always something equine about them. One in Clwyd looked like a large frog. It is sometimes said to look like a great wet mass which throws itself on passers-by. It could be luminous. A type of small Welsh horse known as the merlyn is said to be descended from these creatures, which had possibly mated with Welsh ponies. [H11* S1*]

CELPHIE This beast, described by Solinus, was said to live in Ethiopia. It had a man's hands and feet, but the rest of it resembled a cow.

CENAPRUGWIRION (pronounced *kenaprigwirion*) A kind of large lizard reported from the Abersoch area of northern Wales. It is said to be a foot long and to live in burrows. Karl Shuker speculates that we might have here an imported population of New Zealand's extraordinary reptile, the tuatara (*Sphenodon punctatus*). [S5]

CENTAUR The centaur of Greek myth was half man and half horse. The notion may have come from a tribe of mounted neatherds in Northern Greece. They were sometimes called *hippocentaurs* ("horse centaurs") which distinguished them from *onocentaurs* ("donkey centaurs") and *ichthyocentaurs* ("fish centaurs"). In modern Greek folklore they have been assigned a vast number of shapes and called *kallikantzaroi* in Greece and *planetaroi* in Cyprus. A creature half man and half horse was reported by a number of witnesses in Centerville (Illinois) in 1963. [C12 B11]

CENTRALIA BEAST An odd creature reported in the vicinity of Centralia (Illinois). It was described by one Howard Baldridge as a felid, smaller than a lion with a face like "something on television". The sightings took place in 1971. [B11]

CENTYCORE An animal noted by Solinus, which combined the characteristics of man (voice), bear (muzzle), lion (breasts and thighs) and horse (hooves), not to mention large ears, a large mouth and eyes close together. This creature was to be found in India and I cannot guess on what, if anything, it was based.

CERASTES A four-horned serpent found in bestiaries. The horns are small.

CETACEAN CENTIPEDE This creature is mentioned by Guillaume Rondelet in his *L'Histoire entiere des poissons* (1558). He says the beast is called a centipede by virtue of the number of its feet, while the word 'cetacean' would indicate it is of considerable size. It has large nostrils and a lobster-like tail. Aelian describes a similar beast.

CHAGLJEVI Nocturnal beasts of doglike appearance reported in Montenegro. They are afraid of men.   [#11]

CHAKORA A legendary Indian bird of the partridge family, said to live on moonbeams. [D1]

CHAMP A large serpentine monster reported from Lake Champlain on the American/Canadian border. The Indians call it *tatoskok.* It is described as having a horse-like head, grey skin and green eyes. It spouts water. There is a mistaken notion that Champlain himself saw the monster, but he in fact saw another mystery creature, the chaousarou. Historian M.L. Porter says he (Champlain) saw a 20'/6m serpent, but this clashes with Champlain's own account. A large number of sightings are recorded in the 19th Century. In 1819 Captain Crum observed it in Bulwagga Bay. He said it was 187'/57m long. It apparently came ashore in 1873 and started feasting on livestock. Hunters tracked it to a cave but its growls and aspect frightened them away. It was later wounded by gunfire from a ship.

In 1887 picnickers by the lake were startled to see Champ heading towards them. They fled, but the creature did not actually come ashore. In 1915 it became stranded in Bulwagga Bay, but succeeded in extricating itself. There were sightings in 1939 and 1945. An alleged photograph was taken by Sandra Mansi in 1977. In 1979 possible sonar evidence of Champ was picked up in Whallon Bay. In 1982 the creature was accorded legal protection in the states of New York and Vermont. In 2003 recordings of what sounded like whale communications were made under the lake. As to what exactly Champ is, if it is a mammal or a reptile one must ask how it survives when the lake freezes over in winter.

In June, 2003, bisonar readings were made by Elizabeth von Muggenthaler of Fauna Communications Research which were ten times louder than those of any fish to which the lake is said to play host.

Interestingly, it is recorded in 1775 that there was a boat called *Lake Monster* on the lake. [Z1 B7]

CHAN **1** A Mexican cryptid, supposed to occupy a lake in the Vale de Santiago since Aztec times. Gifts are bestowed on it by locals each September. The lake is small, but it has been suggested that there are subsurface channels leading to other bodies of water. L. Bolanos led an expedition there and actually managed to photograph a shape of some creature in the water.   [K4]
2 In Chinese legend, a huge clam which seems to breathe, the vapours it exudes forming the shapes of palaces and terraces. It is mentioned by the early historian Ssu-Ch'ien. [W*]

CHANGBAI CREATURE A monster with an egg-shaped head and long neck was observed in this Chinese lake in 1980. The creature was said to look like a reptile, to be black in colour and to be 6'/1.83m long.   [B9]

CHANEY BEAST A hominoid reported over the last 150 years from the vicinity of Chaney (Wisconsin). It is known as "Green Eyes".   [121]

CHAOSAROU Samuel de Champlain (1567-1635) observed this creature in Lake Champlain in 1609. It had sharp teeth and was 5'/1.5m in length. This animal should not be confused with Champ, the lake monster which has become so well known to cryptozoologists.   [Z1]

CHARLES MILL LAKE CREATURE *see* **Mansfield Creature.**

CHARLESTON LAKE MONSTER On this Ontario lake Noah Shook shook indeed when he was pursued by a hissing creature in 1897. A dinosaur-like creature was spotted in the lake in 1947. Water disturbance has made locals suspect there may still be a monster here. They have affectionately named it "Charlie".   [101]

CHATENEUF FOREST RIPPER A mystery beast which killed over 300 sheep in France. Its identity was never discovered.   [#8]

CHATTAHOOCHEE RIVER MONSTER The river in question is near Roswell (Georgia). Descriptions of this creature are vague. It has just been referred to as "something".

CHAUS Pliny mentions this animal which, he informs us, looks like a wolf with spots. The Gauls called such an animal a rhaphius.

CHEMOSIT A ferocious creature which Kenyans believe to be at large in their country. This beast would break through hut roofs, killing those within and eating their brains. It is also said to lie on branches and, when people walk beneath, swipe open their skulls to get at the brains within. B. Heuvelmans suggests that here we are dealing with some unknown breed of gigantic baboon; perhaps the supposedly extinct dinopithecus, for example, is not so extinct as supposed. This creature has, unfortunately, become mixed up with the stories of the so-called Nandi bear.   [H9]

CHENOO A hominoid creature in which the Passamaquoddy Indians believed. It is quite possibly the same as the windigo, as it shares its habit of rubbing against resinous trees and then rolling on the ground.   [C16]

CHERNOBYL BLACK BIRD Before the Chernobyl explosion (1986) in the Ukraine, a huge flying creature with gigantic wings and fiery eyes is said to have been seen in the area.   [170]

CHERUFE A strange beast in Chilean belief, apparently composed of lava. It lives in volcanoes and has a taste for maidens. Perhaps it harks back to a time when young girls were sacrificed to volcanoes.   [4]

CHESSIE Name given to a sea monster sighted in Chesapeake Bay (Maryland), not far from Washington, DC. It was a creature of 20'/6m length, but it seemed to be exceedingly slim. Its undulations varied from the horizontal to vertical and one wonders from the descriptions furnished whether the same animals are being described or whether, indeed, we are dealing with an animal at all. The latter supposition would be supported by the fact that it seemed undisturbed by human onlookers. An unsatisfactory photograph was taken in 1977.   [S18]

CHETCO MONSTER A large ape or apelike creature which apparently gave vent to whistles and shrieks heard by those in an Oregon logging camp in 1890. It apparently killed two men who pursued it. Another man actually saw the creature and put its height at 7-8'/2m-2.3m. He said it had yellow eyes and fangs. The local Chetco Indians apparently harboured a belief in manlike monsters in the area. [115]

CHEYENNE CREATURE An unidentified animal observed near Cheyenne (Oklahoma). Its head was described as sitting on its shoulders, indicating a lack of neck. It was quadrupedal and larger than a dog. It was not furry, its skin was compared with a pig's. It seems to have been quite heftily built and was unflurried by the car-travelling witnesses, who honked their horn at it.   [B9]

CHI LONG In Chinese dragon lore, a dragon without horns. [J2]

CHIANG-LIANG A strange ungulate in Chinese lore, said to have a man's face, a tiger's head, long legs and a snake between its teeth. Whether the latter is in fact something the chiang-liang is eating cannot be determined.   [B10]

CHIAWTKW Upper Chehalis Indian name for a BHM.

CHICKEN MAN This beast carried out its depredations in El Reno (Oklahoma) in 1970. It would raid chicken coops, thus earning its name, and it left in its wake footprints and handprints indicative of a primate, perhaps suffering from a manual deformity. Interestingly, the raids began after one Charles Dreeson, who lived near Calumet, had stopped feeding a wild simian creature in the area of his home.   [B7]

CHIEN ROUGE Mystery red doglike or wolflike animal in the folklore of Vienne, France.

CHIHA TANKA Sioux Indian term for a BHM.

CHILEAN HUMANOID One or more creatures answering this description was/were reported in 2002-3. A 4'/1.2m specimen was seen on a roof in Calama in February, 2003. [#9]

CHILLUDO A large hairy hominoid reported from Argentina in 1950. [#12]

CHIMERA A composite creature in Greek myth. It looked like a lion in front, a goat in the middle and a serpent at the rear. It is sometimes depicted as having a head for each beast. It hailed from Caria (in modern Turkey) and was killed by the hero Bellerophon, mounted on the winged horse Pegasus. In recent times the term *chimera* has come to be used to designate an animal hybrid.   [H2]

CHINESE FLYING SNAKE This reptile was supposed to have existed in China in the time of the T'ang Dynasty (618-907).   [E]

CHINESE SEA SERPENT A large sea monster which became stranded on the coast of China in 1863. About 3000 Chinese made a beeline for the beach and proceeded to chop bits off it. All this was reported by Captain Boyle of the *Beaver*, who witnessed the incident. He procured the head, which had been much mutilated. It was like that of a snake, but the eye reminded the good captain of a pig's.

CHIPFALAMFULA   This is the name of a large fish in the legends of Mozambique. It is capable of clogging a river with its huge body and thereby cutting off the water supply.   [K5]

CHITAPO A monster of Lake Kashiba, Zambia, of which it is said it can eat people's shadows.   [E]

CHITTYVILLE MONSTER A BHM described as about 10'/3m tall reported in 1968 in Williamson County (Illinois). It was black in colour, while its face was hirsute and round. As it was seen not far from the Big Muddy River, one wonders if it could be the same kind of creature, though a colour variant, of the Big Muddy Monster. [#9]

CHIYE-TANKA Sioux name for a BHM.

CHOANITO Wenatchee Indian name for a BHM.

CHOLLIER'S APE This was seen by L. Chollier on the Mali/Burkina Faso border in 1938, but he could not decide whether it was a bear or an ape. It was black with thick dark hair. The natives said that large monkeys lived nearby. [H7]

CHONCHON A sort of flying head with vampiric tendencies supposed to inhabit Peru and Chile. The rustics believe that some dead people develop huge ears, their heads lift from their bodies and they go about thirsting for blood.

CH'OU-TI In Chinese lore a creature with two heads, one at the front and one at the back.   [B10]

CHRISTMAS ISLAND WHALE Large beaked whales which could not be identified were photographed off Christmas Island by K. Balcomb.   [S5]

CHUBUT MONSTER A monster with a swanlike neck and a possibly crocodilian body was seen by a farmer named Sheffield in this part of Patagonia (Argentina) in 1922. [B9]

CHUCHUNAA A wildman of Siberia. They apparently hunt reindeer and traces of their supposed habitation have been found in caves on the River Lena. They are known to whistle. They were also believed to venture over to the Aleutians in Alaska at times. Sightings have declined since about 1900. [B3 C3 T1]

CHU-MUNG Lepche name for the yeti.

CHUN GOEROES Apparently a kind of hominoid, smaller than an almas, to be found in the Gobi Desert. [#8]

CH'UNG-CH'I A creature like a tiger with wings which the Chinese believed was to be found in central Asia. It may be identical with the creature Aristeas of Proconnesus identified with the griffin.. [C26]

CHUPACABRAS This strange creature seems to have made its first appearance in Puerto Rico in 1995. The bodies of livestock were found on the island, drained of blood; hence its name *el chupacabras,* 'the goatsucker'. Then sightings of the creature to which responsibility was assigned began to occur. A particularly detailed description of the entity was furnished by Magdalene Tolentino Maldonado. She claimed the creature was around 4' tall, had short, neat-looking hair, walked upright, had three long fingers on each hand, its arms also appeared long, its eyes lacked whites and were entirely dark. Its legs were long and skinny. It had three toes per foot, apparently webbed. Its mouth was a mere slit, it had two noseless nostrils, that is, simply two holes in the face for breathing. It had a complication on its back, looking like a collection of feathers, but, to judge from the testimony of other witnesses, they were in fact spines. A kind of acid battery smell attended it. There was no sign of genitalia or excretory organs. Its movements seemed strangely robotic, while the skin beneath its hair appeared rubbery.

When the creature exsanguinates an animal, it leaves some kind of slime in the area. Its bites are clean, like surgical cuts. Bites are made around the throat or genitalia.

By late 1995 it seems it was generally believed there was a whole population of the creatures on the island. Mayor Soto of Canovanas had a troop of followers on the lookout for it. Other incidents were reported. Two fishermen were actually pursued by a chupacabras. A Senora Gomez, on 15th November, 1995, saw a clawed hand on the end of a hairy arm come through her window and rip up a teddy-bear.

It has been suggested that the chupacabras paralyses its victims with its bites and subsequently sucks their blood.

In the following days, chupacabras reports continued to come in, but now alleged sightings spread to other countries – Costa Rica, Brazil, Mexico, Guatemala, Peru, Hispanic communities in the United States, even Spain. That its attentions were confined so greatly to persons of Hispanic origin may be a cultural phenomenon, a sort of hysteria spread by the Spanish-speaking media. It is difficult, otherwise, to explain the creature's selectivity. It may be that the term chupacabras has been applied by Hispanics in some cases to quite different anomalous creatures. The "chupacabras" that assaulted Senora

Ayala in Mexico, for example, which was a 2'/60cm winged creature, sounds rather different from the entity with which we are at present dealing. However, Ramiro Parra Gonzalez, of the same country, blamed the chupacabras for the exsanguinations of his sheep in 2002. In 2000 an alleged chupacabras was actually shot by J.L. Talavera of Nicaragua. A veterinary scientist was unable to identify the animal and suggseted it might be the result of genetic engineering. Some alleged chupacabras attacks may be due to the depredations of packs of wild dogs, which will kill an animal, but consume only a small amount of it.

With regard to what this creature might be, the notion that it is some kind of genetic experiment cannot be ruled out. It may be, on the other hand, that such creatures were always to be found in Puerto Rico, but managed to remain well hidden until demographic or other factors flushed them into the public gaze. The suggestion has been made that the Taino Indians knew of the creature which they regarded as an evil god, Maboya. This word was used to designate a crop-destroying deity, while Taino *mabuya* is used to signify a ghost generally.

A chupacabras festival is held each August in Zapata (Texas). [C23 D6]

CHUPAGENTE Guatemalan name for a creature thought identical with the chupacabras. [C23]

CHUPASANGRE Guatemalan name for a creature thought identical with the chupacabras. [C23]

CHUTI A catlike creature reported from the Choyang and Iswa Valleys of Nepal. It is possibly identical with the striped hyena (*Hyaena hyaena*).

CHUZENI MONSTER Chuzeni, a lake on Honshu, Japan, is said to contain a monster which causes unusual waves to break on the shore. [C1]

CIGAU Avoid this Sumatran animal, whose name, however spelled, is pronounced *chigow*. It is said to hate man and is feared by local hunters. It is said to combine features of tiger and monkey, and, though smaller than the Sumatran tiger, it is heftier. Its tail is short, its fur yellow or tan and a ruff decorates its neck. [112]

CIGUAPA In the traditions of the Dominican Republic, this creature has reversed feet and lives in underwater caves. It is said to resemble the chupacabras. [C18]

CINCINATTI MONSTER 1 According to the *Cincinatti Post and Times Star*, a strange monster was supposed to be found in the waterways of this Ohio city in 1959. One witness compared it to an octopus. Another seemed to think it was a bipedal creature several times the size of a man. One person described it as indescribable. It is possible that more than one kind of creature was being reported and that a large dollop of hysteria had coloured accounts.
2 A strange creature reportedly seen in Cincinnati about 1893 by two ladies in a buggy. It boasted wings, a head with a beak and clawed feet. W.R. Benedict, writing to the *Fortean Times*, suggests it was a griffin.

CINOMOLGUS A bird said to build its nest from spices by the ancient Arabians, but none knew where the spices were procured.   [N2]

CIPACTLI According to Aztec legend, this is a creature resembling a crocodile which used to be found in the Gulf of Mexico.   [30]

CIRCHOS A sea monster described by Olaus Magnus. It has doubly cloven hooves, with a left leg much bigger than its right, causing it to list to one side. It fastens itself to rocks at times and, once it does that, it is very difficult to dislodge it. [C9]

CIREIN CROIN A sea serpent of Scottish lore, said to be able to devour seven whales at a single meal. However, the term *curtag* (whirlpool) is sometimes applied to it, indicating it may be a zoomorphic representation of a natural phenomenon. [75]

CLEAR LAKE FISH An unidentified fish with a face like a dachshund's, a horizontal tail (which other fish do not have, though marine mammals do) and pectoral fins reminiscent of feet. It was fished up from this California lake, but then thrown back in. [#12]

CLEARWATER RIVER MONSTER One Robert Forbes saw a creature on this Alberta river seize a calf from the bank. He flung stones at it to make it release its victim, but the 20'/6m long creature just swam off.   [K4]

CLEOPATRA SEA-SERPENT A creature with a dog-like head, coloured greenish-brown and about 30'/9m long, seen from the *Cleopatra* in the Indian Ocean in 1849. [H8]

COATASTAPUVAS In Brazilian legends, the alleged hybrids of monkeys and humans. [#8]

COATESVILLE CREATURE A creature said to combine the features of giraffe, dog and deer and to make wailing sounds. This animal was reported in the vicinity of Coatesville (Pennsylvania) about 1945.   [R6]

COBBETT'S CAT Writer William Cobbett (1763-1835) described how, as a child, he saw a strange cat as large as a middle-sized spaniel, in Surrey. When, years later, he was shown in Canada a cat which was called a lucifee, he was convinced it was the same kind which he had seen in his boyhood years. The lucifee seems to have been a lynx. Whether Cobbett was right in stating it was identical with the mystery cat he had seen years before is uncertain.   [S7]

COBRA GRANDE A huge serpent said to inhabit the Amazon. It is a shapeshifter, according to local lore, using this talent to keep fishermen at bay.

COCKATRICE *see* **Basilisk**.

COCKROACH MAN A bent-over creature which, if standing upright, would have been about 7' tall. It was hunched up and seemed to be running on its knees. Its colour was compared with that of aluminium. It may have had arms. It was seen at Chaffee (Missouri) in December, 2003.   [145]

COHOMO A shortened form of Cole Hollow Road Monster. This creature, seen in Illinois, was of the bigfoot type, between 8-12'/2.44-3.66m in height. It was observed by Robert Emart in 1972 and many further reports were received. One said the beast was swimming in the Illinois River. [R2]

COLEMAN FROG A huge frog which was supposedly killed in Killarney Lake (New Brunswick). An hotelier named Coleman claimed to have had it stuffed. It was 5'4"/1.62m long and weighed 42 pounds. It now resides in a glass case in the York-Sunbury Historical Museum at Fredericton. The suggestion that the creature is a hoax has been made, but the authorities at the museum will not allow it to be examined. [C22]

COLOSSAL CLAUDE A name given to a sea-serpent seen many times between 1921-1950 at the mouth of the Columbus River (Oregon).   [101]

COLUMBUS MYSTERY ANIMAL An animal described as being grey with yellow stripes, viewed in a back garden in Columbus (Ohio) in 1938. It was possibly feline, as it was described as being the size of a dozen cats.   [#9]

COLUMBUS MYSTERY CAT In 1999, Andrew Carowick encountered a felid with black velvety fur and grey stripes in a wood in or near Columbus (Georgia). Seeing him, the creature climbed up a tree backwards and then it backed onto a branch and pulled itself upwards, using its hind legs. It bounded to another tree and thence away. [81]

COMEGOLLOS A man-sized hairy humanoid type of creature with brown or black hair reported from Puerto Rico in the latter two decades of the 20th Century. These animals are mainly nocturnal. The creature has a tendency to eat the hearts of plantain trees, eschewing the fruit itself.   [C24]

CON RIT A strange and headless armour-plated creature washed up in Vietnam in 1883. It was 60'/18m long, 3'/90cm wide and divided into segments. The spines at its end looked like tails.   [S6]

CONCORD HOPPER   Concord (Delaware) in 1979 played host to an unusual creature. Less than 3'/90cm tall, it was black and had a long tail with a curl at the end. It progressed by hopping.   [B9]

CONGOLESE FOREST RHINOCEROS   This possibly unknown species of rhinoceros, bearing some resemblance to the Sumatran rhinoceros, has been reported from central Africa. [30]

CONNECTICUT CRAWLER   A small, scaly, bright green animal spotted in the Connecticut River (Vermont) in 1968. A pair of canoists saw it swimming beside them, then it mounted the riverbank and disappeared from view. They were unable to identify it, nor were park officials when they described it.   [C8/A]

CONSER LAKE MONSTER This Oregon lake, now difficult of access, was supposed to house something compared with a white gorilla in the 1960s. It was said to be web-footed. It is supposed to have communicated with a telepath and to have told her it came from outer space and that its name was Flix.   [140]

COOLE LOUGH MONSTER Coole Lough in the west of Ireland is supposedly the home of a monster. [C25]

COONIGATOR   A raccoon-sized creature which has been reported from the area of Mount Pelier (Vermont). Its body looks like a raccoon's, but its face bears a strong resemblance to an alligator's. It seems to be a scavenger by nature. Reports of this creature are increasing in frequency.   [120]

COPIAPO BIRD A strange bird observed over Copiapo, Chile, in the 19th Century. It had wide, shining eyes, its feathers were greyish, its wings huge, it had brilliant scales which clashed together when it turned and it also seemed to have bristles or something of that order. Its story was told in the July, 1868, issue of the *Zoologist.* [S8]

COQ-NINJI   A sabretooth cat in which the Youlou of the Central African Republic believe. It is perhaps identical with the mountain tiger of Chad.   [S7]

CORDIER'S APE The footprints of an unknown species of ape were discovered by Charles Cordier, an animal collector, in the Congo (Kinshasa). Its identity has never been established.   [C20]

CORN MARTEN A mysterious kind of marten reported from Wiltshire, said to be paler in colour than the pine marten.   [D7]

COROMANDEL MAN A hairy creature, perhaps some sort of ape, reported from the Coromandel Peninsula in New Zealand. A cave has been discovered harbouring bones and shells, where the creature may have been living. It has been suggested that it is a gorilla which escaped from a ship off Wai Aro. R.W. Roach, director of the Auckland Zoo, opined that, if the animal existed at all, it was a baboon. No one can say what it really is. However, different colours (red, silver) have been mentioned in describing the beast's hair, which may indicate there is a population of the animals.   [115 S5]

CORSICAN WILDCAT   A subspecies of wildcat (*Felis sylvestris reyi*), once quite common in Corsica. The mystery is whether or not it still exists.   [S7]

CORTEZ   A fish of medieval lore, which had to seek the depths when it rained, as rainwater would blind it.   [151]

COSENZA MONSTER In 1981 a reptilian creature with fur and legs, 12'/3.66m in length, was reported from Cosenza in Calabria (Italy). [B9]

COW-HEADED FISH A peculiar creature said to be found in Canada's Lake Massawippi. [M7]

COX This beast, which seems to combine the features of a cat and a fox, has been seen on a number of occasions by William Russell of Bradford, Tennessee. [2]

CRANBERRY LAKE MONSTER A 12'/3.66m long serpentine monster has been observed in this Nova Scotia lake. [K4]

CRATER LAKE MONSTER This Oregon lake is so clear you can see right through the water to its bottom. In Klamath Indian tradition it is home to monsters. Mrs Mattie Hatcher reported that, when she was in a boat on the lake, she looked over the side to see a huge monster below her. She said that it was as long as a block of buildings. [12]

CRAWFORDSVILLE MONSTER A strange aerial creature observed in Crawfordsville (Indiana) in 1891. It was 20'/6m in length, 8'/2.4m wide, oblong and without a discernable head. Its flight seemed to be maintained by a number of pairs of fins. Witnesses included G.W. Switzer, Methodist minister.

That evening the creature was seen again, evidently in some distress, squirming and wheezing. An eye was visible in it, described as "flaming". It swooped downwards and those on the ground felt the heat of its breath.

Its ultimate fate seems unknown. [C10]

CRAZY BEAR A term for a supposed wildman used by Indians, according to a journal entry for 1888. Though not unique, the specimen in question lived in a cave in Tennessee. He had been left there by what the Indians referred to as "skymen" who had apparently come in "moons". The story was passed on by the grandson of the diarist. [C11]

CRESCENT LAKE MONSTER A monster, nicknamed "Cressie" , is supposed to inhabit this Newfoundland lake. Traditions of the creature date back to Indian times. There have been many alleged sightings, but different estimates of length, from 5-25'/1.5-7.6m, have led people to speculate that a whole family of monsters inhabits its depths. Descriptions portray the creature(s) as black and serpentine. On August 15th, 2003, Vivian Short claimed to have seen the animal. She reckoned it could easily have polished off several swimmers. The lake has been noted for the large size of its eels and perhaps these lie behind the reports of the creature. [Sightings]

CRESTED COBRA A creature reported from Africa, up to 20'/6m long, lacking a hood and having a forwardly inclined coxcomb. The male, in addition, has wattles and can crow like a cock, while the female clucks like a hen. Maggots are supposed to form much of its diet, but it may also have a taste for hyrax. It is supposed to be very poisonous. It will lie on a tree branch and dart down, biting passers-by on the head. A somewhat similar, though smaller, reptile has been reported from Haiti and Jamaica. [S4]

CRETAN PTERODACTYL A creature reminiscent of a pterodactyl was seen over the Asteroussia Mountains, Crete, in 1986. This incident was drawn to public attention by a letter appearing in the Greek newspaper *Ethnos* in 1987.

CRIMEAN WAR BIRD This avian is the subject of a curious legend connected with the Crimean War (1854-6), in which Russia was opposed by Britain, France, Sardinia and Turkey. Some Russians out for an evening ambush observed overhead a gigantic creature like a huge headless crow and, having become disoriented, lost their way and returned towards their own camp where all but one were killed by friendly fire. In another version the people killed were Turks, who fled towards the Russian lines pursued by batlike creatures.   [74]

CROCOTTA According to Pliny, a cross between a wolf and a dog. Such crosses (wolfdogs) do occur, but this does not seem to be the animal Pliny has in mind, for he describes it as omnivorous and capable of breaking anything with its teeth. This sounds as if it might be an hyena.

CROLAN LOUGH CREATURE This Irish lough is located in Co Galway and is connected with Derrylea Lough. A huge eel, so the story goes, repulsive to behold, was once trapped between the two of them. Nobody would approach the beast. It was left to rot. This happened about 1890. A man named Connolly claimed to have seen an unidentified creature in Crolan Lough in 1961.   [H5]

CRYPTOPHIDION ANNAMENSE The scientific name of a snake reported from Vietnam, but the only tangible evidence for whose existence is a photograph. [74]

CU SITH A fairy dog of Scottish Highland folklore. It is the size of a large calf, shaggy and green.   [131]

CUERO UNUDO A South American creature that looks like a tree trunk and hides in the sand. It attacks its victims with its claws and pulls them beneath the water. In the language of the Araucanians it is called *Lafquen Trilque.*   [#12]

CUINO The supposed hybrid of a pig and a sheep, said to have been found in Mexico and Brazil. However, such a hybrid is not scientifically possible. [S8]

CULLONA A huge bird in the traditions of the Saint John River Indians of New Brunswick. It once carried off a child, but, as its nestlings did not seem peckish, it thoughtfully returned it.   [R2]

CULLOO According to Micmac Indian legends, this was a winged creature so large it would bring moose and caribou to its young to eat. Tradition said it was not above carrying off a human.   [H]

CULTIS LAKE MONSTER In the 1990s a monster was reported in this lake in British Columbia. It may have been a giant beaver. [C/H]

CUNARD DIN A creature said to inhabit Guyana and Brazil. The Wapishana Indians think it is some kind of jaguar. [S8/A]

CURINQUEAN A twelve foot hominoid reported from South America. [5]

CURUMIN A small or juvenile curupira. [5]

CURUPIRA A wildman reported from South America. [5]

CYCLOPS A one-eyed giant, its eye in the centre of its head, in classical mythology. Originally three in number, they were later supposed to be a whole race. They were traditionally supposed to live in Sicily and the finding of elephant skulls there that bore some resemblance to human ones, with a single hole in front (nasal) which may have been thought to be an eye-socket may have given rise to or added to the legend. (The elephants' eye-sockets were in fact in the sides of the skull). The most famous classical cyclops was Polyphemus, whom Odysseus blinded. The Basques formerly believed in a cyclopean giant called Tartaro. Cyclopeanism can occur naturally in humans. [C12]

D

DAALZWURM Alternative name for the tatzelwurm. [41]

DAEDALUS SEA SERPENT A creature sighted from HMS *Daedalus* in 1848. It was described by Captain McQuhae as a head and shoulders held above the water, about 30'/9m in overall length and moving without the slightest deviation from its course. It was coloured dark brown and was yellowish-white about the throat. It had a mane like a horse's.

Because of the apparently unmoving nature of the beast, it has been suggested that it was nothing more than a mass of vegetation. This seems unlikely because of its proximity to the vessel. It has also been suggested it was a native canoe with a face painted on the prow. However, we cannot rule out the possibility, especially bearing in mind the professional status of the witnesses, that it was a living and unidentified beast . As a footnote I would add that I am waiting for the day when some crackpot of psychiatric bent will announce that the political disturbances in Europe in 1848 had such an effect on the mariners that they conjured up the image of the sea-serpent to encapsulate their insecurity and unease. [H8]

DAKWA In Cherokee legend a huge fish, known as the father of fish, which dwelt in the French Broad River in North Carolina. [119]

DAMASIA A large, dark, leopard-like creature reported from Kenya. Natives maintain it is a completely distinct animal from a leopard. [S7]

DANAU POSO MONSTER A lake monster on the island of Celebes (Indonesia), reported as having the head of a cow and being 30'/9m long. [E]

DARK BLUE BIRD A flying creature, which the witnesses claimed was too large to be a bat, was reported from the cave system in Chapel-le-Dale (Yorkshire). [146]

DARTMOOR CAVEMEN A friend (gender unspecified) of the noted folklorist Theo Brown was at the uncanny area of Lustleigh Cleve on Dartmoor when he/she saw a family of "cave men", naked and hairy, or perhaps wearing shaggy pelts. They were in the environs of the stone circles there. [#1]

DARWIN SEA MONSTER A creature seen from near Darwin, Australia, in 1980. It had a long neck and was estimated to be more than 75'/23m long. [B9]

DAS-ADDER A creature supposedly found in the Drakensberg Range in South Africa, with a head reminiscent of a hyrax and a body like that of a viper. Its tail is said to be bedizened with red and yellow stripes and it is very poisonous. If it in truth exists, it may be a legless lizard rather than a snake. Attempts to explain it as a monitor fail to convince. [S5]

DAUPHIN LAKE MONSTER In 1948 a monster was reported in this Manitoba lake. It was about 6' long and coloured brownish-black. [R8]

DEATH BIRD These "birds", whose actual existence is not in doubt, live in Lekempti Cavern near Nek'emte, Welega, Ethiopia, coming out at night to drink blood. Nobody knows exactly what they are, but they may be of the vespertilian kind, rather than genuine birds. [31]

DEDIEKA A mystery simian like a chimpanzee. It has a black face. It has possibly sprung entirely from misidentifications of chimpanzees or gorillas. On the other hand, it may be identical with the kooloo-kamba. [F5]

DEER WOMAN In the legends of the Poncan Indians of Nebraska, a woman with the legs and hooves of a deer. She will seduce and kill men. [B7]

DEFIANCE WEREWOLF A werewolf reported from the vicinity of Defiance (Ohio). In 1972 a railroad worker saw a creature 7-9'/2.13-2.74m approaching. It had fangs, was hairy and shuffled. It carried a stick, with which it struck the worker, who identified it as a werewolf. Other reports came in and the police were put on the alert. [132]

DE LERY'S LIZARD John de Lery (whose name was latinized as Lerius) lived in the 16th Century. In the wilderness of South America he descried a human-sized lizard with hard scales. His party lacked firearms and they made no attempt to attack the reptile. [W5]

DELAMERE FOREST ANIMAL   An unidentified creature often seen in this forest near Chester in 1974. In some respects it resembled an Alsatian/German shepherd, but its tail was like a fox's brush.   [B8]

DELAND'S SEA SERPENT   Captain Deland of the good ship *Eagle* made a report in 1830 of a 70'/21m long beast, not unlike an alligator, which he had discerned from his vessel. He fired a musket, striking or grazing the animal, which understandably piqued it. It rammed the ship again and again. It was described as eel-shaped and its back was full of joints or bunches. A smaller serpent was descried in the distance. Fortunately for Deland's crew, the attacking beast did not succeed in sinking the ship.   [F5]

DELAVAN LAKE MONSTER   A monster reported in the 19th Century from this Wisconsin lake. C.E. Brown describes it as "prankish", but does not elaborate. [B16]

DE LOYS' APE   Here we have a rather controversial cryptid, which some have suggested is a hoax. A geologist named F. de Loys, in South America in 1920 with companions, shot a huge spider monkey-like primate, or so he claimed. He set it propped up on a box to show the comparative size. He maintained it was a true ape, for it had no tail. Then he photographed it. Unfortunately, the box's use as a determinative for height was questioned and it was suggested that the only reason the animal lacked a tail was because someone had cut it off. However, if it was a fraud, K.P.N. Shuker pertinently asks why it was perpetrated, as de Loys was a geologist and discovering new species was not really within his field of interest. R. Freeman, on the other hand, is convinced the creature is a red-faced spider monkey (*Ateles paniscus*). *See also* **Mono Grande**. [H9 S4]

DELTOX SWAMP CREATURE   The swamp in question lies in Wisconsin. Some might have thought the creature a bigfoot, but it left fin marks in its footprints, which would indicate another kind of primate altogether.   [C17]

DEMON NIGHTINGALE   A creature with a bird's head and a human body which, in Russian legend, fought the hero Svyatogor.   [134]

DENDAN   Huge fishes of Arabian legend which die if they come into contact with man. [28]

DERBYSHIRE HOMINOID   A hairy humanoid, 8'/2.4m tall, seen near Cutthroat Bridge, Derbyshire, in 1991.   [78]

DERO   A surprising belief in these creatures was for a time quite widespread and they are believed in even today. They are supposed to be a race of subterraneans, some looking like humans and some definitely not, who interfere with surface life and lead a debauched existence. They were first heard of when Richard Shaver (1907-1975) claimed that, while working in an assembly plant, he heard voices coming from his welding implement, which informed him concerning them. He also remembered, he claimed, past lives. He wrote of this to the magazine *Amazing Stories* in 1943. When his beliefs were published, every crackpot who could wield a pen wrote in supporting the idea that the dero existed, some suspecting that this was the true nature of certain of their neighbours. The dero were opposed by a more benign group, the tero. The dero craze died down in due course, but there are still some who credit their existence. [C6/A]

DESCHENE LAKE MONSTER   In this Ontario lake, a boat supposedly struck some kind of underwater creature in 1880. Something resembling hair was afterwards found in the water.   [H14]

DEV   A kind of wildman in the lore of the Tajiks. It is perhaps identical with the Mongolian almas. People do not regard it as dangerous, but it is thought of as an evil omen to meet one. B.M. Zdorik saw one sleeping on its stomach in 1934. He said its feet were not consistent with those of a bear. The Tajiks, he felt, used another name for the creature amongst themselves, but , as the term *dev* was more widespread, used that to convey their meaning to him when he discussed the creature with them.   [T1]

DEVIL BIRD   A bird of Sri Lanka noted for its hideous cry. K. Shuker suggests it may be some kind of nightjar.   [S4]

DEVIL CAT   In Amerindian lore, a black felid regarded as a counterpart of the puma, but very much to be feared. It was said to carry off children. The animal is unlikely to have been a form of puma, as melanism is extremely rare in that species, if it exists at all. However, bearing in mind there are sundry reports of "black panthers" in the United States at present, one wonders if surviving populations of devil cats may not in some instances account for them.   [#11]

DEVIL MONKEY   A term used to signify a mystery animal that looks like a baboon and jumps like a kangaroo. It is, however, rather larger than a baboon, 4-5'/1.5m tall. Feet are flat and three-toed. This creature is thought to exist in the United States and may account for the reports of "phantom kangaroos" that sometimes come from that region. It is possibly identical with an animal known to the Choctaw as *nalusa falaya.* An early sighting may have occurred in 1941 when a cleric named Harpole encountered something like a baboon in Jefferson County, Illinois. From 1941-2 there were a number of further sightings. A band of baboons reported from the Trinity River area of Texas in the 1980s may have actually been devil monkeys.   [C21 C19]

DEVIL PIG *see* **Gazeka**.

DEVIL'S LAKE MONSTER   A monster has been reported on the surface of this Wisconsin lake on a number of occasions. Descriptions are vague.   [A1]

DEVIL-WATER-COW   These beasts, noted for their pungent odour and strange call, are reportedly found in Lake Weatherford (Texas). They have a taste for human flesh, so don't try to stroke one should you happen upon it.   [116]

DHULIGAL   This word, variously spelled, is said to be an Aboriginal name for the yowie. It is found in the Ngarigo language.   It was also used to mean an ogre and a tribal outcast. Aboriginal expert R. Robinson quite firmly says the doolagarl (his spelling) is a man-like gorilla. [S11 H6]

DHULOUGH MONSTER   Three witnesses saw a monster in this Irish lake. One of them apprised Lady Gregory (1852-1932) of the event. It had a mane like a horse's. [C25 G7*]

DIBA Baya name for the badigui. [H9]

DIDI Humanoid creatures, about five feet tall, reported from Guyana, Suriname, French Guiana and Venezuela. They are described as black haired. A British magistrate claimed to have seen a couple of them in 1910. A similar claim was made by an American mycologist in 1987. According to legend, they have opposable thumbs. It is said they live in couples and, were one killed, its mate would find the hunter responsible and strangle him in his hammock. The didi were supposed to be responsible for a long, low whistle heard by C. Barrington Brown, a government surveyor, in 1868. In fact, reports of them go back to about the 17th Century. In 1769 British writer E. Bancroft mentioned them.   [C21 H9 S1]

DIENTUDO, EL   The name of this large, hairy hominoid reported from Argentina means 'the one with the big teeth'. It lives in woods, but it has also been reported in or near the city of Tolosa.   [#12]

DILALI A maned beast reported from Cameroon. It is generally regarded as inhabiting water, except among the mountain-dwelling Youlou. One description gave it a horse's body and lion's claws. Another said it was tusked.   [H9]

DILDO POND MONSTER This body of water in Newfoundland is said to harbour a monster of some kind. They have some strange placenames in Canada.

DINDERI Small hominoids covered with red hair in the Aboriginal lore of Queensland. [S5]

DINGONEK An African monster encountered in rivers flowing into Lake Victoria. It is said to have scales and claws, white fangs (?tusks) in the upper jaw, a lioness-sized head (spotted) and a length of 14'-15'/4.50m.   [H9]

DINOSAUR SWAMP CREATURE   A monster supposedly found in the Singleton region of New South Wales. There is a valley in the area called Dinosaur Swamp locally and here the creature is said to dwell. Reptilian tracks in days gone by were found near a farm of the valley's periphery and farm animals went missing. In 1953 duck shooters claimed to have seen a monster standing in water in the valley. Though it was partially hidden, they could see it had a long thick neck and a head reminiscent of a snake's. White excrement found in the area may also be testimony to the creature's existence. In

1976 Steve Taggart had a good view of the animal, which reminded him of an apatosaurus (which was called a brontosaurus in the days of my youth and vigour). P. Garland claimed to have seen the monster in 1985. He reckoned its length at 25'/7.62m and again a comparison was made with an apatosaurus. [G3]

DIRTY WATER LAKE MONSTER   This Manitoba animal was observed in 1935 and described as looking like a dinosaur. It boasted a horn.   [F4]

DISCO BAY MONSTER   A water monster, black in colour, was reported from this Greenland bay in 1954.   [B9]

DJA RIVER MONSTER   This monster in Cameroon has been described as having a tortoise's head, a long neck and a large body.   [E]

DJUGWE   A huge bowerbird in Australian Aboriginal mythology, who taught man how to erect shelters for initiation ceremonies and how to dance. His spirit continues to be found in lesser bower-birds of today.

DOBHARCHU   In the Irish language, this word can mean either an ordinary otter or a special kind of monstrous otter, called in English the master otter or king otter. The creature is also known in Scotland, where there is a Loch nan Dobhrachan on the Isle of Skye.

In Roderick O'Flaherty's *Description of West or h-Iar Connaught* (1684), we are told of an attack by a dobharchu. It fastened its teeth in an unfortunate wayfarer's head, but the man, though dragged into the water, thrust his knife into the animal and escaped. He said it was black skinned and hairless. An earlier encounter was reported between the beast and a man with a wolfdog. The beast was driven off and what were thought to be its remains were later found decomposed in a cave. There may be some confusion in the first of these accounts with the ordinary *each uisce*.

A dobharchu was supposed to have killed Grace Connolly in 1722 at Glenade Lake, Co Sligo. Her husband, coming on the dobharchu standing over her body, shot it. Another dobharchu emerged from the lake, perhaps its mate. The husband fled, but returned with his brother. The dobharchu pursued them, but the husband at length managed to kill it. Grace Connolly's grave is today to be found in Congbhail Cemetary and there is a dobharchu carved on it. This shows a beast with powerful legs, an otter-like head and a canine muzzle.

It is said in legend that only a silver bullet can kill a dobharchu. It is said to rule over other otters. Sometimes it is said to be white.

Gary Cunningham suggests that an unusual stuffed otter in Hynes' Pub in Crossmolina (Mayo) is a dobharchu. [C2 S8]

DOBSENGA   A mysterious creature reported by natives in both parts of the island of New Guinea. It has a huge mouth, is striped from ribs to hips and is doglike. It bears a considerable resemblance to the thylacine (*Thylacinus cynocephalus*), which was found in Tasmania, but is now thought, perhaps erroneously, to be extinct there. [S6]

DODO The dodo's extinction is proverbial, though stories persist of the occasional specimen's being encountered on Mauritius. Alleged twilight appearances have taken place on the Plain Champagne. These reports are unlikely to be accurate for ecological reasons.   [C2]

DODU This creature, reported from Cameroon, seems to be a large ape. It generally walks upright, but will occasionally proceed on all fours. It has only three fingers per hand and likewise three toes, with claws, per foot. It can reach a height of 6'/1.83m. Its colour is dark grey. It appears to be very ferocious and will attack gorillas.   [S8/A]

DOG-BEAR THING This rather vague name was given to a creature seen near Brookfield (Connecticut) and reported in October, 2003. It was coloured white. It was said to be the size of a bear (somewhat variable, depending on the sort of bear), but it ran like a dog.   [2]

DOG-FACED BEAST In the 1920s this water creature was observed in the Pentland Firth, Scotland.   [146]

DOG-FACED MEN Chinese records mention a ship from Fukien which sailed into the eastern Pacific in 507 AD. The sailors discovered an island where dog-faced men lived. However, it is not possible even to guess where the ship landed or what the creatures were. Baboons or lemurs spring to mind.   [F11]

DOGLAS This creature is believed in India to be the hybrid of a leopard and a tigress. Large leopards with stripes have definitely been seen, but whether they are truly hybrids or a different species has yet to be determined.   [S7]

DOG-LIKE ANIMAL An animal that resembled, but didn't appear to be, a dog was sighted at St Louis (Mo.) in the 1990s. It was the size of a German shepherd/Alsatian or even larger. It had red glowing eyes.   [2]

DOG-LIKE PRIMATE   Creature observed in the woods in Virginia in 2002 and so described.   [2]

DOG MAN A creature sighted a number of times in the Big Thicket area of Texas. [R6/A]

DOG-MAN For more than a century there have been reports of a man with a dog's head in the Michigan woods. It is said to appear every seventh year of each decade. [S8]

DOGSHEADS There were fire-breathing men with dogs' heads who lived in Ethiopia, Herodotus informs us. In the Middle Ages, dog-headed people were said to be found in India. Marco Polo informs us dog-headed people inhabited the Andaman Islands. King Arthur was supposed to have fought with Dogsheads in the region of Edinburgh, according to the obscure Welsh poem, *Pa gur.* H. Butler suggested his adversaries were a tribe of people whose name meant dogsheads. While this is plausible, what are we to make of Carla Randle's brother, Mark, who, at the age of nine, claimed he had seen fully dressed men with dogs' heads in Crewe in the 1960s?   [B17]

DOMENECH'S PSEUDO-GOAT The Abbe Domenech, a missionary whose memoirs were published in 1858, said an American officer had told him of the singular pet of a Comanche woman, which he had seen in Texas. It was the size of a cat, looked like a goat, bore roseate horns and had white fur with the glossy consistency of silk. In lieu of hooves, it had claws. She refused to sell it, but said she knew of a wood where the species abounded, yet no one has ever reported seeing this kind of animal again.   [S8]

DOONONGAES In Iroquois lore, a serpent with horns which lives in the water. It seems to be an individual. It is also a shapeshifter. [134]

DORMIDERA Explorer Percy Fawcett records having heard of a kind of anaconda called a *dormidera* (sleeper) in the Araguaya and Tocatins basins in Brazil. This creature was said to be black and huge, with a propensity to snore.   [C1]

DOUBLE-BANDED ARGUS The existence of this bird (*Argus bipunctatus*) is inferred from a single primary feather. Its home may be on Java or Tioman Island. [71]

DOUBLE-HEADED EAGLE A creature found in petroglyphic form in Mexico and Chile. H. Wilkins tells us that when the Marquess of Vallero was Viceroy of Mexico, he found in a tomb two embalmed heads of double-headed eagles. Wilkins implies a species of such eagles existed, but this seems highly unlikely. If the discovery in fact took place, the bicranial birds may have been fakes or possibly each was a *lusus naturae* specially preserved because of its singularity.   [W5]

DOUBS MONSTER A long-necked monster was seen in this Swiss river in 1934. [B9]

DOVER DEMON At 10.30 p.m. in Dover (Mass.) on April 21st, 1977, three seventeen-year olds were driving along when one, W. Bartlett, espied a strange living creature on a wall in Farm Street. The creature was progressing somewhat gingerly. In the full light of the car, the witness saw the entity had a large head the size of a water melon and a trunk of equal size. The skin was hairless and rough, a kind of deep flesh colour and it seemed to have something black rubbed on it. The body was thin, as were the arms and legs. The hands and feet, however, appeared large. The witness's companions saw nothing.

Shortly after midnight John Baxter saw the creature, which ran into a gully. After looking at it, he withdrew. The next night (April 22nd), it was seen by two teenagers, Will Taintor and Abby Brabham. They made out its face, which had eyes, but no nose or mouth. It also lacked ears and a tail. The eyes had a green glow.

Assuming the episode is not a hoax, the creature's identity remains a mystery. An argument that it was a misperceived yearling moose is unpersuasive. [C19]

DOWA BEAST An unidentified beast which has been reported from the Dowa district of Malawi in 2003. It injures its victims terribly. The suggestion that it could be a rabid hyena seems an inadequate explanation.   [54]

DOWINGTON CREATURE A creature part man, part beast, its outer covering of dirt or hair, reported from Dowington (Pa.) in 1932.   [C19]

DRACONA Draconas featured in Greek mythology. Their upper halves looked like beautiful women, their lower halves like serpents.

DRAGON In its standard form the dragon is scaled, quadrupedal, reptilian, fire-breathing and winged. However, in classical literature the term usually signified a large serpent and it is possible this was its meaning in the earliest English sources. When exactly it assumed its current shape and form is difficult to determine. However, if we look behind classical mythology to the Babylonian period, four-footed dragons are certainly recorded there.

In the classical mind, some distinction seems to have been made at times between serpent and dragon – for example, Hesiod speaks of them as different creatures – but there can be little doubt that, in the mind of the average Greek and Roman, the dragon was no more than a big snake.

Some addition to the standard concept of the dragon may have arisen from the use of the dragon-shaped windsock. Trajan's Column in Rome shows a Dacian holding one, while Flavius Arrianus tells how the Scythians wove these artefacts to look like real flying dragons when the wind filled them. Dragons came to be used as standards by the Roman army and were later adopted by the British Celts.

Martianus Capella wrote in the 5th Century that dragons breathed fire, as did his fellow Carthaginian Blosius Aemilius Dracontius not much later.

At what stage the dragon took root amongst the Germanic nations is another matter. They may have picked up the notion of the beast from the Romans. Words derived from Latin *draco*, such as Old High German *traccho*, are common in Germanic languages. However, we cannot rule out the possibility that they harboured some similar beasts among their own beliefs.

We learn from Anglo-Saxon poetry that dragons guarded treasure. There is a suspicion that in early belief persons buried with treasure turned into dragons to guard it, but that in literature this notion has been excised, as it clashes with Christian ideas of the Afterlife. Amongst the Norse, treasure was called 'dragon's bed' (*orms bedr*). In classical literature the dragon is also regarded as a treasure guard. Cicero refers to dragons' treasure, while in the *Fables* of Phaedrus we are informed that treasure guarding is the dragon's function, assigned it by Jupiter.

By the 13th Century it seems to have been generally established that dragons had four legs. Earlier it may have been held they had two. There is a two-legged dragon on the Bayeux Tapestry (11th Century). Yet as late as the 17th Century there is an illustrationn of a legless dragon in Topsell's *History of Serpents* (1608), while both Aldrovandus and Gesner seem to have thought at least some dragons had merely a brace of feet each. It might be mentioned, however, that Topsell believed in legged as well as legless dragons.

The dragon was also known in Africa. In this context we might mention the dragon Bida, mentioned in the west African *Epic of Dausi*. It lived in a lake near the Niger and devoured a maiden a year.

When we turn to the oriental dragon, we may wonder if we are dealing with the same beast at all. Indeed, it has been argued thet the Chinese *lung* should never have been translated as dragon. While the western dragon was essentially a foe, that of the east was generally beneficent. It is said officially to have a camel's head, deer's horns, rabbit's eyes, snake's neck, frog's belly, carp's scales, hawk's claws and tiger's palms. In practice – for example in art and general belief – dragons were not constructed in so complex a manner. Depictions of them resemble their European counterparts. The physiology of the Chinese dragon is said to be based on the Chinese alligator (*Alligator sinensis*). This notion is buttressed by the belief that they often have a watery habitat. Chinese dragons are sometimes shown with "wings", but these are more properly fin-like appendages. In ancient times in China the Indo-Pacific crocodile (*Crocodylus porosus*) was regarded as a flood dragon. The Chinese distinguish between two kinds of dragon, the smooth-skinned and the rough-skinned. Once again treasure appears in connection with the animal, for there is a special subspecies that guards treasure (*fu-t'sang lung*).

Japanese dragons (*tatsu*) are similar to those of China, except that they have three claws, while their counterparts in China have four or five. The king of the Japanese sea dragons is Ryu-jin, whose underwater court is near the Ryukyu Islands. There are records of some dragons' being kept in temples in Japan and these may have been Indo-Pacific crocodiles.

One might ask if there could be any truth behind the legend of the dragon? Sightings of large snakes and lizards from time to time may have led to belief in them. Carl Sagan has suggested that we may have inherited a memory of dinosaurs from small mammals coeval with such mighty beasts. John Christopher, on the other hand, argues they may have been real animals, but, owing to the combustible nature of their interiors, they exploded on death, thus leaving a world bereft of their remains. I feel both these ideas should be treated with caution. The belief of D.E. Jones is that man's ancestors lived in a world which had three particular predators – the snake, the big cat and the bird of prey – and that these have melded themselves together in the human unconscious to form the dragon. He goes on to relate this fusion to a theory of memory. One cannot just rule out the existence of a real unknown beast behind some of the legends. An actual alleged sighting of a winged dragon crawling in and out of a cave a number of times in 1902 was reported by Chinese soldiers. This is not the only modern report of a dragon.

That the dragon is nothing more than a symbol of greed, Mammon enfleshed, has been postulated by mythologist Joseph Campbell, but he cannot be said to have proven this. It might be added that the term firedrake (drake=dragon) was applied to meteors, which were doubtless thought to be fiery reptiles flying through the sky.

I understand a foodstuff called Welsh Dragon pate is available in Oxford.
[G5 T4 M G8 S7/A C26 J2]

DRAGON-BIRD **1** In Japanese belief a creature (Japanese *hai-riyo*) which has a dragon's head and wings. The body is that of a bird. [J2]
2 A creature in the *Epic of Mwindo*, part of the legendry of the Congo (Kinshasa). It had swallowed, but not digested, a great many people, so when the heroine Nyamitondo killed it, the people inside were freed. [K5]

DRAGONESS A female dragon. The term is quite modern, dating only from the 17th Century.

DRAGONET This word can signify either the young of a dragon or a dragon of small size. It is first found in the 14th Century. Under this heading it might be appropriate to mention an alleged baby dragon of which Aldrovandus speaks. He judged the specimen, which had been killed by an Italian farmer in 1572, to be a juvenile. It had only two legs. Alleged bodies of baby dragons were displayed at Paris in 1557. They may have been specimens of the Asiatic lizard *Draco volans.*

DRAGON-HORSE A creature which resembled a horse in front and a dragon behind. This sort of creature seems to have been known among both the American Indians and the Chinese.   [H*]

DRAGON-WORM A creature reported to have been seen in Switzerland in 1468. It swam out of Lake Lucerne and into the River Reuss. Details of its size and speed could not be determined.   [M7]

DRAKENSBERG UNICORN This cryptid is said to be extinct, but occasional sightings still occur. It is dark brown, with a single horn and very dangerous. It lives in the Drakensberg Mountains, South Africa.   [31]

DREKAVAC A beast of Serbian folklore. Supposedly hairless, it will drag its victims into the River Morava. By some at least it is said to live in the mountains and to make somewhat simian sounds. One was heard in the swamp near Basheid in the 1900s. A supposed dead drekavac was found on the banks of the Kravicke in 1992. It looked like a combination of a dog and a fox with legs like a kangaroo. Locals feared that, despite folklore, it was in fact the result of laboratory experiments.   [#11]

DROP BEAR It is said in Australia that drop bears resemble koalas, but are far fiercer, dropping out of trees to attack helpless passers-by with fang and claw. Some argue that these have a real existence, while others maintain they were invented to scare tourists. [1]

DU A legendary bird of the Houailou, a tribe of the Isle of Pines in the Pacific. It was said to be human-sized, flightless, swift and fierce. To back up the legend, bones of a large flightless bird were discovered in 1974.   [#8]

DUAH A flying creature rumoured to live in Papua-New Guinea. It has been compared to a pteranodon. Its underparts seem luminescent.   [87]

DUENDE, DWENDI Originally a name for a homesprite in Spanish folklore, this term has come to be applied to sundry beings of a folkloric nature in Central and South America and the Philippines. In Belize, however, it may stand for a cryptozoological creature, which is described as 3.5 – 4.5'/ 1.2m tall with thick, tight brown hair and a tendency to hold palm leaves over their heads. They have been seen by many witnesses. [G2]

DUINE EAGALACH A sort of tall wildman said to live on Rannoch Moor in Scotland. His mane is thick and black, while his eyes gleam. His head is described as 'egg-shaped'. In Gaelic, his name signifies a person who instils fear.   [F4]

DUMP CREATURE In 1999 a woman whose name is given as Paula M. was searching for vintage glass in a dump outside a small Oregon town when a strange creature partially emerged from a hole. It was not a worm, but somewhat wormlike. At first the witness could discern no distinguishing features, but suddenly two crystal blue eyes appeared on it. She in fact described it as looking like a tube with eyes, though it never seems to have emerged completely from its hole. It raised itself further upwards and began to sway. Finally, it retreated into the opening whence it had emerged. [99]

DUMPTON PARK CREATURE A strange animal observed by a policeman in this park in Ramsgate (Kent) in 1954. It was the size of an Alsatian (German shepherd) and had claws.   [A]

DUNDASS ISLAND BLACKFLY A large black insect, said to attack in swarms and consume its victims' flesh and blood. It is supposed to be found on Dundass Island (British Columbia).   [30]

DUNDONALD HILL CREATURE This hill in Scotland was supposed for a long time to be the dwelling-place of a huge creature. In 1994 a woman encountered on it a 10' tall bipedal creature with charcoal-coloured hair. She felt it had a spectral character.

DWARF DRAGON In the vicinity of Heidelberg, back in pagan times, it was common to keep dwarf dragons as household pets. They were handy for lighting a fire. Only the males could fly. The females liked water and would come down to the River Neckar. [135]

DWARF HORSE A race of dwarf horses was, in American folklore, said to live in the Grand Canyon. Small horses were kept there by the Havosupai Indians, but they were not as small as the dwarf horses of folklore. In the 1930s a number of circuses were exhibiting such horses and claiming they had been captured in the Grand Canyon. It reached the stage that some scientists were suggesting that the Canyon harboured a relict population of eohippus, supposedly extinct for 35 million years, but none of these animals was discovered in the wild.   [#11 K8/A]

DWAYYO A large hairy creature was supposed to be dwelling in the Gambrill State Park in Maryland in the 1920s. It was said to have been seen in Carroll County in 1944, where it was noted for its screams and loud footprints. A 6'/1.83m tall bushy tailed creature was supposed to have attacked a man named Becker according to the *Frederick News Post* in 1965. In December of that year, the same paper reported that it had been seen chasing cows. The name *dwayyo* itself was not used before 1965, when it was coined by a man named G. May. May asserts that he did not, however, concoct the Becker report. [#12].

DZIWOZONY Wild women in the folklore of Poland. They throw their breasts over their shoulders, a practice attributed to wild women elsewhere. They are hostile to humans, but will sometimes force young men to become their lovers. Perhaps there is a dearth of equivalent wildmen.   [J1]

DZONOQ' A The Kwakiutl Indians give this name to male and female hominoids. [M6]

DZU-TEH Large hominid reported from Tibet and Xinjiang, perhaps identical with the tok, gin-sung and kung-lu. It is thought to be the largest of the three types of yeti and is said to attack cattle. Some have suggested this creature is no more than a misidentified bear. At places supposed to have been raided by dzu-tehs, clawlike ursine prints have been found. R. Messner, an Italian mountaineer, claims to have seen the yeti (i.e., the dzu-teh) four times and that it is in fact a bear. Against this, however, R. Freeman argues that a bipedal gait is atypical of bears and so the dzu-the should not be identified with them.

E

EACH UISCE ("horse of water") A general term for lake monsters in Ireland and Scotland. In Scottish Gaelic the spelling *uisge* is used.

EARTH HOUND A mystery creature of Banffshire, Scotland. It is supposed to be about the size of a ferret, to have a somewhat doglike head and to live in graveyards. It is said to break into coffins and devour corpses. A couple of killings of the creature are said to have taken place in the early 20th Century. The creature is also known as a *yard pig.*

EAST CAPE SEA SERPENT A sea serpent seen off North Island, New Zealand, in 1891 from the *Manapouri*. It had some sort of appendages depending from its sides.

EAST COAST RIVER SERPENT This creature, reported from Trinidad, could not really be a serpent, as it did not move in serpentine fashion. It was 25'-30'/7.6-9m long. [B9]

EASTER BUNNY An animal of children's lore. Its origins are obscure, though perhaps connected with fertility – as you know, rabbits breed like rabbits. The earliest references to the Easter Bunny come from 16th Century Germany. It was brought to the United States by the Pennsylvania Dutch, who were in fact German immigrants, in the 17th Century.

EASTERN BIGFOOT *see* **Marked Hominid.**

EASTERN COUGAR A subspecies of cougar or puma, once found in the eastern part of the United States, but reckoned extinct since 1946. However, there have been numerous reports of the animal since then.   [B6]

EASTINGTON SEA MONSTER A flat-headed green creature with a long mouth which kept opening and shutting, seen off the Yorkshire coast. Mrs J. Borgeest, the witness, said it moved in humped glides.   [#1]

EBO GORILLA Gorillas have been observed recently in the Ebo Forest of Cameroon, where no gorillas were hitherto supposed to have existed. They may belong to an unknown subspecies.   [#9]

ECHENEIS A legendary water creature with a flat head. On this is a disc. Should the disc become attached to the bottom of a ship, it will stop it or impede its movements. [4]

ECHINEMON A creature hostile to dragons. It was apparently able to kill them by covering itself with mud.

ECHO LAKE MONSTER In 1923 or thereabouts, two motorists camped near Echo Lake (Nebraska). During the night they saw a huge animal with a single horn on its forehead and a long neck, like a giraffe's.   [B9]

EDALE CREATURE A mysterious animal of predatory instinct reported from the Edale vicinity of the Peak District (England) in 1925. Many sheep killings were credited to it. It caused much local alarm, but search parties failed to find it.   [C11*]

EDWARDS' PARROT George Edwards (1694-1773) was a painter who was lent a stuffed parrot that had been shot in Jamaica. This he painted. The painting has survived and depicts a parrot of no known species. Jamaicans of Edwards' day were unable to identify it. It remains an enigma.   [S8]

EEL LAKE MONSTER There have been legends and reports of a monster in this lake in Ontario for over a century. One witness, who sighted it around 1990, said it was at least 10'/3m long with a sleek head and huge bulgy eyes.   [99]

EEL-LIKE SHARK A shark that looks, as you may have gathered, like an eel, which has been seen off the coast of Maine.   [31]

EGILSSTADIRVATN MONSTER This Icelandic lake is said to house a monster that has found its way into the nearby town's coat-of-arms.   [E]

EGMONT BAY MONSTER A serpentine sea monster 40-60'/12-18m long was seen in this bay in Prince Edward Island in 1956.   [B9]

EKA-PADA A legendary race of one-footed men of whom the Indian *Puranas* speak. [D1]

EL ISH KAS Makah Indian term for a BHM.

EL ZANJON DOG   A canid of unidentified species which was captured and photographed at this location in Santiago del Estero, Argentina.   [#12]

ELAPHOS KHRYSOKEROS   Golden-horned deer (all female) sacred to Artemis in Greek mythology. Hercules had to capture one as one of his labours. They may be based on the reindeer, whose hinds are horned like the stags. These are not to be found in Greece, of course, but rumour of them may have trickled down from the north of Europe, perhaps along the amber route from the Baltic.

ELBE MONSTER   This creature is said to have been seen in this German river in 1638. It looked like a giant deer with horns on its head. When a sailor was about to harpoon it, it vanished. This caused the sailor to have a fit and he subsequently died. [M7]

ELBST   A monster of the Selisbergsee in Switzerland. It is supposed to be scaly, to look like a serpent and to have feet like claws. This draconic creature had a reputation for coming ashore at night and feeding on cattle. It was said to be able to shapeshift and to have the form of a spectral horse. It was supposed to have supernatural qualities and this was certainly believed as late as 1921.   [M7]

ELEPHANT-DUNG BAT   This creature is said to live in Kenya. Guess what it is supposed to live in. Terence Adamson (whose sister-in-law Joy Adamson raised Elsa the lioness) would kick over piles of elephant dung on occasion. (It's amazing what you'll do when bored). On two occasions when this happened a tiny bat, perhaps a mystery species, fluttered out of it. It is, however, possible that the creature is the one known to science under the name of *Eptesicus floweri.*   [S8/A]

ELKHART LAKE MONSTER   A happy angler at Elkhart Lake, Wisconsin, one day pulled in his line and up came something with a large head and jaws in proportion. He quickly put some distance between himself and his catch.   [R4]

ELLENGASSEN   In 1875 in Argentine Indian lore a certain cave was inhabited by a beast of this name. It was described as like a hairy ox with a human head. Beneath the hair, except on the underparts, was armour. This would tie in with its being a supposedly extinct ground sloth, as a preserved skin of one of these showed they had protective ossicles in their pelt. This may be the same kind of animal as that encountered by Argentine secretary of state Ramon Lista in the 1870s. It had reddish grey fur and, apparently, bullet proof armour.   [S6]

ELMA CREATURE   A very large flying creature with a wingspan of 9-10'/3m, a human body and a head described as "grotesque" was reported near Elma (NY) in 1974. [C18]

EMELA-NTOUKA   This creature, which lives partially in the water, has been at times confused with the mokele-mbembe. In some ways it resembles a rhinoceros as it has a horn on its nose, but this seems to be composed of bone, rather than the compressed hair which forms that of a rhinoceros. Its tail resembles that of a crocodile. Its footprints are as large as an elephant's and show three toes or claws. Should an emela-ntouka encounter an elephant or buffalo, it will disembowel it with its horn. [S6]

ENEMY, THE A term used for dangerous hominoid beings by the Dogrib Indians of the Great Slave Lake in Canada. So fearful are they of these creatures that they build their dwellings on islands in the lake, never on the shoreline. [M6]

ENFIELD HORROR A creature first reported in Enfield (Illinois) in 1973. Its body was short and it had three legs on which it hopped about. Its arms were very short, it was coloured grey and had large, pink eyes. For sounds, it hissed or wailed. It scratched at the doors and windows of houses, as though seeking ingress.   [B7]

ENGBE(RE) A long-haired hominoid of west Africa. [E]

ENGOT A gigantic creature, neither ape nor man, but apparently resembling both to some extent, reported from Gabon. This is its Bulu name. The Fang call it *engungure*. [H7]

ENKIDU A wildman who appears in the Akkadian *Epic of Gilgamesh*. King Gilgamesh may have been an historical character and stories about him survive in Sumerian from about 2000 BC. In the full epic Enkidu is created as a fitting opponent for Gilgamesh, but his description conforms to that of modern wildmen. The poem says:

> *With shaggy hair his body was encap'd;*
> *Like woman's hair the locks on him were drap'd.*

He behaved like a wild animal, eating grass with the gazelle and drinking with animals at the water-hole. He and Gilgamesh became at length companions. Does this mean, perhaps, that the historical Gilgamesh had a wildman for a pet?

ENTZAEIA-YAWA A creature said to live in Ecuador, to look like a cat with long hair and a bushy tail and to spend some of its time in water. White, brown and black specimens have been reported. It is regarded as very fierce.   [30]

ENZINZI A giant "man" supposed to live in the forests of Gabon. Heuvelmans would identify it with the *ntyii*. [H7]

ERCEK LAKE CREATURE A peculiar monster or creature looking like a white horse has been reported in this Turkish lake.   [C1]

ERENSUGEA A legendary Basque snake which lures folk to its cave to destroy them. [122].

ERH FU A race of monocular people who lived in central Asia, according to the Chinese.   [C26]

ERNE MONSTER A monster allegedly seen in the Erne Waterway (Ireland) on a number of occasions. An indistinct photograph was taken in 2003 by S. Walsh. A. Moran, a local swimming club chairman, also claimed to have seen the creature. [60]

ESAKAR-PAKI A small variety of peccary in whose existence the Shuar Indians of Ecuador believe. Descriptions of the animal vary. It will attack unprovoked and is gregarious.   [41]

ESSEX PTERODACTYL This beast was actually described as 'pterodactyl-like'. It was reported near Boreham Village, not far from Chelmsford, Essex. It was seen after nightfall.   [21]

ESTI CAPCAKI Seminole Indian term for a BHM.

ETHIOPIAN BULL The Troglodytes, Aelian informs us, rightly regarded this bull as the king of beasts. Pliny also speaks of these animals. They were impervious to weapons and they could be trapped only in ditches or pits. Their horns were mobile like their ears. They were twice the size of Greek bulls and carnivorous. Their hair seems to have been reddish and they moved speedily.

ETHIOPIAN DEER A cervid of unknown species reported from Ethiopia. It is perhaps a subspecies of the fallow deer (*Dama dama*). [31 S8/A]

ETHIOPIAN HYRAX An unidentified creature, possibly an unknown species of hyrax, reported from Ethiopia. [31]

EUMERALLA RIVER CREATURE This animal was seen in this river in Victoria, Australia, in 1848. Its head resembled that of a kangaroo. [E]

EUROE MONSTER An Australian creature. The passage of this monster was inferred from its footprints. These indicated it was 30'/9m long.   [K1]

EVEREST FLYING CREATURES Two strange creatures observed in the skies above Mount Everest by F. Smythe, mountaineer, in 1933. At least one had wings. Both appeared to have beaks and to be pulsating, as if breathing. Eventually they became concealed behind mist.   [S8]

EWAH *see* **Wampus Cat.**

EZOX In the Middle Ages, a fish supposed to live in the Danube. It was so large it could not be carried in a cart drawn by four horses.   [151]

EZOZOME Alternative name for the enzinzi. [H7]

F

FALKLAND HOMINOID   For two hundred years there have been rumours of a creature living in the area of Falkland (Fife), Scotland. More recent reports speak of a hominoid 4-6'/1m tall, hairy and able to climb or jump into trees.   [31]

FAMH   A sort of dog-mole creature with a large mouth and sharp teeth, reported from the Scottish Cairngorms. One wonders if it is identical with the earth hound or yard pig, reported from elsewhere in Scotland.   [146]

FANGALABOLO   A gigantic bat reported from Madagascar, said to dive down and tear the hair of humans.   [S8/A]

FANTASMA DE LOS RIOS   A large hairy hominoid reported from western Argentina. It has been referred to as an "abominable snowman"   [#12]

FARASAN ISLAND GAZELLE   A specimen of this large gazelle was collected in the first half of the 19th Century. Its alleged point of origin was the Farasan Islands in the Red Sea, but it has not been seen since. Its type is unclassified and it may well be extinct. [B6]

FARMER CITY MONSTER   In 1970, sheep turned up dead near Farmer City (Illinois) while hogs had been disappearing in Marion County. When a number of teenagers camped out on 9th July to the south of Farmer City, they found in the course of the night that outside their tent a creature with gleaming eyes was watching them. When it realised it had been noticed, it ran off on two legs. Our campers also ran off, but presumably in a different direction.   [#9]

FARRISVANET MONSTER   A monster was reported from this small lake in Denmark in the 1840s.   [C25]

FATHER OF ALL BUFFALO   According to the Shawnee Indians in 1762, certain skeletons in the vicinity of the Ohio River were the remains of this species of animal, which had been destroyed by lightning.   [E]

FATING'HO   A large but vaguely described primate that walks on its hind legs. It is found in Senegal and may be identical with the *wokolo* reported from the same region. [31]

FEATHERED PEOPLE   In Chinese geographical lore, a race of people who dwelt in the land of Yu-min kuo. They were supposed to be oviparous and to have wings instead of arms. They had limited powers of flight. Perhaps they are based on some early traveller's account of meeting a large flightless bird such as the cassowary.   [W*]

FEI-FEI A hominoid creature described in a Chinese work, the *Erh-ya* (200 BC). It was said to have long red hair and a human face. This may refer to the orang-utan, which once lived in China, but we cannot be sure. [N1]

FEI-SHENG A bird of Chinese legend which produces live young, which are able to fly from birth. [#11]

FENCE RAIL DOG *see* **Yakhetan Amai.**

FERNANDO DE NRONHA SEA MONSTER The beast in question was seen off this Brazilian island in 1905. It was said its head was the size of a cow's. [B9]

FIJI DWARFS Dwarf-sized hominoids reported by witnesses from the Lautoka Methodist Missionary School, Fiji, in 1975. [B9]

FIJIAN CAVERN CREATURES Kevin Deacon, a diver, found four dead creatures in an underwater cave beneath the island of Matigi, Fiji, in 1990. He could not identify these 30'/9m long animals which he said looked as if they belonged rather on land than beneath the sea. [#12]

FILEY MONSTER In 1934 there had been a number of sightings of some sort of monster off the coast of Yorkshire. Then one night a coastguard, Wilkinson Herbert, was walking along Filey Brig, a sort of projection into the sea, when he heard a growling, as of a pack of dogs, ahead of him in the dark. Switching on his torch, he found himself facing a head with huge saucer-like eyes and a large mouth. The body behind he estimated at 30'. He threw stones at it and it returned to the water. It had a great black body with four little legs with "flappers" attached. The creature growled as it returned to the water. [H5]

FILIPINO CREATURE A strange creature observed by Daniel Carter in 2002. It looked generally like an ape, but was very slim and it was not a mammal. It was between 5-6' tall and was unfamiliar to the Filipinos who were accompanying the witness. [2]

FILIPINO MYSTERY DOG Apparently strange dogs have been attacking Filipinos, it was reported in 2001. One victim said his attacker had unusually short forelegs, while a town official at Valladolid (Carcar) described the animals as more like kangaroos. It is said they can fly. It has also been claimed they are pups by day, fierce creatures by night. A final tale is that one of them is the husband of a tattered old woman. [12]

FILIPINO SECRETARY BIRD A bird resembling the African secretary bird observed in the Philippines in the 18th Century. [E]

FINKSBURG FLYING HUMANOID Mrs Ruth Lundy was returning to her home one night when she saw a figure exceeding 6'/1.83m in height, bipedal, brownish-grey, with wings and a possible beak. It took off and flew away. This happened in 1980 in Finksburg (Maryland). [#7]

FINNGALKN A kind of monster in Norwegian saga. It had a human's head, a beast's body and a heavy tail. In addition its claws were ferocious and each contained a sword. [S7/A]

FIORDLAND MOOSE Although the moose is not native to New Zealand, some were introduced in times agone and it is suspected there may be a relict population of these in the Fiordland district. However, video footage of the alleged moose has proven unsatisfactory. [#3]

FIREBIRD A bird of Russian legend. Its feathers were of golden hue, its eyes like crystals. Its song was said to heal the sick and make the blind see. Its original owner was Czar Dalmat. [D4]

FIRE-BREATHING HOUNDS A pack of these apparently supernatural white creatures has been reported from the area of Wellington (Somerset). [146]

FIRE-QUELLER A legendary Chinese bird which, if thrown onto a fire, will extinguish it. [#11]

FISH-MAN According to the legends of the Showano Indians, this was a water dweller with a face like a porpoise and two fish tails. The Showano were enchanted by his singing voice. When they were plagued with shortages, he led them across the water in their canoes to a land of plenty on the west bank of the Mississippi. [P2]

FISH-REPTILE Creatures with catfish-like heads, long flat tails and four legs were found in 1923 in a pond near Medicine Lodge (Kansas). Their bites were fatal to cows. Some savant seems to have proclaimed that they were salamanders. [#2]

FISKERTON PHANTOM There does not appear to be anything particularly phantasmal about this creature encounterted by young girls near Fiskerton, Lincolnshire. It seemed to be about 4'/1m tall, was black and eating a pheasant. They described it, not as a bear, but as 'bear-like', which would indicate it was to some degree different from a bear as such. [46]

FIVE-HEADED DRAGON About 1990 such a creature was believed in Laos to be inhabiting the Mekong. [#9]

FLASHLIGHT FROG A frog from Cameroon said to have, like Edward Lear's Dong, a luminous nose. [31]

FLATHEAD LAKE MONSTER There have been over seventy reports of a monster in this Montana lake. Its estimated length is 25/7.62m, it undulates, making it unlikely to be a fish, and it is coloured black. It is said to have been known to the Kootenay Indians. On August 18th, 1998, a fisherman near Gravel Bay said a form pursued the fish on his line but added that its shape was consistent with that of a sturgeon. [B11]

FLATWOODS MONSTER In 1952 a UFO was apparently observed landing on a hill near Flatwoods (West Virginia). It was after dark and a local woman and some teenagers ascended the hill to be confronted by a monster, 10' tall and humanoid, with a round face, which hissed and glided towards them. They turned and fled. A mist around them made them nauseous and they spoke of a pulsating light.

However, it has been suggested that the monster was no more than an owl, foliage and branches giving the impression that there was a full body beneath its owlish head, while it was in reality perched on a bough. This is supported by the fact that the monster was alleged to have claws on the ends of its arms.

Many local people thought the UFO was no more than a meteor. The smell may have come from the rather heavy scent of the grass round about and the nausea from the witnesses' terror. The pulsating light can be explained by a nearby beacon. Skid marks and oil on the ground were later established to have come from a car.

Although these sundry explanations are plausible, they are not absolutely conclusive. [S16]

FLINTVILLE MONSTER A hairy humanoid reported from the vicinity of Flintville (Tennessee). In 1976 it attacked a car and almost grabbed a child. Reports continued until 1993. [147]

FLOOD MONSTERS These four colossi were responsible for the Flood in the legends of the Caddo Indians of Arkansas and Oklahoma. They were so large they reached the very sky, but were defeated by Turtle. [138]

FLORIDA SEA MONSTER In 1962 this creature emerged from the mist to devour a skin diver in a grisly meal and pull three more to an untimely death. A fifth, Edward McCleary, made it to a small boat, which the monster proceeded to circle. Its head was the shape of a turtle's. At length it departed. Officials inclined to blame the incident on sharks. [C5]

FLUORESCENT FREDDIE A name given to a hairy and perhaps humanoid monster seen near French Lick (Indiana). It was supposedly green in colour. [#12]

FLYING CAT Flying cats have been blamed for attacking livestock in Canada, particularly in Ontario. They are usually black. These beasts should not be confused with so-called "winged cats", which are actually deformed domestic cats. [B7]

FLYING CROCODILE In 1882 a couple of lumberjacks in California looked up and saw a flying crocodile, with three pairs of wings and six pairs of legs. The beast was supposedly 18' long. In 1891 a couple of not dissimilar creatures were discerned near Fresno. The imprint of one of these animal's feet was found in the mud. It is to be hoped we are not dealing here with mere newspaper hoaxes. [R6]

FLYING CYLINDER These creatures were reported by O. Tchuimbu in Siberia in the early years of the 19th Century. They flew 6'/1.8m off the ground. They were coloured

like flames, but had a silvery sheen and seemed to be composed of something like jelly.
[C3]

FLYING ELEPHANT Some who believe in conspiracies have maintained that the USA has produced flying elephants by genetic engineering. This is supposed to have occurred in 1983. The operation was known as … Project Dumbo. If there is any truth in all of this, these volant pachyderms have managed to avoid public notice, but the appearance of such creatures might, I feel, cause an upsurge in the sale of umbrellas. [W6]

FLYING HORSE In Russian legend, the hero Ilya Muromets, who features in the *byliny* (oral epics), rode a flying horse. In Greek mythology, the flying horse Pegasus sprang from the blood of Medusa the Gorgon. [J1]

FLYING HUMAN Although flying humans have been reported from Brazil, some kind of animal probably lies behind the traditions. They have also been reported from Chile and Argentina. [31 #12]

FLYING LION A creature reported in 1926 by two children from West Orange (New Jersey). [C19]

FLYING TRIANGLE Triangular creatures, apparently alive, with flapping wings, were seen over Norton Acres (Ohio) about 1980. The witness at first took them for kites. [81]

FLYING WOMAN A black, unclothed. furry-skinned woman with wings which were attached to her fingers and emitting a greenish glow was observed by three U.S. soldiers in Vietnam in 1969. [E]

FOREST MONSTER A BHM reported from the Finland/Russian border. It is said to eat bark. [C20]

FORKED DEEP RIVER CREATURE This creature has been sighted twice if reports are true, the first time about 1868, the second in 1871. The river in question, for those not well versed in geography, is in Ontario. The creature had a white, humanlike face, a moss-like substance in place of hair, a body covered as far as the waist (all seen) in black and white spots, a neck longer than a human's and big, black eyes. No arms were visible. [#11]

FORLI REPTILE An animal 15'/4.57m long allegedly attacked a man near Forli, Italy, in 1970. He compared it with a dinosaur. The legs were said to be thick and the breath very hot. [43 B9]

FORRUR ISLAND GAZELLE A gazelle of unknown type reported from this island in the Persian/Arabian Gulf. [B6]

FOUKE MONSTER   In 1965, James Lynn Crabtree of Jonesville, Arkansas, encountered a hominoid, 7'/2.13m tall, with red-brown hair all over its body. It advanced on James, who fired a shotgun at its face, apparently with no effect, after which he wisely fled. His uncle and cousin later revealed that they also had seen the creature. About a year later it was seen again, this time by a woman hunting deer. James' father, Smokey Crabtree, started hearing something screaming outside their house at night, panicking the dogs.

In 1971 the creature is said to have put its head through the window of a house, scaring several females inside. It seems to have changed its residence to the vicinity of Fouke, where it earned the name by which it became known. Orville Scroggins strongly disbelieved in the creature until he saw it in 1973. However, he put it at only 4' tall. This may have been another animal. In fact, rumours grew that there was a family of the creatures in the area.

In 1991 the skeleton, lacking a head, of an unknown biped was found near Fouke. The creature had died of pneumonia. Even without the head, it was 7'/2.13m tall. Its DNA could not be identified.

An ex-sheriff named Greer asserted that here had been sightings went back to 1946. There have been reports of subsequent sightings which may refer to other members of the monster family. N. Arnold, in an exhaustive article on the animal, voices doubts that it is to be identified with bigfoot.

A fictionalised account of the monster was filmed as *The Legend of Boggy Creek* (1972). There were two sequels.   [C2]

FOUR-FOOTED SERPENT According to Burton's *Miracles of Art and Nature* (1678 ed.), such creatures were to be found in part of Poland, were three hands long and were treated as household gods by the natives.   [H12]

FOUR-LEGGED FISH An article in *Popular Science Monthly* in 1872 describes this creature seen crawling on a piece of coral off the northern Australian coast. Though something like a lizard, it had a fish's body and hands at the ends of its four legs. It stood up for a while on its hind legs.   [G6]

FOWLER LAKE MONSTER In the 19th Century a monster like a large otter or beaver was reported in this lake in British Columbia.   [C/H]

FOX-DOG A mystery stuffed animal, kept in a pub near Nomansland, on the borders of Wiltshire and Hampshire. It was variously described as a doglike fox and a foxlike dog, but has now disappeared.   [C1]

FRASERBURGH SEA SERPENT This beast was reportedly 200'/60m in length, with an equine head and long pointed teeth. It attacked a boat off the Scottish coast in 1903 and withdrew when fired on.   [146]

FREIBURG SHRIEKER On 10th September, 1978, coal miners in this German city tried to enter their mine, only to find in their path a black creature with outstretched wings. When the miners advanced on it, it let out appalling shrieks. The men decided to withdraw and, about an hour later, there was an explosion in the mine. The Shrieker had saved the miners' lives.   [120]

FREIDRICHSHAFEN SEA MONSTER   A creature supposedly killed near Friedrichshafen (Germany) in the early 18th Century. A picture of the beast shows a most unlikely creature. The forepart is like a boar, the rear like a two-tailed fish with what might be an eye in each tail. The forelegs end in hooves, the rear feet are like a duck's, but with added claws. That the artist has highly stylised any original model for his picture seems beyond doubt.   [S5]

FRESHWATER SEA-COW   A creature reminiscent of a manatee reported from freshwater lakes in Chad and Ethiopia.   [30]

FROG-LIKE CREATURE   Although looking like a frog, this creature reported from Lake Ontario was 10'/3m long, its mouth resembled an alligator's, its eyes were huge and green and it was said to have flippers close to its head and long horns. A rifle bullet fired at it ricocheted back into the gun. Although there is clearly a piece of folklore here, some truth may lie behind the legend.   [K3]

FUZZY MAN-BEAST   This occurs in an account reported by J. Green, but he cannot find its source. It tells of a humanoid completely covered with yellow fuzz, seen by miners in Oregon in 1899.   [G7]

G

GAASYENDIETHA   A fire dragon in the lore of the Seneca Indians. These creatures are supposed to inhabit rivers and lakes, but can be seen in the sky as fiery tracks and may have been inspired by comets and meteors.

GA-GORIB   A monster of the Khoikhoi (Hottentots). It was overcome by the hero Heita-eibib. No description is to hand.   [4]

GALOS-GANVHIDA   In Cherokee folklore a kind of black bear of considerable size that was nonetheless thin and had small feet.   [NF10]

GALVESTON SEA-SERPENT   An ugly-looking beast with a horn, fins and a long tail tapering to a point. It was seen by the crew of the *Saint Olaf* in 1872. It appeared to be pursuing sharks. The head was serpentine. Below this was a 70'/21m long body of uniform thickness. It had four dorsal fins. The back was greenish with brown spots, the underparts white.

GAMAYUN   A bird which dwells on an eastern island and foretells the future in the legends of Russia.   [4]

GAMBO   A mystery animal whose carcass was discovered by Owen Burnham, schoolboy on holiday, on a Gambian beach near Banjul in 1983. He made careful notes and measurements and, although the beast's head was hacked off by locals, his family and hotel staff buried the body secretly. The creature had not started to decompose, so it cannot have been some known sea animal whose shape had been transformed by rotting. It was 15'/4.5m in length, its jaws were long like a crocodile's, its skin was smooth and it was endowed with flippers. It does not seem to have been of the whale family, for it had no blow-hole. Jonathan Downes, an eminent cryptozoologist, pointed out its similarity to the pliosaur, generally thought extinct for 65 million years. Local fishermen, however, are aware of this creature, which they call *gnalo*.   [C2]

GANBA   A huge serpent believed by the Australian Aborigines to live beneath the Nullabor Plain, though it sometimes goes into the sea.   [B2]

GANIAGWAIHEGOWA   A huge bear in Iroquois lore, invulnerable except for the soles of his feet. [134]

GARADIAVOLO   A kind of malign-looking fish which A.G. Garamendi claimed to have caught in Puerto Rico in 1974. It had a face, tail, solid skeleton (which fish do not have), leg-like appendages and a tubular tail. X-rayed, it was found to be no known species. Another specimen was dissected. Garamendi denied he had manufactured the fish, but argued that they may have come from outer space, left by aliens. They decomposed into a kind of slime.   [C24]

GARGOUILLE   A huge dragon said to have lived in the Seine in the 7th Century. [59]

GARLOCH MONSTER   Hector Boece in his *Scotorum Historiae* (1527) says that a monster the size of a greyhound emerged from this arm of the sea. It had a mighty tail, with which it slew three men, while others had to take to the trees for safety. It then returned to the loch.   [C25]

GARUDA   A large bird of Indian mythology, the enemy of the nagas. In Indonesia it was regarded as dangerous to man. Buddhists think it demonic. The Hindus claim Garuda is the king of birds, with a man's body, but an eagle's talons, wings and beak. Its face is white, its wings red and its body golden. According to the Nepalese, Garuda has a wife called Unnati. Garuda may be a personification of lightning or based on the lammergeier (*Gypaetus barbatus aureus*) [D1]

GASPARILLA LAKE CREATURE   A mystery creature which has been compared with a small dolphin was reported in this landlocked Florida lake in 2003. [2]

GASSINGRAM   A predatory beast reported by indigenes in central Africa in 1937. It was said to be larger than a lion and sometimes to be seen in daylight.   [#4]

GATINEAU RIVER MONSTER   There is said to be a monster in this Canadian river. [M7]

GAUARAGE This is believed to be a creature which lives in Australian water-holes and makes a whirlpool to suck down any so foolish or uninformed to swim in said water-holes. It is referred to as a "featherless emu", but no emu, plumaged or otherwise, is likely to lurk at the bottom of a water-hole.   [S6]

GAZEKA A creature reported from Papua-New Guinea. According to a description furnished by a policeman named Ogi who encountered one, it was 5'/1.5m long and 3.5'/1m wide, with cloven hooves, but a tail like a horse's. It had a lengthy nose and its skin was dark or even black.   It has been compared with a tapir, but may be a swimming diprotodon. This supposedly extinct huge marsupial is known from remains found in Australia and has a superficial resemblance to a tapir. If this creature exists, reports would place it in the Owen Stanley Range.   [#4 S4]

GE NO'SGWA Seneca Indian term for a BHM.

GENEVA LAKE MONSTER A serpentine creature reported from this Wisconsin lake in the 1890s. It was seen at Fontaine and the Narrows.   [R4 B18]

GERGASIS Humanoids in Indonesian mythology. [4]

GERIT A beast-man of Kenya, traditions of which were related to herpetologist J.H. Powell. It lives in the thick forest, is massively built and has a powerful chest. It resembles a man with long hair.   [H7]

GET'QUN Lake Iliamna Athabascan Indian term for a BHM.

GHOST DEER   A legendary deer said to be found in the region of Mount Eddy (California). Its antlers are said to be twelve points on one side, ten on the other. It is asserted that bullets pass through it.   [2]

GHOST ELK A beast seen by the Laird of Ardblair (Perthshire) in modern times. His wife had a separate sighting. His first impression was that it was like an American moose (*Alces alces*). Actually, the European elk is virtually identical with the American moose and is known to have roamed Scotland until about 1300. Could there be a few surviving? The laird seemed to regard it as spectral. He also entertained the possibility that it was the extinct so-called Great Irish elk, which was in reality no elk but a deer with colossal antlers, and which was by no means confined to Ireland.   [F4]

GIANT Giants occur in the lore of many lands, but no evidence that giant humans once existed as a race is currently available. Sometimes stories of giants may have grown up from encounters of smaller races with larger ones; from the discovery of large bones, misidentified as human; from seeing structures made by earlier races which seemed only within the power of giants to erect; or from encounters with apes or humanoids. This is not to say, of course, that giants never existed. Rather, it is a statement based on currently available data. In some mythologies, giants are almost indistinguishable from gods, who are no doubt also thought of as being of gigantic stature. Thus the Titans of

Greek mythology are an early race of gods, while the Jotuns of the Norse intermarry with gods. The giant Mbombo of the Congo (Kinshasa) seems to be actually a creator god. The Ice Giants of Micmac legend, defeated by the hero Glooskap, may contain a reminiscence of the retreat of the glaciers at the end of the last Ice Age.

GIANT AFRICAN HOMINOID There have been reports of sundry hominoids from Africa – Cameroon, Congo (Kinshasa), Kenya and Sudan – some of them nearly 14'/4.2m tall. [218]

GIANT ALPINE RABBIT A large unidentified lagomorph, seen on 26th July, 2003, by H. Harrison. It was observed – and nearly stepped on – by the witness on Mount Laurel, near Mammoth Lakes (California). It was about the size of a cocker spaniel and silvery blue in colour. There had been an earlier report of mountaineers "hallucinating" such creatures.   [2]

GIANT AMERICAN CATFISH There are not supposed to be giant catfish in the United States, yet they have been reported from time to time. Mark Twain (1835-1910) asserted he had seen one 6'/1.8m in length. There are said to be giant catfish in Saguaro Lake, east of Phoenix (Arizona). Reports have come in of such creatures in the Lake of the Ozarks and Lake Mead. A 25'/7.6m long dead one was encountered in the Ohio. In 1971 an 8-10'/2-3m catfish was allegedly espied in Lost River (California).

GIANT ANACONDA On the Rio Abuna in 1907, Col. Percy Fawcett shot an anaconda whose length he estimated at 62'/18.9m. Huge snakes in South America feature in Indian tradition. The killing of a snake of nearly 75'/23m has been reported from Brazil. One report exists of a giant anaconda with horns, but these may, in fact, be growths. [H9]

GIANT ANT Herodotus remarked that there were giant ants to be found in Asia, bigger than foxes, though smaller than dogs. The Chinese also referred to giant ants in central Asia. The animal behind this legend may be the red marmot (*Marmota caudate*).

GIANT AYE-AYE The possible existence of this cryptid has been inferred from a single skin discovered in Madagascar in 1930.   [E]

GIANT BEAVER Native American belief makes mention of giant beavers the size of bears. These legends have been supported by the discovery of the fossil remains of a giant beaver (*Castoroides ohioensis*) in 1837. A reported sighting of a living giant beaver took place at Lake Powell (Utah) in 2002.   [C/H]

GIANT BIRD A huge bird of Papua-New Guinea credited with the ability to carry off dugongs and turtles. Not alone does this creature occur in native tradition, it was also seen by early explorers. Certainly, a bird capable of carrying a dugong would have prodigious strength and no known bird has anything approaching it. Its abilities may well have been exaggerated.   [31]

GIANT BLACK BEAR A huge black ursid in the folklore of Siberia. Stan Bergman is reported to have killed one. It is perhaps related to or even identical with the terrifying short-faced bear (*Arctodus simus*) that once roved America.   [30]

GIANT BLACK FISH This gargantuan piscid rammed a boat in the Missouri in 1970. It was filmed by a man named Haller.   [C/H]

GIANT BLACK PANTHER A felid of very large proportions reported from Peru. [30]

GIANT BUSHBABY This creature has been reported from Cote d'Ivoire and Senegal. [31]

GIANT CALIFORNIAN SALAMANDER A creature rumoured to exist in the Trinity Alps (California).   [B6]

GIANT CONGO SNAKE When flying over the Congo in 1959, R. van Leede snapped a photograph of a huge snake which seemed to be about 50'/15m in length.   [79]

GIANT COOKIECUTTER SHARK The cookiecutter shark (*Isistius brasiliensis*) and the largetooth cookiecutter shark (*Isistius plutodus*) take bites out of other sea-creatures. E. Clark, on the basis of bites found on a narwhal, has mentioned the possibility of a giant species; but other sea-creatures, known to take bites out of carcases, could explain the bites on the narwhal just as easily.

GIANT EAGLE In the myths of the Ata of the Philippines, a giant eagle saved the two survivors of the Flood.

GIANT ELK Monster in Jicarilla Apache legend, overcome by the hero Killer-of-Enemies.

GIANT ETHIOPIAN LIZARD A lizard with a dorsal crest, 10-12'/3.5m long. [E]

GIANT FISH 1 This dangerous piscid was reported to have been seen eating a man, a canoe and a caribou in Kaluluktrok Lake (Alaska).   [E]
2 A large and ferocious pike in the lore of the Chukchi of Siberia. Its size may be judged from the fact that the paddle of a boat could be placed betwixt one eye and the other. You will only see these creatures in deep lakes and they can break a boat in two with their huge teeth.   [J2]
3 In the myths of the Jicarilla Apache, a monster slain by Killer-of-Enemies.

GIANT FLYING CREATURE A strange creature with leathery wings, through which the sun shone, observed in Camden, Maine, in October, 2001. A second sighting occurred later in the winter.   [2]

GIANT FROG This creature is supposed to be found in Silver Lake, Massachussetts. [C/H]

90

GIANT GECKO   A large lizard has been reported among the trees of New Zealand. It is thought it may be the supposedly extinct Delcourt's giant gecko.   [#1]

GIANT HORSE A correspondent of the *Fortean Times*, one Mark Allan Swift, claimed that, as a small boy, he had seen a giant horse in a field containing other horses of normal size. He stoutly maintained that his memory was not at fault. It may be, of course, that he saw some large breed of horse in a field otherwise occupied by ponies.

GIANT HYRAX An early Chinese sculpture depicts such a creature, but we cannot be certain whether it stems from the sculptor's imagination or real life. There have been no modern reports of such a creature.   [S6]

GIANT INSECT A report in September, 2003, from Bridgeton (NJ), refers to insects with 10" wingspans. It has been suggested they are mutant wasps.   [120]

GIANT KANGAROO This creature may not have been an actual giant kangaroo, but according to reports it certainly resembled one. It was sighted in the Tennessee River Valley in 1934. It killed dogs and other farm animals. Its speed elicited comment. [B11].

GIANT LEMUR This animal (*Megaladapis*) is supposedly extinct since the Pleistocene in its native Madagascar. However, this may not be the case. A 17th Century explorer said the natives were often frightened by huge animals with human faces, a description that might well be applied to such creatures.   [22]

GIANT LION   There is a legend of giant lions in Madagascar. This island is not supposed to be home to any members of the cat family, as it has developed its own peculiar fauna due to its isolation from the African continent. What giant lions would be doing there is a complete mystery. How they arrived there is equally mysterious. It may be they represent a relict population of the giant fossa, found on Madagascar in the Pleistocene. [S7]

GIANT LIZARD (INDIAN) Such reptiles, says Pliny, were to be found upon Mount Nysa.

GIANT LIZARD (NEW ZEALAND) The Maoris told Captain Cook that New Zealand harboured giant lizards, but, if such be the case, they have kept well hidden since the coming of the Pakeha.   [C25]

GIANT MOLLUSC Huge molluscs, each weighing about 500 grams, have started to appear at Billings Dam, Sao Paolo, Brazil. Scientists are unable to classify them, but a local resident says they taste like chicken.   [1]

GIANT MONITOR   That the monitor lizard (*Varanus*) can grow to a great size is shown by Indonesia's Komodo dragon. In Australia giant monitors of unknown species have been reported from the Wattingen Mountains and Warragambie Mountains. Both ranges are in New South Wales. An interesting sighting by F. Gordon, herpetologist, occurred in 1979, when he estimated the lizard at 27-30'/8-9m. A guess that these animals represent a surviving population of the huge megalania of prehistoric Australia is no more than that. [S6]

GIANT MONKEY Alternative term for the devil monkey.

GIANT MOSQUITO A huge mosquito in Native American lore which would devour humans. The creature lived in the vicinity of Fort Onondaga (NY). It was eventually killed by the Holder of the Heavens and its blood became small mosquitoes, which proceeded to bite the Holder of the Heavens most annoyingly. The bird-like footmarks of the Giant Mosquito were pointed out by the Indians at Brighton (NY). [S10]

GIANT OWL Huge owls with an appetite for human flesh have been reported in the vicinity of Hemmed-In Holler, which lies near Compton (Arkansas). [H]

GIANT PINK LIZARD These animals were reported in Scippo Creek, Ohio, by early settlers. They seemed to grow to 6'-7'/2m and had horns reminiscent of moose antlers. They appear to have died out in a drought which occurred before 1820. They may have been a larval form of some larger creature. [S6]

GIANT RABBIT Gold prospectors claim to have seen such a creature in Australia. A kangaroo silhouetted against the horizon can look like a large rabbit. Perhaps they saw an unusually long-eared specimen. Giant rabbits have also been reported from Minnesota and Florida. Cryptozoologist Neil Arnold knew someone who claimed to have seen a giant white rabbit in the Robin Hood Wood in Kent. [H9 #1 R3]

GIANT RAT-TAIL What may be a giant variety of rat-tail has been sighted twice, once off Bermuda, once in the Gulf of Mexico. [E]

GIANT RATTLESNAKE Zoologists would not generally admit the existence of rattlesnakes longer than 9'/2.74m, but there have been many tales of giant specimens. A number of them exceeding 17'/5m were allegedly killed in 1714, while in 1750 an 18'/5.49m specimen was said to have met its end in Virginia. Perhaps the longest in legend was a 22'/6.71 individual, not including the head and rattles, killed in 1753. *See also* **Big Jim**.

GIANT RAVEN Birds of this kind, larger than eagles, are said to occupy a valley in British Columbia. [31]

GIANT REPTILE V.S. Kuznetsov in 1971 told of an experience he had undergone in Siberia many years before. He came upon a bonfire at twilight where some sort of religious ceremony appeared to be going on. Singing men were bowing towards the setting sun. Then an unidentified reptile 32'/10m long, like a snake but with forefeet, appeared. It reared up and the singers seemed to be worshipping it. Kuznetsov fled. [C3]

GIANT SERBIAN SNAKE A beast 32'/10m long reported from Mount Ovcar and near Ivanica.   [#11]

GIANT SHRIMP Although this creature is referred to as a giant shrimp, it is only so called because a shrimp is what it resembled.   According to Virginia Staples, a correspondent of *Strange Magazine*, when in a laundry room in Bremerton (Washington), she found herself facing this creature with a bright orange body, spindly legs and antennae. It was 5'/1.5m tall, but it is unclear whether or not it was standing on its hind legs. It advanced towards her, so she wisely beat a hasty retreat.

GIANT SNAKE A creature, yellow in colour, described as looking like a barrel with a maned horse's head. This beast was reported in 2000 at Ezitapile, South Africa. Its presence was said to disturb livestock.   In 1997 it was reported that, in Peru, snakes 130'/40m long had been sighted. Their alleged tracks were shown. Another giant snake 120'/36.6m long was once allegedly killed in Benoud (Algeria). Giant snakes are also said to exist in Siberia. One 32'/10m long was observed in 1946 or thereabouts; a 16'/5m specimen was reported in 1978; a 32'/10m specimen in 1983; while in 1984 a busload of people saw a vast black snake make its way across the road. At a more cosmic level, the Bumun of Taiwan believed a huge snake caused the Flood by damming a river with its body. [#1 45 B9 C3]

GIANT SPIDER A correspondent of the Centre for Fortean Zoology has mentioned seeing a spider whose body alone was around 2'/50cm long. This seems to be a mystery archnid, unclassified by science. However, if this seems large, a spider the size of a human pygmy has been reported from the Congo (Kinshasa) and one the size of a small dog from Papua-New Guinea.   [1 30]

GIANT SQUIRREL In the lore of the Micmac Indians, huge squirrels with a penchant for devouring their wigwams existed in days agone. M. Bradley has suggested that this preserves a memory of ground sloths.   [B12]

GIANT TADPOLE Such a creature has been reported from time to time. One was observed by a shipload of onlookers in 1876, while another, estimated at 40'/12m long was espied by a Captain Brocklehurst in 1880. R. le Serrec claims to have seen a 70'/21m long one in 1967 off Australia and to have photographed it. The photograph shows something indistinct but alive-looking under the water.   [#1]

GIANT TOAD These animals are said to live in Hubei (China) near Wuhnun.   Some scientists were visiting this area in 1987 when they came to a number of freshwater pools. Then suddenly three giant toads emerged. Their skins were of a grey/white colour, their mouths were six feet wide and the scientists averred their eyes exceeded rice-bowls in size. They stood staring at the scientists who had been setting up cameras on tripods. A tongue shot out from one mouth, encircled the cameras and tripods and drew them away, while the other two toads voiced eerie screams. Then all three ducked under the water. The scientists were struck with shock and one of them actually fell to his knees and threw up.   [31 S13]

GIANT TROUT This huge piscid is said to be found in Lac d'Alfeld (Haut-Rhin), France.   [E]

GIANT TURTLE Huge turtles have been reported in the Atlantic, east of Canada. One was even mistaken at first for an upturned ship. A large turtle of unknown species called *ndendeki* exists in the traditions of the Congo (Brazzaville), but this is much smaller than those of Atlantic report. Aelian mentioned the existence of huge turtles in the Indian Ocean in ancient times, as did the Arab writer Idrisi in the Middle Ages. [M1 S6]

GIANT UKRAINIAN SNAKE According to an article written in 1841, the Cossacks said that, not long before, there had been giant snakes in the reed banks of the Dneister. They enjoyed killing man and beast. They could pursue a man on horseback and hunt him down, as no horse was able to outrun them.   [C1]

GIANT WASP The Chinese work *Hai Nei Pei Ching* (1st Century AD) alludes to such creatures. As to what they looked like, they do not keep us guessing – they looked like wasps!

GIANT WHITE BEAR An Alaskan white bear which occurs in popular legend. It is said to be larger than a Kodiak bear and to have furry paws.   [30]

GIANT WOLF A Canadian animal, probably identical with the waheela. [30]

GIANT WORM 1 The *Robert Ellis*, a.small ship, was making its way from the Welsh island of Anglesey or Mon to the shore in 1805, when a huge worm from the sea managed to wriggle aboard and established itself on the deck, coiled up under the mast. The sailors summoned up their courage and managed to push it overboard, but it continued to follow the vessel for a time.   [H5]
2 N. Redfern says he has received reports of giant worms in tunnels underneath Wiltshire and at Stonehenge.   [R4*]

GIASTICUTUS A large bird supposed to have been seen in Howell County (Missouri). It was said to have a wingspan of 50'/15m and to carry off full-grown cattle. The term was later applied to non-existant creatures in fairground hoaxes. [H]

GIGANTIC OCTOPUS Unlike the giant squid (*Architeuthis*), the equivalent form of octopus is not recognised by science. The remains of what might have been such a creature were washed up on the shore near St Augustine (Florida) in 1896, but they were not conclusive, though A.E. Verrill of Yale favoured an octopus identification. Remains found on Bermuda in 1988 were equally inconclusive. The epithet *gigantic* rather than *giant* is used of this hypothetical creature to avoid confusion with the Giant Pacific octopus (*Enteroctopus dofleini*). [E2]

GIGELORM A name which would seem to derive from a Gaelic term. The creature it denotes is found in Scottish lore. It is microscopic, so small it could nest in a mite's ear. As it has never been actually seen under a microscope, one wonders how the Scots came to know of this creature.   [F4]

GIGLIOLI'S WHALE A whale said to have two dorsal fins. Reports would indicate it is widely distributed among the world's oceans.   [30]

GIN-SUNG A large hairy primate rumoured to inhabit central China. It is perhaps a completely distinct animal from the yeren and its range extends into Tibet. It has also been identified with the *Dzu-teh* known to Himalayan dwellers. [5 C21]

GIRT DOG OF ENNERDALE A savage predator which flourished in north-western England in 1910. It killed livestock, sometimes doing little more than sucking their blood. When sighted, it was said to be tawny with stripes. Sheepdogs feared it and it drove off a pack of pursuing hounds, killing a number. People were now suggesting it was a lion, a tiger or perhaps even a supernatural creature. When it was eventually killed, it had been so badly torn to pieces by hounds that it defied identification. Its fragmented remains were somehow mounted in Keswick Museum, but disappeared with the closure of that museum in 1876. It has been suggested that it was a thylacine, an escapee from some travelling menagerie. It was unlikely to have been a striped hyena, as it eschewed poisoned carrion left out by the locals. No striped form of dog is known, so a canine identity seems very unlikely.

GLACIER ISLAND CREATURE A carcass of a 25'/7.6m animal was washed up on this island off Alaska in 1930. It had a trunk of 3'/1m and was covered with white fur. It was described as "elephant-like". It bears some resemblance to a number of other monsters; *see* **Trunko; Sea Elephant; Kintyre Creature.**   [E1]

GLASLYN MONSTER Two travellers in Snowdonia (Wales) saw, in this lake, the long body of a creature rise to the surface. This happened in the 1930s. [W3]

GLAUCUS A rarely seen fish of medieval belief. [151]

GLAWACKUS A mystery dog or cat, variously described as brown or black, reported in the vicinity of Glastonbury (Connecticut). Reports continue, but it seems clear that more than one kind of animal is being described.

GLENDARRY LOUGH MONSTER The lake in question is situated on Achill Island, Ireland. There is a tradition of monster sightings here. In 1968 a man called Cooney saw a monster cross the road in front of him, while two girls later in the same year claimed to have seen a "dinosaur", also on land. This has been photographed, but P. Costello thinks there might have been hoaxing involved.   [C25]

GLOBSTER *see* **Blob.**

GLOUCESTER SEA SERPENT   A large monster sighted off the coast of Massachussetts from time to time from 1817. Indeed, reports continued to be made for nearly a century. It was summertime visitor. It swam vertically. Generally, it looked like a line of humps, each pursuing the one in front. It was described by a Colonel Perkins as being chocolate coloured, at least 40'/12m long and boasting a horn. The horn was also mentioned by W. Foster, but not by other witnesses. It may have had its length underestimated by the good colonel, for another calculation placed it at 75'/3m. [S6]

GLOWING OWL   A creature (or creatures) observed in Norfolk in 1897 and 1908. Apart from glowing, they looked like specimens of the barn owl (*Tyto alba*). [146]

GLOWING-EYED MAN   A small man with glowing eyes reported from Ain-el-Turck, Algeria, in 1954. Perhaps it was a hominoid of some kind.   [B9]

GLYPTODON   A large shelled mammal whose remains are found in both North and South America, bearing some resemblance to an armadillo than which, however, it was much larger. It is thought to have become extinct about 10,000 years ago. However, the Indians of Argentina say it still exists. They know it by the name *tatu-carreta*. [C6]

GLYRYVILU   A kind of lake-dwelling monster, a fish or dragon, in the lore of the Indians of Chile. The name means 'fox-snake'. Descriptions of the creature vary. [M7]

GOAT-HEADED MONSTER   The Black Lake near Posen (Poland) was supposed to harbour a monster. In 1578, the lake was frozen and fishermen made holes in the ice to draw out fish. The net drew up what looked like the head of a goat with large horns and glowing eyes. The fishermen fled.   [#9]

GOATMAN   A creature said to be found in Prince George's County (Virginia). It is supposed to resemble the Greek god Pan, man to the waist and goat beneath it. It also boasts horns. Some say goatman is a creature indigenous to the area and represents an unknown life form. Some say he was a scientist who experimented with goats, but something went terribly wrong, turning him into Goatman. There are scientific facilities nearby, including the National Agricultural Research Center. He hates both humans and animals, they say he wields an axe and Fletchertown Road in Bowie seems to be one of his favourite haunts. A possible sighting occurred on 3rd November, 1971, when April Edwards and friends saw a large creature in the dark and April's dog was killed. Another possible sighting that year took place on November 17th when various girls saw a humanoid figure enter some woods after alighting from a pickup truck.

GOAT-WOMAN   A creature combining features of both woman and goat seen at Limonas, Peru. A report of this featured in the Argentine newspaper *La Razon* in 1972.

GOB MONSTER   A monster supposed to be found in mines in Illinois. It will attack miners when their lights go out.   [1]

GOGGAU SEE FISH A fish with a ridge looking like the teeth of a saw on its back is said to live in this Austrian lake.   [E]

GOGIT Haida Indian term for a BHM.

GOLDEN BIRD A pair of these birds occur in the Flood legend of the Lisu, who live in the Yunnan area of China. It was they who warned children of the oncoming flood.

GOLEM In Jewish legend it was believed that certain wise men could, by magic, make an image come to life. Such was the golem.   [4]

GOO TEE KHI Chilkat Indian term for a BHM

GORGONIY A beast of Russian legend that keeps mortals out of Paradise. [57]

GORO MONSTER This creature takes its name from the vicinity of Goro, Italy, where it was reported in 1975. It was 10'/3m long and looked like a snake with legs.   It was said to have scared one Maurizio Tombini, a man of serious bent. It was compared by Tombini to a huge lizard. It was also reported to howl like a wolf.   [43 B9]

GORYNYTCH A dragon with three heads and seven tails in Ukrainian legend, killed by the hero Dobrynja.   [135]

GOSSE'S WHALE Naturalist Philip Gosse (1810-1888) observed a school of whales, brown on top with white underparts and white pectoral fins. They were 30'/9m in length. This species has never been identified.   [B6]

GOUGOU A huge creature in which the Micmac Indians of New Brunswick believed. They told Samuel de Champlain (1567-1635) that it looked like a woman and that the masts of Champlain's ship would only reach its waist. It was supposed to have a "pocket" into which it could place prisoners and which was big enough to contain a ship. The beast was said to reside in a certain island and make frightening noises. In the Micmac language the word *gougou* as a common noun signifies an earthquake. [C22]

GOUIN RESERVOIR MONSTER This Canadian reservoir was formed from a number of small lakes. In the 1970s a man named Geoffroy saw what he described as a prehistoric monster quit the shore and enter its waters.   [M7]

GOUROCK SEA SERPENT This is the name given to a carcass discovered on the shores of the River Clyde, Scotland, in 1942. Because of the wartime situation, it was buried promptly. It was described as about 27'/8.2m in length with large pointed teeth. Its eyes seemed somewhat to the side. Its only bone seemed to be the spinal column. It had bristles of a sort growing on its skin. The teeth were inconsistent with those of a basking shark.   [S8/A]

GOWDIE'S SEA SERPENT A creature killed off the Shetland Islands in 1881 by a man called Williamson. The skull was huge. [C3*]

GOWROW A strange creature said to lurk in the Devil's Hole Cave, Boone County, Arkansas. Much noise could be heard from the depths of this cave, causing the proprietor, E.J. Rhodes, to climb down 200'/61m. It then became too narrow for further descent. Later a group of men lowered a flatiron into the hole. After a time, considerable hissing was heard. Pulling up the rope, they found the iron bearing possible teethmarks and its handle bent. They then lowered a stone on a rope. After more hissing, the rope was drawn up stoneless. A gowrow is supposed to have been killed by a man named Miller in 1897. The locals think the gowrow to be a giant lizard. [B11]

GRAMIUS' SERPENT Nicolas Gramius was a Norwegian cleric who said that, in 1636, a serpent that had been living in the Rivers Mjos and Branz emerged and crossed the fields. It looked like a long ship's mast and huts or trees that lay in its path it knocked over.   [M7]

GRAND BANK SEA MONSTER A sea monster or sea serpent reported off the Newfoundland coast in 1913. The sighting was made from a ship called the *Corinthian*. It had liquid blue eyes and a 20'/6m long giraffe-like neck. Its head was surmounted by three fins resembling horns.   [G1]

GRANT COUNTY MONSTER A creature reported from Grant County (Kentucky) in 1964. It was described as 7'/2m tall with shining eyes and was observed at a rubbish dump off US 36. Rumours concerning it circulated rapidly. Ursine footprints were said to have been found. Reports of other sightings came in. Police felt the monster was merely an eccentric with whom they were well acquainted.   [#2]

GRASSMAN A bigfoot-like creature reported from Ohio. It was noted near Akron, where there is an area of forest. A sighting of 1988 describes a creature 7'/2m tall. Support for its existence has been found in the form of a "bigfoot bed" about 10'/3m long fashioned from sticks and weeds.   [89]

GRAVUS A fish in medieval lore with an eye in the top of its head, which guarded it against attack from above.   [151]

GREAT ELK A legendary animal in the traditions of the Tuscarora Indians. Pere Charlevoix, a missionary, said in 1744 that the Indians beyond the Missouri believed in a Great elk. Other elk seemed like ants compared with this creature, which is described as being so large that it could easily progress through 8'/2.44m of snow. It had an arm coming out of its shoulder. This sounds suspiciously like a mammoth, as H. Wilkins notes. [W5]

GREAT LEECH The Cherokees told that the Valley River in North Carolina was home to this monster. It had red and white stripes and looked like a huge leech. Its apparent method of ensnaring its prey was to send a jet of water in its direction, washing it into the river. A possible attack on two Cherokee women was recorded in 1835. [H14]

GREAT QUISQUIS A monster in the legends of the Tuscarora Indians, the last nation to join the Iroquois Confederation. It supposedly attacked a village near Lake Ontario. The word *quisquis* means pig, but we should not infer from this that the monster was necessarily porcine.   [W5]

GREAT RABBIT According to Cherokee lore, this huge lagomorph once lived on Gregory Bald Mountain (North Carolina) and was king of the other rabbits.   [119]

GREAT SALT LAKE MONSTER The *Daily Corrine*, a Utah newspaper, claimed there was a monster in the Great Salt Lake in the 19th Century.   [12]

GREAT SANDY LAKE MONSTER In 1886 a hunter is supposed to have taken a pot shot at a monster which reared out of this Minnesota lake.   [C1]

GREAT SERPENT An evil supernatural ophid in Chippewa (Ojibway) legend, fatally wounded with an arrow fired by the hero Nanabozho. While dying, this creature caused a great flood.   [131]

GREAT SNAKE A monster said to occupy Lake Erie. It was first mentioned in 1819. In 1892 Captain Woods of the *Madeline* saw it and estimated its length at 50'/15m. Its eyes sparkled "viciously" and its head was large. It was dark brown in colour. A Captain Beecher who observed it from the shore in 1896 said its eyes looked like silver dollars, its back was black or dark brown, but its underside was lighter. Its head resembled that of a dog. Captain Beecher estimated its length at 35'/10.7m.   [C22]

GREDPO *see* **Migoi.**

GREEN DWARF 1 Reported from Derry (New Hampshire) by a man gathering Christmas trees in 1959. The creature did not look very human, had a high domed forehead, was green with wrinkled skin, had no nose (just holes), green glossy dorsal spines and grey/green body hair. His feet had no toes and his hands were like stumps, one suspects lacking fingers.   [B9]
2 An unidentified green humanoid reported from a number of areas in General Acha, Argentina, in 2003.   [A]

GREEN HILL MONSTER A BHM said to have scared a student in 1970 in Oklahoma. There have been numerous reports of such creatures in this state, dating from the 19th Century. Sightings have been reported from nineteen counties.   [12]

GREEN HORSE Green horses exist in African mythology. They live, not on land, but in the Indian Ocean. Their Swahili name is *Farasi Bahari*.   [K5]

GREEN LION Such a creature has been observed, but only once, in Uganda.

GREEN MALE MONSTER A creature so described was reported from Somerville (New Jersey) in 1949. No further details are available.   [C19]

GREEN MONSTER An alternative name for the Flatwoods Monster.

GREEN PIG An animal which is supposedly seen at times in mines in Bolivia. It is said to be of a preternatural character.   [#12]

GREEN TURACO An unidentified bird reported from Uganda. [30]

GREEN-FACED MONKEY A monkey resembling no known simian reported from Churston Woods, Devon, in 1996. It was described as 4-5'/1.3m tall and flat-faced. [21]

GREENWICH CREATURE This chicken stealing animal was shot by a farmer at Greenwich (NJ), but then none could identify it. In size it was compared to an Airedale, a tall dog, in fact the tallest of the terriers. Its fur was black and compared with astrakhan. Its forelegs were higher than its back legs, which were in a crouched position. Its hind feet were webbed and there was nothing canine about its jaws. It had been seen making its way about by hopping.   [B9]

GRENDEL The monster slain by Beowulf in the Old English poem that bears his name. Beowulf also slew his (Grendel's) mother. They were water-dwelling creatures. It has been generally felt that they were humanoid of the wildman type, but one author has contended they were surviving dinosaurs.   [C12]

GRIFFIN The griffin was said to combine the features of eagle (head, wings) and lion (body). It often appeared in Iron Age sculptures, in western Asia, Crete and mainland Greece. From the latter the Scythians of the Ukraine adopted it.

Aristeas, a Greek traveller of the 7th Century BC, set out on a journey into Asia where he stayed awhile with a nation called the Issedonians. They told him of certain animals which Aristeas identified with the griffins of iconography. These animals guarded gold from the Arimaspians, a one-eyed race. Gold was to be found in the parts of central Asia assigned them.

This seems to be confirmed by the Chinese *Shang Hai Ching* which speaks of one-eyed men and winged beasts like tigers, which could well be the beasts Aristeas identified with griffins.

Actual belief in these griffins may have stemmed from the bones of Proceratops, a dinosaur whose skeleton combines to the unschooled eye features of mammal and bird. Their remains are still to be found near to the sources of gold.

Griffin-like creatures were produced by heraldry and literature. The *opinicus* was a thin version of the griffin used for heraldic purposes; the *grifaleon*, a mixture of griffin and lion, featured in the saga of *Amadis de Gaula*; while the *hippogriff*, a mixture of horse and griffin, is an animal in Ariosto's *Orlando Furioso*. This latter term was also applied to a supposed monster seen in Lake George (NY) in 1904. This is generally thought to have been a hoax, but a recent argument contends it was based on misperception. *See also* **Brentford Griffin.** [C26 #6]

GROOT SLANG A water monster reported from South Africa, said to occur in the Orange River and the tributaries of the Vaal. Locally, belief in this creature is widespread. Some hold it to be a snake, some an eel. [#4]

GROTON LIZARD An 8-10'/3m lizard looking like a small dinosaur, which crossed the road near Groton (Vermont) in front of a couple called Desorda in the 1960s. It had a rather humped back, a tan colour, short legs and big webbed feet. Its head seemed definitely saurian. [C8/A]

GROUND SHARK A shark reputed to inhabit the sea between Timor and Australia. It is said to be larger than the great white shark and to have only a small dorsal fin. It gets its name because it lies on the sea bed awaiting prey, rather than actually pursuing it. [A13]

GRUAGACH A creature in Irish folklore, a giant, ogre or magician. The name means 'hairy one' and it probably originally referred to a wildman. The word was also used in the Louth area to mean a champion warrior, indicating that it was regarded as tough and robust. It should not be confused with the more supernatural gruagach of Scottish folklore. [C12]

GRYPHON *see* **Griffin.**

GRYTTIE An unidentified creature reported from Lake Gryttjen, Sweden. There is some speculation that it may be a kind of pinniped. Strange tales have been associated with this lake for many years. [37]

GUADALCANAL REPTOID Guadalcanal is one of the Solomon Islands. Japanese troops stationed here during World War II are said to have encountered strange reptoids, creatures combining human and reptile characteristics. It is even said they constructed a statue somewhere on the island of a reptoid with a ray beam weapon clutched in its tail. [129]

GUALLIPEN An animal in the lore of the Araucanians. It has a calf's head and a sheep's body. [J1]

GUAURABO CREATURE A strange marine animal described as "long-shaped" which attacked a Cuban mother and her children in 1998. They were partially paralysed by the creature and sent to hospital. No further details are available. [#11]

GUAYAZI A diminutive hominoid said to be found in South America [5]

GUBGANANA This is a Circassian word used in the region of the Caucasus to signify a female hominoid. [T1]

GUDENA RIVER SNAKE A mystery snake about 6'/1.83m long, in colour yellowish-brown, seen in this Danish river in 1943.   [6]

GUERNSEY SIREN A kind of fish-tailed mermaid in Guernsey belief. However, the Guernsey siren looks old and wrinkled, unlike the conventional depiction of a mermaid. [P2]

GUGU *see* **Orang Pendek.**

GUGWES A kind of ape or monkey in the lore of the Micmac Indians. It has big hands and a bearlike face. It will attack and eat humans and sometimes makes a noise like a partridge.   [M6]

GUIJE Creatures combining features of monkey and man, said to be found in eastern Cuba. [E]

GUISCHAN BEAST A beast with a hairy frill or mane around its neck, seen by a crofter in this Scottish deer forest. Perhaps it was a creature of the Loch Ness type ashore. The sighting is undatable, but occurred before 1934.   [C25]

GUIVRE A kind of serpentine dragon with deadly breath in medieval lore. However, when people discovered it was embarrassed by naked men, so that the prospect of one rendered it harmless, this fact was used to combat it.   [S3]

GUL A name given to a wildman in Tajikistan. It is derived from Ghul, a type of jinn in Islamic lore.   [B3]

GUL'BIYAVAN A name for a wildman in Afghanistan and the Pamirs. A.G. Pronin saw one of these in the distance, standing out distinctly against the snow, about 1958. In 1939 it is recorded that a hunter wrestled with a gul-biavan. It was described as being covered with wool rather than hair and left the hunter unconscious. [S1]

GULF CRYPTID In 1973 two fishermen saw a shiny object sporting an amber light in the Gulf of Mexico off the mouth of the Pascagoula River (Mississippi). A coastguard vessel was unable to haul it aboard. Some have suggested it was no cryptid but a machine, but its behaviour seems animal-like. [#11]

GULF ISLAND MONSTER A sea monster seen by duck hunters in the region of the Gulf Islands (British Columbia) in 1934. It had a head like a horse's, lacking ears or nostrils, and piscine teeth. Its estimated length was 40'/12m.   [C22]

GURRANGATCH A huge fish which Australian Aborigines believe existed in the Dreamtime, the period when the gods who founded tribes walked the earth.

GUYANA WILDMAN Wildmen, perhaps living in groups, have been reported by the Arawaks in this country. [12]

GWIBER A Welsh word for a viper, but it could mean a viper of monstrous proportions. One in Penmachno had wings and had dwelt there for hundreds of years. It killed a hunter in a story which involves the well-known triple death motif. There was supposed to have been a gwiber's lair near the summit of the waterfall of Pistyll Rhaeadr. It was overcome by the stratagem of an old wise woman. She told the people gwibers were made furious by the colour red. They draped a red cloth over a pillar. The gwiber attacked it, only to be impaled on the spikes underneath the cloth. [C/H]

GYONA PEL In Komi folklore, a name for a hominoid. It indicates the hominoid has hairy ears. [B3]

H

HABARBAR In Jewish legend, a man named Adnah was the first to crossbreed the horse and donkey, producing the mule. God was not pleased, so he crossed the serpent and the lizard, the result being the habarbar, which mortally wounded with its bite. [G4]

HADJEL A feline beast rumoured to be found in the Ouadai district of Chad, it is perhaps identical with the mountain tiger, said to exist elsewhere in that country. [S7]

HADLEY HEATH BEAST A beast observed emerging from Hadley Heath near Droitwich (Worcestershire). It had a long snout and a big red mane, but was otherwise bald. The witness, Mrs Harris, said it was larger than a fox. [113]

HAI HO SHANG This monster, whose name means, strange to say, the bonze (Buddhist cleric) of the sea, is noted for its ferocity and its tendency to overthrow boats. It looks like a large fish with a bonze's head instead of an ichthyous one. Amongst the Chinese, feathers are burnt to ward off its attentions. A ritual dance was also deemed efficacious against it. [C14 L4]

HAIETLIK A serpent in the lore of the Nootka Indians. It is associated with lightning and the thunderbird. [M7]

HAILO' LAUX Name of a race of giants, perhaps identical with bigfoot, in the lore of the Lillooet Indians of British Columbia. [C16]

HAIR-EEL A kind of eel with a mane, long said to be found in Loch Ness before ever it became famous for its monster. [143]

HAIRLESS CREATURE A two-foot long hairless creature with a nine inch tail had to be beaten off a dog with a pipe at Hillsboro (Wisconsin) in 1992. Identity remains a mystery, although the police favoured a raccoon – presumably suffering from some kind of disease that made its fur fall out. [17]

HAIRY CREATURES These creatures were observed by three prospectors east of Thomas Bay (Alaska) in 1900. They were said to be smaller than men and to be neither men nor monkeys, but they seem to have had a generally primate-like configuration. [B8*]

HAIRY FISH A creature which is mentioned in early Japanese sources. In unfishlike fashion it would come ashore, make noises and kill, but not devour, men. In fact, this does not sound like a fish at all. It may have been some sort of mammal. [#1]

HAIRY-NECKED PYTHON A supposed resident of the Sahara. [S4]

HAIRY VIPER A snake reported from Algeria in 1852. It was said to be brownish and about 22" long. [S8/A]

HAKUWAI A large bird in Maori legend. No one is ever supposed to have seen it, as it lives too high in the sky. Its cry has been heard, however, as has the beating of its wings. [#8]

HALATA A viviparous fish of medieval lore. The female would remove her young from inside herself, take a look at them and, if they were not fully developed, put them back inside again. [151]

HALF-MAN A strange creature said to look like half a man with the other half looking like a horse or a cow reported from Helix (Oregon). [99]

HALF-TIGER A newspaper story circulated in November, 2003, said a woman who was half human, half tiger was on the loose in Tehran. A mob apparently tried to attack her and fifty arrests were made. [2]

HALF-WOLF A mystery creature so-called was attacking sheep in Yorkshire in 1865. What, exactly, it was has never been discovered.

HAMLET *see* **Lake Elsinore Monster.**

HAN RIU A striped species of Japanese dragon, which can grow to a length of 40'. [J2]

HANDALE WORM A serpent of English legend that had a crested head, a dragon's fiery breath and a wyvern's sting. It was slain by a man named Scaw and the place where once it had lurked was named Scaw Wood in his honour. [#1]

HANGLEY CLEEVE CREATURE This was an animal that inspired horror in the man who saw it. It was crouching so that it resembled a rock, was covered in matted hair and had pale flat eyes. The sighting was in Somerset and there are barrows (burial mounds) nearby. The witness was not normally frightened and later went on to become a big game hunter. [#1]

HANNA'S FISH   A fish 25'/7.62m long and 10"/25cm in diameter, looking largely like an eel, with the upper part of its flat head projecting over its mouth, a pair of small fins behind its head, a triangular fin above them and an eel-like tail was captured by Captain S.W. Hanna at New Harbor (Maine) in 1880. The good captain threw the fish (which was dead) back into the water and its species remains a mystery. However, it bears some resemblance to the frilled shark (*Chlamydoselachus anguineus*) found in the Pacific. [S5]

HANTU JARANG GIGI   A hairy, bigfoot-like but shy creature reported from Malaysia. Recent alleged sightings have been in the Endau-Rompin Park.   [84]

HANTU SAKAI   A name bestowed on either pygmies or larger hominoids – it is not clear which – in which the Semang of Malaysia believe.   [S1]

HAPYEXELOR *see* **Muskrat Lake Monster.**

HARIMAN JALOR   A tiger reported from Malaysia of which it said the stripes run horizontally rather than vertically.   [S7]

HARRINGTON ANIMAL   This creature was seen in Delaware in 1984. No one seems to know what it was. It may have been feline.   [B9]

HARRISON LAKE MONSTER   A creature in this British Columbian lake referred to as *Chunucklas* by the Indians round about. In 1908, a serpentine head was seen to rise out of the water to a height of 12-14'/4m. No body was visible.

A curious report from 1936 describes the creature as being in three sections and joining itself together. This seems absolutely unbelievable, but there have been more credible sightings since.   [K4]

HASELWURM   An alternative name for the tatzelwurm.

HATCUKLIBA   The Creeks, Alabamas and other Indians spoke of this creature, a giant lizard, said to be found in sundry parts of the south-eastern United States. [119]

HATTHILINGA   A gigantic bird in the lore of Myanmar. [N2]

HAWKESBURY RIVER MONSTER   According to cryptozoologist Rex Gilroy, hundreds of reports exist of a monster in this Australian river. He claims the creature looks like a plesiosaur and suggests it breeds at sea, coming inland to lay its eggs. It is greyish in colour and length varies from 23-78'/7-24m. It was known in the lore of the Aborigines as *moolyewonk* and *mirreeular.*

HAWLEY HIM   A BHM found in the vicinity of Peerless (Texas) and the Sulphur River Bottoms.   [B7]

HEADLESS MEN Pliny, in his *Natural History*, speaks of the Blemmyes, who lacked heads but had eyes and mouths in their chests. He applied this name to a tribe living in North-West Africa, but it was later used for an Ethiopian tribe. They were also known as *Akephaloi* ('headless ones'). Sir Walter Raleigh later wrote of a headless race in South America called the Ewaipanomas, with eyes in their shoulders and mouths in their chests. A headless man, perhaps a preternatural creature, has been reported from Beech Hedge, Meikeleour, Scotland. In fact the creature may have been holding its head lowered forward, so it was not visible, and was perhaps an ordinary wildman.   [D2 F4]

HEADLESS WINGED CREATURES These were reported from Sweden in 1946.

HEBER SPRINGS WATER PANTHER This Arkansas creature looks to some extent like a furred human, but also seems to have some puma-like characteristics and is said to be able to breathe both on land and under the water. It lives in the vicinity of Greers Ferry Lake and the Little Red River. It utters a most unpleasant shriek.   [33]

HECAITMOMIXW A Quinault Indian name for a BHM. It literally means 'devil of the forest'.   [90]

HEDGEHOG-BEAR A bear covered in spines like a hedgehog, reported by Grizzly Adams (1812-1860), who claimed to have seen it in California. It has been suggested that the sighting was genuine, but the creature was not acrually a bear.   [30]

HENDERSON ISLAND MONSTER Details of this creature are to be found in the *Tacoma Daily Ledger* (July 3rd, 1893). Men on a fishing expedition who had come to this island off Puget Sound, together with surveyors, saw the "creature" concerned. A loud noise was followed by a strong electric current and strong lights. Two men who touched the water were rendered senseless immediately. The monstrous creature which seemed to be the origin of both light and sound dived beneath the water, but the light it engendered remained visible.

  The creature was described as 150'/45.7m long and, at its thickest point, 30'/9m in circumference. The body itself appeared oval and its upper part appeared to be covered with rough hair. The head was larger than that of a walrus, but resembled it in configuration. Its eyes – it apparently had six – were large and dull. The electricity appeared to come from "copper bands" encircling its body. It flung out electricity - filled water from hornlike protruberances on its head. Its tail seemed like a propellor and revolved.

  Loren Coleman seems to think we are dealing with a machine here, rather than a living creature. The witnesses seemed to think differently. Facts may be adduced in support of both arguments. Even if it was a machine, however, where would such an engine come from in the 19th Century?   [C17]

HENGE A general term for were-creatures in Japan. [122]

HENHAM SERPENT According to a pamphlet published in 1669, which claimed to be based on eyewitness accounts, a serpent, 8-9'/2.5m in length, with small wings and eyes the size of a sheep's, had been about in this area of Essex. It was chased away by locals, but an annual fair in its honour, at which model serpents were sold, was inaugurated and continued until 1939.   [W3]

HERRINGTON LAKE MONSTER   There are many caves surrounding this Kentucky lake and these may be the habitat of a 15'/4.57m lake monster, swinish of snout and tail, reported here by a Professor Thompson in 1972.   [B11]

HESSA SEA SERPENT   This was observed off the Norwegian coast by A.H. Molvaer and his son. It was 65-98'/20-30m long and had a dorsal fin. Later they came back and took a film. Despite the fin, it reminded the witnesses of a long snake, like an anaconda. It is alleged that several other persons witnessed the animal. [126]

HIASCHUCKALUCK   Native American name for the Sproat Lake Monster.

HIBAGON   A 5'/1.5m mystery creature with simian characteristics reported from near Hiroshima. It smells dreadfully. Some say hibagons are a mutated species, resulting from the dropping of the atomic bomb in 1945. The hibagon has a triangular and bristly face.   [C21]

HIBLA-BASHI   In Iraqi folklore, a creature part man and part goat which will suck your blood.   [C12]

HILDE   This mysterious creature of Chilean folklore resembles nothing so much as a cowhide stretched upon the sea with eyes all around its edges and four more prominent eyes in an area supposed to be its head. It is described as an octopus, so presumably it has tentacles.   [B10]

HIPPELAPH   According to Athanasius Kircher in his *Arca Noe* (1675), a cross between a horse and a deer.

HIPPOPARD   According to Athanasius Kircher in his *Arca Noe* (1675), a cross between a horse and a leopard.

HIPPOPOS   A creature mentioned by Aldrovandus, something like a centaur, having the upper half of a man set atop the two-legged rear half of a horse.

HOAN KIEM TURTLE   This, possibly a new species of turtle, is to be found in Hoan Kiem Lake, in the centre of Hanoi. There may be but a single specimen in the lake. It has been filmed. In the 1960s three similar turtles quitted the lake and died. A stuffed specimen can be seen in a temple on an island in the lake. Whether it is identical with the Chinese species *Rafetus swinhoei* or whether it is an hitherto unknown species to be classed as *Rafetus laloii* is disputed by zoologists.[S8/A #9]

HOAT   A creature whose parents were supposedly a Poland China hog and a goat. It was asserted to be an hybrid of the two. This seems very unlikely, if not downright impossible. It was eventually purchased by Tom Slick, the well-known pursuer of Abominable Snowmen. [#8]

HOCKWURM Alternative name for the tatzelwurm.

HODAG To most cryptozoologists, the hodag is an outright hoax, exposed and unworthy of consideration. Certainly what was termed a hodag was shown towards the end of the 19ᵗʰ Century at various exhibitions. Its career started out at Rhinelander (Wisconsin). Investigation proved the hodag to be made of wood and ox-hide, with wires to control its movements. However, some sources say the hodag fake was based on a real creature, as yet outside the annals of zoology, ranging in size from a collie to a bear, which favoured a diet of rabbits. The swamps of Vilas and Oneida are said to be home to this creature. [A1]

HOG-FISH Alternative name for the angulo.

HOKIOI *see* **Hakuwai**.

HOLADEIRA A dolphin with toothlike projections on its back reported from South America. It has been seen and photographed, but whether it is a new kind of dolphin or merely an injured specimen is not certain. [#9]

HO-LO Legendary Chinese fish with one head but ten bodies. [#11]

HOLLOW BLOCK LAKE MONSTER This Indiana lake is said to play host to a most peculiar looking creature resembling a square in shape. It gives out screams, which probably keeps unwanted attention at a safe distance. [E]

HOMBRE ORSO A bigfoot-type humanoid that has been reported from various parts of Mexico. Its name means 'bear-man'. [C23]

HOMO MARINHO A kind of merman supposed to dwell of the coast of South America. They look like humans, but will strangle humans they capture. [C14]

HONEY ISLAND SWAMP MONSTER A humanoid monster reported from the Honey Island Swamp (Louisiana). L. Coleman asserts firmly that it is different from bigfoot. It is said to be 7'/2m tall and have orange-brown hair. Witness Harlan Ford claims to have stood face to face with it and to have been startled by its amber eyes. [58]

HONG KONG MYSTERY ANIMAL This creature, resembling a cat, was seen in 1976. It was the possible killer of a number of dogs. [B9]

HONG KONG SEA MONSTER In 1969 a black sea monster, 20-30'/6-9m long, was seen off the coast of Hong Kong. It had green eyes. It made a loud crying sound. This is not the only time a monster has been espied off the Hong Kong coast. In 1901 a dragon-like sea-monster was seen from the customs launch *Lung-Tsing.*. When sailors were sent in a boat to attack the creature, it understandably bit one of their oars in two. It was 40-50'/12-15m long. [B9]

HOQUIAM A Puget name for a BHM. [S1]

HORNED HUMAN It has been asserted that a race of horned humans once existed. In the 1880s a burial mound was supposedly excavated at Sayre (Pennsylvania). The skeletons inside appeared to be those of 7'/2m humans with horns. Other horned human skeletons are said to have been excavated in Texas and New York state. Individual horn-growing persons are not unknown.   [121]

HORNED SNAKE A creature in the legends of the Creek Indians. It dwelt in the water. The elders would sing a magical song, drawing it to the shore. Then its horn would be cut off and carried into battle.   [C/H]

HORNED WATER LIZARD *see* **Sil:quey.**

HORNY CHESSMAN TROLL The Horny Chessman camping grounds lie outside Seaside (Oregon). A 7'/2m tall hairy monster, referred to as a troll, has been reported lurking there in the past.   [140]

HORSE-EEL General term applied to Irish water monsters.

HORSE-HEADED WOMAN This is supposed to occupy Bay Lough in Co Tipperary (Ireland) and to appear from time to time.   [D3]

HOW-HOW On totem poles in British Columbia this is a depiction of this feline creature which the Indians assert really exists, but which has not to be identified with the puma. [S7]

HRAESVALG A huge bird in which the early Norse believed.

HSIAO In Chinese lore, this is an owl-like bird with a man's face, an ape's body and a dog's tail.   [B10]

HUA-FISH A fish with bird's wings in Chinese lore.   [B10]

HUALLEPEN This creature, the Chileans say, lives in the water. It has a calf's head and a sheep's body. It is described as being both fierce and shy. It will engender offspring on ordinary ewes and cows. These look like their mothers, but canny Chilean shepherds can distinguish them by their twisted hooves. They sometimes have deformed muzzles also.   [B10]

HUANACO CREATURES Manlike, scaly beings reported from Peru. In 1977, a hapless student fell into a marsh. Four creatures, covered with scales, three-fingered and about 3'/90cm tall, helped him to extricate himself by holding out branches to him. [B9]

HUEKE-HUEKE' This is a fierce and dangerous creature supposed to be found in the rivers and lakes of South America. It looks not unlike a sting-ray, but it can appear to be a stretched animal hide floating on the surface of the water.   [120]

HUIA A supposedly extinct bird (*Heterlocha acutirostris*) of New Zealand. However, despite the fact that huias are supposed to have died out in 1907, there have been a number of reports of more recent sightings, one of them by prominent cryptozoologist Lars Thomas.   [E]

HUILLA This serpentine creature has been reported from Trinidad. It is said to live in bodies of fresh water, moving from one to another. It undulates horizontally and its length has been estimated at 25'-30'/7.6-9m.   [#4]

HUMAN-ALMAS HYBRID In the Mongolian monastery of Lamyn Hegen, there had been a very learned and intelligent lama known as "son of the Almas". His father had been captured by almas and fathered a child on one of them. When he escaped, he took the child with him. This information came from an old Mongolian named Gendun, whose father had been a contemporary of the lama in question.   [T1]

HUMAN-DOG HYBRID According to Eskimo mythology, a woman mated with a dog and produced five dogs and five monsters. The dogs became the ancestors of the white men, while the monsters became the ancestors of the horrific Adlet, also called the Erqigdlit. These were fierce monsters with a taste for human flesh. In China, a dog-human hybrid was supposed to be the progenitor of two minority races, the Miao and the Yao. [J1]

HUMAN-DOLPHIN HYBRID Any scientist would have forty fits if told such a thing could occur, but in Brazilian folklore it is believed that dolphins disguise themselves as females and have relationships with humans. The hybrids produced look human, but have a beak and a blow-hole. In the same area male dolphins are said to rape girls who sometimes give birth to fishlike children.   [M7 #15]

HUMAN-ORANG UTAN HYBRID According to Edward Long (1734-1813) such hybrids were not alone possible, but actually occurred from time to time.   [K8]

HUMAN-SISIMITE HYBRID In an article in the journal *Inexplicata* we are informed that there exists the belief that sisimites from time to time carry off women and father children on them.

HUMAN-TARMA HYBRID The tarma is itself a cryptozoological primate supposed to live in Peru. It is believed there that hybrids between humans and tarmas are produced.

HUMAN-WOLF HYBRID Such a thing is not genetically possible, but it is said that, along Devil's River in Texas, some time in the 19th Century, a girl was raised by wolves.

Having reached maturity, she mated with them. Her offspring looked like wolves, but had human eyes. Their descendants are believed to be still living in the vicinity. [B7]

HUMAN-YETI HYBRID In folklore, such hybrids are said to have occurred. Yetis themselves are supposed to be descended from the union of a Chinese or Tibetan girl and an ape. [L1]

HUMAN-YOWIE HYBRID The yowie, which features elsewhere in this dictionary, is a legendary hominoid of Australia. A bizarre story in the *People Magazine* in 1979 by three alleged witnesses told of events said to have happened about a century before when a woman, having been violated by a yowie, subsequently gave birth to a female half-yowie child. This creature was locked away. It was described as looking like a girl, but covered in orange hair. When the woman died, the husband, who had refused her request to kill the child, released it into the wild. If there is any truth in this yarn, the genetic implications are indeed interesting. [M6]

HUMPED FISH According to the *Caspar Star-Tribune* (7th April, 1983) an unidentified fish with two humps was seen by a married couple in Pathfinder Lake (Wyoming).

HUN GOROOS A Mongolian term (meaning 'man beast') used for hominoids. One can also find *hun har garoos* ('black man beast'). [T1]

HUNGARIAN REEDWOLF A mystery canid which is possibly, but not certainly, extinct. Specimens of the creature are to be found in museums, but its exact nature is unknown. It may be a jackal or small wolf. [135]

HUSE-BJORN A were-bear in Norwegian legend. [T2]

HUSPALIM A legendary Ethiopian animal. In some respects it resembles a marmot. [45]

HVITA MONSTER It was said that in 1595 a monster was seen in this Icelandic river. Its head looked like a "sea-dog's" and it had tall spines on its back. *See also* **Okind**.

HVOKO CAPKO An animal in the lore of the Seminole Indians. It is not unlike a horse, but its head is wolflike. Its ears are long. It is coloured grey and about 3'/1m high. It stinks somewhat. [G6]

HYDRA One of the labours of Hercules was to kill the many-headed hydra, a serpentine beast. Authorities vary as to the number of heads with which this creature was endowed, but one figure says it had nine, a main head and eight not so important. If you cut off a head, however, two more grew in its place. Bringing his trusty nephew Iolaus, Hercules cut off each head and, before new ones could regrow, Iolaus applied a burning brand to the place whence they would have sprouted. R. Carrington is sure the hydra was an octopus, with a major head and eight tentacles. Sometimes octopus tentacles will re-grow if severed and this, he suspects, lies behind the story. D.E. Jones, however, would suggest that belief in polycephalic draconic creatures such as the hydra have their origin in artistic attempts to depict motion by a multiple image. Gesner spoke of an hydra that had lions' heads. It was a water creature, he claimed, which had been brought from Turkey to Venice in 1530 and then sent to the King of France.   [C5 J2]

HYNISH WEREWOLF A creature reported on the Scottish island of Tiree, blamed for killing dogs.   [146]

HYTHE MOTHMAN *see* **Kent Batman.**

I

ICEGEDUNK A peculiar form of land seal or seal-like beast reputedly to be found in British Columbia. It is said to propel itself forward with appendages that resemble wheels more than legs of flippers.   [120]

ICELANDIC RIVER CREATURE A mystery creature that did not look like a fish that hastened towards a swimmer in this Manitoba river in 1988. The swimmer was unscathed. [R8]

ICHITAPA A monster said to live in Lake Kashiba, Zambia.   [C/H]

IEMISCH A creature in Argentine lore. It is to be found in the region of Patagonia, bears a number of characteristics of the otter, yet is said to be very fierce. B. Heuvelmans feels that, when the jaguar became extinct in Patagonia, the natives attributed its ferocious aspects to this creature. R. Mackal would suggest that the iemisch is a large species of otter, which is fearsome in its own nature, owing nothing of this to the memory of jaguars. When we speak of an otter's being large, it is pertinent to ask how large. South America is home to the giant otter, known to reach a length of five feet. However, the Araguaia river in Brazil is rumoured to be home to otters as long as twelve feet and Peter Fleming (brother of James Bond author Ian Fleming) averred he saw an otter seven feet long in this river. A giant otter in Patagonia could be a substantial creature indeed. [H9 M2]

IGOPOGO A water monster reported from Lake Simcoe, Ontario. It is said to be "dog-faced" and its length has been estimated from 20'-70'/6-21m, indicating more than one specimen may exist. Indeed, as it has been observed for many years, there may well be a breeding population in the lake. A notable sighting by a boating party occurred in 1963. [C22 C20]

IGUPIARA A singularly unpleasant water-dwelling creature in the legends of Brazil. They look just like humans and the females are beautiful. However, they will seize and kill real humans and eat their eyes, noses, genitals and the tips of their fingers and toes. However, in 1554 a Portuguese captain, Balthasar Ferreira, fought with and killed one that didn't seem all that human, for it had claws and its body had hair. [M7]

IKIMIZI Mystery cat reported in Rwanda in 1921. It is supposed to be grey with dark spots and to have a beard. [S7]

IKUGAN A large monkey of Filipino folklore. It has a long tail with which it can pull helpless human victims into the trees where it strangles them. Genrally speaking, monkeys with prehensile tails are found only in the New World. The Manobas of Eastern Mindanao believe in this creature. [R1]

ILE DU LEVANT CAT The Ile du Levant is one of the Iles d'Hyeres off the French coast. This cat has been observed, but scientists have never examined a specimen. It seems quite large. Bernard Heuvelmans actually saw one in 198. Whether it is a subspecies of wildcat or an hitherto unknown species has yet to be determined. [S7]

ILLIGIAN DOLPHIN A dolphin observed from the islands of Indonesia. The back is brown, the sides are yellow and the underparts are pink. [30]

ILLINOIS MONSTER This hominoid put in a number of appearances in 1972. It was supposed to have long grey ears shaped like the letter U, its face was long and grey and its mouth red with sharp teeth. It was the subject of numerous reports, one of which says that it was 10'/3m tall and looked like a cross between an ape and a caveman. Teenager Randy Emert described its colour as "kind of white", which may mean off-white, but could also be cream, light yellow, etc. [#9]

ILLINOIS STRIPED CAT A large mystery cat, described as black with stripes, was seen in Champaign County (Illinois) in 1963. [C19]

ILLUYANKAS A dragon of Hittite legend which was first made drunk (as were its offspring) and then killed. It was fire-breathing, had a feathered crest and horns and was legless. (particularly after it had been made drunk). [59 J2]

IMAP UMASSOURSUA A somewhat flat sea monster, the size of an island. It is supposed to be found in the vicinity of Greenland. [M7]

IMOGEN SEA SERPENT An apparent sea serpent observed in the North Atlantic in 1856. It was seen from the ship *Imogen* and judged to be 40'/12m in length.

INDESTRUCTIBLE WINKLE A legendary Chinese crustacean. If it seems dead due to lack of water, it can be revived by being placed in vinegar. [M9]

INDIAN OCEAN SEA SERPENT A report published in 1834 mentioned a creature seen to the east of Madras. It had a large mouth, a dorsal fin, a tail, a lizard-like head and its body was covered in brown spots. There were fish, perhaps dogfish, round about it, with which it seemed on the friendliest terms. In 1979 a sea serpent was observed in the Indian Ocean from the ship *Priam*. A possible Indian Ocean sea serpent was seen off Madagascar in 1889.

INGOT An unidentified wormlike creature encountered by French troops in Indo-China in the 1950s. A French regiment was said to have disappeared in 1953 and many ingots were reported from the area where this is supposed to have taken place. In the mind of some French soldiers this meant that they were imbued with a paranormal element. [99]

INK MONKEY Chinese writings claim that scholars were once assisted by tiny monkeys, which could prepare their skin, turn their pages and pass them brushes. They would also consume the leftovers of ink. There seems little doubt they once existed, though what they actually were and whether they were true monkeys remains unknown. A recent report of the finding of a living specimen seems baseless.   [S8/A]

INKANYAMBA A monster in South African lore. It is supposed to be a water-snake with flippers. Inkanyambas occur in cave-paintings. They are not observed in summer and this leads people to believe they go into the sky and cause summer rains. A famous member of the species is said to dwell at Howick Falls and has been nicknamed "Howie". Sightings of Howie were reported in 1964, 1981 and 1995.   [40]

INORIK A two-horned beast in Russian folklore, it rules all the other animals. It is even friendly to humans, helping them in times of drought. Its name is a corruption of the word *unicorn*.   [D4]

INTULO A sort of lizard with human features in Zulu folklore. [4]

IOLA THING Iola is in Kansas and, about midnight in 1903, a man's shout cleft the air in its general vicinity. Others ran to see what had distressed the caller. They then saw a creature standing upright. It had horns, long hair and large eyes.   [R6]

IPILYA A gigantic gecko that lived on Groote Eylandt in Australia's Gulf of Carpentaria (according to Aboriginal legend). It was said to live in the Numenka Swamp and to be 300'/91m long.   [G3]

IRISH WILDCAT Evidence for the existence of such a creature has been scant, though there were a number of reports of possible wildcats in the 19th Century. The term wildcat is sometimes used in Ireland merely for a feral. The general consensus among scientists has been that they do not exist. However, a number of reports have come in in modern times. A Tipperary psychologist and her daughter saw a wildcat a number of times in 2002. She was adamant that it was neither a feral nor a pine marten. It had a thick, banded tail. In 1999 a school vice-principal had observed a wildcat in the nearby Keeper Woods. Not far away are Dundrum Woods where a ranger in 1993 saw a cat twice the size of a domestic and averred that, had he been in Scotland, he would have described it unhesitatingly as a wildcat. Reports of wildcats are now coming in from Wicklow. At the other side of the country in Co Sligo, there is supposed to be a population of wildcats. It is believed locally that a family imported Scottish wildcats in the 1880s and that they have interbred with ferals.   [D3]

IRIZIMA   A creature with a trunk like an elephant's, a lizard's head and a hippopotamus' legs has been believed to occupy Edward Lake in the Congo (Kinshasa). [C1]

IRKUIEM   A large unidentified white bear from the region of Kamchatka in Siberia. It is said to have a slim body, a small head and larger front than back legs, which means it proceeds with a remarkable gait, jumping with its forefeet and dragging its back legs after it. It is rumoured to sometimes cross from Siberia to Alaska on ice floes. Scientist R. Sivolobov was given an alleged skin of the animal in 1987, but, as it was accompanied by neither tooth nor skull, there was nothing to distinguish it from the skin of a polar bear. [S6]

ISA BERE   A dragon of African legend, who was said to have drunk up the Niger river. It was killed by King Samba and his trusty bard Tarafe and its bones then released the water. Those bones are said to lie under the river yet.   [75]

ISNACHI   A kind of monkey, about the size of a chimpanzee, reported from Peru. It lives in the forested areas of mountain ranges. It is sometimes seen in groups, but more often on its own or in company with spider monkeys. It is also called *camuenere* and *makisapa maman.*   [31 C25]

ISSIE   Lake monster reported from Lake Ikeda, Japan. A photograph taken in 1978 reveals a serpentine form with alternating rings of black and white. A photograph taken later in the year apparently revealed two monsters.   [S18]

IT   I do not pretend to know what *it* looks like and neither do the Shetlanders who believe in it, for they credit it with the power to assume any shape it wishes. It could look like a legless beast, a jellyfish or something inanimate.   [F4]

ITALIAN WATER MONSTER   This was seen in marshes near Perugia about 1933. These marshes are connected with the sea by the Tiber.   [B9]

ITALIAN WILDMAN   A couple of reports of a yeti-type creature have been made from Italy. In 1996 some people in a car saw what looked like a cross between a gorilla and a man near Sealza. The same creature or another like it was later seen in the same area and estimated to be 2m tall.   [31]

IU-WUN   A mystery ape reported from Myanmar.   [#4]

IVORY-BILLED WOODPECKER   This bird (*Camephilus principalis principalis*) is supposedly extinct, the last ones having died out in Cuba in 1990. It was supposed to have become extinct in the United States in 1960. David Kulivan, a student at Louisiana State University, claimed to have seen a pair on 4th November, 2000. More sceptical persons claim he saw pileated woodpeckers. However, on a more encouraging note, in 2003 Bob Russell of the US Fish and Wildlife Service heard what he thought might be the bird.   [#1]

IZCUINTLIPOTZOTLI   A mystery animal that once inhabited Mexico.   While its quondam existence is not in doubt, there has been speculation as to what it actually was. It does not seem to have survived beyond 1850.   Clavijero's *Historia Antigua de Mexico* (1780) describes a beast with a head like a wolf, small ears, a kind of hump along its back and forelegs shorter than hind legs.   Canine and rodent identities have been proposed for the beast, but nothing can be pronounced with certainty.   [S8]

J

JACKALOPE   A horned hare, this creature is rarely regarded as a true cryptid, but rather as an invented creature, perhaps made up by Douglas Herrick (died 2003). However, there is some evidence that the jackalope goes back to a legendary animal of the Ogalala Sioux, who referred to these creatures as dust devils.   Moreover, there is a virus called Shope papilloma which can give lagomorphs the appearance of being horned.

JACKO   According to reports, what may have been a young bigfoot captured in the 19th Century.   Unfortunately, there appears to be little doubt that the story of Jacko is a hoax.

JACULUS   An alternative name for the amphiptere.

JAGO-NINI   A creature of central Africa which is perhaps identical with mokele-mbembe.   [61]

JAGUARETE   An unknown animal of the cat family reported from South America in the 18th Century.   The jaguarete mentioned by G. Marcgrave in 1648 seems to have been a melanistic jaguar, but a "black tiger" described by T. Pennant in 1771 had light underparts, which do not occur in melanistic jaguars, so we may here have the true jaguarete.   The jaguarete's existence was once accepted by scientists, but they do not now consider there is sufficient evidence to warrant firm belief in the animal. [S7 S8/A]

JAK-ANYWONG   A large serpent reported from the swamps of the Upper Nile. Heuvelmans thinks it is a kind of catfish.   [#4]

JAVAN TIGER   A tiger subspecies thought extinct since 1984, yet signs of a surviving population have been found and it has been alleged that a photograph of one has been taken.   [B6]

JERSEY DEVIL   A strange creature reported from the Pine Barrens of New Jersey. Belief in it goes back at least to 1790.   It looked somewhat like a kangaroo, with leathery wings, ram's horns and a forked tail, but considerably different descriptions of it have been furnished over the centuries.

It was the subject of various stories in the 19th Century.   In 1840-41 it was blamed for the death of livestock.   Sightings were reported from 1859 onwards.   In 1870 it was seen in the company of a mermaid. On other occasions it was seen with a golden-haired girl and a pirate's ghost. In the 1880s, it was said to be carrying off livestock once more.

The week of January 16th-23rd, 1909, was one in which many sightings were reported. Police Officer James Sackville saw the beast in Bristol (NJ) and opened fire on it, making it take off with a scary cry. The postmaster, E.W. Minster, saw it flying that night. At 2.30 on Tuesday, the Devil favoured Gloucester City with a visit, where Mr and Mrs Evans saw it on their shed roof. A sketch by Mr Evans gives it a somewhat horselike head. It was seen by a policeman and clergyman back in Burlington on Wednesday. The policeman declared it had no teeth. Two separate witnesses placed its height at 3'. Sightings continued till the end of the week, when the Devil left inhabited areas for the time being. Large numbers of tracks were found. There may have been some chicanery in all of this, as persons for reasons of their own were said to have tried to use the general scare to lower house prices in the area. In fact, Ivan Sanderson had what he understood was the fake foot used to make footprints. However, this by no means indicates all the sightings were hoaxes. There does nor seem to be evidence that the entire scare was orchestrated.

In 1951 the Devil was supposedly sighted in Gibbstown. In 1966 Stephen Sikotch was horrified to find two large dogs, four cats, three geese and thirty-one ducks slain. Some suspected that the Devil was involved. Reports of the creature have continued up to 2003. One rumour has it living in a body of water called the Blue Hole in woods in Winslow Township.

Also known as the Leeds Devil, it was possibly so-called because it was often reported about Leeds Point. However, it was also said thar it was the offspring of a Mrs Leeds, of whose existence some evidence survives.

There is now a Jersey Devil Café in Medford. A local hockey team is called the New Jersey Devils. [T8 C19]

JERUSALEM MONSTER A ferocious beast, supposedly slain near Jerusalem in 1725. It had a leonine head, was the size of a horse and had a brace of horns. It boasted wings, scales and claws, not to mention an aquiline beak and long ears that hung down. It was a female, having a cow's udder.   [T2/A]

JETETE An unknown species of flamingo reported by locals in Chile. [S8/A]

JEZ-TERMAK A form of wildman reported from Tibet. Its shaggy hair is said to be dark black and it is said to have copper fingernails – this would refer to the colour, not the composition. [S1]

JHOOR An animal that is lizardlike, perhaps identical with the buru, reported from the Gir region of India.   [C20]

JIAO LONG In Chinese dragon lore, a dragon with scales [J2]

JIMBRA A mysterious simian creature described by Aborigines to three explorers in Western Australia in 1861. *Jingra* is given as an alternative form of the word. [S11]

JINSHIN-UWO This huge eel of Japanese mythology lives underneath Japan and causes earthquakes. [73]

JIUKAM-YAWA Some kind of feline animal said to hunt in groups in the belief of the Shuar Indians of Ecuador. [41]

JUBOLAI ISLAND BIRD An unidentified bird reported in the 18th Century from this New Zealand island. It was coloured brown, about the size of a kite, with a tail that was yards long and at first mistaken for a flock of smaller birds flying in its wake. [#8]

JUGHEAD A blob which turned up on the coast of Oregon in 1950. Many people cut pieces from it for use as souvenirs.

JUMAR A supposed cross between a horse and a cow. Such a hybrid is not scientifically possible. The dissection of supposed jumars revealed them to be mules. [C8]

JUMPING CREATURE This was seen in Tucson (Arizona) on 6th November, 2003. It was a dark hominoid creature that crouched and jumped like a frog and made hissing noises. [145]

JUNGLE LION An animal bearing a distinct resemblance to the lion (*Panthera leo*), but reported from Peru. [30]

JUNGLI ADMI A kind of hominoid, known to the Sherpas. It is about four feet tall. It likes living in high ground, but chilly weather will drive it into the valleys. Its hair is long and yellowish brown. It seems to be both terrestrial and arboreal. [5]

JUNJUDEE A small hairy hominoid of Australian Aboriginal folklore. They are supposed to be found in Carnarvon Gorge (Queensland). Their heads seem long and their limbs simian. They make cackling noises. [S8]

K

KA RIU A small species of Japanese dragon, only 6'/1.8m long. [J2]

KADIMAKARA A large marsupial said to be found in the centre of Australia. It bears some resemblance to a rabbit and may be identical with the giant rabbits reported from that country. [31]

KAHUI-A-TIPUA A race of beings in Maori lore. Some said they had the faces of dogs. They were regarded by some as a form of maero. [C12]

KAI TSI The Japanese believed in this creature, but not that it was to be found in Japan. It looked something like a lion, but had a single horn. It was also known as *Sin You* and it had a moral sense. The Chinese called this animal *Hiai Chai.* [03]

KAKAI BESAR A sasquatch-like creature said to inhabit Malaysia. [5]

KAKUNDARI Unknown primates the size of a child. C. Cordier felt them to be identical with the agogwe. They are given the name *kakundari* by a number of central African peoples, while the Bakumu call them *amajungi*. On the left side of the Congo river they are known as *lisisingo*. [H7]

KALA'LITABIQW Skagit Indian name for a BHM

KALAMALKA LAKE MONSTER This beast has been discerned only once, in 1978. Most of it was submerged, the only definite feature beings its fins, but it was estimated at being 100' long. This lake is in British Columbia. [K4]

KALANORO A hominoid in the lore of Madagascar, but the term means different things to different groups on that island. The Sakalave say it is under 3'/90cm in height and will try to lure the innocent passer-by into lake water to his doom. It has three toes on each foot. The Bara say kalanoros are long haired men and will go foraging in villages after nightfall. In the north of the islands it is said to live in caves and will fight humans only in self-defence. The Betsileo regard it as female and call the males *kotokely*. Around Lake Aloatra it is believed to be something like a mermaid. [H9]

KALIMANTAN BEAST-MAN This creature, 9'/2.74m tall, was reported from the western part of Kalimantan, the Indonesian part of Borneo, in 1983. [B9]

KAMLOOPS LAKE MONSTER In this British Columbia lake a 10'/3m long eel-like creature with humps which lowered and resurfaced repeatedly was observed by two witnesses in 1966. [K4]

KAMMAPA A gigantic amorphous beast in the beliefs of the Basuto. It was also called Khodumodumo. It swallowed every animal it encountered. It once swallowed a complete village, but its stomach was cut open by the hero Ditaolane, who thus saved man and beast within, although in cutting he injured a disgruntled swallowee's leg. [W2]

KANGAROO MAN According to a story in the *Rosenburg Review* of 1900, this creature was seen in the Sixes River area of Oregon. It looked like a handsome man, was 9'/2.74m tall, its body was covered with hair and its hands reached almost to the ground. It seems to have proceeded by bounding. Its footprints were 18"/45cm long and showed five toes. [G7]

KANGAROO MONSTER A creature observed by two witnesses at Dayton (Tennessee). It was nearly 6'/1.83m tall and looked like a kangaroo, but it had hooves and horns. [99]

KANGAROO-LEGGED CREATURE A strange creature reported from the Buin-Maipo route in Chile. It is about 1.5m tall, with taloned hands, a face like a wolf's, a rattle on the end of its tail and a mane down its back. It has been seen with a dead animal in its mouth. Its legs enable it to make considerable leaps. It has been sighted by a number of drivers. Scott Corrales of the Institute of Hispanic Ufology has nicknamed it "killeroo". It has also been dubbed the Viluco Monster.

KANIMAS A term for a hominoid used in Venezuela. [#4]

KAP DWA In 1900 a stuffed two-headed giant known by this name was exhibited in Britain. Since 1980 it has been shown in the United States. It is said to have been killed by Spaniards in 1673. [69]

KAPPA Creatures in Japanese folklore. There is some evidence that a real animal lies behind them. Kappas are amphibious, with a head like a monkey's, webbed feet, a shell and eyes like triangles. Each kappa has a hollow in its head, containing water from which it derives its strength. If you meet a hostile kappa, bow to it. It will bow back (for they are well-mannered) dislodging the water and rendering it too weak to harm you. They enjoy eating cucumbers and they can also use those for purposes of flight. [C21 J1]

KAPRE A bigfoot-like species reported from the mountains of the Philippines. It is not considered dangerous. However, it is said to be taller and heftier than bigfoot and it has been described as smoking cigars or even a pipe. It is thought kapres may live on Mount Makiling in caves. One legend gives the kapre the magical power to turn into a banana tree if shot at. [31 57]

KAPTAR A BHM reported from the region of the Caucasus. The males seem to be found a-wandering in the upper parts of the mountains, the females further down. There is supposed to be a small variety, but these may be only younger ones. Its voice makes a singular sound. [S]

KARKOTAK NAAG A monster said to occupy Lake Taudaha, Nepal. [C/H]

KARSHIPTA A talking bird of Persian mythology. [4]

KASAI REX This animal has been reported from central Africa. It looks like a dinosaur, is bipedal and estimated to be 40'/12m tall. Witness John Johnson (or Johanson) saw one attack a rhinoceros in 1932 and actually fainted from shock during the experience. Heuvelmans considers this sighting a hoax. It has been stated that there were other sightings, but I have been unable to find any details. [2]

KATARAGAMA MOTH Yellow moths of unknown species appeared at Kataragama (Sri Lanka) and nearby areas in December, 2003. [2]

KATCITOWACK A Cree name for a monstrous animal in their legends. It means 'stiff-legged bear' and may just possibly preserve a memory of the terrible short-faced bear (*Arctodus simus*) which is thought to have become extinct about 3000 BC.

KATE-KATE   In the lore of the Mapuche Indians of South America, a flying head which uses its ears as wings.   [#12]

KAUREHE   A mammal of New Zealand in which the Maoris believed. Rarely seen, it is whitish in colour and comes out after nightfall. Its name would indicate it is endowed with spines. Bernard Heuvelmans misspelled the name of this animal.   [H9]

KAVAY   The Tsimihety people of Madagascar will warn you about this animal. It lives in water, but will emerge to tear your eyes out.   [H9]

KELLAS CAT   A Scottish felid of mysterious origin. It was first heard of in 1984, when one was trapped in Scotland. It may have resulted from hybrids of wildcats and feral domestics breeding with other wildcats and feral domestics or else be a separate race of the Scottish wildcat (*Felis sylvestris grampia*).   Animals bearing a startling resemblance to the Kellas cat have recently been reported in North Carolina. [S7 #9]

KELPIE   In Scottish legend, a creature in the guise of the horse, which is found near water. However, if you mount it, it will dive into the water with you. There is some possibility that some Scottish lake monsters so resemble horses that people have tried to climb onto them, only for the monster to jump into the water. At any rate, we hear so often of lake monsters having horselike heads that they may lie behind belief in the kelpie.   [J1]

KENT BATMAN   A figure that looked like a bat of human size was seen on the ground at Hythe (Kent) in 1963. Its appearance coincided with that of a UFO overhead. [K1]

KENYAN BLACK SWIFT   An unidentified bird reported from Masabit Mountain, Kenya.   [30]

KESSINGLAND SEA-SERPENT   A sea-serpent has been reported off Kessingland near Lowestoft (Suffolk). It is first mentioned in 1750, when it is described as having a dog's head and a lion's beard. It was often reported in the 19th Century and in 1912 Lilias Rider Haggard, daughter of H. Rider Haggard, wrote to her father saying she had seen it. It was observed by a naval ship in 1923 and by an anonymous correspondent of the *East Anglian Magazine* in 1978.

KETOS   A large sea-creature in Greek mythology. It had a propensity to devour maidens. One of them was rescued by Perseus, another by Hercules.

KHANAS LAKE MONSTER   This Chinese lake harbours a monster which is said to attack people and cattle. It is said to be possibly a red fish, about 30'/10m long. It has been claimed a picture has been taken. However, scientists say the lake is too cold for, and does not contain a sufficient number of fish to support, such a creature.   [10]

KHEYAK Name given to the wildman in the Russian area by the Sea of Okhotsk. The kheyak is supposed to have hypnotic powers. [B3]

KHODUMODUMO A monstrous creature in South African lore which makes nocturnal raids on farms and kraals. It will carry off a sheep, goat or calf. It leaves mysterious and unidentifiable footprints.   [H9]

KHYA A term used in the Newar language for an abominable snowman. [L1]

KIIK-ADAM A Kazakh term for a BHM. [T1]

KIIK-KISH A Kirghiz term for a BHM. [T1]

KIBAMBANGWE A mystery predatory beast in Kenya – possibly an unknown form of hyena. Its only noteworthy features are its size and blackish colouration. [S7]

KICKING MONSTER A monster in the legends of the Jicarilla Apache, overcome by Killer-of-Enemies, the defeating of monsters being his forte. [K]

KIDOKY A mystery animal of Madagascar, which seems to be an unknown form of lemur. It is reported to have dark fur, with a white spot on its forehead and another below its mouth.   [#9]

KIKITUK A large sea monster with saurian characteristics in which the Eskimo of the Point Hope region of Alaska believe. It is supposed to be man-eating, venturing ashore to engage in this prandial activity.   [J2]

KIKIYAON A fearsome creature in the legends of the Bambara of Senegal. It looks like a large owl in some respects, its talons are said to be terrible, but it has greenish/grey hair all over its body and some accounts mention a tail. You are likely to hear its cry before you see it. It lives in the very depths of the forest.   [40]

KIKOMBA An unknown ape of Africa, of which C. Cordier wrote. It dwells in the forests of the easterly portion of central Africa. It is noted for its howl and it eats honey. It also relishes a tuber called mele-mele. Cordier once met a man who claimed his arm had been rendered useless by a kikomba.   [H7]

KILKERRIN BAY MONSTER In 1910 a sea monster with a brown hairy body was seen here off the coast of Galway (Ireland).   [B9]

KILLER, THE Name applied by Oliver Goldsmith (1730-1774) to an animal known to New England fishermen. These killers were supposed to attack whales and overcome them as a pack of dogs would a bull. Goldsmith avers that they themselves are of the whale family.   [F2]

122

KILOPILOPITSOFY A mystery animal of Madagascar, whose name means 'floppy ears'. It is also called a *tsomgomby*. The general appearance seems to be that of an hippopotamus. There were once two small species of hippopotamus in Madagascar. At least one may still survive. [#9]

KIMBALL BEAST What was described as a prehistoric beast graced Kimball (Tennessee) with its presence in 1936. It was seen in the South Pittsburg area and what was believed to be its den was discovered on the banks of the Tennessee River. Grenades were flung and machine-guns fired into this. Whether or not it was in fact the beast's lair, it was not seen again. [B11]

KINEPIKWA A lake monster with one horn, but otherwise serpentine, in which the Shawnee believe. [M7]

KING A one-horned beast in Chinese lore. It looks like a large stag and has an ox's tail. [G5]

KING SNAKE A bluish coloured snake in the legends of northern Germany. This serpent is reckoned a king among its fellows and even wears a crown. It is supposed to live near Flensberg. Possession of its crown confers immortality. It should not be confused with the king snake (*Lapropeltis getulis*) of modern zoology. [T2]

KING SQUIRREL An unidentified animal the size of a cat observed among squirrels in Indiana. [31]

KINGSTON SEA SERPENT A water creature reported from the waters near Kingsron (Ontario). The earliest extant report dates from 1867. In 1881 ir was variously estimated from 25'-40' long. It had a large head, many feet and a long, powerful tail. A man named Parks fought against it with a fishing pole in 1892. A sighting took place in 1931 and the creature is still supposed to exist. It has been given the nickname *Kingstie.*

KINIE GER An animal in the traditions of the Australian Aborigines, eventually defeated by the Owl and the Crow. He had the head and body of a cat, with human limbs. [134]

KINNARA A creature half man and half bird in Thai lore. [K7]

KINOSO A name given by Indians to a mysterious white animal with a humped back which is said to dwell in Cold Lake (Alberta). [E]

KINTYRE CREATURE A creature the size and general shape of an elephant, but lacking a head, was washed up in 1944 on the coast of Kintyre (Scotland). It was pronounced a polar bear, but seems to have been too large and the wrong shape. It may have been an elephantoid sea creature like those reported elsewhere. *See* **Glacier Island Creature; Sea Elephant; Trunko.** [E1]

KIOH TWAN A beast of Chinese lore, with a horn on its nose, a horse's tail and the general appearance of a deer. It was of a greenish colour. [G5]

KITALARGO Mystery cat of Uganda.   [61]

KITSUNE A were-fox in Japanese belief. [122]

KIWAKWE A kind of cannibal giant in whom the Penobscot Indians believed. [M6]

KNUCKER This seems to have been a term used in Sussex to mean a dragon generally or a certain kind of dragon. They lived in holes. A specific Knucker Hole Monster lived at Lyminster, with a brace of wings and four legs.. There are various stories about how it was killed. One is that it was given a huge plum pudding, causing it great indigestion, especially as it had scoffed the horse and cart which brought this provender to it. Its head was cut off by Jim Puttock. His gravestone used to be in Lyminster churchyard, but is now in the church itself. [W1]

KOAO A mystery flightless bird of the Marquesas Islands. It has been said that no one has ever captured one because they are so fast. One was encountered by no less a personage than Thor Heyerdahl in 1937.   [S8]

KODIAK MONSTER In Raspberry Strait off Kodiak (Alaska), a 200'/60m long unknown animal was located by an electronic device in 1969.   [101]

KOERAKOONLASED A race of creatures in Estonian legend that were part man and part dog. Some thought them to be dog-headed men with a single cyclopean eye. Some held they were dogs down one side and humans down the other. They lived at the end of the world and were hostile to humans.

KOKOTSHC *see* **Marked Hominid.**

KOLOR HIJAU A man-beast reported from Indonesia since November, 2003. Despite its bestial nature, it is said to wear green underwear and this is what its name signifies. A report by two women that this creature tried to rape them is regarded by police as a hoax. According to the *Jakarta Post* (26th January, 2004), police claim one of the girls has retracted her story.

KONDLO An unidentified bird of South Africa, black, with red beak and legs. The most recent report of this creature is that of a sighting about 1956.   [#8]

KONGAMATO A flying creature said to live in the Jiundu swamps of Zambia. It is described as reptilian by natives, who claim it has a wingspan of 4'-7'/1-2m. On seeing pictures of a pterodactyl, they identified it as kongamato.   In 1956 J.P.F. Brown asserted he had seen "prehistoric-looking birds" west of Lake Bangweulu. Each was 4'-5'/1m long with a 3' wingspan and their beaks were filled with teeth. Dr R. Smithers of the Southern Rhodesian National Museum said the birds were shoebills. Shoebills, of course, do not have teeth, but perhaps Dr Smithers thought they had been fitted with dentures. Where Zambia borders the Congo (Kinshasa) dwells a tribe called the Awemba who have a tradition of "flying rats" which would attack wayfarers. It is said that a man was attacked by a "strange bird" near Fort Rosenbury and a drawing he made of this creature looked much like a pterodactyl. However, the kongamato as generally reported would look like some other kind of pterosaur.

A "flying dragon" reported from Kenya seems very similar to the kongamato. These were said to be found in the vicinity of Mt Kilimanjaro. A. Blayney Perceval in 1928 found the tracks of a two-footed creature with a tail. The locals assured him this creature flew down from Mt Kenya under cover of darkness. The actual term for the Kenyan creature is *Trappe pterosaur*. [H9]

KOOLOO-KAMBA A supposed ape of equatorial Africa. It may be a discrete species, but misindentifications of other species may be involved. It is unlikely to be a chimpanzee-gorilla hybrid, as has been suggested. The skull of one shot in the 19th Century is preserved in the British Museum of Natural History. That the animal boasts characteristics of both chimpanzee and gorilla is implicit in its Akela name *koula-nguia* (chimpanzee-gorilla). [F5]

KOOTENAY LAKE MONSTER A monster has been seen a number of times in this British Columbia lake. A boy who saw it in 1900 claimed it had four legs. A drawing by another witness showed it had much in common with descriptions of ogopogo. [K4]

KOPROVINKA MONSTER A creature with a long neck and small head seen in the Koprovinka River in Croatia in 1999. The river is connected with Lake Soderica where a swimmer apparently died of fright when a strange wake was seen near him, from which some have inferred he might have seen a strange creature heading in his direction. [125]

KOSHI SERPENT A huge eight-headed serpent in Japanese mythology. It covered large tracts of land, but was at last slain by a warrior to stop its devouring a princess. [73]

KOSORUSH An unidentified creature of scary reputation, reported from south-east Europe. It may be a cryptid. [#11]

KOULA-NGUIA In Gabon, these mystery creatures are believed to be gorilla-chimpanzee hybrids. This is their name in Bakota, while the Bulu call them *ebot*. [#9]

KOYOREOWEN A kind of hominoid, perhaps the same as the yowie, supposed to exist in the southern parts of Australia.

KRA-DHAN A large bipedal monkey in the lore of Indo-China, also called *bekk-bok*. [C21]

KRAKEN Erik Pontoppidan describes this huge sea-creature, also called *kraxen, krabben, horven, soe-horven* and *anker-trold*. He bases his description on fishermen's accounts. Although no one had ever seen a complete kraken, he computed its back as 1.5

miles in circumference. He opined that the beast was harmless. The kraken is now known to be an exaggerated account of the giant squid (*Architeuthis*). [M8]

KSI-GIIK A central Asian wildman covered with camel-like hair. It is said to have a sloping forehead, arched brows, a small nose and a huge jaw. This creature is said to be quite different from the almas. [S1]

KTING *see* **Linh Duong.**

KU BIRD A bird in a Yaqui Indian legend which owes the other birds plumage and therefore continually hides from them. It is supposed to live in a waterhole and Yaquis are said to have heard it singing. [131]

KUCHENA Siberian term for a wildman. [T1]

KUL A name given to the wildman of Siberia. It probably has the same origin as the Tajik word *gul*. In about 1960 two kuls were observed by a hunter on the banks of the Gornaya Ob. [B3]

KULTA In Australian Aboriginal legend, a huge, small-headed, long-necked quadrupedal creature. It lived in swampy terrain and seems to have been vegetarian. When the forested land gave way to desert, the creature died out. [G3]

KUMIHO A nine-tailed fox that can transform itself into a seductress in Korean mythology. [4]

KUNANTHROPOS A were-hound according to the writer Paul Aegineta (7th Century AD).

KUNG-LU Large hairy primate of China and Myanmar, perhaps identical with the gin-sung and the dzu-teh. Its name means 'mouth man' and it is supposed to be 20' tall. [S1 106]

KUNG-READ A large hominoid reported from Myanmar. [77]

KURANDA JELLYFISH As the *Kuranda* was sailing through the Pacific in 1973, the fore portion dipped into the choppy waters and, when it came up again, a huge tentacled nightmare had seized it. Its horrid head was visible to the hapless mariners and it swished its tentacles across the deck, actually catching an unfortunate sailor by the arm, so that his companions had to free him. Some of the tentacles seemed 200'/60m long and there was fear that the monster would pull the craft under the waters of the pitiless ocean. Luckily, another ship, the *Hercules*, drew near and dislodged the beast by spraying it with steam. No one is sure of what this creature really was. Analysis of the slime it left reposing on the deck suggested it might be an immense form of the lion's mane jellyfish (*Cyanea capillata*). Sherlock Holmes enthusiasts may remember the Great Detective once encountered a normal-sized specimen of this creature. [S8]

KURREA A monster said by the Aborigines to dwell in Boobera Lagoon in New South Wales. [B2]

KUSA KAP A legendary huge hornbill of the Torres Strait, said to be capable of carrying off a dugong. While the latter attribute is highly unlikely, a large unknown species of hornbill may lie behind the legend.   [#8]

KUSCHKA Alternative name for the tatzelwurm.

KUSHTAKA Tlingit Indian term for a BHM .

L

LA LA Amongst the Bella Bella Indians, this term was used for a female hominoid with an appetite for men – for eating them, that is.   [M6]

LAC DE MORAT MONSTER *see* **MURTENSEE MONSTER.**

LAC-DES-PILES MONSTER This Canadian lake is supposedly haunted by the ghost of a drowned man. It is said he was eaten by a monster in the lake.   [M7]

LACKAGH LAKE MONSTER The lake in question is near Killarney, Ireland, and is supposedly home to a monster with a long neck and stumpy horns.   [S2/B]

LAGAR-ORMSSMARIN A lake monster said to be found in Lake Fijot (Iceland). [#8]

LAGARTATUGA No less a person than Christopher Columbus described this creature, which was the size of a whale and had a turtle-like shell. It may have been the same as the giant turtles reported from the North Atlantic.   [#12]

LAGO PELLEGRINI MONSTER In the 1930s a monster, said to look like a dinosaur, was reported from this lake in the province of Rio Negro, Argentina.   [E]

LAKE ABAYA HAYK CREATURE A beast the size of an hippopotamus reported from this lake in Ethiopia.   [E]

LAKE AMANNINGEN MONSTER This lake is in Vastland, Sweden. It is generally shallow, but contains a deep area known as Bo's Cauldron. A monster was seen here in the 1830s, but, as it was strong and intelligent, it evaded capture. It has not been reported recently.   [34]

LAKE ANSEN MONSTER A witness claimed that, in this Swedish lake, she had seen a monster that covered an entire island.   [M7]

LAKE ARENAL MONSTER A cow-headed serpentine monster was seen in this Costa Rican lake in the 1970s. Recently crocodiles have been reported in its waters. They had hitherto been apparently unnoticed. [12]

LAKE AYLMER MONSTER A fast-moving monster was reported from this Quebec lake in the 1950s and 1960s. It has not been seen in recent times and there has been a suggestion that it perished due to pollution.   [M7]

LAKE BAIKAL MONSTER This huge body of water in Russia contains, amongst other things, its own species of seal. It is also said to house a monster, which some feel is a member of the seal family, while others regard it as looking like a sturgeon. [120]

LAKE BAROMBI MBO MONSTER Two long-necked monsters were observed by children in this lake in Cameroon in 1948 or 1949.   [B9]

LAKE BITOBI MONSTER A monster is reported to inhabit this Canadian lake. [M7]

LAKE BROMPTON MONSTER A monster has been reported from this Canadian lake for some time. One description compared it with a grey camel.   [M7]

LAKE BROSNO MONSTER This Russian lake, very deep in parts, is supposed to house a monster with a serpentine head. There have been a number of sightings and an indistinct photograph. One of its eyes was seen and said to be large. There have been reports of this monster from 1854. The lake is regarded as too small to harbour a population of fish sufficient to support a population of monsters and some have said the sightings are to be blamed on a large but elderly beaver or pike. It has also been suggested there is a volcano in the lake whose eruptions may have occasioned supposed sightings. Echo soundings in 2002 revealed no monster but did discover a jelly-like mass. Fishermen's legends in the area relate to a "huge mouth" that sometimes swallows fishermen. Another legend says that, during World War II, the beast consumed an enemy aeroplane.

   Legends regarding a monster in the lake are nothing new. One such states that Baty-khan Tartars were on their way to attack Novgorod when they paused at the lake. A monster emerged and commenced to dine on men and horses. Horrified, the Tartars retreated and Novgorod was saved.

   The beast has been named *Brosnya.* [15 C20]

LAKE BULLARE MONSTER This Swedish lake-monster was supposed to have a neck 12' long and a calf-sized body.   [C25]

LAKE CATEMACO MONSTER A monster was reported from this lake in Mexico in 1969. It was described as large and serpentine with two horns.   [B9]

LAKE CHUZENI MONSTER The lake in question lies to the north of Tokyo and strange tides at night are blamed on the monster's moving about.   [C25]

LAKE DESERT MONSTER A creature with a horselike head and bumps has been reported from this Canadian lake.   [M7]

LAKE DUCHENE MONSTER The monster in this lake, which straddles Ontario and Quebec, was reported in 1880. It was dark green and reckoned to be about 12' long. [G2*]

LAKE DULVERTON MONSTER A creature reported from this lake in Tasmania in 2002. As the lake was dry for fourteen years, it has been suggested that we have here a hoax with a view to promoting tourism. However, it is not impossible that a monster could have reached the lake overland.   [7]

LAKE DUOBUZHE MONSTER A most peculiar monster from this Tibetan lake was said to have been killed by Chinese soldiers in 1972. It was described as looking like an ox, having curly horns and a turtle's feet.   [B9]

LAKE ELIZABETH MONSTER A huge creature the size of a whale with bat-like wings and possibly underwater legs and flippers was reported in this California lake in the 19th Century. It gave a screaming roar that was possibly a development of a hissing sound. In 1883 a local rancher reported seeing a huge flying monster at night.. Three years later another witness in the area said he had seen a winged monster the size of four elephants, 45'/13m in length, with wings, six legs and a bulldog-like head. Apparently the witness opened fire on the beast: most of the bullets were flattened against its hide and one ricocheted and hit the witness. This, at least, was what was reported in a Los Angeles newspaper.   [R6]

LAKE ELSINORE MONSTER A monster or strange creature has been reported from time to time in this California lake since 1884. This is surprising, since the lake dried up twice in the 20th Century and no monster was revealed. One Bonnie Prey claimed to have seen a monster there twice in 1970, saying it was 12/3.66m feet long and black. Another claimed it had a head, ears and tail. The suggestion made by one onlooker that it was a catfish should not be lightly treated – such a creature could have been introduced into the lake and some catfish can attain considerable proportions. Because of the lake's name, the monster is sometimes called Hamlet.   [M5]

LAKE ERIE CHOMPER A mystery fish or creature which takes bites out of swimmers in this lake. It has made its presence felt since August, 2001. Many kinds of fish dwelling in the lake have been ruled out as suspects.   [120]

LAKE ERIE MONSTER A monster was reported from this lake in 1817. It was said to have bright eyes and to have been of a mahogany colour. Estimates of its length varied. [G2*]

LAKE EUFALA MONSTER A monster was reported from this lake in Oklahoma in 1973.   [B9]

LAKE FAGUA MONSTER A Paris broadsheet of 1784 claimed this was a Chilean lake monster with a human's face, a mane, a bull's horns, an ass's ears, bat wings and two tails, one with which to capture its prey, the other with which to stab it.   [M7]

LAKE FEGEN MONSTER   The Chairman of the Local Board of Fisheries saw a monster in this Swedish lake in 1969. It made a gurgling sound and moved speedily. At least a score of people saw it that year.   [34]

LAKE FOLSOM MONSTER   This lake in California is said to house unusual monsters. Their appearance is supposed to be somewhat crocodilian. A suggestion has been proffered that they are giant salamanders.   [K4]

LAKE GALILEE MONSTER Lake Galilee is situated in a remote part of Queensland (Australia) and is said to be the home of a monster which has been sighted a number of times over the years. It has a head like a snake's and a long neck. 19th Century descriptions provided by Aborigines said it had flippers and its tail looked like an eel. Possible Aboriginal paintings of the animal have been discovered.   [G3]

LAKE HANAS FISH A large reddish fish reminiscent of a salmon observed by a Chinese biologist and his students in 1984. Its estimated length was 33'/10m.   [B6]

LAKE HODGES MONSTER The lake in question has been changed into a reservoir. It is situated in California on the San Dieguito River. The Lake Hodges Project commenced in 1916, though Indians warned that the lake was tenanted by a monster. Reports of a monster were circulating amongst whites by 1930, one claiming to have seen a lizard-like head. A trap in the form of a cage with a sea-lion as bait was constructed in 1932. The bait was apparently taken, but no monster was apprehended. An underwater photograph, when digitally enhanced, certainly showed what looked like a monster. In 1956 the lake was poisoned to get rid of all the fish and then restocked. The poison may not have been strong enough for any monsters, for in 1966 a creature was spotted in the lake by picnickers and a photograph of a hump was taken. The monster has been nicknamed *Hodgie*.   [39]

LAKE ILIAMNA MONSTER   There have been regular sightings of this monster, named "Illie", which is said to lurk in this Alaskan lake. Some reports say it is snake-like. A biologist flying over the lake in 1963 said he saw it and it was 25'-30'/7.6-9m long. A report of a huge seal in the lake in 1998 would appear to refer to another creature. [15]

LAKE JAMES MONSTER Lake James in North Carolina is said to house a monster of dragon-like appearance.

LAKE KATHLYN MONSTER   In the legends of the Bulkley Indians of British Columbia, a huge serpentine monster in this lake devoured a chief's daughter. Boiling rocks were thrown into the lake, which caused it to seethe and the monster's corpse to come to the surface.   [K4]

LAKE KEGONSA DRAGON   A vaguely described water monster in this lake in Wisconsin, seen off Colladay Point and Williamson Point.

LAKE KHAIYR MONSTER   There had been rumours of a monster in this Siberian lake and a scientific team was sent to investigate. A biologist named N. Gladkika was there when the monster came ashore. It had a small head, a long neck (which gleamed), a jet-black body and a fin which stretched vertically along its back. The leader of the expedition and two workers subsequently saw the monster swimming in the lake. [UU]

LAKE KILVAELD CREATURE   In 1986 a mystery animal was reported in this Danish lake.   [B9]

LAKE KLEIFFARWATN CREATURE   In fact, a pair of these has been observed. They emerged from this Icelandic lake, played about and left hoofprints cloven in three on the shore. The two witnesses failed utterly to identify them.

LAKE KOSHKONING MONSTER   Indians claimed a creature in this Wisconsin lake was always damaging their nets, while a white farmer asserted it had attacked his pigs. [H14]

LAKE KUTCHARO MONSTER   This monster is said to be long-necked. The lake from which it takes its name is on the Japanese island of Hokkaido. It has been given the nickname "Kussie".   [K4]

LAKE LABYNKR MONSTER   A black monster looking like a dinosaur was reported in this Siberian lake in 1964. Later in the year Soviet scientists saw three humps in the water.   [C25]

LAKE LBJ MONSTER   This Texas lake is supposed to house a monster that has been described as "prehistoric". One writer claims that her father was actually attacked by it around 1990.   [99]

LAKE LEELANAU MONSTER   A monster in this Michigan lake observed by W. Gauthier in 1910. He went up to it in his boat, mistaking it for a tree. To his shock, it opened its eyes and dived into the water.   [101]

LAKE LICKASJON MONSTER   This Swedish lake monster is said to be 10-16'/3-5m long. It is reported every summer.   [34]

LAKE LOUKUSA MONSTER   A white monster has been reported from this Finnish lake. The earliest known observation was in 1958.   [B9]

LAKE LUNDEVATTNET MONSTER   A monster, which had a considerable number of fast-moving humps, was reported from this Norwegian lake in the 18th Century. [K4]

LAKE MALGOMAJ MONSTER A monster was reported from this Swedish lake in 1917. It had humps and was 82-100'/25m-30m long.   [32]

LAKE MANITOU MONSTER The Potawatomi Indians maintained there was a monster in this Indiana lake and in 1835 the *Logansport Telegraph* reported a number of sightings. Unkind opinion has suggested these reports were a hoax perpetrated by the editor, a man named Dillon. R. Mackal says the Indian legends may have been inspired by the discovery of mastodon bones near the lake.   [M2 B11]

LAKE MARACAIBO MONSTER A serpentine creature with three heads was witnessed by a number of onlookers in this lake in Venezuela in 1965. [#12]

LAKE MEMINISHA MONSTER This lake is on the Albany River in Ontario. The Cree Indians contend it contains a fish-like monster.   [G2*]

LAKE MENDOTA MONSTER This Wisconsin lake is said to be home to a creature with a snakelike or dragonlike head. It startled a fisherman in 1917 because of its fiery eyes and huge jaws. On another occasion that year it started flicking the sole of a sunbather with its tongue. She described its head as dragonlike. It is given the name Bocho.

LAKE MICHIGAN MONSTER About 1900 a fierce looking monster was descried by some fishermen off Jones Island in this lake. Some time later some young men claimed to have seen a serpentine animal at rest. What was considered the same beast was later viewed in the Milwaukee River. *See also* **Lenapiska** *and* **Winnebozho.**

LAKE MINNEWANKA FISH An unidentified species of fish with a long neck is said to lurk in this lake in Alberta.   [#12]

LAKE MJOSA MONSTER A Norwegian monster of which the historian Olaus Magnus wrote, saying it had been seen in 1522 and adding that its appearance portended a change in the kingdom. It was supposed to be multi-coloured and had two large eyes. People were still of the opinion it was in the lake in the 19th Century.   [C25]

LAKE MOFFAT MONSTER A monster was reported in this Canadian lake around the end of the 19th Century. Its estimated length was 15-20'/5m. It was once seen on the shore and described as looking like a burnt log, but it rose up and ran into the lake. The creature has not been reported in some time.   [M7]

LAKE MONONA MONSTER There were several reports of this creature in the 19th Century. An account in 1896 said it was about 20'/6.1m long. This lake is in Wisconsin. [B11]

LAKE NATSILIK MONSTER This lake in Greenland is connected to the sea by a canal. Monsters have been reported in the lake while in the canal a huge fin was observed in 1954.   [B9]

LAKE NORMAN MONSTER   A monster in this North Carolina lake has been described as snakelike, dark yellow with brown spots and having a beak-shaped mouth. [117]

LAKE OKOBOJI MONSTER   On 23rd June 2001 a monster was sighted in this Iowa lake by an anonymous witness and her children. They saw first a hump, then a head and a small portion of the neck. It opened its mouth once and gasped for air. A somewhat stumpy tail was also observed. It had scales like a snake's, not like a fish's, or else a scale-like pattern.   [79]

LAKE ONTARIO MONSTER   In 1829 a 20-30'/6-9m long monster was reported in this Canadian lake. A sleeping monster with an eel-like head and a mane, 50' long, was seen in 1882.   In 1891 a Mr and Mrs Parks became affrighted when a monster approached their boat too closely and beat it off with a paddle. A natural resources officer saw the monster in 1970.   [K4]

LAKE ORIGUERE CREATURE   This unidentified creature is said to lurk in the Bolivian lake which gives it its name. It is believed to capsize canoes.   [#4]

LAKE PATENGGANG MONSTER   This lizardlike monster of Indonesia is feared by the natives, so they burn opium on the lakeside to keep it in a state of blissful tranquillity. [S6]

LAKE PAVIN DRAGON   The beast in question seems to have lived not in, but next to, this French lake. It had both feathers and scales, two horns and a peacock's plume. A pamphlet published in 1632 claimed it attacked and was killed by a man named La Briere, but the bites he suffered were infected with plague.   [M7]

LAKE PILATE MONSTER   This lake is at the top of Mount Pilate in Switzerland. Pontius Pilate, now transformed into a monster, is said to inhabit its depths. [M7]

LAKE POCKNOCK MONSTER   There is supposedly a monster in this Canadian lake. It is thought to live in a cave.   [M7]

LAKE POHANKA MONSTER   About 1992 a creature with smooth skin, about the size of an alligator and with flippers (more than two) was seen threshing about in this lake in Maryland.   [S7]

LAKE POHENEGAMOOK MONSTER   This Quebec lake is said to house a monster, noted for speed, silence and a black and draconic appearance.   [G2*]

LAKE RASVALEN MONSTER   A monster exceeding 16'/5m was reported from this Swedish lake. Sightings occurred in 1950 and 1953.   [32]

LAKE REIN MONSTER According to folk tradition, this Norwegian monster died and it is buried under a cairn near the lake.   [K4]

LAKE REPSTADSVATTNET MONSTER A monster with a neck bearing a mane like a horse's has been reported from this Norwegian lake.   [K4]

LAKE ROMMEN MONSTER In the 18th Century a monster with a head like a calf and a body like a log was reported in this Norwegian lake. There were other sightings in the 1930s. In 1975 a busload of schoolchildren saw what they thought was a large animal in the lake, but an academic pronounced it to be marsh gas. Another account dealt with what appeared to be a large slug on the shore: this inched its way forward into the lake, having come from another body of water.   [K4]

LAKE ROOT MONSTER A couple of monsters were observed in this Swiss lake at the end of the 18th Century. At least one of them would come ashore and leave slimy tracks. The impression given is that it dragged itself along and did not have feet. [M7]

LAKE SAINT-FRANCOIS MONSTER A Canadian lake monster, sometimes described as having a head like a horse's and said to be 15'/4.5m long. One of the locals is quite convinced it is a 30'/9m sturgeon.   [M7]

LAKE SAINT-JEAN MONSTER A monster has been reported from this Canadian lake, but the reports have been treated with unwarranted contempt. The monster has also been observed in the Ashuapmouchouan River, which flows into the lake. A 1978 sighting in the river estimated its length at 50-60'/15-18m long. The local Ouiatchoua and Montagnais Indians believe in the creature, but do not like to talk about it for fear of unmerited white ridicule. G. Goguon, Director of the Saint-Felicien Zoo, has also expressed a belief that something unusual may lurk in the waters.   [M7]

LAKE SALSTERN MONSTER The monster of this Swedish lake, of which there have been sightings since 1870, is described as a snake with a mane.   It was seen in 1930, but has not been reported in modern times.   [32 34]

LAKE SANDSVATTNET MONSTER A Norwegian lake monster. In 1910, a rowing boat banged into it. The woman rower saw a wide animal, 16-19'/5-6m long. Sightings of this creature or similar ones are reported every summer. It is thought the beast may come ashore, as tracks have been found. They show cloven hooves.   [K4]

LAKE SELJORD MONSTER This monster with a horselike head has been reported from this Norwegian lake since 1750. In 1980 Gunhild Bjorge killed what she described as a lizard when it came onto the lakeside. She thought this to be an offspring of the monster.

   J.-O. Sundberg conducted tests with an echosounder which proved very revealing in that they picked up sounds of at least three large objects moving about in the lake. On a couple of occasions he feared his boat would be rammed, but whatever was approaching the craft underneath the surface stopped before making contact.

In 2003 a witness alleged he had seen two monsters chasing one another. The nickname "Selma" has been given to this creature. [K4]

LAKE SENTANI SHARK Natives of New Guinea contend there are sharks in this lake, as did American scientist George Agogino, but as yet they have not been studied and accepted by the full scientific establishment. [S13]

LAKE SONDERDRACH DRAGON A dragon is supposed to live in this Austrian lake. If anyone tries to measure the depth of the lake, the dragon has threatened to devour him. [135]

LAKE STENSJON MONSTER This Swedish monster has been supposedly known since the 19th Century. It has been described as having a head like a horse and to be 32'/10m long. There have been no recent reports. [34]

LAKE SVARTTJARN MONSTER A lake monster of the 'upturned boat' kind was reported from this lake near Stockholm in 1933. [34]

LAKE TAHOE MONSTER *see* **Tessie**.

LAKE TAUPO MONSTER A monster was reported in this New Zealand lake in 1980. [B2]

LAKE TAVELSTON MONSTER A creature in this Swedish lake, it was at first mistaken for an upturned boat. The first report of its existence was in 1943 and it has been regularly seen since in the summertime. Despite a popular theory to the contrary, it is not a catfish, which could not survive in the climate. [34]

LAKE TESLIN MONSTER A poorly observed mystery creature has been seen in this Canadian lake. It was dark and had black spots. [K4]

LAKE TINGSTADE MONSTER This lake is on the Swedish island of Gotland in the Baltic. A monster was seen here by sundry people in 1976. The lake is not deep, but there is said to be much mud at the bottom, a possible dwelling place for a mystery creature. [34]

LAKE TITICACA MONSTER This Peruvian lake is supposed to be home to a 12'/3.6m monster. [B9]

LAKE TOPLITZ MONSTER This Austrian lake monster is said to be on the fearsome side. It is believed to be 49'/15m long and to weigh perhaps a ton. [K4]

LAKE TORNE MONSTER A monster in this Swedish lake has been reported in modern times. It was also seen sixty years ago. [34]

LAKE TOYA MONSTER   Three monsters were reported rising from Lake Toya, Kyushu, Japan, in 1978.   [K4]

LAKE UMANAK MONSTER   A white monster was reported in this Greenland lake in 1954.   [B9]

LAKE UTOPIA MONSTER   A 100'/30m long creature believed by both the red man and the white to live in this New Brunswick lake. A Micmac medicine man told how he and a fellow Indian had once been pursued in their canoe by the monster, which had a large head. The New Brunswick Museum houses a well-known engraving of the monster by B. Kroup.   [C22]

LAKE VAN MONSTER   A creature said to inhabit this Turkish lake. An estimated length of the animal is 49.5'/15m. Descriptions have been furnished by about a thousand witnesses. Some say it is black with a hairy horned head and spiny back. Some say it is white with a black stripe on its back. On one occasion two have been reported together, which may account for the disparity in descriptions.   A film proved unsatisfactory. The beast is called *Canavar.* It has been suggested it is a hoax to promote tourism.   [40]

LAKE VATTERN MONSTER   A rarely seen monster is said to occupy this Swedish lake. A photograph taken of it in 1973 was inconclusive.   [34]

LAKE VOROTA MONSTER   A grey monster was observed in this Siberian lake in 1953. It had a dorsal fin, which would apparently put it in a different category from creatures reported from Loch Ness and Lake Okanagan. Its eyes were set widely apart. The body was 32'/10m long, huge and dark grey. It moved in forward leaps.   [C25]

LAKE WABASH MONSTER   This lake near Huntingdon (Indiana) was said to house a large animal, its skull like a whiskered lion's which was the size of a boy of twelve years. It was witnessed by what Skinner calls three "truthful damsels".   [S10]

LAKE WALGREN MONSTER *see* **Alkali Lake Monster.**

LAKE WASHINGTON MONSTER   There was supposed to be a duck-eating monster in this lake. Although a large sturgeon found on the shore was supposed to lie behind the sightings, sturgeon do not eat ducks.   [C/H]

LAKE WILLIAMS MONSTER   A monster, described as a serpent with a body the size of a flour barrel, 30-40'/9-12m long has been said to inhabit this Canadian lake. [M7]

LAKE WORTH OGRE   This beast is not your usual type of lake monster. It is a humanoid creature reported from the vicinity of the lake. There is a considerable possibility of some hoaxing where this creature is concerned. It has been variously described as a seven foot hairy creature showing signs of aging and as a creature half man and half goat.   [B11]

LAKE ZEEGRZYNSKI MONSTER A monster with a black head and ears that stuck up like a rabbit's, 20'/6m in length, has been reported from this Polish lake. This is an artificial lake, so one might question how a monster might have entered it. [B9]

LAKE ZWISCHENAHN MONSTER A monster is supposed to lurk in this German lake. Veteran cryptozoologist Ulrich Magin thinks it may be a giant catfish. [S5]

LAMBS POINT MONSTER The possible existence of this sea creature was inferred from footprints found on a beach in New South Wales (Australia). The prints were large and appear to have been made by fins. [G3]

LAMIA A kind of mermaid in Basque lore, not to be confused with the horrid lamia of classical mythology.   [4]

LAMPALAGUA A large snake of Argentine lore. It may be identical with the boiuba. [#12]

LANCASTER HOPPER   In 1979 some Amish men encountered this creature in Lancaster County, Pennsylvania. It hopped like a kangaroo, but they were sure it wasn't one. Its features were somewhat human and it was covered with rough, sandy hair. It had a peculiar effect on one of the witnesses, giving him what felt like an electric jolt which made him cry and utter strange words. The creature began shouting at him in what the men took to be an unintelligible language and then made off speedily into some woods.   [R6]

LAS PERLAS SEA SERPENT Its head looked like that of a horse, but it had a pair of horns which seemed to remind the witnesses of those of an unicorn. It had four legs or double-jointed fins. It was coloured brownish with large black spots. Its tail seemed to divide into two parts. It was witnessed by a boatload of sailors from the whaler *Hope On* in 1883 near the Las Perlas islands in the Pacific. It is said there had been a number of other sightings of this kind of creature by mariners of the Pacific Mail Company.

LAST MOUNTAIN LAKE MONSTER This lake in Rowan's Ravine (Saskatchewan) is said to play host to a most peculiar monster which resembles groups of objects attached together. It was seen in 1964.   [G2]

LAU A huge snake said to live in swamps at the source of the White Nile, leaving furrows in the mud as its tracks. It is brown or dark yellow. It has tentacles or prehensile hairs on its head that it uses to ensnare victims. It is said to make an occasional booming cry, which should be impossible for a snake and which might indicate it is in fact something else.   [H9]

LAURISIOR CREATURE In 1949 an unidentified creature was seen in Laurisior, a body of water in Australia. It propelled itself by its ears, which were long and shaggy. [B9]

LAWALAWA Strange small nocturnal creatures in which the Coos Indians believe. They attack people and bombard their houses with stones. [4]

LEGGED WHALE Whales with legs and sometimes with two heads have been reported from various parts of the world. [30]

LEMUR-LIKE DOG A strange creature observed in 2002. It looked to witness Anthony Mudge (who had studied lemurs at college) like a cross between a lemur and a fox. The sighting occurred on a farm in Sherborn (Mass.). [2]

LENAPIZKA A water monster of the Peoria Indians, which could also live on land. Its watery habitat was Lake Michigan. Seen by whites in the 19th Century, it was described as "serpentine" and "ferocious-looking". [M7 R2]

LENIN One might well ask how V.I. Lenin (1870-1924), Russian leader, earns a place in this dictionary, but a zoomythological legend attaches to him. In Siberia it was believed amongst the tribesmen that Lenin started life as a bear. He was captured by being made drunk on a quantity of vodka left out for the purpose. He was then trained as a dancing bear, but at length escaped. Then he became a man and the rest was history. Does this make Lenin a were-man? [S17]

LETAYUSCHIY CHELOVEK The Russian name of this creature means 'flying man'. It is found in the region of Vladivostok, is humanoid in appearance and its wings are described as webbed like a bat's. It was chiefly seen in the 1930s-40s and it has been reported occasionally since. It is said to live in the Pidan Mountains. One wonders if it was the same kind of creature observed in Siberia in 1908 by Vladimir Arsen'ev, who claimed to have seen a flying man. [#1]

LETICHE A monstrous humanoid said to haunt the bayous of Louisiana. The story is that he was an abandoned baby raised by alligators, which is said to explain his appearance. His skin is pale and wrinkled, he is scaly and clawed, his digits are webbed, his fangs are fearsome. His features are difficult to discern, as his face is covered with swamp matter, but his eyes are large and green and glow in the dark. He has an abiding hatred of humans, whom he eats, sharing their bodies with other swamp creatures. However, he keeps their hearts and brains for himself. [B7]

LEUCROCOTTA The Roman natural historian Pliny describes this beast as being donkeylike in size, with a badger's head. In this reposed no teeth, but rather a continuous bone. Its mouth, when open, looked like a great slash across its face. It had cloven hooves. It was considered to be a cross between a lion and an hyena.

LEVIATHAN A huge sea monster in Hebrew legend. It eats fish and to drink requires all the Jordan water that empties itself into the sea. Its fins give out such light that it hides the sun and its eyes often light up the sea. Unfortunately, it gives off an awful stench. Originally there were two leviathans, but their combined strength posed a danger to the earth, so God killed the female. To stop leviathan getting out of hand, the stickleback, for which it cherishes no little respect, keeps it in order.   [W]

LEWIS WEREWOLF A whole colony of werewolves was once supposed to have lived on the Isle of Lewis, Scotland.   [146]

LIBREVILLE SEA SERPENT In 1883 a sea serpent was observed from a ship off Libreville, Gabon. Its head looked like a spear, it was 50-65'/15-20m long and it had a 20'/6m long black and white tail. The colour of the creature was whitish. The sighting was recorded in the log of the German ship *Elisabeth.*

LICKING RIVER MONSTER A report from this Kentucky river mentions a tentacled creature like an octopus with a "lopsided" crest. It actually crawled onto the bank, so it clearly could survive, at least for a time, outside water. This occurred in 1959. [C1]

LIK A water serpent of the Grand Chaco of South America. On its back it carries a palm tree.   [M7]

LIMERICK BEAST This animal made its appearance in 1874 in Limerick, Ireland. It was described as "wolf-like". It attacked a number of people who later went insane, perhaps infected by bites.   [65]

LINDORM A sort of dragon in Scandinavian legend. Writing in 1885, G.O. Hylten-Cavallius gave them a length of 10-20'/3-6m. Old ones had long hair or scales like a horse's mane. The existence of such old ones would negate the earlier theory of Erik Pontoppidan that lindorms were born on land, but then entered the sea to become sea-serpents. Lindorms had forked tongues, flat, round or square heads, no legs and teeth white enough to delight any dentist. Many witnesses claimed to have seen lindorms. Sometimes more than one witness had seen a lindorm at the same time. Fights between men and lindorms were recorded in the 19th Century. Although Hylten-Cavallius did much work in trying to show the lindorm to be a real animal, after his time science came to regard it with scepticism.   [C10]

LINGUIN Mystery swamp-dwelling reptile mentioned by Percy Fawcett as being reported from Borneo.   [S6]

LINH DUONG A goat or goatlike animal of south-east Asia, known to science only by its horns. The above is its Vietnamese name. To the Cambodians it is known as the *kting.* It has been given the scientific name of *Pseudonovibos spiralis.* [S8/A]

LIPANI Molala Indian name for a BHM

LISISINGO *see* **Kakundari.**

LITICAYO A hominoid reported from Guatemala.   [#4]

LITTLE RED MEN OF THE DELTA Small primates which make much vocal noise, they are sometimes arboreal, sometimes aquatic. They are said to live in Mississippi. [#11]

LIVING FIREHOSE This glowing and gigantic creature was observed by workers on undersea oil rigs in the Gulf of Mexico in the 1970s. It moved very quickly. [#11]

LIVING FIREHOSE EATER The creatures described in the previous entry are apparently preyed upon by a huge undersea creature, seen and described by George Hale (died 1998). It was so huge he could give only limited details of it. He said it was as large in proportion to him as a human is to an ant. Its skin texture he compared with a sea anemone's. He also spoke of its pallor. [#11]

LIZARD MAN There have been sundry reports of humanoid lizards and reptoids over the years. A man named Shufelt averred he had been told by a Hopi Indian that his people harboured a tradition that a race of lizard men had once flourished along the Pacific coast of the United States. A lizard man wearing shirt and trousers was supposedly seen on Mount Shasta (California) in 1976. A lizard man was said to have visited Pass Christian (Mississippi) in 1983. A small boy described it as having green scales, blazing eyes and big teeth. In 1987 a Baptist minister's wife and son reported a man-shaped but scale-covered creature's emergence from a pond. Its head was small, its mouth like a slit. They saw no ears. This happened near Charlotte (NC). A lizard man was reported from Scape Ore Swamp (South Carolina) in 1998. One Christopher Davis (17) had stopped to change a wheel. A strange beast which looked like a bipedal lizard leaped out of the woods. Davis jumped into the car. The creature grabbed the door handle, but Davis drove off. The rough-skinned creature was coloured green, had three fingers on each hand and long nails. During the following month (July) a 7'/2m tall creature was seen running across the road by two couples in a car in the same vicinity.

It might be added that some UFO believers say that a race of reptoids – or even several races – is regularly visiting the earth. Examination of such assertions, however, does not really fall into the limits which this work has set for itself. [M5 A1 S16]

LLAMIGAN-Y-DWR A Welsh creature. Specimens were said to be found in several bodies of water. It looks like a giant legless toad with wings and a tail. It is said to feed on unwary drinking sheep.   [W3]

LLANABER SEA-MONSTER At Llanaber (Gwynedd), Wales, half a dozen schoolgirls saw an animal perambulating along the strand. It was 10'/3m long, with a long neck and long tail. Its eyes were green and big. In due course it entered the sea. [E]

LLANDUDNO SEA-MONSTER This monster was seen off the coast of Wales in 1882 by three witnesses. It was described as "snake-like".   [H12*]

LLYN CYNWCH MONSTER The lake lies to the north of Dolgellau and, according to legend, it once harboured a monster, but a shepherd killed it with an axe. [H12*]

LLYN Y CADER MONSTER A serpentine monster was supposed to have killed a man in this Welsh lake in the 18th Century.   [C1]

LO-AN An hominoid reported from the western portion of Australia. It is perhaps identical with the yowie.

LOCH.... In entries on lake creatures beginning with this word, the reader should assume the lake concerned is in Scotland. It is also wise to remember that the word *loch* sometimes signifies an arm of the sea.

LOCH ALSH SEA SERPENT This animal was seen in Loch Alsh, an arm of the sea east of the Isle of Skye, in 1893. It raised itself as high as the mast of the yacht from which it was observed.   [R]

LOCH ANALT MONSTER According to R.L. Corrie in *The Monsters of Achanalt* (1935-6), this lake contained a number of monsters, including a nine hundred foot colossus. He had no doubt these beasts were reptiles and he named one of them Gabriel, but allowed that his lack of spectacles may have affected his perception. In fact, Corrie claimed to have seen monsters in other lakes as well and on land. One cannot avoid the suspicion that his work is a practical joke. [H5]

LOCH ARKAIG MONSTER This was observed in the 19th Century. Its head resembled that of a horse. One could see only its long neck and hindquarters (=?neck and hump). It was seen by a stalker and later by his three children.   [C25]

LOCH ASSYNT MONSTER A monster was supposedly seen here in the years agone. Lord Ellesmere wrote an article on it, but it has not been traced.   [C25]

LOCH BEISTE MONSTER A monster was rumoured to be in this lake in the 19th Century. Indeed, its very name means "beast loch". The landlord's measures to catch it were unsuccessful.   [C25]

LOCH CANISH MONSTER One Kenneth MacKenzie was crossing this loch in a boat when a long neck with a head like a hind's rose above the stern – doubtless an unnerving experience.   [C25]

LOCH CON MONSTER A Scottish lake monster said to look like a huge dog. Perhaps it is a dobharchu, as the loch's name translates as "hound's loch". [F4]

LOCH DUVAT MONSTER Ewen MacMillan saw on a hazy day what he took to be his mare, despite poor visibility. An hideous scream rent the air and MacMillan realised it was in fact a lake monster and ran home. This occurred in 1893. [C25]

LOCH EIL MONSTER BB (pseudonym of writer D.J. Watkins-Pritchford) in his *September Road to Caithness* (1962) mentions that he saw a strange creature here, resembling the head of a monstrous worm.[H5]

LOCH FYNE MONSTER This monster was reported about 1570. It was able to raise itself to the height of a ship's mast.   [146]

LOCH GARTEN MONSTER A Scottish lake monster said to have looked something like a horse, something like a bull. A crofter is said to have drowned it by attaching a stone to it.   [F4]

LOCH GARVE MONSTER This monster seems to have been an affable creature. It was said to have kidnapped a young girl and kept her in an underground building. When she complained of the cold, it brought humans down to install a kind of heating system. As a result, that part of the lake never freezes over.   [H12*]

LOCH KYNE MONSTER A 30'/9m monster seen washed ashore at Loch Kyne in 1934. [C3*]

LOCH LOCHY MONSTER There have been various reports of a monster in this lake. A photograph taken of the alleged beast was diagnosed as showing a mass of rubbish by prominent zoologist Maurice Burton, a Loch Ness sceptic. There is a belief that underground tunnels connect this loch directly with Loch Ness.   [C25]

LOCH LOMOND MONSTER In 1724 it was stated there was an unknown creature in this lake. In 1964 a couple of sightings of a monster were reported here. In addition, some form of monster or unknown fish is said to be found in Loch Lomond (New Brunswick), Canada.   [C25]

LOCH MORAR MONSTER *see* **Morag**.

LOCH NA MNA MONSTER According to a story set down by James Boswell in the 18th Century, this loch had once contained a monster that ate a man's daughter. The man lured it ashore and killed it with a red hot spit.   [C25]

LOCH NAN DOBHRACHAN MONSTER There was an unsuccessful attempt to net a water monster here in 1870. Because of its name, one suspects the monster concerned was a dobharchu.   [C25]

LOCH NESS GIANT FROG A huge froglike animal allegedly encountered in Loch Ness by diver Duncan McDonald in 1880. Although regularly told, the source of the story cannot be pinpointed.   [#8]

LOCH NESS MONSTER Loch Ness, 24 miles/38.6 kilometres long, 1 mile wide and 100'/30m deep cuts a swathe through central Scotland. To give some idea of its size, the world's population of humans could fit into it several times over. It is connected to the sea by the Caledonian Canal and the River Ness. The bottom is mud covered and has been compared to a peat-bog.

Modern sightings and widespread knowledge of the lake's supposed monstrous denizen began in 1933. At this time a new road on the northern shore of the lake afforded greater visibility to the passer-by. Mr and Mrs Mackay perceived the beast in the form of two humps in the water followed by a huge wake. The story hit the headlines in the *Inverness Courier.*

Shortly thereafter, the monster was seen ashore. On July 23rd a couple named Spicer saw it cross the road in front of them to disappear into the bushes fringing the lake. They described a long neck and a large body. There was some complication on the neck that may have been hair. It was grey in colour and Mrs Spicer was repelled by its texture.

Since that time, thousands have claimed to have seen the monster. A head on a neck has been mentioned or humps. Pre-1933 sightings also came to light. Indeed, St Adamnan's *Life* of St Columba has him encountering a monster in the River Ness in the early Middle Ages.

About fifty people in cars and tour buses asserted they saw the animal at the same time in 1936 near Urquhart Castle. In Urquhart Bay in 1953 five people observed it and said the front part looked horselike. To give a full listing of witnesses over the years would be impossible in an article of this size; but, if there is really a monster, a good idea of forming an impression of its appearance consists in studying sightings of the beast on land. The Spicers' sighting has already been mentioned. In August of the same year, Mrs M.F. McLennan saw a dark grey animal on a lochside ledge. She placed its length at 20'/6m and said it had legs that ended in trotter-like feet. It had a humped back. In December, a Mrs Reid saw a creature reminiscent of an hippopotamus, about 10'/3m long with a mane and thick legs in the lochside bracken. Next month (January, 1934), Arthur Grant, tootling along on his motor-cycle, saw an object plunge into the loch. 15-20'/4-6m long, it had a long neck, a long tail and a pair of flippers deployed at either end. In 1933 William MacGruer said that, back in 1912, when he was a child, he and other children saw what looked like a small camel, sandy coloured with long legs, enter the water. A more recent land sighting by Donald MacKinnon described a creature that emerged from a wooded area and entered the loch. It was grey, had a small head, a long neck, was 24' long and had four feet, each boasting three "fingers". This occurred in 1979.

Despite inconsistencies in these reports, they are not irreconcilable, bearing in mind the limitations of human perception, the fallibility of memory and the fact that, if one monster dwells in the loch, it is almost certain a whole population does, some of which may exhibit individual differences. Photographic evidence for the monster has proven controversial, to say the least. One of the most well-known snapshots of the monster, the so-called "surgeon's photograph", taken by R.K. Wilson on April 1st (!), 1934, is now known to be a hoax. An impressive-looking photograph by P. O'Connor, taken in 1960, has had its authenticity challenged. F.C. Adams' photograph (1934) is obscure and others show unidentifiable floating objects. The Academy of Applied Sciences took impressive looking underwater photographs, one of a flipper-like appendage attached to a large body, one of the underside of a plesiosaur-like animal and one of what appeared to be an hideous head. The latter may have only been a log and doubts remain about the other photographs as well, though they appear supported by sonar evidence taken at the same time. Film evidence has hitherto proven unsatisfactory.

Some sonar tests have been more positive. Those carried out by D.G. Tucker and H. Braithwaite of the University of Birmingham seemed to show animate objects 20'/6m long swimming in the lake. They were probably not air-breathing animals. Additional material has been adduced by mobile sonar searches. However, sonar investigations by GUST in 2001 and the BBC in 2003 proved fruitless. The BBC's claim to have covered the entire lake, using sonars EM2000 and EM3000, has been challenged: it has been asserted complete coverage would not have been possible. The BBC also used satellite technology for positioning, but this cannot discern anything at a depth of more than 40m.

The suggestion has been made that the monster surfaces more often than is known because it is nocturnal. One group performed a night-time stakeout of the loch and during the night saw what looked like a single finger stick up out of the water. Perhaps the monster was trying to convey some message to the observers.

The creatures could, of course, avoid detection in a number of ways. They could hide in a lochside cave, though no evidence has shown so far that any such cave exists. However, the Edwards Deep depression in the loch bed may lead to an underwater cave or even a network of them, where monsters could easily lurk. The contention that the Deep is simply the result of an underwater avalanche is challenged by the lack of appropriate debris in the vicinity. They could be mud-burrowers, as there is much mud to be found on the bed of the loch.

Undoubtedly many alleged monster sightings can be quite easily explained by witness misperception, especially by visitors hoping to catch a glimpse of the loch's mysterious denizen. Maurice Burton is convinced that "monster" sightings were in fact those of masses of rotting vegetation rising suddenly to the surface. Waterfowl, otters, sturgeon and the like can appear to be monsters very easily. But if there actually is an unknown creature in the lake, what could it be?

As early as 1933 a plesiosaur was suggested, but for such a creature to survive in the Loch it would have had to undergo a number of adaptations. The BBC documentary seems to have argued that a plesiosaur was the only kind of possible monster in the loch and then to have taken pains to show that there was no possibility of one living there. Actually, many investigators would not support a plesiosaur identification. A zeuglodon or basilosaurus, a serpent-like whale with feet, has also been suggested. Objections have been voiced that it would be hard to explain away the gap in the fossil record where these animals are concerned. Others have postulated unknown species of seal or eel. Indeed, R. Freeman has argued that there exists in the loch a number of infertile eels which never leave its waters to spawn and therefore just remain there, growing ever larger. A. Shields suggets it may be an unknown cephalopod. We will need a lot more data to support any positive identification.

The monster has been given the nickname of *Nessie* and the Gaelic form *Niseag* has been coined for it.

LOCH NESS WHITE MICE Mystery creatures videotaped and photographed on the bed of Loch Ness. They look like silvery-coloured mice. The animals could not be identified by an expert at the British Museum (Natural History). [Z2]

LOCH OICH MONSTER A monster traditionally inhabits this lake. There is a story that children once found "a deformed pony" on its banks. One of them mounted it and it bore him into the lake. A witness claimed a monster sighting in 1936. It was 6'/1.83m long, furry looking and had a dog-like head. In 1961 a hoax monster was placed in the lake and a photograph of this was published by the press. A river connects Loch Oichy with Loch Ness. [C25]

LOCH PITYOULISH MONSTER This monster is said to be found in a submerged human dwelling in the loch. [M7]

LOCH POIT NA H-I MONSTER This creature is reported from the island of Mull, Scotland. [146]

LOCH QUOICH MONSTER A monster has been reported here, both ashore and in the water. [C25]

LOCH SCAVAIG MONSTER A monster was observed in this loch in the Isle of Skye in the early 20th Century. [146]

LOCH SHIEL MONSTER *see* **Seileag**.

LOCH SHIN MONSTER A water horse which supposedly occupied this loch was said to have helped people to build a church. [146]

LOCH SUAINBHAL MONSTER There was an old tradition of a monster in this lake. Lambs were once thrown into it to feed it. [C25]

LOCH TREIG MONSTER This lake lies below Ben Nevis, Britain's highest mountain. Legend credited it with ferocious monsters. An hydroelectric scheme was introduced into the lake and divers working on it reported monsters lurking in it. Some resigned from their jobs as a result. The man in charge, B.N. Peach, stated this in 1933. [C25]

LOCH URABHAL CREATURE In this loch on the Isle of Lewis an unidentified creature was observed by two teachers in 1961. [C25]

LOCH VENNACHAIR MONSTER In 1800 this lake was supposed to have contained a monster. [C25]

LODSILUNGUR A trout covered with hair, found in Icelandic rivers and lakes, according to legend. [S8/A]

LOFA In the legends of the Chickasaw, a long-haired humanoid with the power of speech. [147]

LOMIE This beast was supposed to have been found in days agone in the Czech Republic. It had under its neck a bag of boiling water, so that if hounds on its trail approached it, it could quite literally dampen their ardour by scalding them while it made its escape.   [H12]

LONDON FLYING SNAKE   Two reports of such a creature were made to the *Gentleman's Magazine* in 1798.   [S8]

LONG LAKE MONSTER   A monster reported in 1994 in this Wisconsin lake. Its face was like that of a dragon, but its body resembled a swan's. A further sighting may have occurred in 1998. [A1]

LONG POND MONSTER   A report of a monster in this Newfoundland lake saw light in 1967. It was described as being like an eel and 30'/9m long, but its head was reminiscent of a salmon's and its body of a trout's.   [C1]

LONG-NECKED CREATURES   At Fritton Wood (Norfolk) two creatures of generally human shape but with long necks were seen by witnesses in 1997.   [146]

LONG-TAILED PEOPLE   Creatures of diminutive stature with a generally human appearance in the folklore of the Wintun Indians of California.   [R7]

LONG-TAILED WILDCAT   An unidentified kind of wildcat reported from Pennsylvania.   [32]

LOS ANGELES LAKE MONSTER   A silvery and serpentine monster with a taste for sheep reported from this lake in Peru.   [#9]

LOTA ENTITY   The Chilean paper the *Concepcion Cronica* (4th September, 2003) tells of a strange entity that has been killing dogs and poultry in Lota. The rigidity of the muscles of four of the dogs suggests that whatever killed them terrified them. The entity responsible has been supposedly seen in the area of Alta Lota, but no fuller description is available.

LOU CARCOLH   A monster resembling a huge snail in French folklore. It lives in a cavern under the town of Hastingue (Les Landes).   [M7]

LOUGH....   In articles on lake monsters beginning with this word, the reader should assume the lake concerned is in Ireland.

LOUGH ABISDEALY MONSTER   A creature seen in 1914. It had a flat head and long neck with loops going in and out of the water. It was perhaps 35'/10m long.   [C25]

LOUGH ATTARIFF MONSTER   This was witnessed by fishermen in 1966. It was long, dark and brown and its eyes glittered.   [D3]

LOUGH AUNA MONSTER   This was the locale of a number of monster sightings, even though it is a small lake.   [H11]

LOUGH BRAY MONSTER In 1963 a man claimed he and a friend had seen a monster in Lower Lough Bray in Co Wicklow. He compared its hump to a rhinoceros' back and its head to that of a turtle. [C25]

LOUGH BRIN MONSTER *see* **Bran.**

LOUGH CLOON MONSTER The boggy area of this lake is said to be home to serpentine monsters. [143]

LOUGH DERG MONSTER 1 Monster in Lough Derg, Co Donegal. It is supposed to have been wounded by the hero Fionn mac Cumhaill, its blood given the water a reddish tinge. It is called the Caoranach. [See the present writer's *Dictionary of Irish Myth and Legend* (1979)]
2 Large unidentified life form in Lough Derg on the Shannon, which should not be confused with its Donegal namesake. Sightings are modern. Mrs J. Glanville in 1978 saw humps and estimated the creature's length at 6'/1.8m. There was a further sighting in 1983 which put the length at 12'/3.6m or more. [143]

LOUGH DUBH MONSTER The monster reported from this lough is different from most of those allegedly seen in other Irish lakes. A schoolmaster named Mullaney and his son were fishing here. Something took the bait and then emerged from the water. It was a quite unrecognisable animal, the size of a cow or donkey, with a head like that of a hippopotamus and a white pointed horn on its snout. The animal tried to clamber onto the land and the Mullaneys took off. There had been earlier reports of animals in the lake, three having been discerned on one occasion in 1961, one large and two smaller. [C25]

LOUGH ESKE MONSTER A monster of vague description was seen by several witnesses in this Donegal lake in 1989. [#1]

LOUGH FADDA MONSTER A creature observed by Georgina Carberry, librarian, and fellow anglers in this Co Galway lake in 1954. There were two humps behind the head. The body seemed to be in perpetual movement. Lionel Leslie, monster hunter, gelignited the lake to create a shock wave to unsettle the beast in 1965. Ten seconds later something blackish, but difficult to discern, and threshing came to the surface about fifty yards from the shore. A subsequent netting operation was not successful. [H11]

LOUGH GRANEY MONSTER There was a traditional story of a monster in this lake which pursued a swimmer, who happily made it to the shore. [C25]

LOUGH INAGH MONSTER A serpentine creature with a mane was reported from this Connemara lake in 1897. [32]

LOUGH MAJOR MONSTER A monster which was seen in this lake by two teenagers and a boy. They claimed it had a hairy head and two horns. It made for them when they threw stones at it. A local man also claimed to have seen the animal.   [C25]

LOUGH MASK MONSTER In 1963 a monster with a head, tail and two humps was observed here.   For an earlier encounter with a strange animal in this lough *see* **Dobharchu.**

LOUGH MUCK MONSTER A monster was seen in this lake in Donegal by a young woman around 1885. It continued to be observed for a couple of years afterwards. It had humps and large eyes.   [C25]

LOUGH NAHOOIN MONSTER This tiny lough was the scene of a monster sighting in 1968. Witnesses saw a head emerging, then two humps and it had projections from the top of its head. To suggest this lake could support even one monster seems ludicrous, but another witness claimed he had seen this creature on land, which would indicate these animals travel from lough to lough.   [H11]

LOUGH REE MONSTER This large lake on the Shannon was the scene of a sighting in 1960 of a monster by three priests. One of them sketched it. They described the head as being like that of a python. The sketch resembles the long necked monsters of Scottish lore. There had been a tradition of a monster in the lough and there had been accounts by anglers of fishing lines being caught by something strong and unidentified under the water.   Investigation by submarine tracking devices have produced sounds like bodies propelled by flippers.   [C25]

LOUGH SHANAKEEVER MONSTER This lake lies in Co Galway. A witness said that in about 1963 he noticed a disturbance in the water and saw a creature which he could not identify, 7'-8'/2.3m long. A story told about this lake was that, perhaps in the late 19th Century, a creature had actually emerged from the water. A woman who saw it described it as looking like a horse in front and an eel behind.   [H11]

LOUGH WASKEL MONSTER A strange creature which was brown/grey blotched with cream was hooked in this lough in the 1940s. [E]

LOVELAND FROG It is sometimes said that this was an animal or entity that looked like a frog or lizard, stood upright and had leathery skin and was seen by two policemen in Loveland, Ohio, in 1972. The officers are supposed to have seen the creature on separate occasions. However, one of the officers told an interviewer that all he saw was a lizard, that it did not stand upright and that there was nothing particularly unusual about it. It has been suggested that he changed his story because he was annoyed by unwanted attention.

    In addition, this is not the only alleged sighting of a bipedal batrachian in the Loveland region. In 1955 a driver claimed to have seen three creatures like frogs walking on their hind legs near the Miami River. One seemed to be holding something that gave

148

off sparks. In the same year Mrs D. Johnson, while swimming in the Ohio River, found herself grabbed by a clawlike hand, which she eventually fought off. [79]

LU Chinese legendary animal like a donkey with one horn. It had cloven feet. [G5]

LUD CHURCH BEINGS Darkeyne's *Legends of the Moorlands and Forest in North Staffordshire* (1860) says that a strange race of beings was to be found beneath Lud Church. Unfortunately, she does not elaborate.

LUKWATA An unidentified creature said to live in Africa's Lake Victoria. When Sir Clement Hill was crossing this stretch of water, one emerged and unsuccessfully tried to snatch a native. The lukwata has a reputation for fighting with crocodiles and is noted for its loud bellows. [H9]

LUMUT MYSTERY CREATURE A decaying and unidentified creature, 20'/6m in length, washed up on Lumut beach in Brunei. Whenever unidentified monsters of this nature turn up, they often prove to be basking sharks, which, when they decay, have the disconcerting habit of not looking like basking sharks. [97]

LUNKASOOSE A large animal with a mane like a lion's, which was to be found in Maine, according to a newspaper report of 1836. For those who would argue with Loren Coleman that there is a still-existing species of American lion in America, the account can be adduced in support of this. [C19]

LUPIN A kind of werewolf in Norman lore. Lupins are said to gather around graveyard walls and howl.

LUSCA An unknown creature with tentacles said to live in the blue holes off Andros Island in the Bahamas and the pools or lakelets called banana holes on the island itself. Similar creatures have been reported from Great Bahama and the Caicos Islands. Its nature cannot be determined from the data currently available. [C20]

LYCOPANTHER The hybrid of a wolf and a panther, according to Topsell.

M

McCAMUS' MONSTER An unidentified and really undescribed, but evidently frightening, creature, mentioned by a pilot on the *Alvin*. He said it was at least 40-50'/12-15m long. [B6]

MACFARLANE'S BEAR A bear of huge size and yellow colouration was killed by a couple of Eskimoes. The MacFarlane from whom the ursid takes its name shipped skull and skin to the Smithsonian. It corresponded to no known bear and may represent a species as yet unclassified by science. It may also have been an abnormal grizzly bear or a grizzly/polar hybrid.   [B6]

McGREGOR LAKE MONSTER McGregor Lake is a reservoir in Alberta and the monster seen here – the head and neck were discerned – must have swum in from elsewhere. Its estimated length was 10'-14'/3-4m   [K4]

MACHLIS A creature like the elk, Pliny informs us, but, having no joints in its legs, it had to sleep leaning against a tree. These animals lived in Scandinavia.

MADUKARAHAT A Karok name for a BHM. It simply means a giant. [12]

MAERO Also called *maerero*, these are the wildmen of New Zealand according to Maori lore. They are supposed to have arrived in New Zealand by canoe, settled in the South Island (and possibly also the North) and been displaced by the Maori. So bony are the fingers of the maero that they could use them to kill their prey. They live in he Eyre Mountains and Bayonet Reefs. One special tall kind of maero were the Maerero-repuwai, who had beautiful women. It has been suggested that the maero were in fact a people called the Ngati-memoe, who were exterminated.

   Occasional encounters with hairy bipeds, possibly maero, have been reported. In the 1850s one was said to have attacked a man in Fiordland, South Island. Two hairy creatures were spotted in the Dusky Sound area in 1947. Tracks were reported from Dusky Sound in 1974. One Les Lisle, proprietor of an ostlery, found a hominoid helping himself to vegetables from his patch in 1991.   [C12 R5 #3]

MAGDALENA RIVER MONSTER This creature, which someone identified as an iguanodon, was seen in this Colombian river in 1921.   [C1]

MAGGOT A sea-serpent reported from Swangler's Cove in Newfoundland.   [B7]

MAHAMBA A huge crocodilian reported from the Congo (Brazzaville). It is said to be 50'/15m long, but it is not merely a large crocodile, say the inhabitants. A Belgian explorer is said to have sighted some possible mahambas.   [25]

MAHONI A race of hairy giants, said by the natives to live in the area of the Porcupine and Peel rivers in Canada. Sometimes they wander further west, to the locality of Kandik Creek. They eat humans and cannot make fire.   [M6]

MA-HUA A legendary ape of western China. They are supposed to carry off women and win their affections by plying them with (presumably purloined) jewels and clothes. [#11]

MAIPOLINA This unknown cat of South America was described by a witness as having tusks like a walrus, which would make it a sabretooth. Its feet have claws and its ears droop. Its size was estimated at 9.75'/3m. The maipolina is also known as the popoke.   [S7]

MAJORCAN WILDCAT A subspecies of wildcat (*Felis sylvestris jordani*) which may still exist.   [S7]

MAKALAKA A legendary bird in the lore of the Wasequa of central Africa. It is supposed to be able to fly, yet is reportedly the size of an ostrich. It has plates on the tips of its wings, which it crashes together to make a loud noise. If you wish to hunt the makalaka, you lie down and play possum, whereupon a passing makalaka will descend with luncheon in mind. Before he can commence his grisly feast, however, you kill him with your spear or other appropriate implement. This, at least, was the method the Wasequa claimed to use. Karl Shuker opines that, if aught real lies behind the legend, it is likely to be an unknown species of secretary bird.   [#8]

MAKARA A kind of dragon in Indian mythology, generally regarded as water dwelling. It is generally thought to have a crocodile's head and legs and a snake's body. Belief in this creature is found well beyond India itself. It is also called *kantaka, asita-danshtra* and *jalarupa*. It is sometimes depicted with an antelope's head and forelegs and a fish's body. It is the sign Capricorn in the Hindu zodiac. [J2 D1]

MALACCA SEA SERPENT A large serpent striped black and yellow seen by the captain of the *Nestor* in the Straits of Malacca in 1876.

MALAGASY WILDCAT Officially, wildcats don't exist on Madagascar, yet there is evidence that in fact they do. The Malagasy language has a word for the wildcat (*kary*) as distinct from the domestic cat (*pisu*). L. Dollar of the University of Tennessee recently trapped two possible wildcats on the island. They may represent a population of the African wildcat (*Felis lybica*) or an entirely unknown species. As early as 1950 R. Decary suggested that a wildcat existed on Madagascar. In the zoo known as the Parc Tsimbazaza there was on display in 1998 a cat that may well have been a specimen of this animal.   [#9]

MALAGNIRA A tiny and unknown species of lemur reported from Madagascar. [S8/A].

MALAITAN HOMINOID A diminutive quadrupedal hominoid, covered with hair, reported from the Solomon Islands.

MAMA MUTU A creature which reportedly lives in Lake Tanganyika. It is said to look like a fish-tailed man, to eat its victims' brains and to suck their blood. Its name signifies 'crocodile man' in Swahili.   [#5]

MAMELEU A large scaled sea serpent in which the West Visayans of the Philippines believe.   [C1]

MAMFE POOL MONSTER A creature the size of an hippopotamus with a seal-like head was observed in this body of water by Ivan T. Sanderson and G. Russell in 1932. [C1]

MAMI WATER A kind of mermaid supposed to live off the West African coast. It is perhaps a manatee.   [#9]

MAMLAMBO Originally the name of a monster in Xhosa legend, in more modern times this has been applied to a river monster in South Africa. It is supposed to inhabit the Mzintlewa River and to attack people, eating off their faces and sucking out their brains. It is said to have the features of a horse and to look like a fish. It has been estimated at 67'/20m long and has been said to have stumpy legs. Police attributed the deaths of its alleged victims to drowning.   [15]

MAMMOTH A member of the elephant family, formerly found in both the Old and New Worlds. The general consensus amongst scientists is that mammoths became extinct about 11,000 years ago, except for a population on Wrangel Island, off the Russian coast, which survived until about 5000 years ago. The question asked by cryptozoologists is whether there is any evidence of survival of this creature until more recent times.

Mammoths have sometimes been found frozen in ice in Siberia. This gave rise to the Chinese idea that the mammoth was a huge rat which died as soon as it reached the surface of the earth. But there is some evidence for mammoths that were all too alive wandering about. In 1580 a Russian officer named Timofeyvitch encountered a large "hairy elephant" on the eastern side of the Urals, while a hunter claimed he had seen two "elephants" in the Siberian taiga in 1918. In 1873 the *New York World* reported that an escaped Russian convict named Batchmatchluk had, in the course of his flight, arrived at a hidden valley which contained a population of mammoth. On the American continent, Indians in Alaska told C.F. Fowler in 1877 that they had killed two mammoths or mastodons. From a sketch these seemed to have four tusks apiece. Apart from this, a Dr Frizzel claimed to have found mammoth tracks in the Aleutians in an article in the *Nome Semi-Weekly News* in 1903.   [H9 F3]

MAN-DRAGON A skyborne beast reported from China in 1927. Its appearance was supposed to presage the destruction of the Xaou Te Dam.   [120]

MAN MOUNTAIN A 13'/3.7m primate which was shot by a hunting party in the Okefenokee Swamp, according to a newspaper story which appeared in 1829. [46]

MANABAI'WOK Menomini Indian term for a BHM.

MANAHA A creature similar to momo, reported from the Great Lakes area of North America.   [30]

MAN-BIRD A bird like a raven but of human size, reported from Marlow's Sands, Wales. The sighting took place in 1998.   [#9]

MANDE BURUNG A yeti-like creature reported from the state of Meghalaya (India). It had last been seen in 1992, before one Nabilson Sangme claimed to have encountered it in 2002, while Dipu Marak made a video recording of what looked like its nest. [12]

MANETUWI-RUSI-PISSI A water monster in which the Shawnee Indians believe. [M7].

MAN-FACED CAT Christopher Columbus, in a letter of 1503, wrote to the king and queen of Spain of this feline animal, much larger than an ordinary cat, with a face reminiscent of a human's. It was shot by a crossbowman, but, even after this, it was so fierce its killer had to cut off two of its legs. With its remaining foreleg it killed a wild boar that was nearby, having first encircled its snout with its tail. No other reports of such an animal are known to the present writer.   [S7]

MANGDEN A mystery animal, apparently of the deer kind, of south-east Asia. Its supposed antlers have been discovered.   [51]

MAN-HEADED BIRD This creature was reported from Point Pleasant (West Virginia) in the 1900s, the very area where Mothman was to be said to flourish in later times. It was also spotted by country dwellers in various counties of the state. I will not make any facetious remarks about a sighting from Looneyville. The creature was said to have had a 12'/3.65m wingspan and dark reddish feathers that the sunshine caused to glisten. [C18]

MAN-HEADED HORSE This terrifying creature was witnessed by a couple in Louth (Ireland). They described it as having, on a horse's body, a man's head with bulging eyes. A similar creature has been reported from Lincolnshire. [D3 #1]

MANINGRIDA This three-headed 60'/18m long monster is supposedly lurking in Gudgerama Creek (Northern Territory), Australia.   [E]

MANIPOGO A serpentine monster, blackish-brown and perhaps 30'/9m long, which has been reported from Lake Manitoba, Canada. The earliest report was in 1909. In 1957 a cave was discovered on the lakeside showing traces, it was alleged, of some sort of serpent, plus the remains of animals on which it had feasted. In 1960 twenty picnickers saw the monster. Its head was described as flat and three humps followed it. A few weeks later seventeen witnesses had a sighting of three animals. A rather unsatisfactory photograph of the creature appeared in the Winnipeg *Free Press* in 1962. J. Kirk avers that since that year there have been no sightings, but J. Colombo contradicts this.   [C22 C20 K4]

MANITOWAC MONSTER In this Wisconsin locale in 1998 two teenagers were scared by a large white animal with dirty fur. They had heard what they had first taken to be the sound of a train. Then they realized it had come from the unidentified creature. [17]

MAN-MONKEY OF RANTON When about a mile from the village of Woodseaves on the way to Ranton (Staffordshire) in 1879, a horseman had a horrifying experience. A creature, black in colour, that seemed part man and part monkey, jumped from the trees and landed on the horse's back. When the man tried to fight with it, his whip seemed to go through it. Eventually, it vanished.

MANORO A giant worm with quills reported from South America. [#12]

MANSFIELD CREATURE Charles Mill Lake near Mansfield (Ohio) was the scene of a rather frightening episode in 1959. Three witnesses claimed to have seen a hominid with green eyes and apparently no arms emerge from this body of water. It left flipper-like footprints. It was reported again in 1963, when it was said to be luminous.   [C18]

MANTA According to the lore of the Araucanians, if you are standing in the water and a hungry manta is nearby, it will feast on you. If, however, you are lucky enough to find a quisco bush to hand, you can use a branch of this to slay him. The manta is conceived to be a huge kind of cuttlefish and should not be confused with the manta ray. [J1]

MANTICORA A curious Indian creature described by Ctesias, who claims to have seen one. He called it *martihora*, but subsequent writers used a corrupt form of the word. It had the face of a man, the figure of a lion, a scorpion-like sting at the end of its tail and shootable spines which were deadly unless you happened to be an elephant. It seems the tiger lies behind this beast, for there was a belief that it could shoot its whiskers at its foes and it was said a little claw on the tip of its tail resembled a scorpion's sting. However, why Ctesias thought it had a human's face is anybody's guess.   [C26]

MAN-TIGER A curious creature exhibited in England during the reign of Queen Anne (1702-1714). From below the head it was described as manlike, implying that the head itself was the tigrine portion. Its hinder parts were hairy. It would drink ale from a glass and engage in bouts with the quarterstaff.   [T2/A]

MANX SEA-SERPENT When Major W. Peer Groves and his family were boating off the Isle of Man (a UK dependency between Britain and Ireland) , the last thing they expected to see was a sea-serpent, but nonetheless one stuck its head up out of the water. It was bewhiskered and had a diamond-shaped ctanium. Michael Peer Groves, describing it, said he was struck by the sweet and gentle expression on its visage. He drew a sketch of it which would remind one of the illustrations in Tove Jansson's Moomin books. [H8]

MAOREN An alternative name for the yeren, meaning 'hairy man'.   [D5]

MAPINGUARY A mysterious apelike creature reported from Brazil. It is supposed to have a distinctly human appearance. Its hair flows. Curiously, it is reported to have but a single leg. This monopod progresses by making huge leaps, thereby leaving a print in the ground, looking as though a bottle has been stuck into it, hence its name of 'bottle foot' (Portuguese, *pe de garrafa*). B. Heuvelmans has suggested the tracks may be of meteorological origin, the one-leggedness being inferred from the tracks. There is a belief that the mapinguary is covered in armour and has only one vulnerable spot, in the vicinity of the navel, which you must hit in order to kill it. A hunter who shot and wounded what he thought to be a mapinguary disputed this. The creature is also known as the *pelobo*. The suggestion that the mapinguary might be a surviving species of ground sloth has been made.. In eastern Brazil, stories of the mapinguary sound more far-fetched than those found in western regions. In one tradition, it has a single abdominal eye. One tradition gives it an additional mouth in its belly from which it emits a protective stench. This may refer to scent glands. Despite its simian or anthropoid features, it may in fact be a sloth. [H9 S6]

MARA RIVER CREATURE An animal seen on a large log in this river in Tanzania. Its head was like that of an otter and it had both scales and spots. [C1]

MARAKIHAN A gigantic sea-monster in Maori legend. With its huge tubular tongue it draws sea craft into its cavernous maw. It is described as having a man's head and a fish's body. [26]

MARGATE SEA SERPENT A creature with a long head and horselike ears was observed off Margate (England) in 1950. [E1]

MARIBUNDA A large type of monkey, about 5'/1.5m tall, supposedly living in the northerly regions of South America. It is said to have a tail, which, like those of other South American monkeys, is prehensile. [90]

MARKED HOMINOID A general term for a form of hominoid said to exist in North America, but to be not so tall as a sasquatch. The term is also applied to Siberian hominoids, including Mecheny, the one studied by Maya Bykova at close range in 1987.

MARKUPO A huge snake in the lore of the West Visayans of the Philippines. Its mouth boasts a brace of white tusks. The end of its tail is split. It is known to sing, but its breath is venomous. [R1]

MARMORE RIVER CREATURE In 1931, Harold Westin, an explorer of Swedish provenance, spied on the banks of this river in Brazil a creature with an alligator-like head, a body reminiscent of a boa-constrictor and four little legs. Its eyes were scarlet. Westin tried to shoot it, but either he missed or the creature proved impervious to the bullet. [S6]

MAROOL A sea monster reported off the coast of Scotland. It was described as a fish of large proportions, covered with eyes. It had a crest made out of flame and it would raise its voice in song if a ship's crew were drowning. [F4]

MAROZI An animal which combines features of both lion and leopard, according to Kenyan lore. It looks like a small lion with spots and lives on higher ground than lions. A "spotted lioness" and her cubs were killed by a game warden named Blayney Percival and he reported this in 1924, while one G. Hamilton-Snowball actually seems to have seen a pair of marozi in 1923. A man named Powys Cobb gave chase to a possible marozi. Two apparent marozi skins have been obtained from animals shot by a hunter named Trent. Further reports of this creature occurred in 1952. We may have here a subspecies of lion, a freak or two of the lion clan or, as the Kenyans maintain, an animal wholly different from the lion.   [H9 S7]

MARSABIT SWIFT A black variety of swift reported from Marsabit Mountain in Kenya.   [S8/A]

MARTIAN BUG-LIKE CREATURE A. Austin interprets a photograph taken on the surface of Mars (orbital camera image M0201837) as showing a living bug-like creature. [A3]

MARTIAN DARKER CREATURE A. Austin argues that Mars orbital camera image M0000063 may show a darker creature with legs consuming a paler creature. The picture is from the southerly pole region of the planet.   [A3]

MARTIN MERE, MONSTER OF A large creature in this English lake that appears to attack swans. While its identity remains uncertain, it seems very likely that it is a wells (*Silurus glanis*), a type of catfish which can grow to monstrous proportions and live for at least a century. It may have been deliberately introduced into the lake.   [R7]

MARU CREATURE In May, 2003, a panic occurred in the town of Maru, Nigeria. A creature said to be half man, half horse, was reported from various sectors of the town. This resulted in women being afraid to venture out.   [2]

MARVIN The name given to a monster seen off the coast of Oregon in 1963. A video-recoding was made of it. It showed a creature 15'/4.57m long with barnacles attached. The jury is still out on what exactly Marvin is. His movements through the water resemble the twists of a corkscrew.   [101]

MASBATE MONSTER A 40'/12m long creature which could not be identified, this was washed up on the shore of the Philippines in 1996. It had four fins and a long tail. It was variously said to have resembled a plesiosaur, a turtle or a cow, so goodness knows what it was.   [101]

MASCARENE EEL A huge kind of eel, said to be found in pools on the island of Mascarene (Reunion).   [S8/A]

MASTERTON CREATURE A strange animal with a propensity for killing dogs reported from Masterton, New Zealand. Observers said it was large with curly hair. It had a broad muzzle and short legs.   [K1]

MASTODON   This huge creature has been supposedly extinct for 8-10,000 years. However, Captain S. Cochrane reported a sighting of living mastodons in South America in 1820. He describes the creatures as "carnivorous", but here he may be speculating. J. Ranking in *Historical Researches Concerning the Conquest of Peru* (1827) averred that mastodons were yet to be found in the Andes in his day.   [W5]

MATA-CHUPA   Guatemalan name for a creature thought identical with the chupacabras.   [C23]

MATAH-KAGMI   A humanoid, perhaps the same as a sasquatch, but showing some singular features. These creatures are supposed to dwell on Mount Shasta, California, which has a reputation for strangeness. They have hair all over them and had been known to trade with an old Modoc Indian, whom they subsequently cured when he had been bitten by a snake by somehow cutting the wound and letting the poison run out. Their alleged presence ties in with a prospector's stories of hairy giants with long arms and short legs living on the mountain. [B8*]

MATLOX   A monstrous creature with a humanlike head and black animal hair. It was reported from Vancouver Island by Mariano Mozino who visited there in 1792. This was the name used for the creature amongst the Nootka Indians.

MATTHEWS RANGE BIRD   An unidentified bird reported from this mountain chain in Kenya. It has a long tail and a greyish colour.

MATUYU   Wildman reported from South America. [5]

MAU MEN   Small hominids reported from Kenya. Their faces and bodies are covered with long black hair, while their skins are white.   [H9]

MAUI BIG CAT   For fifteen years or more there have been rumours of an unknown big cat on the Hawaiian island of Maui. In 2003 these rumours came to a head with reports of sightings in the vicinity of Olinda. Clawmarks on trees have been adduced in support of its existence. However, attempts to track the creature down have proven unsuccessful and its existence has been called into doubt.   [142]

MAURETANIA SEA MONSTER   A 60'/18m long humped monster was seen from the ship *Mauretania* east of the Bahamas in 1934.   [B9]

MAWAS   A mystery hominid in Malaysia. Two were espied in 1999, one six feet tall and black-haired, the other five feet tall and brown-haired. Because *mawas* in Indonesia can sometimes mean an orang-utan, it has been suggested that these creatures represent a relict population of this creature in Malaysia.   [10]

MAYANJA ANIMAL A wild cat-like creature said to have a tiger's head, a lion's claws and a leopard's rosettes. It was supposedly on the loose in Kenya, busily eating domestic animals, in 1974. [S7]

MAYMAYGWAYSHI The Chippewa (Ojibway) Indians believed in these small hairy humanlike beings, noted for their stench. They lived by lakes. [B7]

MAY'S POINT MYSTERY FISH May's Point is a fishing pond on a tributary of Finger Lakes (NY). Here a nocturnal fish has been observed by anglers who cannot identify it. It is said to be 4'/1.2m long, to have a huge hump and a circular tail. Its epidermis boasts patterns near its flank. It has been said to scratch its back against a lock dam. Although it is referred to as a mystery fish, we cannot be certain that it is a piscid. [120]

MBIELU-MBIELU-MBIELU This beast is reported from the Likouala region of the Congo (Brazzaville). It lives partially in the water and is described as having plates on its back. It looks like the prehistoric stegosaurus, but, insofar as we know, this dinosaur had no interest in gadding about in water. [S6]

MBILINTU A strange animal, said to combine characteristics of elephant and hippopotamus, reported from central Africa. Some say it looks like a huge lizard, its neck like a giraffe's, its tail a full 30'/9m long. It is supposed to live in the region of Lakes Bangweulu, Meu and Tanganyika.

MBOREVISU In the legends of the Guarani Indians of South America, a beast of burden they once domesticated, but which is no longer known. [#12]

MECHUNE *see* **Mirgola.**

MEDFORD REPTILE MAN A man-sized humanoid with wings, green scales and the ability to fly reported from the vicinity of Medford (Wisconsin). Although several people are supposed to have seen this creature, the whole story comes from a reptile dealer and is notable for its lack of names or dates. [17]

MEDICINE WOLF A creature in Navaho lore. The Navaho are vague regarding its exact nature – it is perhaps a spirit, perhaps a shapeshifter. A sighting of a strange canine creature in modern times was regarded as a sighting of a medicine wolf. [G6]

MEE SING Delaware/Leni Lenape name for a BHM.

MEGALANIA A supposedly extinct monitor lizard (*Megalania prisca*) which exceeded 30' in length and was terrible to behold, as those who saw the computerised version in the BBC series *Walking With Beasts* will realise. However, reports dating from the first half of the 19th Centuty, indicate it may still exist. In 1979 Frank Gordon, an herpetologist, saw a 30'/9m lizard. Reports tend to be concentrated in New South Wales. [49]

MELON HEADS Deformed humans said to inhabit the woods near Chardon and Kirtland (Ohio). They are said have been originally human children with hydrocephalus who were experimented on by a scientist. The latter made their heads grow to a huge size and retarded them mentally. Grown to adults, they are now said to be found in these woods and are regarded as dangerous.

MELVILLE ISLAND SEA MONSTER A monster with a huge head, estimated to be at least 40' in length, was observed from this location in northern Australia in 1980. [B9]

MEMPHIS MONSTER A mysterious animal has been on the prowl in Memphis (Tennessee) in 2003. No one has seen it, but it has been heard making loud noises. Dogs' and cats' disappearances have been blamed on it. People are wondering if it will begin attacking humans.   [120]

MEMPHRE A monster of Lake Memphremagog, on the American-Canadian border. It has certainly been known since the 19th Century. It is said to have a dragon-like head and a long neck. Its length has been estimated at 15'-45'/4.5-13m. One unusual report in the 1940s said it was 150'/45m long. It seems to come to the surface with some frequency. Photographs taken have shown humps, while video footage has not proven very satisfactory. While reports have been generally consistent, an exception is one made in 1816, which said it had 12-15 pairs of legs. W.B. Bullock in *Beautiful Waters* (1938) averred the legend of the monster to be of Indian origin. Under a mountain called Owl's Head, the lake water is very deep. The monster is thought to live here. [S13 M7]

MERICOXI A large hairy hominoid reported from Brazil.   [#12]

MERIGOMISH SEA MONSTER In 1845 a sea monster was observed by fisherman who hailed from this Nova Scotia locale. It was in the shallow water, endeavouring to return to the deep, which it eventually did. It was 100'/30m long, black, with possible humps and a head like that of a seal.   [C22]

MERLION Yuan Chao, in a posting dated 2003, spoke of seeing in south-east Malaysia a water animal with a red skin and furry mane. He thinks it a new form of sea-lion and has named it a *merlion.*   [2]

MERMAID The mermaid is traditionally described as being like a woman to the waist and below that like a fish. Her male counterpart, the merman, sometimes has a fish-tail, sometimes legs. Some regard the dugong (*Dugong dugon*) or the manatee (*Trichechus*) as the original of the mermaid. While such creatures may have been mistaken for mermaids on occasion, traditions of mermaids and sightings often come from areas where these creatures are quite unknown, which makes it most unlikely that the mermaid has not a rather different origin. Singing mermaids of the classical fish-tailed type were known to the Micmac Indians of Canada.

A full account of the mermaid legend would require a book of its own. Here, I will furnish a few examples of sightings, though these are not exhaustive.

In Wales in 1826 a farmer and his family, gazing at the sea, discerned a short-haired and beautiful mermaid. Her skin was absolutely white. She appears to have been upright and they were not sure whether they could discern a tail.

One of the sailors accompanying Captain Wedell in an Antarctic expedition in 1822-4 was left on Hall Island to guard stores. He reported seeing a reddish mermaid, who raised her head and shoulders out of the water.

About 1830 a small mermaid, perhaps a juvenile, was spotted off Benbecula in the Hebrides. A boy flung a stone at her and struck her. Some days later her body was washed ashore. Her upper part was like a young child with a developed breast and the lower like a salmon, but lacking scales. The local sheriff had her bried in a coffin, so she must have looked very human.

In 1900 in Scotland Alexander Gunn saw a beautiful mermaid of human size stranded on the shore, waiting for the tide to take her out to sea. Her hair was reddish-yellow and her eyes were of a blue-green colour. Not long before there had been a number of sightings off the Orkney Islands, commencing in 1898.

In 1947 a Scottish fisherman saw a mermaid sitting on a herring box. When she saw him looking at her, she dived into the water.

In 1961 a mermaid was seen off the Isle of Man by the Mayoress of Peel and others.

One of the scariest incidents involving a mermaid occurred in 1988. Robert Foster, a professional scuba diver, was scuba diving off the Florida coast when attacked by what he said was certainly a mermaid, the upper half woman, the lower half fish. He said her eyes were full of evil and hate and he was sure she meant to kill him. Foster sped to the surface and thus escaped. So shocked was he that he gave up diving.

I will not venture to guess what creature lies behind these supposed sightings, but it sounds startlingly like the traditional mermaid of lore and legend. Speaking of mermaids, D. Cohen says we know there are no such creatures. I would hesitate to be so dogmatic. [C12 P2 B5 C13]

MERMAN The male of the mermaid, not always depicted as tailed. The Wild Man of Orford, a merman supposedly captured in England during the reign of King John (1199-1216) was not tailed, but endowed with legs. He seems to have eaten only raw food – meat and fish. He was also bald. He eventually escaped back into the sea. A merman with webbed fingers was seen in the Strait of Canso, Canada, in 1656. In the 19th Century there was a family in the Hebrides that claimed descent from a merman. The *Aberdeen Chronicle* (20th August, 1814) mentioned a sighting of a merman off the Scottish coast. Sailors saw him from a ship. They said he was human to the waist, after which his body seemed to taper, but they weren't sure if it tapered into a fishtail. There was a report of mermen and mermaids dancing together on Unst in the Shetland Islands. Sometimes, in Scottish belief, merfolk's tails are really overgarments and can be removed for such terpsichorean recreations. [C12 F4 B7 C22]

MERRIFIELD LIZARD A giant lizard reported from Merrifield, Virginia, in the 1990s. [30]

MESHE-ADAM Azerbaijani name for a wildman.

MESSIE A long-necked monster reported from Lake Murray, South Carolina. Reports have been coming in since 1973. One witness described it as a fish, but was quite definite that it was not a sturgeon, which can be quite easily mistaken for a monster. [32].

MET'CO A large bird in the beliefs of the Indians of Labrador. According to one legend, it carried off a boy to its nest. The child was not eaten. Having stayed in the nest all summer, he clung to the leg of the bird when it flew off and thus returned to the ground.   [R2]

METRO MAGGIE A water snake believed to inhabit Lake Ontario. It was said to be the cause of disease.   [B7]

MEXICAN PTEROSAUR Pterosaur-like creatures have been reported from eastern Mexico.   [30]

MICHICHIBI A creature reported from the south-eastern United States in the 18th Century. It looked like a wolf with a lion's mane and claws.   [C19]

MICHIGAN CREATURE A creature seen crossing the road in the Upper Peninsula of Michigan in 2000. It was 4'/1.2m or taller, its front legs were longer than the hind legs, causing its back to slope. Its hair was silver grey with black or dark brown streaks in it. Its face was round and flat. Its ears also were flat.   [2]

MIDLANDS FIRE CREATURE In 19th Century England in the Midlands there was a belief amongst those who strove in iron works that, if the fires were not extinguished from time to time, something (though it never seems quite clear what) would be engendered in them. The something, one infers, would not be pleasant. [H12]

MIEHTS-HOZJIN A creature of Lapp/Saami legend. It was black with a tail and prized silence in its sylvan retreat. If people broke this, it would muddle them so they became lost.

MIGO On the island of New Britain, part of Papua-New Guinea, lies the lake known to the locals as Dakataua or Niugini. No fish are found in its waters, but it does have a legendary monster, the migo. As there are no fishes, this creature often comes to the surface to eat swimming birds. It has been videotaped and seems to be over 33'/10m long, undulating vertically. However, it has been argued that the so-called "animal" is in fact three crocodiles swimming in a line.   [S6]

MIGOI The Bhutanese name for the Abominable Snowman, to be found at an altitude of 3500-5000m.   It has a hairless face and red-brown to black-grey hair. Migois are generally seen singly or in couples. The migoi does not fear fire, is an herbivore, it will attack humans, but is also curious about them. Migois live in caves in which they build nests. The migoi can make itself visible or invisible at will, because it has a magic charm called a dipshing which it keeps under its right arm. The dipshing, I would inform those on the lookout for one, resembles a twig. The migoi is also called a *gredpo*. [C7]

MI-GOMPO A Tibetan term for the yeti.

MIHIRUNG A large and supposedly extinct bird of Australia. Its name is taken from Aboriginal legend. Fossil evidence shows mihirungas were still around 26,000 years ago. Its memory is also preserved in rock art. The legends and pictures argue that it survived much longer than the fossil evidence would indicate. It may even have survived into modern times, for in 1967 a couple named Rollo saw a 9'/2.74m tall bird which resembled a huge emu in a New South Wales forest.   [#8]

MIITIIPI Kwaisu Indian term for a BHM.

MILKBIRD A creature in the lore of southern Africa. It supplies, not exactly milk, but amasi, a kind of yoghurt.   [K5]

MILNE *see* **Mystery Black Bear**.

MILTON LIZARD An unidentified lizard seen around 1975 in Milton, Kentucky. It was black and white striped with orange blotches. More than one animal may have been seen. The witnesses were two brothers named Cable. One of the possibly two lizards seen was estimated at 15'/4.5m long. The lizard was thought to be responsible for a recent attack on a dog.   [29]

MINETY MONSTER Name given to an unidentified creature that killed animals in the area of Minety (Wiltshire) in 2002.   [149]

MINHOCAO A South American creature, described as a giant worm. Large furrows in the soil were ascribed to its progress. It is ssaid to be water dwelling and to seize passing animals in the abdominal region. It is said to boast horns. One description of what was probably a minhocao said it was the size of a house. A. de Saint-Hilaire suggested it was a giant lungfish, which is not implausible. It can hardly be said to be a surviving glyptodon, as its description bears scant relation to such a beast, despite this being a proposed identity. No reports of this animal came in during the 20th Century. [S6]

MINIBIRD An unidentified tiny avian reported from Sumatra in the 1950s. The general colour is yellowish. It has a dark brown belly and stripes.   [S8/A]

MINIO These are horned and hairy creatures in the beliefs of the Cheyenne. They will drag unwary travellers into the water.   [J2]

MI-NI-WA-TU An animal believed by Indians to dwell in the River Missouri. It has red hair, one eye, a straight horn and a bison-like body. It is said to light up. [M7]

MINNESOTA ICEMAN An apparent hominid in a block of ice, placed on exhibition in Minnesota. It was observed by prominent cryptozoologists Ivan Sanderson and Bernard Heuvelmans. It was covered with dark brown hair and one of its eyes seemed to dangle from the socket; the other was missing. It was also wounded in the left arm. Heuvelmans accidentally caused some of the ice to melt, leading to a smell of rotting flesh. As this had occurred as an unexpected mishap, the stench cannot have come from a piece of rotting meat placed in the ice-block to discourage too-close examination. Therefore, this would argue that a genuine animal and not a model lay encased in the ice. It had a nose resembling that of a Pekinese and hardly any lips.

At some stage, however, the animal was replaced by a dummy and Hansen, the exhibitor, claimed the original had been returned to its millionaire owner. As to what it was, Heuvelmans emphatically identified it as a Neanderthal man, while Sanderson asserted just as firmly that it was not. As it has disappeared from general ken, further research is currently impossible.   [C16 R3]

MINOTAUR A bull-human hybrid of Greek mythology, housed in the labyrinth at Knossos, Crete. Its story probably stems from a garbled memory of the bull cult of the Minoan civilization.

MIRGOLA The name by which the smaller kind of yeti is known to the Bhutanese. It occupies the forested areas 1.5miles/2500m high in the mountains and above. In height they are about 4'/1m tall and generally flee if they encounter humans. The mirgola is also known as a *mechune.*   [C7]

MIRII DOG A creature in the beliefs of the Wiradjuri tribe of Australian aborigines. These dogs are supposed to emerge from water. When first you see them they can be small, but the more you look at them the larger they grow. The dogs are reputed to occupy the Aborigine sacred site of Mirrigana.   [S8]

MIRYGDY A name for a wildman in the language of the Lamut, who are to be found on the Chukchi Peninsula, which juts out into the Bering Sea. The creature is supposed to be tall and secretive.   [B3]

MISABE A long-haired giant in which the Grand Lake Victoria Band of Quebec believed. It is possibly the same as bigfoot.   [C16]

MISIGABENIK A general term for lake monsters amongst the Algonquians.

MISS WALDRON'S RED COLOBUS MONKEY This simian of the Cote d'Ivoire and Ghana was thought extinct in 2000, but there is evidence that there are some lingering specimens.   [2]

MISSISSIPPI WILDMAN A simian creature, perhaps identical with the nape. [30]

MITLA This animal was described by the explorer Percy Fawcett as a black, doglike cat. It was about the size of a foxhound. R. Mackal thought it might be the bush dog (*Speothos venaticus*) while K.P.N. Shuker suggests the short-eared dog (*Atelocynus microtis*). The latter's felinity of movement might account for its being thought of as a cat.   [S7]

MI-TSHEMPO A Tibetan term for the yeti.

MNGWA A large felid said to live in Africa. Its name means "strange one". It is also called *nunda*. It is said to be the size of a donkey, with stripes resembling those of a tabby cat. It is to be found, we are told, on the coast of Tanzania. It features in a Swahili war song of the 12th Century.

The mngwa was credited with the killing of two police constables in 1922. In 1937, a man who had been attacked by this mysterious animal received medical attention. Its spoor is said to look like that of a lion-sized leopard. The mngwa may belong to one of the species of African felids generally thought to be extinct. [H9 S7]

MOA A flightless and completely wingless bird (*Dinorthis*) of New Zealand, believed extinct. Moas ranged in size from 12 to 3 feet/3.66m-90cm. Maoris say the last moa was killed at Lake Rotorua. While it has been questioned whether the moa was still in existence when the Maoris arrived (?13th Century), the Maoris contended they had indeed known it. An old Maori told Governor Fitzroy in 1844 that he had actually seen a moa in 1771. Another claimed to have actually taken part in a moa hunt some time before 1800.

However, one might ask if the moa still exists. Sir George Gray, who later became prime minister of New Zealand, claimed that Maoris had told him in 1868 that they had recently killed a small moa, one of a little flock. A newspaper report of 1878 claimed a sighting of a living moa. In modern times in South Island a turkey-sized bird which may be one of the smaller moas has occasionally been reported. Due to an error, some people term this creature *roa-roa*, which in fact means the largest variety of kiwi. In 1993 a man named Freaney and two companions alleged they had encountered what they took to be a moa. An unsatisfactory photograph was taken.[H9]

MOALGEWANKE A creature that emitted a booming roar and looked like a red-haired mermaid was mentioned as occurring in this South Australian lake in 1879. The name is presumably Aboriginal. [C1]

MOBERLY LAKE MONSTER A mysterious creature with a horse-like head has been seen from time to time in this Canadian lake. [K4]

MOCHEL-MOCHEL An Australian mystery animal, generally thought to be a local name employed by Aborigines in Queensland for the bunyip. In the 1850s one was seen by T. Hall. He claimed it looked like a low-set sheepdog, its head and whiskers were like an otter's and the back of its head resembled that of a bald Aborigine. [S11]

MOCHIS CREATURE A creature that looked like a dragon, 35'/10.7m tall, which was said to have killed ducks, chickens and a goat. It was said to have long fangs. It was seen at los Mochis (Sinaloa) Mexico. [C23]

MOCKING LAKE MONSTER There have been reports of a monster in this lake in Quebec for decades. It is said to be 12-18' in length, coloured brown or black. [G2*]

MOHA-MOHA A large kind of sea creature observed by a Miss Lovell in Queensland in 1890. It had a long neck and a carapace covered both that and its head. As she looked on, it raised a wedge-shaped tail like a fish's out of the water. Certain features of the description have caused suggestions that it may be due to poor observation or mendacity. The name of the beast seems to be identical with the *mochel-mochel*, sometimes identified with the bunyip. The form *moha-moha* would not occur in an Aboriginal language, as they lack the letter *h*. [B2 #9]

MOKELE-MBEMBE A large creature reported from the Likouala area of the Congo (Brazzaville). Descriptions of the beast furnished by natives assert that it has a long neck, a head distinguishable from it, a body reminiscent of an elephant's, thick legs and a long tail. Its colour is red-brown. It lives in and often beneath the water. It is a vegetarian, but it will attack and kill hippopotamuses and it will upset canoes, slaughtering their unhappy crews. In 1959 pygmies are said to have killed and eaten a specimen they encountered at Lake Tele, but they all died shortly afterwards, indicating that the flesh is poisonous to man or riddled with bacteria or viruses. R. Mackal, a well-known cryptozoologist, made two expeditions to the Congo collecting data on the beast. He did not see the animal itself, though on his second foray he seems to have come within a hair's breath of doing so, actually hearing it descend into the water. More fortunate was Congolese zoologist Marcellin Agnagna, who actually saw the beast in 1983. A more recent sighting was by two guards who reported seeing the beast in the Boumba River in April, 2000. Reports of a horn on the beast's snout seem due to confusion with the emela-ntouka, another legendary creature.

Although noted explorer Redmond O'Hanlon (who once offered to delineate the symptoms of a malady called shaggers' disease on a television talk show, only to have his offer declined), feels no monster exists and sightings are due to mistaken glimpses of partially submerged elephants, but there does seem a case for the existence of an unknown animal, However, although a sauropod identity has been suggested for this creature, this does not commend itself to palaeontologists, as such creatures are now thought to have been terrestrial rather than water-dwelling. [H9 M1]

MOKO-HIKU-WARU A kind of reptile in the legends of the Maori. [#3]

MOMO The name of this creature is an abbreviation of "Missouri Monster". It has been described as humanoid, six or seven feet tall, with its head covered with black hair. It was spotted in Missouri in 1972, carrying off a dog. Another dog nearby, though apparently untouched, was violently ill. Dogs in the area had been reported missing. Hairy monsters had been reported in Missouri since the 1940s. Creatures similar to momo have been reported in Michigan. [C21]

MON ISLAND SNAKE A mystery snake seen on this island in a woodland area of Denmark. It was black on the back, while the underparts were lighter. [6]

MONGOLIAN DEATH WORM The native name of this creature is *allghoi khorkho*. It is a dark red worm, thick as a man's arm. No eyes, mouth or nostrils can be discerned on it. It is to be found in the Gobi Desert and keeps generally underground, except in the warm months of June and July. (Remember, the Gobi is a cold desert). It has been reported to be as long as 5'/1.5m, but smaller estimates would seem to occur more regularly, e.g., 1'6"/50cm. The skin is smooth and has blotches. If attacked, it is said to rear up and squirt poison at its foe. It is said to be able to kill people by touch or at a distance. The last is possibly accomplished by electricity. [#8]

MONKEY MAN 1 In 2001 a strange panic gripped parts of India. A monkey or a man in a monkey mask was allegedly running amok attacking people, either scratching or biting them. India's capital, New Delhi, was one of the scenes of its activities. Its eyes were red. It was said to have red and green lights on its chest and an ability to speak Bhojpuri. One "authority" claimed it had three buttons on its chest, one to turn it into a monkey, one to give it extra strength and one to make it invisible. It was suspected it might be an alien or a robot. Police ascribed the whole scenario to mass hysteria. Do not confuse this beast with **Monkeyman**. [#9]
2 The name "monkey man" was given to two brownish simians which were reported from the jungle on the banks of the Mekong in south-east Asia. Their species was unidentified. [K1]

MONKEY-LIKE CREATURE Ian Harper, bicycling home in Ontario one night, encountered a white creature, about 3'/90cm tall, with a large head. Then came a strange noise like a grunt or blast. He described this sound as "sub-sonic". It seemed to surround him. It frightened his dog. [18]

MONKEYMAN Hoboken, New Jersey, is supposed to be home to this hairy primate. It is said to frequent schools, throwing teachers from upper windows and kidnapping children. For the similarly named Indian creature, *see* **Monkey Man**. [B7]

MONO GRANDE A simian animal – monkey or ape – reported from eastern Venezuela. It may be the same as the controversial de Loys' ape. They are said to attack using branches as weapons. One was sighted by G. Samuels, mycologist, in 1987. The animal has been reported from the 16th Century. It may be identical with the didi. It is said one was actually captured and kept for a time in the Santa Cruz Zoo in Bolivia, but this has not been verified. [C10 115]

MONO REY An alternative term for the mono grande.

MONOCEROS *see* **Unicorn**.

MONONGAHELA SEA SERPENT The captain of the *Rebecca Sims* (in some accounts miscalled the *Gipsy*) handed in an account he had been given by the captain of the *Monongahela* when the two ships had met in 1852. The *Monongahela* had encountered a gigantic sea serpent over 100'/30m long, which those aboard slew. It looked generally serpentine, but had four little paws and two blow-holes. They cut off its head to bring home. Alas, after passing on the message to the captain of the other ship, the *Monongahela* was never seen again. It presumably sank. Its name board was found washed up in the Aleutians. Some commentators have considered this tale a hoax, but this is by no means necessarily the case. [C/H]

MONROE CREATURES Vague large creatures have been reported in the vicinity of Monroe (Michigan). These seem to be but indistinctly discerned, but their presence is said to be indicated by frogs' falling silent. One of the creatures is supposed to have grabbed a girl (? with a hand), while a girl of fifteen saw, by the light of the moon, something big, black and terrible. [B11]

MONSTER CAT This cat was once supposed to be seen from time to time on Sturminster Newton Castle, an earthwork in Dorset. It was said to have eyes the size of saucers. [#6]

MONSTER OF GLAMIS A strange creature, reputed to have lived in Glamis Castle, Scotland, home of the earls of Strathmore.

Glamis has a great reputation for the number of ghosts it is said to harbour. Yet Sir Walter Scott stayed there in 1794 and, although he averred that the castle was said to contain a secret room, he makes no mention of ghosts, which suggests stories about them became current only in the 19th Century. One of these is supposed to be that of Beardie, a former earl; another to be the Mad Earl, heard walking on the roof. Strange noises came from the secret room according to F.G. Lee's *Glimpses of the Supernatural* (1875). Then rumour seems to have started about an awful but unspecified secret. An article in *All the Year Round* for 1880 claims a man who discovered this was given a payoff and sent to Australia. Augustus Hare, writing in 1896, felt the secret had something to do with a 14th Century event. For the first time it is suggested that this secret had to do with a half-human monster by Charles Harper in *Haunted Houses* (1907). This is only one of a number of suggestions he proffers. A theory grew up that this monster was the offspring of one of the Strathmore family, hideous and deformed. The presence of a monster, whether the scion of the lordly family or not, would account for some of the supposed sightings of ghosts and the noises associated with them. The only thing that can be said with certainty is that there was *some* secret. It is said this was passed down from earl to earl and that the last to know of it may have been Patrick, the fifteenth earl. Perhaps, if there was a monster, it died in his time. [#13]

MONSTER OF THE WOODS A monster reported in Co Cork, Ireland, in 1921, by Thady Byrne. The woods were near a sea-inlet. It was the size of a greyhound, looked like a cat, had a naked tail and would growl and bark like a dog. It had a wide chest and shoulders, while the body tapered. Other locals claimed to have seen it. [C25]

MONSTROUS FISH A prickle-headed fish with long horns and huge eyes, 20-24'/6-7.6m long and black in colour, described by Olaus Magnus in *Historia de Gentibus Septentrionalibus* (1555).

MONTENEGRO HOMINOID A wildman was seen in a cave by Bozo Radovic and he passed this on to folklorist Vujica Ognjenovic. He described it as being hirsute and muscular.

MONTEROSE DRAGON This seems to have been a large lizard with a green and yellow body seen north of Rome. It was observed over a number of years, a notable occasion being in woods in 1935. [B9]

MONTICELLO CREATURE An anthropoid or humanoid about 4'/1.2m tall with smoky black hair was observed by hunters at this Utah location in 1959. [B9]

MO-O A kind of huge sea-creature in Polynesian belief. One used to live in Pearl Harbor, but is said to have migrated. [N2]

MOOCH NOCHVA A mysterious manlike being with claws who plucks flesh from the mouth and other parts of his victims, causing much distress in Uttar Pradesh, India, where it has attacked a considerable number of persons. The creature's claws have been compared with those of a tiger and it has been said to give out a red and green light. [12]

MOOMEGA Variant name for the yowie. [H6]

MOON WOMAN According to Aldrovandus, a woman who could lay eggs from which giants were hatched. [53]

MOORE'S BEACH MONSTER A stranded creature found on National Bridges State Beach (California) by one Charles Moore in 1925. Various persons felt it was a prehistoric monster. Some time before this incident, sea-lions had been seen battling an unidentified beast nearby. The mouth was like a duck's bill and the creature was covered with what the *Santa Cruz News* described as "semi-hair or feathers" (a sort of down?). It was bigger than a barrel, had "elephant-like legs" at regular intervals with "ivory toenails". Its aroma was uninviting. It is by no means impossible that it was some kind of beaked whale or a basking-shark. [121]

MORAG A now quite famous monster, said to inhabit Scotland's Loch Morar. It was seen by Sir Theodore Drinckman in 1895 and there were said to have been earlier sightings. In 1946 it was seen by a group of children and their supervisor, a man named MacDonnell. It was on shore, but dived into the water. It was described as being the size of an Indian elephant. In 1948 a boatload of tourists saw it. It was regularly seen thereafter. In 1969 men called MacDonnell and Simpson were in a boat which was struck by the monster. When MacDonnell tried to fend it off with an oar, it proved quite solid. Simpson fired a rifle at it and it pursued them no further, perhaps scared by the noise. They said it was 25'-30'/7.6-9m long with three humps. Its skin was rough and dirty brown. In all, this monster has been sighted about fifty times. [M9 C25]

MORGAWR A monster supposed to be found off the coast of Cornwall. There certainly have been reports of monsters in the area. Harold Wilkins claimed to have seen two "saurians" off the coast in 1949, saying they were 19-20'/6m long. In 1975 a Mr Riley and his friend Mrs Scott saw a hump-backed creature with stumpy horns and bristles down the back of its neck. It dived, then reappeared with a conger eel in its mouth. In 1976 the *Falmouth Packet* printed photographs of an alleged monster taken by "Mary F.". J. Downes is quite certain they are fakes. As to who faked them, some suspicion has fastened on the flamboyant Anthony Shields, but Downes points out that they lack the finesse usually associated with his productions. A John Gordon has also been the object of suspicion.

In 1986 Sheila Bird and her brother saw a large sea-creature from the top of a cliff west of Portscatho. It had a long neck, a small head a hump and a long tail. Its length was estimated at 17-20'. [C2]

MORRISTOWN MONSTER A creature observed in New Jersey in 1965-6 (two sightings). It combined scales and hair, seemed to lack a face and walked stiffly on two legs. It was estimated at being 7'/2m tall. [C19]

MOSES LAKE MONSTER A monster of reptilian nature was reported from this lake in Washington state in 1992. [K4]

MOSQUETO In the legends of the Oneida, this was a monster living in Lake Onondaga in New York state. The tale says it once rose up from the water and slew a number of Indians. [C19]

MOTHER OF FISHES A large fish in German folklore, said to live in the River Esler. [M7]

MOTHMAN A creature supposedly observed near Point Pleasant (West Virginia) in 1966. It was sighted by two couples in a car, the Scarberrys and the Mallettes. It was humanoid and had two glowing red eyes. When they tried to flee, it pursued their vehicle on the wing, sometimes attaining a speed of 100 m.p.h.

Linda Scarberry, in an interview for a book published many years later, gave co-author D. Sergent considerable detail of the encounter. Although its face could not be made out, its eyes seemed to exert a fascination. It had muscular arms and legs like a man's. (This contradicts a statement made by a commentator that it was armless) When they first saw it, one of its wings had been trapped by a wire and it was endeavouring to free it with its hands. Initially, it impressed the witnesses as perhaps being scared. In their last view of it, it was seated on a flood wall, its arms around its legs. Some time later the witness was to see it again, seated on her own roof. The Mothman did not strike her as malign. She said she knew of 30-40 other people who had seen it and she believed it was connected with a UFO seen in the area at the time. It is possible these couples were not the first witnesses: a number of possible sightings had preceded theirs, beginning on 1st September.

On 16th November Marcella Bennett, her daughter and a couple called Walmsley were heading back to their car between 8-9 p. m. when a figure rose out of the darkness behind it. Taller than a man, it had red, glowing eyes.

Other sightings occurred. A businessman saw Mothman on his front lawn. Teenagers saw it at Campbell Creek. Thomas Ury, purveyor of footwear, saw it at 7.15 one morning. He claimed its wingspan was 10'/3m.

On November 26th Ruth Foster saw it and managed to get a look at its face. She described this with the words *funny* and *little*. She saw no beak. Its height she put at about 6'. Sightings continued.

An earlier sighting of a Mothman-like creature at Point Pleasant had taken place in 1961. A winged man was seen standing on the road by a motorist. It took off and disappeared into the sky.

It cannot be said with certainty when Mothman sightings stopped. The *Athens (Ohio) Messenger* of 5th June, 1967, describes something which sounds very like Mothman scaring three boys camping out for the night near Lewis Street, Point Pleasant.

A Native American copper sculpture bearing some resemblance to Mothman is to be found in the Peabody Museum, Harvard (catalogue no. 88-45-10/46959).

Mothman seemed to defy the laws of aerodynamics by flying. He does not seem, incidentally, to have flapped his wings when doing this. He had an hypnotic gaze, but did not necessarily seem malignant and he may have been connected with the UFO phenomenon. One theory was that a government experiment was somehow involved. The notorious Men in Black or MIBs were reported in the area. Some UFO believers assure us that Mothman is one of a population of such creatures that migrated hither from the constellation Draco and live underground. It has even been suggested that Mothman is a temporary physical form acquired by a human having an out-of-the-body experience. I can, however, offer one conclusive piece of analysis: Mothman is a mystery. [K1 C18 S2 #9 150]

MOUNTAIN BONOBO The bonobo (*Pan paniscus*) is a discrete kind of ape, which was formerly regarded as a pygmy chimpanzee. As well as the known species, there is some evidence that the mountain bonobo, an hitherto unestablished species, may exist. [C20]

MOUNTAIN BOOMER A 6'/1.8m tall bipedal lizard reported from the western parts of Texas. [31]

MOUNTAIN DEVIL Hairy hominid creatures credited with the power of invisibility which attacked a miner's cabin according to the *Seattle Times* in 1998. The incident is said to have occurred in Washington state. [C11]

MOUNTAIN MEN 8'/2.4m tall hominoids in the lore of the Nahanni Indians. [M6]

MOUNTAIN TIGER This creature is rumoured to be found in northern Chad. The Zagaoua claim to know all about it. It has red fur, no tail and is feline. It has protruberant teeth like a sabretooth, which it possibly is. [S7]

MU JIMA A kind of hairy merman in Japanese folklore. [C21]

MUCKROSS LAKE MONSTER In August 2003, an acoustic survey of char stocks in this lake at Killarney (Kerry), Ireland, revealed a huge mass like a whale. Here we have a possible monster. [#9]

MUGWUMP A monster supposed to inhabit Lake Temiskaming (Ontario).   [E]

MUHLAMBELA A snake reported from southern Africa, said to have a crest and to emit sound. It sounds like a smaller version of the crested cobra, *which see*, but it may be a black mamba with unsloughed skin forming a crest on its head.   [S4]

MUHURU A dark grey lizard, 9-12'/3m long reported from Kenya. It has a strange structure reminiscent of a sail on its back.   [E]

MULAHU A large mysterious primate, presumably an ape or hominoid, said to live in central Africa.   [41]

MULEN A Tungus word for a Siberian wildman. It means 'bandit' and has perhaps been so-called because of the creature's tendency to raid the outbuildings of human dwellings. [C20]

MULILO In the Congo (Kinshasa) and Zambia belief is (or was) to be found in the loathsome mulilo. 6'/1.8m long and 1'/30cm wide, it is like a giant slug. It is black as pitch and its breath envenoms the very air. Pieces of mulilo are used as charms which indicates that it is probably not really a slug, for fragments of such a creature would probably be impossible to preserve. The only accounts we have of this beast seem to date from 1940. [S5]

MUMULOU On Guadalcanal in the Solomon Islands lie the mountains of Laudari, where this creature is said to dwell. It is humanoid, tall, hairy and long-nailed.   [#4]

MUNDESLEY SEA SERPENT A creature with five humps seen off Mundesley (Norfolk) in 1936. It was moving at astonishing speed. An earlier sighting off the Norfolk coast had taken place in 1930.   [146]

MURTENSEE MONSTER A number of anomalous creatures have been reported from this lake in Switzerland. Two witnesses claimed to have seen four monsters in the lake in 1992 while another claimed many previous sightings. A photograph of what may have been one of these creatures was taken by A. Trottmann.   [#1]

MURUNG RIVER BEAR This animal has been reported from Borneo. It resembles a bear, but may not really be one.   [30]

MURU-NGU A striped felid of legendary status in the Central African Republic. It is described as larger than a lion but striped, and is said to live in water. There are several different names in African languages for sabretooth beasts, some of which may be identical.   [S7]

MUSHUSH An Akkadian name (formerly deciphered as *sirrush*) found indicating a creature in bas-relief on the Ishtar Gate at Babylon. It is a four-legged reptilian animal with a horn on its nose. R. Koldeway. who excavated in 1902, was sure it depicted some lingering species of the iguanadon family. It has also been suggested it is based upon reports of the mokele-mbembe, but there is no evidence that the Babylonians had any contact, direct or indirect, with central Africa. (An argument in favour of this involving a glazed brick has been superseded). If this piece of artwork shows some beast that genuinely existed, its identity is currently unknown. [H9 S6 L1/A]

MUSKRAT LAKE MONSTER This Canadian lake is said to be home to a monstrous creature. In 1968 D. Humphries claimed to have seen a monster here. It had a large head with a single tooth depending from the upper jaw. There were two front flippers. In colour it was silver-green. The estimated body length was 24'/8m, but the witness later changed his mind about this, claiming it was considerably shorter. The witness bestowed the name "Hapyxelor" on the creature.

An anonymous witness whom M. Bradley calls Mrs B. saw it with her husband and daughter in 1976. It came within 50'/15m of them and remained in sight for about ten minutes. It had a large head and virtually no neck. It gave an impression of submerged front flippers. Another witness, a boy, said it had no neck.

Possible sonar tracings of two underwater creatures were made by M. Bradley in 1988.   [B12]

MUSTELINE HYBRIDS It has been asserted from time to time that different species of mustelid have been crossbred. In 1898 it was alleged that polecat-marten and polecat-weasel hybrids had been produced. It has been said that a pine marten and a sable were once crossed in Russia. A poacher told Jonathan Downes he had succeeded in crossing a polecat-ferret with a mink and showed him the what he averred to be the offspring. [D7]

MUTONKOLE In Lake Kisala in the Congo (Kinshasa) it is said there dwells a snake which resembles a floating clay pot. [E]

MUTTON ISLAND SEA MONSTER In 1935 a sea monster was shot by a lighthouse keeper on the coast of Galway, Ireland. It was 48'/15m long and 28'/9m round the middle. The fate of the body seems unknown.   [B9]

MUTURANGI A form of giant octopus in the legends of the Maoris. [#3]

MYNDIE A huge snake ten miles long which spread smallpox at the hest of the deity Pund-jil, according to the beliefs of the Yarra Yarra tribe of Australian Aborigines. The Myndie was served by little myndies, which it would send out to spread disease. [B2]

MYSTERY APE An unusual kind of ape, traces of which have been found in the Congo (Kinshasa). It lives on the ground, like a gorilla, but otherwise seems to be more like a chimpanzee – indeed, it looks as if these apes may be giant chimpanzees, which have abandoned an arboreal existence due to size.   [2]

MYSTERY ARTHROPOD This has appeared on undersea photographs taken in 1989 in the Pacific. Its exact nature remains unknown.   [S8/A]

MYSTERY BAT   This orange and black male bat was captured in the Maha Chana Chan region of Thailand in 2003, but it later died.   It may belong to a completely unknown species.

MYSTERY BLACK BEAR   An unknown variety of black bear, large in size, reported from Colombia and Peru.   It is known locally as the *milne*.   As A.A. Milne was the inventor of Pooh, there is a certain humour in the name.   The fictitious bear has (I nearly wrote bears) no resemblance to this creature.   One cannot even count on big words bothering it.   [30]

MYSTERY CERAM FISH   An unknown fish, which looks like a mudskipper, reported from Ceram, one of the Indonesian islands.   It pulsates, glowing red, at night.   [F8/A]

MYSTERY DOLPHIN   This animal, seen in the Indian Ocean in 1960, had characteristics of both the bottlenose dolphin and the Malabar dolphin.   It may even have been a hybrid.   [B6]

MYSTERY EARTHWORM   An unidentified grey kind of earthworm which science has failed to identify was discovered in Tennessee in a wood off US 129.   These creatures seem to eat everything in their path.   [120]

MYSTERY GOAT   A goat of unknown species reported from Mongolia in modern times.   It has a shaggy coat.   [30]

MYSTERY LORIS   This creature was seen and photographed in an animal dealer's stall in Hanoi in 1994.   It was much bigger than the slow loris and its colour was paler.   [S8/A]

MYSTERY NORWEGIAN FOX   A mysterious breed of fox, black in colour and much bigger than the red fox (*Vulpes vulpes*), has been plaguing the county of Sogn og Fjordane, Norway, since about 2000.   It is a fierce beast, attacking both humans and animals and apparently killing, not just for food, but out of ferocity.   [2]

MYSTERY SHARK   A shark that has been both seen and photographed in the Pacific off Colombia, but which cannot be identified and seems to be an unknown species.   It is estimated at being 20'/6m long.   It is currently being investigated by Colombian biologist F. Sarano.   [#9]

MYSTERY SNAKE   A snake with a flat head.   The first third of its body is also flat, the rest round.   This curious animal was reported from South America by explorer Percy Fawcett.   [C1]

MYSTERY STONE PARTRIDGE   A subspecies of this bird reported to exist in Senegal.   It has a spotted head.   [S8/A]

MYSTERY TERRAPIN Two specimens of an unknown type of terrapin turned up at Portsmouth University in 2003. They could not be identified and are possibly hybrids. They are currently to be found at the Centre for Fortean Zoology, Exeter. [#9]

N

NAGA In Indian mythology, nagas are supposed to look like men to the waist down. From below the waist they appear to be serpents. Female nagas are called naginis. They sometimes have legs. They live beneath the water and the earth. The term naga, however, is also applied to a mysterious water creature in the Mekong river in Thailand. There was a considerable infusion of Hindu culture into Thailand and this may have brought with it the idea of the naga, whose name was then applied to the Mekong creature. Sightings have been reported in modern times. An old lady allegedly saw one in the river about 1995. She and a friend observed a huge black snake from a bridge. The chief of police at Phon Pisai and others claimed they saw a creature 230'/70m long in the river. R. Freeman suggests this may have been in fact several nagas swimming together. Freeman also met a man who claimed to have encountered a naga in a cave. He asserted that what he could see of its body was 60'/18m long. [L4 #1]

NAHUAL A lycanthrope of Mexican tradition. He is often a were-coyote. [122]

NAHUELITO A lacustrine monster with fins, humps and a long neck reported from Lake Nahual Huapi in Argentina. Tracks indicate it has at times come ashore. It is said to be 33'/10m long. Indian tradition knew of a monster in the lake. There were notable sightings in 1989 and 1994. [M7]

NA'IN A sasquatch-like creature in the lore of the Gwich'in Indians. Some said these creatures were social outcasts that went wild, some that they were not human at all. [48]

NAITAKA Indian name for the ogopogo.

NAKANI Hairy hominoids (the word is plural) in whom the North Athabascan Indianas of Canada and Alaska believe. Along the Yukon river the supposition is that they are generally nocturnal. If you enter their territory, they will angrily fling sticks or rocks (?stones – in American usage a rock is a stone) at you. They are noted for their high pitched whistle. They occupy the woods in summer, when leaves protect them from view. In winter they live underground, eating dried meat. It is said they wear scarves and shoes. [M6 C11]

NALUSA FALAYA Choctaw Indian term for a BHM.

NAMIBIAN FLYING SNAKE The Namaquama of the Namib Desert, Namibia, tell of a flying snake, speckled and with wings sprouting from its neck or mouth, with horns that curve backwards and a light on its forehead. One is here reminded of the French vouivre and the South American carbuncle. It may be that the so-called wings are merely membranes that help it glide, for the manner of its flight is that it jumps from a ledge and "flies" down to the bottom.   [S8]

NAMORODO A creature in the beliefs of the Australian Aborigines of West Arnhem Land. They are flying creatures, formed of skin, bone and shreds and the wind whistles through them as they fly.

NANDI BEAR A creature reported from Kenya. Unfortunately, much confusion surrounds this beast It has been identified with the chemosit, a mythical beast in which the Nandi believe; but there also seems to be a less mythical form of the chemosit, which may be an undiscovered form of giant baboon. Some people seem to think of it as some kind of bear and its Swahili name seems to be related to the Arabic word for this animal. It may in fact be a ratel, which is very ursine in appearance, especially as a ratel of advancing years can lose its distinctive stripe. It has been suggested that hyena-like descriptions of the beast may mirror the existence of a supposedly extinct ungulate with claws, such as the chalicothere, which would look like a horse-sized hyena, but such an animal cannot be blamed for the Nandi bear's alleged depredations. The odd hyena with erythraism, which imparts a reddish colour to the skin, may have added to the confusion. [H9]

NANNUP TIGER A mystery animal reported in Western Australia in the 1970s. It may have been one of a surviving population of thylacines.

NANT'INA Denaine Athabascan term for a BHM.

NAPE This word is an acronym for North American Ape, coined by Loren Coleman, who holds that such creatures exist in the United States and are quite distinct from sasquatches. Unlike recognised apes, they walk and run upright and they appear able to swim. From reports he has gathered he argues they are tailless, 4-6'/1.5m tall, brown or black in colour, with occasional grey or white specimens, perhaps due to aging. He tentatively suggests they are surviving dryopithecines.   [C19]

NARANJITO BIRD This was a bird with black feathers, 3-4'/1m tall and with a lupine muzzle rather than a beak observed on a roof in Naranjito, Puerto Rico, in 1995. [C23]

NASNAS Name given to a wildman by the Tajiks. It is recorded from the 10th Century when it is used by the Arab writer Makdisi. Nizam al-Arudi uses the same term in the 12th Century.   [T1]

NAWAO Tall hominoids covered with hair in Hawaiian tradition. They subsisted on bananas and are now thought extinct.   [S5]

NAZARETH DODO A dodo, perhaps a distinct species from that of Mauritius, mentioned by the explorer Cauche in 1638. He seems to have placed this on the island then called Nazareth, now called Ile Tromelin in the Indian Ocean. It is by no means impossible there are still dodos here, as there is no record of their being wiped out. There may also be dodos on other islands in the area.   [S5]

NDALAWO A mystery animal reported from Uganda. Its fur is black on the back, but the lower parts are grey. It is said to hunt in small groups and to give voice to hyena-like laughter, but to be fiercer than an hyena.   [LS7]

NDAMATHIA Kikuyu term for the dingonek. [#4]

NDENDEKI *see* **Giant Turtle**.

NDESU A large hominoid found in the Congo (Brazzaville). It is on the ferocious side, with a taste for human flesh, but singing and dancing distracts it from anthropophagous intent.   [E]

NDZOODZOO A kind of unicorn reported from South Africa in the 19th Century. Only the males bore horns. It was about the size of a horse. The horn was flexible, but would stiffen if the beast were enraged. [G7]

NEGINLA EH Yukon Indian name for a BHM.

NEITHER In English folkore of the New Forest, the hybrid of a grass-snake and an adder, held to be longer but thinner than the latter..   [C1]

*NEOSHO TURTLE **A gigantic turtle weighing, it is said, over 400 pounds, seen in the Neosho River (Kansas) in 1937.   [C/H]***

NEPALESE MYSTERY CREATURE A report dated 3rd August, 1999, claimed there was a mystery beast in western Nepal with a tendency to bite. It looked like a Tibetan dog, but it had a white stripe on its neck. Its tail was bigger than a normal dog's and most of its body seems to have been white. It was supposed to have actually killed a man in 1996.   [84]

NEPALESE TREE BEAR According to local lore, there is a bear in Nepal smaller than the Asiatic black bear that frequents trees. It is called by locals *sano reech*. A number of skulls have been found and a living specimen was discovered in Kathmandu Zoo. These bears may be nothing more than juvenile Asiatic blacks (*Ursus thibetanus*), despite Nepalese assertions to the contrary.   [S5]

NEVADA GIANT WORM The *Weekly World News* informs us that Nevada is home to giant carnivorous worms that will attack and devour small animals.

NEW CALEDONIAN MONITOR A monitor known to science only from a fossil, yet locals aver it still exists.   [B6]

176

NEW HAMBURG CREATURE A creature described as "lizard-like", three toed, four legged, scaly tailed and greenish brown, was frequenting the town of New Hamburg, Ontario, in the 1960s. It was seen by quite a number of people, including the chief of police. It was thought it had emerged from the Nith River, which flows through the town.   [C22]

NEW JERSEY DRAGON This existed in Indian belief and they named the area in Bucks County it was thought to frequent "Dragon Place". In 1677 Swedish explorers found dragon-like footprints in the area.   [C19]

NEW MUNSTER CREATURE In 1992 a woman in New Munster (Wisconsin) saw a creature she could not identify, bigger than a dog and smaller than a cow. Because of its peculiar appearance, she took particular notice of it, which she would not have done had it seemed a normal kind of animal.   [A1]

NEW YORK FLIER This creature was reported from New York state in 1974. It had a body resembling a human's, a monstrous head and a wingspan of 9-10/3m..   [R6]

NGOIMA A large bird described as having wings 9-13'/3-4m, said to be found in the Congo (Brazzaville). The beak is aquiline, the colour dark brown to black. [25]

NGOLOKO A large apelike creature which has been reported in northern Tanzania. [H9]

NGOROLI An animal supposed to dwell in the River Vovodo in the Central African Republic. It is said to have tusks or prominent teeth, to be hairy and to be 10'/3m long.

N'GUGU Masai name for the Gerit. [H7]

NGUMA-MONENE This looks like a large snake, yet it has a serrated ridge on its back and the natives say it is not actually a serpent. However, one must be careful here, as its tongue is supposed to be forked like that of a snake. It lives in the Dougou-Mataba River in the Congo (Brazzaville).   [M1]

NGUOI RUNG A wildman reported from South-East Asia, believed to flourish particularly where the borders of Laos, Vietnam and Cambodia meet. In fact, we may be dealing here with more than one species. Some of these creatures are reportedly small and can make fire. Some are distinctly larger. It is said that sometimes when people are sitting around a fire a nguoi rung will come and join them, sometimes making noises interpreted as words. One type is said to be of fearsome aspect and will pierce banana trees in order to obtain the juice. There is a story that, during the Vietnam War, two nguoi-rung fell into the hands of Korean soldiers, but nobody knows what befell them. [2]

NIAGARA RIVER MONSTER Sightings of a monster in this US river have been reported since 1817.   [C1]

NIAN A creature from Chinese mythology. This monster was in the habit of hunting people until an old man suggested they scare it off with gongs, fireworks and bonfires. The stratagem worked. The tradition has been kept up to celebrate the Chinese New Year.

NIGHT THING A sea creature reported from Dominica. It seems similar to the St Lucia thing. On this island, however, it is believed to be nocturnal. [10]

NIMBUNJ A small hairy hominid of Australian Aboriginal lore.

NINGPO SEA SERPENT In 1881 a sea serpent was observed from Ningpo, China. It had a flat head, was estimated at 120-140'/36.6-42.7m long and had large yes.

NINKI-NANKA A horned mystery animal said to dwell in the marshes of Gambia. This creature, which has dragonlike features, is said to have claimed victims as late as the 1990s. It is very much feared. [85]

NIP CREATURE A small unidentified creature, reminiscent of a monkey, was seen on an island called the Nip near Brockton (Mass.) in 1980. [B9]

NIRIVILU A large serpent with wolflike characteristics reported from South America. [#12]

NITTAEWO Small hominids reported from days gone by in Sri Lanka. They are now possibly extinct. Their hands were adorned with claws and they were hairy. They used their claws to disembowel animals. They were said to possess a twittering language which was comprehensible to the Veddas, a pygmy race of humans who were their enemies. The Veddas' bows and arrows gave them a distinct advantage when fighting with the nittaewo. The Veddas are said to have eventually driven the remaining nittaewo into a cave and then started a bush fire, which suffocated them. This is thought to have happened about 1800.   [C21 H9]

NO MAN'S FRIEND POND MONSTER The "pond" in question is a thickly wooded swamp in Cook County, Georgia. No description of the monster has been accessible.

NOB HILL BOOGER Nob Hill lies near Springdale, Arkansas, and its vicinity was said to boast a hairy man, perhaps a bigfoot, and certainly an albino. It was not reported after the 1970s.   [Y]

NOGGLE An animal of the kelpie kind in the lore of the Shetland Islands.

NO-KOS-MA A creature like a bear in some respects, with a large snout, in the beliefs of the Cree Indians.   [M7]

NOOCONA A South Australian name for the yowie. [H6]

NORFOLK CREATURE A mystery animal spotted in Norfolk, England, in 1994. It could have been a large cat, a dog or a pony, but R. Trew, who photographed the beast, did not think it was any of these.   [#1]

NORTH SASKATCHEWAN RIVER MONSTER This beastie, 50'/15m long, chased Chief Walking Eagle in 1939.   [K4]

NOVA SCOTIA SEA MONSTER The *Halifax Herald* reported that on 25th June, 2003, a monster, at first mistaken for a log, was sighted off the Nova Scotia coast. The creature had a turtle-like head. The body was about 26'/8m long. There have been over thirty sightings of monsters off the Nova Scotia coast in the last 140 years.   [12]

NOVI KNEZEVAK SHEEPKILLER A mystery animal killed many sheep in this part of Serbia in 2001. Guard dogs did not oppose the creature, whatever it was.   [E]

NSANGA An animal described by P. Gratz as a 'degenerate saurian'. I take it this means a saurian of diminished prowess rather than one given to drink and debauchery. It resides in Africa, is smooth-skinned and clawed. It may be some kind of monitor (*Varanus*).   [H9]

NSANGUNI A water monster said to dwell in Luanshya River (Zambia). [E]

NTAMBO WA LUY A creature bearing some similarity to the dingonek, found in the Congo (Kinshasa). It is about 25'/7.5m long and can be found both in and out of the water. It has a single horn.   [S6]

NTARAGO *see* **Rurutargo**.

NTYII In Gabon, this is supposed by natives to be a form of gorilla unknown to zoologists. [H7]

NUNDU A monster of African legend. At times it is thought to be a lion or leopard of gigantic proportions. Some say it is invisible. According to some, no one has ever described it as none who has seen it has lived to tell the tale. It may be a personification of disease or drought.   [K5]

NUNYENUC A gigantic bird in which the American Indians believed. They distinguished it from the thunderbird.

NYALMO A Nepalese and Tibetan apeman, said to be 10'-13'/4m tall. Nyalmos are reported to have an unintelligible language and to perform dances in which one of them plays a drum.   [C21]

NYAMA Legendary monster of the Ituri River (i.e., part of the Aruwini) in the Congo (Kinshasa), with a small, crested head and a body of hippopotamine proportions. [C1]

NYAMI NYAMI Monsters of this name have been reported from Lake Kariba and the River Zambezi, which separates Zambia from Zimbabwe. They are said to be larger than any other denizen of the river and they perhaps attain a length of 130'/40m. Sightings of them involve conflicting reports.   [79]

NYAN A large creature like a great serpent which lived or lives in rivers in Bengal and Myanmar. It had a tendency to eat elephants. It would wrap itself around them and drag them into the water.   [75]

NZEFU-LOI An animal of the waters in the Congo (Kinshasa), with a body of almost hippopotamine dimensions, a horselike tail, tusks of ivory and a long neck. A man called Le Petit claimed to have seen these creatures on a couple of occasions. They resembled elephants, but their necks were about twice the length of those animals'. Their heads seemed to be more egg-shaped than an elephant's. It is not impossible that we have here surviving dinotheriums, in which case their tusks would have pointed downward rather than upward, a fact on which Le Petit does not seem to have voiced a statement. [H9]

O

O BICHO A creature reported from Brazil. It is said to be a bipedal reptilian creature, dark grey in colour, with thin arms and long claws. It was blamed for the loss of livestock and B. Steiger thinks it identical with the chupacabras.

O GONCHO A Japanese dragon that turns into a bird with a golden plume every fifty years. This is when the term *o goncho* is correctly applied to it. It sings an awful song, portending sickness. The last such singing was reported in 1834.   [J2]

OAXACA FISH In 1648 at santa Maria del Mar in the Mexican state of Oaxaca, a fish of awful aspect came ashore. It had forefeet and a pillar-like tail and was over 40' long. It died on the beach.   [C3*]

OCEANIC SEA SERPENT Captain Brocklehurst of the *Oceanic* saw this creature a short distance under the waters of the North Pacific. It was pale yellow and he estimated its length at 40'.

OCHEYADAN CREATURE A boy saw a 6'/1.8m long creature drinking from this Iowa lake in 1976. Though unidentified, it may have been a bigfoot. [B9]

OCONOMOWOC LAKE DEMON A monster reported from this lake in Wisconsin. [R4]

OEH A Quinault Indian name for a BHM. It is believed to be man-eating and consequently to be avoided by the cautious traveller.   [90]

180

OGOPOGO The most famous of Canada's lake monsters, this cryptid is said to inhabit lake Okanagan (British Columbia). The Indians knew of it, calling it *Naitaka*. They thought it lived at Monster Island and also seem to have associated it with Squally Point. Although reports of the creature go back to early times, there were notable sightings in 1926. In that year the name Ogopogo, taken from a popular song, was applied to it.

We are not, of course, speaking of a solitary beast. A population of the creatures must exist. They are described as being 30-70'/9-21m in length. The head is shaped like a horse's (or sheep's), with horns or hornlike protruberances. Various shades of colour are mentioned, dark green, black, etc. This may imply no more than different perceptions due to light and visibility. The eyes are said to be large, the skin scaly and the back has humps or else is coiled. The animal has been credited with four legs or flippers. The tail is forked or else divided into two flippers. Ridges spring from its back.

Indian legend said the beast was in fact a murderer whom the gods turned into a serpent in punishment for his crime. Whites first seem to have seen it in 1860 and a specific sighting was made by Susan Allison in 1872. A brace of the animals were espied in 1890. Over the years numerous people claim to have sighted the beast. It is claimed it sometimes comes ashore. A dinosaur-like creature with four legs was actually reported swimming alongside a boat in 1979. In January, 1984, a reward of $1,000,000 was offered to whomsoever should prove the creature's existence. John Kirk and others had a sighting in 1989 and described the animal's skin as being like a whale's. Later in the year Kirk saw two animals at the same time.

Photographs and film footage of the alleged monster have been taken. There was a noteworthy film taken by A. Folden in 1968. John Kirk filmed a 40'/12m creature in 1986. An animal leaving a long wake was filmed by a television cameraman in 2001. A further ninety seconds of footage of the beast were shot in 2002.

The species now enjoys legal protection. [G1]

OGOPUP The term applied to the young of the ogopogo. Ogopups were allegedly seen in 1948. [G1]

OGUA A serpent sighted in the Monongahela River (West Virginia). One was supposedly killed by settlers in the 18th Century. It was found to be roughly 20'/6m long. Others are supposedly still there. It is said to weigh 500 lbs and to be 20'/6m long. It is said to emerge at night and kill deer. [S15 #17]

OHIO CREATURE This strange creature, seen on 11th December 2003, seems to combine the characteristics of deer and bear, had a slender muzzle, very thin legs and was covered in black hair. Its eyes were red. It was about 6.5'/2m in height. [2]

OHIO RIVER MONSTER In 1959 a couple of reports by telephone were made to police regarding some strange creature in the Ohio. Neither witness seemed able to describe what he had seen. [#2]

OHIO WILDMAN A wildman covered with hair and of gigantic height is reported to have attacked a man in an equipage in Ohio in 1869. He and his daughter fended off the attack. The creature was believed to be living in the woods near Gallipolis. [#2]

OH-MAH An alternative name for the sasquatch or bigfoot formed from Hoopa *oh-mah-ah*. The Yurok use the term *ohmah*.

OIECHEK In the United States this legendary little beast is supposed to look like a shrew, but is animated by a voracious appetite, which causes it to attack sleeping human campers. It burrows into them and devours them from within. It takes the bones of its victims to make its den.   [A]

OI-UMAINA A creature said to live in the Amala River (Africa). Its head is said to resemble a dog's. Its neck is short, as are its legs, which have claws on the end. It is said to be 15'/4.5m long. [C1]

OIL PIT SQUID These creatures resembling squid were found in 1996 in the toxic liquid in a sludge pit in Indiana.   [E]

OIL SQUEEZER A legendary water bird of China. If you kill it, squeeze the oil out of it and throw it back into the water, it will revive.   [#11]

OJANCANU A large cruel giant in the lore of Cantabria, Spain. The female (*ojancana*) has the habit of throwing her breasts over her shoulders, like various wild women in folklore. The ojancanas are cyclopean. They lodge in caverns from which they rarely emerge.   [4]

OKEFENOKEE GIANT There is some evidence that the Okefenokee Swamp in the southern USA was once occupied by giant humans. Spanish explorers claimed the trees changed into giants which fought them. In the 1920s giant skeletons were found in a mound on Floyd's Island. More were discovered on a mound on Chesser Island in 1969. [46]

OKEFENOKEE TIGER Tigers, apparently just like the Asiatic variety, were reported from the Okefenokee Swamp in Georgia (USA) between 1835 and 1845. Around 1840 a Mr James shot one. Another, missing a paw, was also killed. The missing paw had been apparently hacked off by a determined woman with a hoe some time earlier. Another tiger attacked and injured a boy named Stewart. This (or possibly a similar beast) was killed by pursuers subsequently. Whether these tigers were the descendants of escapees, had been set at liberty or were some native American species cannot be determined.

OKIND A large creature described as a serpent often seen in the River Hvita in Iceland in 1636. It may be the same kind of creature as the one supposedly seen there in 1595. *See* **Hvita Monster**. An unidentified creature of some sort was seen in the river in 1702. [H8]

OKLAHOMA LAKE BEAST A strange creature reported from several lakes in Oklahoma. It is red-brown, has leathery skin, small eyes and tentacles. It may be a kind of freshwater octopus.   [30]

OLD HAIRY A strange creature washed up at Delake (Oregon) in 1950. Various savants pronounced on its nature, but no final identification was ever made. It was supposedly covered in hair, had the body of a cow and boasted nine tails. [101]

OLD LYME ANIMAL In Connecticut in the summer of 1986 a strange animal was reported which seemed to combine the characteristics of dog and rabbit. It was over 18"/45cm tall with a rabbit's head and floppy ears. The rest of its body seemed doglike. It had a long, thin tail.   [B9]

OLD MAN OF MONTEREY A sea serpent that has been seen many times from the vantage point of Monterey (California).   [B7]

OLD SHEFF Apelike creature reported by more than sixty people in Crawford County, Kansas, in 1869.   [C19]

OLD WALLEYES A creature in Ozark folklore. He is very large, has four legs, clawed feet and vacant eyes, which may indicate he is blind. This will not stop him from chasing and devouring you, should he fancy a snack. He is supposed to live in a cave. Of course, if a genuine mystery animal lies behind the folkloric creature, there are probably several living in several caves.   [Y]

OLD YELLOW TOP A large humanoid reported from Ontario. It seems to have generally dark hair, while that about the head is lighter. It was first reported in 1906. Another sighting took place in 1923. It crossed the road in front of a bus driver named Latreilla in 1970. If all these sightings refer to the same kind of animal – on this timescale we are hardly dealing with a single creature – there may well be a species like, but distinct from, bigfoot/sasquatch in the region.   [C21]

OLETAGY MONSTER A large unidentified creature reported from the Oletagy River (Ohio) in 1982. Witnesses included firemen and policemen.   [C1]

OLITIAU A black, flying creature, the size of an eagle, with pointed teeth in its mouth, encountered by zoologist Ivan T. Sanderson in Cameroon. He identified it as a kind of bat, yet it was a bat unkenned by science. Natives became extremely scared when they were told it was in the neighbourhood.   [H9]

OLIVER This ape's unusual gait gave rise to the suspicion that he might be the hybrid of a human and a chimpanzee; but scientific investigation proved he was merely a chimpanzee with an unusual gait.

OL-MAIMA Masai term for the dingonek. [H9]

OLO-BANDA A mystery ape reported from Assam, perhaps identical with the bar-sindic.   [#4]

OMAXSAPITU A large bird in the lore of the Blackfoot Indians. Some reports of this may have been inspired by sightings of condors or golden eagles (the bird's name means 'big golden eagle'), but one reliable report says it carried off a hunter with a deer on his back – a feat far beyond the capacity of any known bird. The hunter, White Bear (died 1905) lived to tell the tale.   [H]

ONE-EYE A monster said to be found in Lake Granbury, Texas. Since the Spanish period there have been stories about a monster in this lake. Most sightings report a serpentine beast, though the possibility that it is a freshwater octopus has been mooted, as a boatman in 1998 reported that his craft had been attacked by tentacles. The lake is well stocked with fish, which would supply food for large denizens.   [38]

ONE-LEGGED MEN The reference is, of course, to races of men believed to be one-legged by nature, not by mishap. The Baronga believe in a race of one-legged men with wings. The Zulu also believe in a one-legged race called the Amadhlungundhlabe. [W2]

ONGLO The East Visayans of the Philippines believe in this species of giant, which lives in swamps and breaks shellfish with its hard knees and elbows.   [R1]

ONIJORE A water monster in the lore of the Iroquois. [F1]

ONONDAGA LAKE MONSTER The Onondaga and Iroquois Indians held in their legends that this lake contained a monster able to quit its habitat and cross the land. The coming of the paleface has led to the most appalling pollution of this body of water. Any monster would need to be on the tough side to survive there. Yet a monster, looking like a dragon, was reported there by cub scouts in 1977.   [120]

ONZA A large felid of America which for many years was suspected by cryptozoologists of being an unknown animal. However, investigation has revealed it is actually only a puma (*Panthera concolor*), perhaps with some specialised adaptive features.

OOGLE-BOOGLE There is supposed to be a population of these monsters to be found in Lake Watherton (Montana). Each is supposed to have no less than forty horns, but perhaps prongs are actually meant.   [B7]

ORANG BATI A flying creature said to live in Indonesia, on the island of Ceram. Its wings are black, its skin is red. It looks like a human 4-5'/1.3m tall. It comes out at night only and it is said to lurk in caves around Mount Kairatu.   [87]

ORANG DALMO A large, apelike creature said to be found at the head of the Endau River in Malaysia. The height of this creature is said to reach twenty feet. [C21]

ORANG GADANG A large primate with bushy hair, said to exist in Sumatra. Its height is reported as 7.5'-12'/2-3.66m.   [5]

ORANG KUBU   Walter A. Gibson in *The Prison at Waltervreden* (1855) mentions a hominoid so called. He saw one being used as a slave in Palembang (Indonesia). It was hirsute and chinless, but had a pleasant expression. It may be another name for the Orang Pendek, which is sometimes called Orang Gugu.

ORANG PENDEK   In Indonesian lore, a small hominoid, also known as the gugu or sedapa, believed to range from 2.5-4'/45cm-1.2m in height. It is supposed to be covered with brown hair, this hiding a pinkish brown skin, and it is said to be abdominous. It seems to stay mainly on the ground. One observed in 1916 ran on its hind legs. A Dutch settler reported an encounter which he shared with an overseer in 1910. Another settler, who saw one in 1917, said it was definitely not an orang-utan, but resembled a siamang. However, siamangs are arboreal. A man called van Herwaarden claimed to have seen one close to in a tree in 1923. He described it as being hairy on the front and back, but said the face was virtually hairless and seemed to come to a point more than a man's would. More recent sightings include one by Deborah Martyr in 1994. She has since seen   the creature on a number of occasions. Creatures seen after an earthquake near Liwa in 1995 were said to look like orang pendek.   It was said a specimen was actually captured in 1958, but disappeared in a time of political turmoil. Alleged tracks and feeding places and possible sample hair of the orang pendek have been found.   It has been suggested that this animal forms a relict population of *Homo erectus*, but this is very hypothetical.   Deborah Martyr has said the creature is gracile yet strong looking, resembling a siamang on steroids.   [H9 #1]

ORANG SANAT   Sumatran name for Orang Dalmo.

ORANGE EYES   A creature with bright orange eyes said to sneak up on couples amorously involved in motor vehicles. One description says it was orange all over and 11'/3.15m tall. Some people say it has a bigfoot-like appearance. Those of a more sceptical bent say it is merely a hermit. Folklore makes it impervious to bullets. It is supposed to be found near Ruggles Road, close to Milton (Ohio). [C13]

ORANGE MOUND CREATURE   A mystery creature from the region of Memphis (Tennessee). It has never been seen, but many dead cats and dogs have been ascribed to its depredations and growling noises thought to originate from it have been heard. [1]

ORANGE RIVER MONSTER   Since 1890 there have been various reports of a monster in this river in South Africa. In 1910 a creature with a huge head and a curving 10'/3m long neck was seen.   [C1]

ORCHUN   A sea monster of medieval lore with a propensity to attack whales, first wounding them and, on their sinking to the bottom, pelting them to death with stones. [151]

OREGON CRITTER   A creature observed in a pond of 5-6 acres. The witness claimed it was a large black animal with an orange shell-like centre and tentacles. [#11]

OREL BEAST In 1895 a mysterious predator was reported from Russia. Various identifications were proposed for the beast, such as panther, tiger or dog. It eventually devoured a couple of poisoned sheep and went off into the woods. There, presumably, it died. In fact, there may have been more than one beast involved and they may have belonged to different species.   [S7]

ORIGES In days of yore this was supposed to be a beast whose hair grew backwards in the direction of its head.   [H12]

OROCOVIS CREATURE A creature with an approximately manlike form with a shining yellow-orange skin, observed in Orocovis (Puerto Rico). The same creature or similar ones were later seen in the same area and in Morovis in 1995.   [C23]

OSHADEGA A large eagle in Iroquois lore, it is the cause of rain, for, when it flaps its wings, water comes down from the lake on its back.   [N2]

OSLOFJORD SEA MONSTER A sea monster estimated at 60' in length with humps was seen in 1902 in this location off the Norwegian coast.   [B9]

OSOYOOS LAKE MONSTER A huge monster, 100' long, has been reported from this lake in British Columbia. The only sighting seems to have been in 1923. [K4]

OSSUM LIZARD A giant lizard was reported from this location in France in the late 19th Century and also in 1939.   [B9]

OUUAHI A kind of anthropoid whose hair is reddish. It is supposed to live in South America.   [E]

OWLMAN A strange winged being sighted in Cornwall. In 1976 it was seen by two children named Melling in 1976 near Mawnan Old Church. They said it had an owl-like head, a human body with wings with claws and no separate arms. Later a sighting by a mother and daughter was reported at Lamorna. It was seen by two girls, Sally Chapman and Barbara Perry, both 14. At first they thought it was a man, but then it took off. Their drawings correspond to the Mellings' description, though they added crab-like claws to the feet. In 1978 a man named Opie claimed his daughter had seen it. Three French girls made a similar report. In 1998 or 1999 a couple with the pseudonyms Gavin and Sally claimed a sighting. They said the Owlman was about 5' tall. The eyes glowed. The colours were grey and brown. Gavin said there was an ankle halfway up each leg, but no knees.

An explanation of the nature of the Owlman cannot yet be provided. It has been suggested that it was a hoax by the flamboyant Doc Shiels, but veteran cryptozoologist Jonathan Downes does not believe this to be the case. That it could be something like the tulpa of Tibetan lore has also been proposed. This is supposedly a creature that can be created by human mental energy. [D7/A]

OZAENA A sort of evil smelling polyp in Spanish lore. They usually dwell on the sea bed. Although they are generally small, they have been known to grow to very large proportions and even to attack shore dwellers. [4]

OZENKADNOOK TIGER An animal reported from Wimmera District (Victoria), Australia. A photograph was taken in 1964, but the animal is only partially visible among the undergrowth. Some think it is a surviving thylacine, but the stripes in the photograph are to the front, not towards the rear. It could, however, be a freakishly striped specimen, but the obscurity of the picture makes this impossible to ascertain with any certainty.

P

PA SNAKE A gigantic snake of Chinese legend, which was said to swallow elephants and eject their bones three years later. [G7]

PADDLER A monster supposed to be in Lake Pend Oreille (Idaho). It may be no more than a large sturgeon. It has been suggested that the US Navy fostered stories of the monster to cover up secret operations in the lake.   [C20]

PAINT RIVER MONSTER A humped creature was reported from this Michigan lake in 1922.   [125]

PAL RAI YUK *see* **Tizheruk.**

PALMYRA WHALE An otherwise unknown whale observed in 1868 off Sri Lanka. [E]

PAMA-YAWA A huge, grey cat, said to be 7'/2m long, reported from Ecuador. It is believed to prey on tapirs.   [30]

PAMBA A monster said to live in Lake Tanganyika. If a red reflection can be discerned on the lake, it means the pamba is about, looking for canoes to swallow.   [M7]

PANGUICH LAKE MONSTER A monster reported from this lake in Utah in the 19th Century.   [79]

PAO'O FISH A kind of divine fish in Hawaiian mythology. There was more than one of them and they were brothers to the sea-dwelling woman Lalohona.

PARADISE PARROT This Australian bird (*Psephotus pulcerrimus*) was believed extinct, having last been seen in 1927. However, there are now reports of its survival. [#9]

PARAGUACO RIVER MONSTER   This river in Brazil was the location of a reported sighting of two monsters reminiscent of dinosaurs. Each had a fierce-looking head and a neck 6' long. The total length of each monster was said to be 30'/9m.   [C1]

PARKER'S SNAKE   An unknown snake with quick-acting poison reported from Papua-New Guinea.   [E]

PARTRIDGE CREEK BEAST   In 1903 some hunters in the Yukon followed the tracks of what appeared to be a huge animal. The tracks led to Partridge Creek, a gulch. The hunters then betook themselves to the Indian village of Armstrong Creek. Here, joined by a Jesuit named Lavagneux and a hunter named Dupuy, they decided to return to Partridge Creek to discover the beast's identity. They observed a huge saurian, 50'/15m long and having an estimated weight of forty tons, scaling a ravine. Its skin was grey-black and it had a horn on its nose, which was probably why the Jesuit identified it as a ceratosaurus. The creature, which had been clearly visible, then bounded down from the ravine. The Jesuit saw the beast once again on a later occasion, crossing a frozen river, a caribou in its jaws. If it was indeed a ceratosaurus, it would need to be warm-blooded to survive in the cold of the northern Canadian wilderness.   [S6]

PASSENGER PIGEON   This bird (*Ectopistes migratorius*) was supposed to have become extinct in 1914. It may still exist, as reports of it have come in from Michigan, New Jersey and Wisconsin.   [30]

PATAGONIAN GIANT   A race of giants was once said to live in Patagonia (Argentina). Pigafetta, who accompanied Magellan, claimed to have seen a man twice the normal size there in 1520. Drake had a brush with tall men there in 1578, when their height was estimated at 7'6"/2.3m. In 1592 A. Knyvet measured dead bodies of some Patagonian giants, saying some were as tall as 12'/3.6m Sebald de Weest in 1598 spoke of Patagonians 10' tall. In 1764 very tall Patagonians were reported, but their height was said not to exceed 9'/2.7m. An attempt by French captain A. Guyat to bring some home by ship in 1766 was unsuccessful. After this they may have intermarried with other tribes leading to a reduction in height. Their height may have been exaggerated by early observers in the first place.   [K2]

PATAGONIAN PLESIOSAUR   Whether this creature in an apparently unnamed Argentine lake was actually a plesiosaur or not, this nickname was applied to it. It was reported in 1922 by a man named Sheffield, who said the neck was like a swan's and who deduced the body resembled a crocodile's. An expedition led by C. Onelli failed to find the creature.   [C25]

PATAGONIAN UNICORN   In the old days, say the natives of Patagonia (Argentina), there were many unicorns about, but now they have been killed off. However, paintings of these animals have been found in caves.   [31]

PATUKI A fish in the legends of Easter Island. Its description bears some similarity to the coelacanth.

PAVAWKYAIVA In Native American mythology, an otter or otter-like animal, said to live in Arizona nad New Mexico. [30]

PAVUS MARIS In medieval lore, a creature that combined features of peacock (above) and fish (below). [151]

PAYETTE LAKE MONSTER A creature said to inhabit Lake Payette, Idaho. It was reported in 1944 as being 35'/10.7m long with camel like humps and a seemingly shell-like covering. There have been other reports. The monster is known by the nickname of "Slimy Slim". [B11]

PAYMUR A term used in Siberia for certain lacustrine monsters. Their bodies resemble those of crocodiles, while their heads are similar to that of the giant species of catfish, the wels (*Silurus glanis*). [C3]

PAYSHTA Anglicised form of Irish *peiste* (also found as *piast, peist*) used to mean a lake monster in general. In current Irish the term is more often used to mean a worm and has also been used to translate 'reptile'.

PE DE GARRAFO *see* **Mapinguary.**

PEARL TURTLE Six-legged turtle reported to exist in China. [E]

PECTEN In medieval lore, the pectin was a fish to be discovered in sandy ground and, if disturbed, it would wink. [151]

PEEL STREET MONSTER A creature which attacked children in Wolverhampton in 1933-4. Eventually George Goodhead struck it in self-defence with a brick and assorted passers-by kicked it to death. The creature could not be identified. A female coati was found nearby, leading some to think this was the identity of the mystery creature, but its behaviour was not consistent with that of a coati (*Nasua nasua*). Some anonymous person suggested it was an ant-eater. [126]

PEEWAUKEE LAKE MONSTER A creature that spouted water like a whale, but looked more like a serpent and was green in colour was reported from this Wisconsin lake in the 1890s by a number of witnesses. [A1]

PEGASUS In Greek mythology, the winged horse ridden by Bellerophon. Pliny uses it as a common noun to mean a kind of horned winged horse which he understood to be found in Ethiopia.

PEGGY SEA-SERPENT This creature was seen in 1852 from the ship *Peggy*. It looked like a huge conger-eel, 100'/30m long, with a snake's head. [H8]

PEG-LEG Among bigfoot-like creatures, this one is indeed unusual, for it has a wooden leg. It tended to be seen on Georgia highways in the 1970s. Perhaps it was an ordinary bigfoot with an arthritic limb.   [B7]

PELOBO *see* **Mapinguary.**

PEMBROKE DOCK SEA MONSTER Pembroke Dock is in the Milford Haven waterway in Wales. An unidentified creature with a snake-like head and a dorsal fin was spotted here in 2003.   [12]

PEN MONKEY *see* **Ink Monkey.**

PENINSULA PYTHON A huge snake reported by several witnesses in Ohio in 1944. Its estimated length was 18'/5.5m. While its existence was not in doubt, no one can tell how a beast of such proportions came to be in that area. It eventually disappeared. [C19]

PENNOCK ISLAND MONSTER Off this Alaskan island a creature with a bovine head and dorsal fins was reported in 1947. [B9]

PENNSYLVANIA CREATURE A seven foot tall humanoid which smells like a wet dog, has short brown hair and a face which is covered with hair from the eyes down. An anonymous professor who used the pseudonym 'Jan Klement' noticed this being in the vicinity of his cabin in Westmoreland County, Pennsylvania. He left out apples for it and was able to study it from nearby. It was carnivorous – he saw it killing a deer – and he eventually found it dead and buried it. The professor claimed the creature did not really look like either a human or an ape.   [C21]

PENNSYLVANIA MOTHMAN In June 2003 a creature of the mothman kind was seen near Harrisburg (Pennsylvania).   [28]

PE'PIR Yurok Indian name for a BHM which is perhaps considered at a psychological level to be part of an otherness of existence, perilous to the nation.   [W]

PERUVIAN TIGER A striped unidentified animal reported from Peru.   [30]

PERUVIAN WATTLE-LESS GUAN   An unidentified guan of Peru, perhaps a completely new species.   [30]

PERYTON A winged deer. Its feathers are blue or dark green and, surprisingly, it cast a man's shadow. We are told the species originated in Atlantis, but this is late information, coming from a 16th Century rabbi who claimed he learned it from a late Greek source. [57]

PETER POND LAKE MONSTER A creature has been seen going in and out of this lake in Saskatchewan. It has been described as scaly and nicknamed Puff, perhaps after the dragon in a well-known song. (There is a groundless legend that the same song is a metaphor for drug-taking).   [K4]

PETEY A furry creature that looks like the trunk of a tree. It tends to be reported from the same areas as the South American caa-pora.   [#12]

PEWAUKEE LAKE MONSTER A huge green monster, spouting water from its head, was reported in this Wisconsin lake in the 1890s. A spear thrown at it bounced off it. [R4]

PHANTOM KANGAROO The term applied to kangaroos said to have been seen in the United States, where kangaroos would not normally be. An early example is a sighting in 1899 at New Richmond (Wisconsin). Some of these may in fact be wallabies, which have become naturalised in Britain and could conceivably do so as easily in the United States. Some may be sightings of the cryptid devil monkey, which bears a superficial resemblance to the kangaroo. Out of place kangaroos are not unknown elsewhere. For example, one was reported from Beckenham Park, Lewisham, London. One has also been noted at Bosberg, Belgium, while a whole population of them, anything but phantasmal, escapees and/or their descendants, are to be found in Rambouillet Forest, west of Paris.

PHOENIX Herodotus tells us of the phoenix. It was supposed to visit Egypt every 500 years. It would place its father in an egg-shaped lump of myrrh and carry it to Egypt. Herodotus claimed to have seen pictures of the phoenix, saying it was the size of an eagle, partially red and partially golden.

Pliny wasn't sure it existed, but said if it did, it was mainly purple in colour. It was a single individual.

A phoenix was reported to have visited Egypt in 35 AD.

It is only towards the close of the ancient era that we first find the tradition that it sets itself alight and rises from its ashes.

The colouring of the painting Herodotus saw is consistent with that of the golden pheasant (*Chrysolophus pictus*). This bird is found in China, but the occasional one may have been brought to Egypt by merchants. However, the traditional home of the phoenix was Arabia. It has also been suggested that the phoenix was in origin the Bennu Bird, the sacred bird of Osiris.

There is supposed to be a Chinese phoenix called the Feng-Whang, with a cock's head, swallow's chin, turtle's back and fish's tail. The *feng* was the male, the *hwang* the female. In Japan it was known as *ho* (male) and *o* (female). P. Costello argues that it is in origin Rheinhart's crested argus (*Rheinath ocellata*) found in Indo-China and Malaysia. [D8 #6]

PHOSPHORESCENT CREATURE Three such creatures were spotted by those aboard Thor Heyerdahl's famous *Kon-Tiki*, during the expedition of 1947. They had huge shining backs and were beneath the water, so detail of their appearance is lacking. [B6]

PHOSPHORESCENT SEA-SERPENT In 1966, John Ridgway and Chay Blyth rowed a boat across the Atlantic. On the night of July 25th, Ridgway was rowing while Blyth snoozled. Looking to the right (or starboard, as jolly tars call it), he beheld a long creature, perhaps exceeding 35'/10.5m, lit up with a phosphorescence reminding him of neon lights, heading towards the boat. It dived under the craft and he heard it come up briefly on the port side. [H8]

PHYSETER A sea creature which, Pliny informs us, was to be found in the Atlantic. It could stand up like a great column, higher than the sails of a ship.

PIAO A one-horned beast in Chinese legend. It is a kind of deer. One was supposedly captured during the reign of Emperor Wu (BC 141-87). It may be identical with an animal called the *chang*.   [G5]

PIASA Louis Joliot, a Canadian, commenced his exploration of the Mississippi in the 17th Century, accompanied by a Father Marquette. On cliffs overlooking the present day Alton (Illinois) they saw paintings of two huge, bizarre creatures. Of one only the head remained, erosion having destroyed the body. The other was still intact in its full glory. This was the *piasa*, a creature which featured in the lore of the local Indians. Father Marquette penned a description: it was horned, horrific, red-eyed, beared like a tiger, somewhat human-faced and sporting a tail that wound back around the body, passing over the head and between the legs, with a fish-like end. He does not mention wings. The pictograph was in three colours, green, red and black.

We don't hear anything further of the piasa until after 1800. By this time the head of the second creature may have disappeared, leaving only one form to gaze down on the waters below. This did not have long to last – it vanished between 1852 and 1867. It was said that, in days agone, passing Native Americans used to fire arrows at the picture. When they graduated from the bow to the gun, they showered the monster with bullets, which were said to have destroyed the image. Others said that quarrying in the vicinity had caused the cliff face to collapse.

Although the picture was gone, an article written in 1883 by an eyewitness described it as being red, black and blue in colour, though these hues had become much faded. The head was like a bear with a mouthful of teeth and faced the onlooker. It had the antlers of a wapiti, a scaly piscine body and wings. The tail was long enough to be thrice wrapped round the body and was spearheaded.

The Miamis seem to have been the Indians who were wont to fire arrows at the creature. It was said that, in a battle, the piasa had carried off two of their chiefs, much to the delight of their opponents, the Michegamies, who had in fact made the piasa image.

The Illini, it is said, spoke of a single – or perhaps only a certain – piasa which had acquired a taste for human flesh. They destroyed the beast by letting their chief Ouatago (also referred to as Massatoga) act as a decoy. When the winged gourmet appeared with hungry intent, hidden Indians ended its career with poisoned arrows.

A John Russell averred he had visited the piasa's cave in 1836 to find the floor covered with human bones. However, some say Russell invented the story of Ouatago and the bones. Some would identify the piasa with the thunderbird, but its anatomy has singular features which make such an identification doubtful. The good burghers of Alton have, in modern times, had a new image of the piasa painted on the cliff face. [H]

PICTISH BEAST The Picts (in their own language, *Priteni*) were one of the early peoples of Scotland. A beast which defies identification appears amongst their carvings in stone. It has legs, a dolphin-like beak and a strange attachment which has been compared with a trunk coming out of the back of its head. As it occurs on a number of stones, it has been argued that it is not an imaginary creature. A. Shields feels it might be an unknown kind of cephalopod, identical with the Loch Ness Monster. He calls this the elephant squid. [S8]

PIG-EAR-EATER This peculiar animal was seen, but could not be identified. It was black and grey, had short ears and a shaggy tail, was almost as tall as a human's waist and would attack pigs, but eat only their ears. Its depredations occurred in 1977 near Bay Springs (Mississippi). [B9]

PIGMAN A strange creature reported from Vermont about 1971. It began when people in the Turkey Hill area found their cats and dogs disappearing. Then one night a farmer disturbed a man-sized creature going through his garbage. This being was covered with light-coloured, perhaps even white, hair and had the face of a pig. The same creature scared the living daylights out of four youths who surprised him in a sand pit. Jeff Hatch, a high school student, and others decided that a nearby pig farm might yield some answers to what the creature was. The farm seems to have been abandoned, though hogs of large size were roaming about it. They also discovered a small room attached to the barn which contained some hay, flattened as if someone had slept on it. There were dead dogs and cats in the room, perhaps partially eaten.

Near to the farm motorists started having sightings of the Pigman and one, who emerged from his vehicle, was attacked by it. He mentioned that his assailant had clawed or taloned hands rather than swinish trotters. The Pigman was said to have taken up residence in a cave. There was speculation that it was a human-pig hybrid. It has not been seen for many a year. [C8/A]

PIKELIAN A hominoid in the lore of the Evens of Siberia. It is said to be of human stature with grey/brown hair. Pikelians will eat roots and are said to steal reindeer meat; this they keep fresh by storing it in puddles. [B3]

PIKE-LIKE HEADED CREATURE Lady Gregory was told by an informant that he was troubled one night by something unidentified lying on his body. One night subsequently, when he had a light on in the room, he saw the terrier he was keeping there fighting with some creature whose shadow on the wall showed it had a head like a pike's. This happened between Waterford and Tramore, Ireland. [G12*]

PINATUBO MONSTER A name given to a number of animals seen in the Tiklo River in the Philippines. They are said to be 7'/2m long, 3'/90cm wide. [9]

PING-FEN A porcine creature with a head at either end, said by the Chinese to inhabit Magical Water Country. [B10]

PINK ALLIGATOR Two encounters with this creature were reported in 1976 near Andytown (Florida) by the *Fort Lauderdale News.*

PINK AND WHITE SEA SERPENT This curiously coloured beast was observed by Captain Roberts of the *Emblem* in 1885. Its back was striped pink and white, its underparts pink. The good captain estimated its length at 60'/18m. The sighting took place to the south of the Azores.

PINK CREATURE It was big, pink, resembled a worm and was espied in an artificial swamp in New Jersey by I.T. Sanderson in the 1950s. [C1]

PINK-FOOTED DUCK A species of duck (*Rhodonessa caryophyllacea*) supposedly extinct since the 1940s. However, reports of alleged sightings show it may still exist. [S4]

PINK GOANNA A large pink lizard of unidentified species seen and photographed in Australia in 2002. [#1]

PINK GRASSHOPPER Unidentified grasshopper observed in North Carolina. [120]

PINKY For many years there have been reports of a pink-coloured reptilian-looking creature in the St Johns River, Florida. There was a clear sighting on May 10th, 1975. A pink head, reminiscent of a dinosaur's, came up from beneath the water, striking one of the witnesses as though its skin had been removed, exposing bones beneath. Horns, with knobs atop them, were like those of a snail. On its neck it had gills or fins. Its eyes were slanted. [S6]

PIRANU A horse-headed black fish which dwells in rivers. It has a reputation for ramming boats and is said to be found in Argentina. [M7]

PISHO PALANG A mystery animal reported from Afghanistan in 2003. Some describe it as feline, some as vulpine, some as canine. Whatever they are, Afghans have little doubt there is a population of them on the loose. Some declare they may be man-eating feral cats. Many suspect they were introduced to the country by the Americans. [201]

PISTRIS A creature of Greek mythology. It had a dragon's head, fins in lieu of forelegs and a fish-tail. Andromeda was about to be sacrificed to it, but she was saved by Perseus. [B13/A].

PITMAN'S WHALE This unidentified whale is to be found in the eastern Pacific, according to R.L. Pitman, who wrote of it in 1987. It can be either black and white or grey/brown. It is not certain if it is a new species. [S8]

PITT LAKE CREATURE Creatures noted in Pitt Lake (British Columbia) have been referred to as "alligators", but alligators would not thrive so far north. It has also been suggested they are giant salamanders, which is more plausible. Indeed, on one occasion they were described as "lizards" and it was even alleged that three were captured. [K4]

PIWICHEN A South American flying snake which is said to suck blood. [#12]

PLANCTOSPHAERA PELAGICA An acorn worm of whose adult form science knows nothing. Specimens were collected in 1932 in the Bay of Biscay. [S8/A]

POH A very fierce animal in Chinese legend. Pohs could be used in place of warriors. They were to be found in Mongolia. They looked like horses, had single horns, their bodies were coloured white and their tails black. Their teeth were likened to those of a saw. They had tigrine claws and, indeed, both tigers and leopards formed part of their diet. Their howling was like a drum roll. [G5]

POISONOUS MEN Peter Heylyn, a writer of the 17th Century, asserts there was a race of men who were poisonous, so poisonous they could even poison a snake. These people were called the Psylii and lived in Libya. [H12]

POLISH MYSTERY BEAST A mysterious animal, supposed by some to resemble an hyena, made various attacks upon sheep about 1716, but always evaded hunters. Its identity was never discovered. [#8]

POMOLA According to the Wabanaki Indians of Maine, you should keep away from Mount Katahdin, the state's highest eminence, or you will antagonise the birdlike pomola that lives there. [4]

PONIK Name given to a monster said to live in Lake Pohenegamook in Quebec. A description given about 1874 puts its length at 35'-40'/10-12m This is the first recorded sighting, but it has been reported up to modern times. It is said to have a dorsal fin. In the nearby town of Saint-Eleuthere, a Ponik Festival is held regularly. [B9]

POOLE ISLAND MUTANTS In the US Army research centre at Poole Island (Maryland) it has been alleged mutant creatures have been produced and it is said there are such things as fish with deer's feet to be found here. [C23]

POPOBAWA A cyclopean dwarf with talons, vespertilian wings and a hairy body reported a number of times from Zanzibar (including Pemba) where it was said to have sodomised shocked sleeping Zanzibaris. [#9]

POPOKE *see* **Maipolina.**

PORTSMOUTH SEA-CREATURE A strange serpentine creature with a large head, estimated at about 15'/4.57m long, chased swimmer Rachel Carney off Portsmouth

(Rhode Island). The animal was greenish-black with white underparts. The incident occurred in 2002.   [12]

POSKOK   A jumping snake reported from Croatia, Serbia, Montenegro and Herzegovina. It is said to be venomous. Some think it identical with the nose-horned viper (*Vipera ammodytes*), but uncertainty attends this. It may be that the term *poskok* is applied sometimes to this, sometimes to another variety of snake.   [S8/A]

POTOMAC PATTIE Alternative name for Chessie.

POTTSTOWN CREATURE A strange creature described in a variety of ways, which seemed to have had a most impressive tail, but to have made a variety of animal noises. It was being blamed for killing chickens in Pottstown (Pa.) in 1945 and was said to have intimidated children by snarling at them.   (Speaking as a schoolmaster, I have endeavoured to do the same thing on occasion).   [R6]

POUA-KA On Mount Torlesse in New Zealand the Waihata tribe of Maoris claim this gigantic bird dwells, a huge eagle with a taste for human flesh. The legend of this avian may preserve a memory of *Harpegornis*, a gigantic extinct variety of eagle.   [#8]

POWNAL WILDMAN In 1879 a wildman was seen near Pownal (Vermont) by two hunters. It was red-haired and had a beard. One of the hunters fired at it and it chased them off. Years before there had been a supposed wildman in the Green Mountains. [47]

PRAATZELWURM Alternative name for the tatzelwurm.

PRAIRIE FIEND An unidentified animal exhibited in Mander's Travelling Menagerie in England in 1869. The proprietors said it came from North America. It had an hippopotamus-like head, an ursine body, tigrine claws and equine ears. The knowledgeable zoologist Clinton Keeling suspects it was in fact a chemosit, the cryptozoological animal from Africa.   [#16]

PRESSIE A monster reported from Lake Superior. Sturgeon and catfish, both of which can grow to prodigious size, have been suggested as possible explanations. The monster takes its name from the Presque Ile River.   [40]

PRESTONBURG ANIMAL This unidentified dog-like creature jumped on the back of a pony in Prestonburg (Kentucky). It was brown with a long tail and larger than a fox. [B9]

PRICCOLITSCH A were-dog in Romanian belief. [S17]

PRIMIHOMO ASIATICUS Kazakhstan and Kyrgyzstan are an area where there are many reports of hominoids. In 1914 zoologist V. Khakhlov gave the above Latin name to the wildmen of this area.

PRINCESS SEA-SERPENT   An extraordinary sea-serpent, supposedly seen in the South Atlantic from the ship *Princess* in 1856. It had a long back (20-30'/6-9m) and a long tail. Its head was like a walrus's and it had twelve fins.   [H8]

PRIVATEER SEA SERPENT   In 1887 this creature was sighted by the captain of the *Privateer* in the Atlantic. It was very black and looked like a long snake.

PROCTOR VALLEY MONSTER   A 7'/2m tall hairy monster in the lore of South County (California).

PROTO-PYGMY   Term used by cryptozoologists to designate small hairy hominoids. Some of these may simply be the young of bigfoot.   [C20]

PSEUDO-STEGOSAURUS The name is my own coining for the creature seen by P.G. Lavesque near Bloomfield, Vermont, about 1971. He said it was small, but bigger than a woodchuck, covered with black shiny fur and it rocked from side to side as it walked. However, it had the "posture and mannerisms" of a "stegosaurus or something". I am not sure how anyone could know much about the posture, let alone the mannerisms, of a stegosaurus, but who am I to quibble? An old hermit told Lavesque he had seen two or three of these animals in his lifetime.   [C8/A]

PUCK BIRD A bird of English folklore said to spread disease among cattle. It seems to have been regarded with a certain horror. One was reported around Fittleworth (Sussex) in the 19th Century.   [#1]

PUERTO RICO LAMPREY An unidentified lamprey spotted by Jonathan Downes in Puerto Rico, where no lampreys are supposed to be found. It looked like a European lamprey, but was a little larger. As he did not retain the specimen, its identity remains a mystery.   [#1]

PUGWIS A sea-swelling hominid with a face like a fish's and a pair of incisors in the lore of the Kwakiutl Indians. It is supposed to lurk in Puget Sound in Washington state. [C18]

PUK A small dragon in Germanic lore. It lived in a human's house and brought its master riches. It measured about 1.5'/45cm.

PULULUKON A horned water serpent revered by the Hopi, Zuni and Kere Indians. [J2]

PUMINA A very long python reported from the Congo (Kinshasa). It is said to reach 40' in length.   [#4]

PUMPKIN-MONSTER A huge living gourd in Swahili tradition. It was able to speak, lived in a lake and swallowed a great many humans. Another human-swallowing pumpkin-monster is to be found in the traditions of the Anitamba of Tanzania. [W2]

PURPLE MONSTER A vaguely described creature reported without details of place or date on an Internet site. The witness claimed it was purple and shining and had an ugly head. It was standing on top of a neighbour's storage building.   [99]

PYGMY BROWN BEAR A small variety of brown bear reported from Peru. It is presumably not called Paddington. [30]

PYGMY ELEPHANT Although alleged pygmy elephants have been captured and actually kept in zoos, many scientists are reluctant to regard them as a separate subspecies of the African elephant (*Loxodonta africana*). Some, however, have argued for the uniqueness of pygmy elephant skulls, which they feel confirms their separate identity. These beliefs would refer to pygmy African elephants. However, it has now been established that there is a population of undisputed pygmy Asiatic elephants living in Borneo.   [B6]

PYGMY GORILLA It has been argued since 1877 that there is a separate species of pygmy gorilla . However, many scientists believe that any specimens adduced in such arguments are merely abnormal ordinary gorillas.   [B6]

PYGMY PLESIOSAUR A name given, perhaps quite inaccurately, to two long-necked animals, apparently reptilian, which have been observed in the Auyan-Tepui, a river in Venezuela.   [C1]

PYGMY RHINOCEROS A small species of rhinoceros, rumoured to be found in Liberia and farther afield.   [H9]

PYRAGON According to Porta (17th Century), a strange creature generated in the fire, which flew about over the flames. However, should it venture away from the fire into the cold air, it would undoubtedly perish.   [H12]

PYRALIS A winged insect with four feet mentioned by Pliny, who maintained it could fly in and out of fire unhurt. It was also called a *pyrausta*. The name clearly comes from the Greek *pyr,* 'fire'.

Q

QATTARA CHEETAH A kind of cheetah reported from the Qattara Depression west of the Nile since the 1960s. It is paler than the normal cheetah and has a heavier coat. Ibrahim Helmy Alaa has appealed on the Internet for help to prove it is a separate subspecies. There is a report of a specimen being killed in 1967.

QIQION The Eskimo say the qiqion is to be avoided, as it causes the beholder to fall into a fit. It has hair on its mouth, ears, feet and the tip of its tail. No other details seem available. [H2]

QIU LONG In Chinese dragon lore, a dragon with horns. [J2]

QOQOGAQ In Alaskan Eskimo lore, a white bear with ten legs.   [E]

QUAGGA The quagga , a member of the zebra family, brown in colour and striped only in the foreparts, is generally regarded as having become extinct in 1875, but there have been a few reports of the animal in Namibia. Heuvelmans doubts that these are genuine quagga.   [#4]

QUANG KHEM Called "the deer that moves slowly".   The supposed skull of this Vietnamese creature, unknown to science, has been discovered. The horns on the skull were no more than spikes and its DNA did not match any known animal's. [51]

QUATO Term used in Guyana for a sort of hominid covered in hair.   [#4]

QUEEN RAT I am not in the habit of frequenting the London sewers. In Victorian times, however, there was a class of people called *toshers* who did so, fishing for any useful objects they might find. Strangely enough, few careers advisers today recommend this as an occupation. Amongst them the legend of the Queen Rat flourished. This rat could change herself into a beautiful girl, but she had claws in lieu of toenails. Her eyes in the light would resemble animals'. She had a tendency to seduce toshers, in the process perhaps giving them a rat bite on the shoulder or neck. This seems to have been quite harmless, despite the fact that rats' teeth are usually caked with bacteria. [S9]

QUEENS BIRD An owl-like bird with blazing eyes started flying into the faces of startled New Yorkers in the borough of Queens in 1934.   [B11]

QUEENSLAND TIGER Although the term *tiger* is applied to this creature, it may not be feline, but rather a marsupial with a catlike appearance, filling in the niche which big cats occupy in other ecosystems. Remains have been found of an animal called the *thylacoleo*, a marsupial creature looking like a large cat, and Queensland tigers may constitute a surviving population. The earliest recorded sighting was in 1864 and others followed. The stripes of the animal are yellow or grey and black, they come up from the abdomen and may not join up at the spine. It is said to be the size of a dingo and to have a long tail. Its habitat is the northern part of Queensland, which was largely unpenetrated by whites before 1890. It seems to be identical with a fierce animal called the *yarri* by the Aborigines. White old timers who spoke of the tigers do not seem to have regarded them as uncommon. Science for a while looked benignly on the tiger's existence, but then, as no one had ever produced a dead body or a pelt, zoologists became sceptical. However, reports continued at least into the 1970s and the animal may still thrive. Indeed, according to researcher D.A. Wright, there are as many as five sightings of thylacoleo per day. [H6]

QUICKFOOT Term applied to a 6'/1.8m tall hominid reported from the Bathgate Hills (Lothian) Scotland.   [E]

QUINCY CREATURE A peculiar and unidentified animal with short legs and a tail which it dragged behind it, said by one witness to have the "sleeky" (?shiny skinned) look of a seal or an eel, has been reported in the city of Quincy, Massachussetts, from time to time. [B11]

QUINQUIN A name applied to the Australian yowie. It was, however, more widely applied. The Yalingi said that most quinkins were small, but one had been a hairy giant named Turramulla, who had three clawed digits on each hand and foot. Cave paintings which apparently depict Turramulla were discovered in the 1970s. [H6]

R

RABBIT-DOG A creature described as having the body of a dog and the head of a rabbit, seen in the vicinity of Old Lyme, Connecticut, in 1986. It had long floppy ears and hopped about in the manner of a rabbit. [B9]

RABBIT-FOX In 1990 it was reported that three people in Poland claimed to have seen a mysterious animal with a rabbit-like nose and a tail resembling that of a fox. [#12]

RABBIT-LIKE CREATURE It was the size of a dog, had a catlike head, rabbit ears and body and an elongated neck which bore tangled spotted hair. Its eyes were black and oval. It proceeded by hopping. It was seen in Roseburg (Oregon) about 1999. [2]

RACCOON-CAT HYBRID Although such an hybrid would be quite impossible genetically speaking, a belief once obtained that such hybrids had indeed occurred and were the origin of the Maine Coon cat, a now well established American breed of domestic cat. An equally unlikely scenario is that these cats are descended from hybrids of domestic cars and bobcats.

RAICHO A crow-sized legendary bird of Japan, which makes a huge noise and lives in a pine tree. [K7]

RAINBOW SERPENT A huge serpent in the legends of the Aborigines of Australia. It is also called *Ngalyod, Almiedj, Yulungu, Julunggul.* It is just possibly based on a 10-16'/3-5m long snake *Wonambi naracoortensis* which is known from the fossil record and may still have been in existence 30,000 years ago. The Yoruba of Nigeria also belive in a rainbow serpent called *Oshunmare* and this belief is shared by persons of Yoruba descent in Brazil. Amongst the Ewe of western Africa the rainbow is said to be the reflection of the giant serpent Anyciwo. [4 84]

RAJU A strange creature in Japanese lore which seems to be a primate with a slim body and badger-like claws. It is said to become agitated during thunderstorms, during which it develops a yearning for human flesh. [120]

RAKSHI-BOMPO A small kind of humanoid or anthropoid in Himalayan lore. [T1]

200

RAM HEAD SEA MONSTER Near this location in Victoria, Australia, a sea monster was observed by the crew of a steamer in 1902. It was 30-35'/9-10.5m in length, the head was larger than a seal's and it had four fins.   [B9]

RASSELBOCK Horned rabbit in the folklore of Thuringia (Germany).

RAT-CREATURE A creature that looks like a rat and weighs eight pounds was captured by soldiers in Beijing in 1995. They could not identify it.   [22]

RAURACKL A hare with horns in which Bavarians believed in the 16th Century. Horned hares or rabbits seem to have been taken seriously by zoologists of old. Gesner makes reference to *Lepus cornutus* and horned rabbits are mentioned in P.G. Schott's *Physica Curiosa* (1667). Buffon also believed in them. There is a disorder called Shope papilloma which may cause a lagomorph to appear horned.

RAZOR-BACKED HOG A ferocious animal with a spiked back reported from parts of Florida.   [30]

RED-BACKED POLECAT This animal, of which a population exists in Co Durham, is of a copper-red colour. No known ferrets or polecats are supposed to have this colouration, but locals in Durham seem quite familiar with them. They may represent a separate subspecies.   [21]

RED CAT 1 There seems to have been some kind of legend of a singular red cat in the north of England. The cat is sculpted as a capital in the chapel of Brimstage Hall, built in 1376. In Brimstage village there was a small pub so-called, destroyed before World War I. Another Red Cat pub is to be found in Crank, there is a Red Cat Lane in Burscough and a Red Cat Hill in Harrogate. To continue the tradition, a Red Cat Inn has been built in Greasby; but what exactly this red cat was or is supposed to have done is known no longer.   [W4]
2 A cat with a bright red coat was reported in the vicinity of Mavagissey (Cornwall) in 1995 and was blamed for killing deer.   [146]

RED CEDAR LAKE MONSTER In the 1890s a serpentine beast was reported on a number of occasions in this Wisconsin lake.   [R4]

RED CHEETAH These have been seen from time to time in Tennessee. It is not impossible that they are a surviving population of mircaonyxes, cheetahs that flourished in prehistoric America.   [32]

RED DOG FOX *see* **Yakhetan Amai.**

RED HORSE LAKE MONSTER A greenish-black creature said to have breathing tubes in its head and to be 60-80'/18-24m long has been reported a number of times from this Ontario lake.   [101]

RED MOUNTAIN BEAR A mystery bear observed in the Andes of South America. [30]

REIFFINGER SEE MONSTER A monster is reputed to inhabit this lake in Austria. [#9]

REMORA Pliny assures us that the remora is a kind of fish. It will adhere to the keel of a ship and slow its progress.

RENXIONG Alternative name for the yeren, meaning 'man-bear'.   [D5]

REPTILE-FISH The *Washington Post* in 1923 reported strange fish with reptilian features in a pond near Medicine Lodge (Kansas). Their heads were like those of catfish, but they had four legs. They used their tails for swimming. They seemed to be confined to a single pond on the farm of one A.J. Shaw. Their bites had proven fatal to some cattle.   [47]

REUNION SOLITAIRE A mystery bird reported from the Indian Ocean island of Reunion. It is perhaps an ibis, as ibis fossils have been found on the island. [E]

REUSS MONSTER In 1556 a monster was reported from this Swiss river. It came out at night and attacked calves.   [M7]

REYNOLDS LAKE MONSTER Described as a giant snake with a very big head and large eyes, this creature was reported from Reynolds Lake, Kentucky, in the 1960s. [29]

RHINOCEROS DOLPHIN These have two dorsal fins and may be either dolphins or whales. Reports of these creatures come from both the Pacific and the Mediterranean. [32]

RHINOCEROS WHALE *see* **Giglioli's Whale**.

RHONE MONSTER Monsters were reported from this long French river in 1954-5 and one was seen at its mouth in 1964.   [B9]

RI This was thought to be an unknown merbeing of Oceania. However, cryptozoologists investigating the matter demonstrated it was actually a dugong.

RI RIU A species of dragon which can see prey a hundred miles away. [J2]

RIDGE-BACK DOLPHIN A pinkish-brown dolphin in the lore of the Amazon Indians. A photograph of this creature has been taken.   [30]

RIJS HOUND A large phantasmal hound said to be found on the Rijs-Oudemirdam Road in the Netherlands.   [A]

RIMI A carnivorous hominoid supposed to live in the Himalayas. [L1]

RINGDOCUS *see* **Shunka warak'in**.

RIO ACRE CREATURE A creature reminiscent of a dinosaur reported from Acre state in Brazil.

RIO DE JANEIRO SEA MONSTER A 100'/30.5m long sea monster with green scales and a long neck was seen from this Brazilian city in 1982.   [B9]

RIO DE LA PLATA CREATURE A strange creature which could not be identified, with large fins, a turtle-like shell and a fan tail, was pulled out of this river by Uruguayan fishermen.   [#9]

RIO GUAPORE CREATURE In this area, on the borders of Bolivia and Brazil, a dinosaur-like creature has been reported.

RIVER DINOSAUR In Colorado there have been reported over the years lizards, estimated at 5' long, said to be able to walk on their hind legs. The first report seems to have come from Pagosa Springs in 1982. A witness in Monte Verde described it as being 3.5' long and having a similar width. It appeared to run on two legs and wasn't a lizard. Its tail was two feet long.   Two women described it as having a long neck and skinny legs when it ran across the road in front of them in 2001.   [9 12]

RIVERSIDE CREATURE When C. Wetzel was driving his car in 1958 near Riverside (California), he noticed static on his radio. Then he was faced by a creature with a head reminiscent of a scarecrow's, lacking ears or nose, with a protruberant mouth. Its skin was scaly: the scales looke like leaves, but were definitely not feathers. The eyes were fluorescent. The legs were joined to the torso at the sides, not underneath. It both gurgled and screamed. It jumped on the bonnet (or, to use American parlance, the hood) of the car and clawed at the windshield. Then it fell off and the car ran over it. When police turned up, there was no sign of the creature. The next night something black frightened a motorist in the same area.   [C19]

ROA-ROA *see* **Moa.**

ROC An enormous bird of Arabian legend, capable of carrying an elephant in its talons. It may have been inspired by the elephant bird (*Aepyornis*) of Madagascar or merely by the discovery of its eggs. The sighting of an occasional albatross may have contributed to the myth.

ROCK HALL FLYING DEVIL A humanoid with wings that used to scare people in the vicinity of Rock Hall (Maryland). It was seen in the woods, it used to fly around Kent County and was once seen sitting on a post near Church Creek. [#7]

ROCK LAKE MONSTER A monster has been reported from this Wisconsin lake on a number of occasions. In 1867 a saurian was sighted, not alone in the lake, but also ashore. Two men were on the lake rowing a boat in 1882 when the monster appeared next to them, affrighting them considerably. One witness from the shore thought it looked like a dog. The last report of the monster on record is a sighting in 1943.   [R4]

ROD Rods – or, as they are sometimes called, Roswell Rods – were first discovered by Jose Escamilla. They are creatures supposed to move faster than the human eye can follow, but are susceptible to perception by camcorders. They have been caught on film both indoors and outdoors and similar things are said to have been found under the sea. Some people actually think it may be a form of fish in the sky and it is sometimes called a *skyfish*. R. Freeman argues for a possible invertebrate identity. In May 2003 rods were reported as having appeared on a wedding video taken near Alexandra, New Zealand. One appears to show up over Baghdad on a film taken for television during the Iraq War of the same year.   [12 14]

ROGGENWOLF A kind of werewolf in German folklore. It is represented by the last sheaf of corn and is supposed to have a mother called the *Kornmutter*. One wonders if the entire notion of lycanthropy is due in some cases to the effects of ergot, giving rise to the connection with corn.

ROOGAROO A hairy wildman in the folklore of Texas. Roogaroos are supposed to emerge from water to attack fishermen, according to the Sabine Indians. Amongst some Cajuns the term *loup-garou* (werewolf) is applied to them.   The term *rugaru* is used amongst the Chippewa (Ojibway) for a hominoid.   [R6/A]

ROPEN The meaning of this creature's name is "demon flyer". It has leathery bat-like wings, a tooth-filled beak and very sharp talons. It is said to occupy caves on New Britain and Umbi, islands which form part of Papua-New Guinea.

ROUMANI MONSTER According to a report of 1931, a supposedly unknown monster was found half interred in the sand at Roumani, Egypt. Its skeleton was transported to Cairo Zoo.   [C3*]

ROUND HEADS When Thor Heyerdahl was making his celebrated voyage aboard the *Kon-Tiki* in 1947, round-headed creatures (bodies not visible) surrounded the raft on a number of nights, staring at it. They had gleaming eyes and their heads were about 2-3'/60-90cm in diameter.   [B6]

ROUND SNAKE A snake of Chinese legend. It looks like a round and beautifully coloured stone, but if you pick it up it may bite you. Its poison is deadly. [#11]

ROW A large saurian supposed to have been observed in the 1940s, but some writers have expressed doubts about the authenticity of the sighting, which is alleged to have taken place in New Guinea. It is described as having a small head, a bony hood, a long neck, a huge body, triangular plates on its backbone and a tapering tail with a horn on the end. [H9 S5]

RUFFED CAT A mysterious cat of which Ivan Sanderson saw two pelts in Mexico in 1940. [S7]

RUGARU Chippewa Indian term for a BHM.

RUNNING MAN A speedy type of hominoid in Scottish lore, different from the Big Grey Man. Its features are described as being at once human and not human. It will tear along beside a car and look into the windows. [30]

RUSH CREEK MONSTER An unidentified monster at Rush Creek (Ohio), which hounds refused to follow. It left clawmarks, but was never actually seen. [132]

RUSH MONSTER A hairy biped said to live near Straight Creek in the Rush (Kentucky) area. In 1964 or 1965 a trio of investigators caught a strange creature in their headlights. One of them opened fire and the animal, very sensibly, ran away. The witnesses discounted the possibility that it was a bear, as it ran off on its hind legs. [40]

RUTURARGO This animal is also known as the *ntarago*, but that is its plural form. It may be another name for the marozi. Its cries were heard by big game hunter E.A. Temple-Perkins in Kenya. [H9]

S

SACALENGUAS Guatemalan name for a creature considered identical with the chupacabras.

SACRAMENTO RIVER MONSTER A creature with a lizard's head reported from this California river in 1891. [C1]

SACRAMENTO RIVER SALAMANDER A salamander less than 3'/90cm in length caught in this California river. It is of the same genus as the Asiatic *Megalobatrachus*, but its colour was very different from Asiatic members of this group and it may have belonged to an unknown variation. [B6]

SACRAMENTO SEA-SERPENT The helmsman and captain of the *Sacramento* reported seeing a sea-serpent in the Atlantic in 1877. Its head was like an alligator's, it looked generally like a large snake and seemed to be 50-60'/15-18m long. It had a pair of flippers and its colour was reddish-brown. [H8]

SADDLE LAKE MONSTER A number of reports had been made of a monster in this Canadian lake, with the result that an Alberta Government helicopter overflew it in 1984, but without spotting the creature. The monster itself was said to be horselike and 75-150'/23-45m long. [C19 B9]

SAGINAW MONSTER A hominid, perhaps on the scaly side, reportedly emerged from a river in Saginaw (Michigan) in 1937 and leaned against a tree, after a while returning to the water. [C18]

SAHAB A sea monster described by Olaus Magnus. Though huge, it has tiny feet, except for one big one that it uses to grasp food and to defend itself. [C9]

ST CROIX RIVER CREATURE A head with enormous green eyes popped out of this river in New Brunswick, startling a number of fishermen in 1903. [B9]

SAINT HELENA MANATEE A manatee or sea-cow, reported from this Atlantic island (where Napoleon spent his exile) until 1810, when it became extinct. There is some possibility it was an unknown species of manatee, for it would come ashore, which is not consistent with the behaviour of known species. However, others have suggested that the creatures described were merely sea-lions or sea-elephants. [#1]

ST JOHNS RIVER MONSTER A creature reported from time to time in this river in Florida. Mark A. Hall notes its resemblance to thescalosaurus.

SAINT LAWRENCE SERPENT A huge water serpent of Canadian folklore, 80'/25m long, said to be found in the Gulf of Saint Lawrence and to wreck many craft. [M7]

ST LEONARDS SERPENT A creature said to be still living in *A Discourse Relating to a Strange and Monstrous Serpent or Dragon* (1614) in St Leonards Forest near Horsham (Sussex). It had killed both men and cattle, the pamphleteer informs us, by its strong and virulent poison. It left behind it a trail of glutinous and slimy matter, not unlike that of a snail, though proportionately larger. It was said to be 9'/2.7m or more in length. It was thick about the middle and smaller at each end. Its back scales seemed blackish, its underparts red.   It killed two mastiffs set on it, but did not devour them. It was thought to subsist upon rabbits. Amongst witnesses to the beast are cited John Steele, Christopher Holder and a widow woman dwelling near Faygate.

ST LOUIS THING A peculiar creature, described by juvenile witnesses whom the police regarded as sincere, as half man, half woman, with half a bald head and half a head of hair. There is also some evidence that this creature was encountered by an adult. All this happened in 1963. One has to ask if the "thing" might really been a peculiarly dressed person with a strange haircut or wigs. [C17]

ST LUCIA LAKE MONSTER A 90'/29m long monster was reported from this South African lake in 1933. This lake is linked to the sea, where a similar creature was seen that night. [B9]

ST LUCIA THING There are reports of creatures of the coast of St Lucia called, simply, "things". One witness, a diver, spied two of them. Neither head nor tail seemed discernable. Each was about 7-8'/2.1-2.4m long. The same sort of creature has been reported from Dominica. [10]

SAINT-MAURICE BEBITE A strange creature whose remains were discovered near the Saint-Maurice River in Canada. Its head was lozenge-shaped and it boasted a tail and paws. Local speculation focussed on a possible extraterrestrial origin. [M7]

SALAAWA A creature reported from Egypt in the 1990s. Though doglike, they seemed to be smaller than dogs. Each had a brace of fangs. They were black. The hair of their coats was soft. [A]

SALAMANDRA A bird believed by the Arabs of yore to be the source of asbestos, which formed its plumage. [N2]

SALPA A fish of medieval lore which could be killed only if beaten severely with implements. [151]

SALTSJOBADSODJURET A sea monster with a thick head and humps observed off the coast of Sweden. [34]

SALVAJE A large mystery monkey reported from Venezuela and Mexico. It is said to be 5' tall. Its hair is reddish. It is credited with large lips. [C21]

SAN CLEMENTE MONSTER A sea monster seen off the California coast. It had a thick, long neck with a mane. Its eyes were protruberant.

SAND WHALE Writer A. Austin maintains there are living creatures on the planet Mars, capable of survival without oxygen. In support of this he adduces photographs which show forms he interprets as "sand whales" among others. Notable amongst these is Mars orbital camera image 45904a showing forms near the Martian polar regions. Image 53408 shows less distinct shapes which he interprets as "feeding microbes". One photograph he reproduces shows what he interprets as the skeleton of a sand whale. [A3]

SANDEWAN A legendary creature of Zimbabwe. There are no descriptions of this animal, as no one pretends to know what it looks like. It leaves bloody trails. [#12]

SANDMAN The Seminole Indians of Florida use this name for a BHM. [G7]

SANTA ANA CREATURE A 6'/1.8m beast covered with leafy scales which emerged from the Santa Ana River (California) and clawed at a car on 8th November, 1958. [A1]

SANTA CLARA MONSTER A marine monster was struck and either killed or severely injured by the ship *Santa Clara* off North Carolina. The creature's length was 45'/13.5m and it was said to have had a head like an eel's. [F5]

SANTER A fierce cat, unafraid of men, reported a number of times in North Carolina towards the end of the 19th Century. In fact, it appears that behind the reports lie a number of different animals, but some may refer to a genuinely unknown species of cat. Sightings of a mystery animal, identified as a santer, were made in 1934. [S7]

SANUWA A hawk of mighty strength in Cherokee folklore. It could carry off a child. [F10]

SAPO DE LOMA A large toad rumoured to live in South America. [S13]

SARGON This fish is mentioned by the writer Porta (17th Century) and, although he gives no description, he tells us that it greatly loves goats – not, apparently, to eat. Each sargon wants a goat to be its chum! Cunning fishermen disguise themselves as goats, so, when the sargon comes bounding towards them, they ensnare it. [H12]

SASA A ground bird the size of a barnyard fowl as yet unidentified by science, but to be found in Fiji, unless it has become extinct. [E]

SASABONSAM In the lore of the Ashanti of Ghana, a creature with a human face, a beard, small horns, stubby arms, vespertilian wings, wry legs and toes on the end of its feet. There are actually said to be three types of this creature. An account occurs of one being killed in 1928. It was about 5'/1.5m tall with a wingspan of 20'/6m. [35]

SASQUATCH An alternative name for bigfoot, used particularly in Canada. It is derived from Halkomelan *sossq'tal*, 'timber giant'.

SAT-KALAUK A former cryptid which has been identified as the yellow-throated marten (*Martes flavigula*).

SATOYCHIN A beast in the legends of the Tuchone Indians of the Yukon. These animals are supposed to live in the mountains east of Frenchman's Lake. Indians have noticed the resemblances between this creature and pictures they have been shown of ground sloths. The satoychin is supposed to eat beavers, but may be actually devouring the vegetable matter of their lodges. It has been reported in modern times. [#1]

SATYR A creature of Greek legend, combining features of goat and man. Satyrs were conceived as human to the waist, below which they were goatlike. At first they were thought to have human feet, but later these were replaced by caprine hooves. Early satyrs were merely represented as wild looking men with horse tails. Some of them may have been thought of as having canine parts. To what extent the cult of Pan, the goat god, contributed to their hircinity is perhaps difficult to evaluate. It has been argued that belief in satyrs was first brought to Greece from Illyria (i.e., the area north-west of Greece), but this is by no means established. [O C12]

SAUROPHIDIAN [literally, 'lizard-sepent'] A term applied by escaped convict Chariton Batchmatchnik to a creature which he claimed to have encountered in a Russian lake. During his flight from the authorities he claimed to have reached a hidden valley, which contained this lake-dwelling creature and a population of mammoth. He regaled a correspondent of the *New York World* with this information and it was published in 1873. He described the creature as 30'/9m long, with scales and large teeth. He once saw one attack a mammoth, which after a long struggle freed itself.   [C3]

SAVANNAH CREATURE In the late 1880s a long green serpentine animal pursued a woman along the banks of the Savannah River in Georgia. A serpentine creature had earlier been seen in the Savannah and subsequently at its mouth in 1854.   [F5]

SAY-NOTH-KAI Salish Indian name for the Sproat Lake Monster.

SCALED HOMINID Alfred Hulstruck, a New York state conservation naturalist, asserted in 1977 that a scaled hominid was appearing from the water in the southern part of the state seeking food in the uplands. It seems to have favoured a vegetarian diet. [C17]

SCALED RHINOCEROS A kind of rhinoceros supposed to exist in Java. It has been asserted to differ from the Javan rhinoceros (*Rhinoceros sondaicus*), but they may, in fact, be identical.   [S4]

SCHELCH A creature referred to in the *Nibelungenlied* (13th Century), a major German heroic epic. It has been suggested that the so-called Great Irish elk (*Magaloceros giganteus*), which was actually a giant deer, is the animal concerned. This creature is supposed to have become extinct over 10,000 years ago, but the above argument points to its existence into medieval times. However, it has also been suggested that the word means the elk proper (*Alces alces*) or even a wild stallion.   [S2]

SCHMIDT'S MONSTER In 1907 Franz Schmidt and Rudolph Pfleng were travelling on the Solimoes River in Colombia. On the shore they saw a huge head rise above 10' tall bushes. This possessed a snout reminiscent of a tapir's. The creature emerged from the trees and they saw it had clawed flippers instead of forelegs. The two men calculated its shoulder height at 8'-9'/2.5m   [S6]

SCHOMBURGK'S DEER A species of Asiatic deer (*Cervus schomburgki*) thought to have become extinct in 1938. However, there is some possibility a relict population still survives in Laos.   [74]

SCIAPODES A race of one-legged men of whom Pliny and Ctesias speak. They could lie on their backs and shelter from the sun under their single feet.

SCOFFIN A creature with a deadly glance in Icelandic folklore.

SCORPION-MAN A creature in Akkadian legend, scorpionlike to the waist, manlike below. They feature in the celebrated *Epic of Gilgamesh.*

SCOTTISH MOTHMAN This creature, described as looking like half man and half bird, was seen in 1992, perched on the branch of a tree in Edinburgh.   [F4]

SCOTT'S DOLPHIN An unidentified dolphin reported from the Straits of Magellan. [30]

SCRAG WHALE Although this animal (*Agaphelus giddosus*) is known to science, there is uncertainty about whether it is really a separate animal or merely the young of the right whale.

SCYRITAE According to Megasthenes, a race of people in India who have holes in their faces instead of noses (two holes to a face) and pliable feet, like serpents' bodies. [A2]

SEA ARMADILLO A creature described as looking like a cat surrounded by the shell of a lobster, according to Erik Pontoppidan.   [M7]

SEA BISHOP A fish supposed to resemble a bishop, for example, the top of its head looked like a mitre. In 1531 it was said one had been captured in Poland. Presented to the king, it at length signified it would like to return to the sea, so it was duly returned. (The King of Poland at this time was Sigismund I).   [L4]

SEA BULL A mysterious water beast which legend places in the Schwarzsee in Switzerland.   [M7]

SEA COBRA A horrifying sea-serpent, hooded like a cobra and extremely swift of movement, which fought with two men on the Alaskan shore. Jack Ross, a deputy marshal, who told the story to the *Juneau City Mining Record* in 1894, saw S.A. Keller lifted into the air in the creature's mouth. He shot the beast, making it release Keller, then shot it again and cut off the end of its tail, which wriggled back into the water. The creature then swam off. Ross estimated its length at 200'/60m.

SEA COW These seem to have featured originally as the kine of the merbeings of folklore. An illustration of one, with the foreparts of a cow and the hindquarters of a fish, appears in John of Cuba's *Hortus sanitatis* (1491). Belief in these creatures persisted at least until the 18th Century.

SEA DRAGON 1 A creature reportedly captured off the Suffolk coast in 1749. It had fins which could also serve as wings; it was scaly and had hooves and there were six rows of teeth in each jaw. It was about 4'/1m long and had a lizard-like head. It was reportedly netted with mackerel. It seems to have died and been put on exhibition. [#9]
2 A creature mentioned by Aldrovandus. It had forelegs ending in flippers, no hind legs and a beaked face. One wonders if it was inspired by a beaked whale, washed ashore and partially decomposed. [H12]

SEA ELEPHANT In modern zoology, this is just another name for the elephant seal (*Mirounga*).   However, Pliny avers that in the reign of Tiberius (14AD-37AD), many strange creatures were washed up on the shore, including "sea-elephants" that looked like elephants, except that they were white.   A French engraving of 1550 shows a sea creature with elephantine characteristics that is supposed to be based on an actual sighting.   [B5 S5]

SEA-GREEN MACAW This unidentified species of bird has been both seen and photographed, but its classification remains uncertain.

SEA HARE This creature was said to have a hare's head, ears and legs and a fish's body. On land it was rather fearful, but it was a fierce creature in the sea.

SEA HOG This fish was said to have the foreparts of a hog and the rear of a fish. [H2]

SEA HORSE A creature of classical lore, said to have the foreparts of a horse, including two legs, giving it its Latin name *equus bipes*, and the hindquarters of a fish. In the west of Ireland, it was believed that a kind of horse lived in the sea. A man told Lady Gregory he had actually seen one. [G7*]

SEA LION This is not the animal with which most of us are on terms of back-slapping familiarity, but a strange beast in which zoologists of yore believed. It had a rather rounded head, scaled body, four legs and a tail. It is described by Rondelatius in a book published in 1554.   [H12]

SEA MONK This was supposed to have a head like a tonsured monk, a cowl-like appendage, fins instead of arms and a fish tail.   [L4]

SEA OF GALILEE MONSTER The Sea of Galilee is a lake on the River Jordan, Israel. It is said to harbour a monster that has some of the features of a crocodile. [E]

SEA RAM According to Pliny, a creature washed up on the shore in the reign of Tiberius (14 AD-37 AD).

SEA SCORPION This creature , which resembles a large scorpion, has been seen off Miami Beach (Florida).   [30]

SEA SERPENT Undoubtedly one of the most well-known of cryptids and one which has had the odd friendly nod from mainstream zoologists. Gesner affirms there are two kinds of sea serpent, one yellowish and harmless if undisturbed and another which can reach a length of 200'/60m and will seize sailors from ships. Olaus Magnus, writing in 1555, assures us the beast is to be found off the coast of Norway and can reach 200'/60m in length. It has neck hair, is black in colouration, has shining eyes and will devour men. The good Burgomaster of Malmo claimed to have seen a sea serpent off the Norwegian coast, as Olearius informs us, in 1666. Ramus tells us of a sighting in 1687.

A rather spectacular sighting was described in a report given to Hans Egede, a Lutheran pastor in Greenland. From a ship off the coast of Greenland, it said a serpent was seen to raise itself up from the water. Its body was broad as the ship itself but longer and its head reached as high as the mainmast. It spouted from its nose and it had rough skin and paws or flippers. A Pastor Bing sketched the creature. It is perhaps interesting than Egede himself, in describing the animal, does not employ the term *sea-serpent*. There is a mistaken belief that Egede himself actually saw the creature.

In 1779 an American officer, E. Preble, saw a sea-serpent 100'/30m long and the length was confirmed by another witness. In Canada a schoolmaster called J. Wilson saw a sea-serpent in 1846 and placed its length at 70-100'/21-30m. A number of sightings occurred off the Norwegian coast in the 19th Century. The celebrated *Daedalus* sighting took place in 1848 and is the subject of a separate article. In the same year a similar animal was espied from the decks of HMS *Plumper* in the Atlantic. Over the years there have been sundry sightings, not all apparently of the same kind of animal. A number of these are given separate articles in this dictionary.

Pictures of sea-serpents generally show them undulating vertically. As true snakes undulate horizontally, this would indicate they are not true serpents ar all. It was reported that some sea-serpents would throw themselves over boars and sink thjem with their weight,

There have been various reports of stranded sea-serpents, but these often tend to be the corpses of basking-sharks (*Cetorhinus maximus*). This fish often looks like a saurian monster when the initial parts have rotted and probably accounts for the Stronsa beast of 1808 and the Zuiyo Maru "plesiosaur" of 1977.

To those who have studied reports of the beasts, it is clear that more than one kind of animal has been observed over the centuries. Bernard Heuvelmans proposed the following system of classification:-

[a] the *super-otter*, a somewhat seal-like creature;
[b] the *many-humped*, a lengthy creature with dorsal humps;
[c] the *many-finned*, a large creature, the so-called fins projecting from its sides;
[d] the *merhorse*, noted for its horselike mane;
[e] the *long-necked*, which, when going very fast, will look like a serpent;
[f] the *super-eel*. comprising a number of species;
[g] the *marine saurian*, which has a head like a crocodile's;
[h] the *father-of-all-turtles*;
[i] the *yellow belly*, which looks like a large tadpole.

Heuvelmans attaches a geographical range to each species. However, his classification has since been queried. G. Mangiacopra proposed a different system, but subsequently abandoned it. A more recent classification is by L. Coleman and P. Huyghe. A totally acceptable system can be constructed only when further data are available. [H8 B15 E1]

See also **Cadborosaurus, Daedalus Sea- Serpent, Santa Clara Sea-Serpent, Cleopatra Sea-Serpent** *and sundry others. Because sea serpent sightings are unlikely to refer invariably to the same animals, a number of articles have been devoted to individual sightings.*

SEA SOW An animal mentioned in the works of Aldrovandus. This scaly beast with webbed feet had, besides eyes in the usual places, several eyes distributed on its sides. [H12]

SEA UNICORN These days, this term is applied to the narwhal (*Monodon monoceros*), because it has a long single tusk like a horn which protrudes from its upper jaw. In days agone, however, there was a belief in actual sea-unicorns, that had the foreparts of a unicorn and the hindquarters of a fish. [H12]

SEA WEASEL It was said in the Middle Ages that, if this creature which combined features of weasel and fish, felt her young to be imperilled, she would swallow them, hie herself to a safer place and spew them forth again.   [151]

SEA WORM A huge monster that tended to swim into the Solway Firth (Scotland) and devour the fish on which the local economy relied. Eventually a palisade was erected below the tidal level and on this it spiked itself. The story cannot be dated. [W3]

SEAHAM CRAB A tiny crab found at Seaham-on-Sea (Co Durham). Although its existence is not in dispute, it seems quite unknown to science. It may be a colour variation of a known species.   [#1]

SEAHAM SEA SERPENT A creature espied off the coast of Britain by a number of girls in 2003. One of them, however, Terri Curtis, thought it likely to be a row of seals. [C3*]

SEARRACH UISGE In Gaelic, 'water colt'. This term was applied to a monster which looked like an upturned boat in a lake on the Scottish island of Lewis. It was reported in 1941.   [C25]

SEDAPA *see* **Orang Pendek.**

SEGAMAT GIANT An 18'/5.5m giant was reported by soldiers at Segamat (Malaysia) in 1966. [S4]

SEHITE One of a race of brown-haired hominoids, supposed by the natives to occupy forests in the Cote d'Ivoire. Trading between natives and hominoids is supposed to have continued until about 1935. A native told a Professor Ledoux that he had once seen one of the creatures caged. An elephant hunter named Dunckel claimed to have killed an unknown primate in the region, perhaps a sehite, in 1947. There may be some confusion between hominoids and traditions of pygmies who once dwelled in the area. [H9]

SEILEAG A monster supposed to inhabit Loch Shiel in Scotland. An old woman saw a speeding monster with three humps in 1874. A sighting occurred in 1905 from a witness aboard the steamer *Clan Ronald*. In 1926 the monster was observed through a telescope coming ashore at Sandy Point and a local hotelier said in 1933 he had been told it came ashore occasionally.   [C25]

SELKIE There is a belief found in Scotland and Ireland that there is a race of people in the sea of this name that cover themselves with sealskins, but will sometimes doff these when they come ashore. A recent book by J.M. MacAulay *Seal Folk and Ocean Paddlers* (1998) argues that its origin lies the occasional visits to Scotland by Lapps/Saami in kayaks, dressed in sealskins. There are supposed to have been unions at times between humans and selkies. The MacCodrum family claims to be of selkie descent.   [F4]

SELMA *see* **Lake Seljord Monster.**

SENMURV A legendary Persian flying creature, with a dog's head, a lion's body and an eagle's wings and talons.   [S8/A]

SERBIAN BLOODSUCKER Whatever this mystery animal was, it would kill sheep and suck their blood. This happened in 2000. An expedition to hunt down the beast proved fruitless.   [E]

SERDLERNAK A legendary bird of the Eskimo. [H]

SERPENT OF DALRY A white monster that wound itself about Mote Hill in Scotland. A local blacksmith made himself a suit of spiked armour, allowed the serpent to swallow him and then wriggled about inside, so that the spikes cut up the beast's interior, killing it. [W3]

SERPENT WOMAN A giant creature, the upper half woman, the lower half snake, who dwells in Lakes Huron and Erie, or so the Iroquois said. She drags men into the water to be her lovers and changes them into snake men.   [B7]

SERRA In medieval belief, a large flying fish.

SEVIER LAKE MONSTER A lake monster reported from this body of water in Utah in the 19th Century.   [79]

SEWANAWYTACH Columbian Indian name for a BHM. [H3]

SEYCHELLES WHALE Beaked whales of an unidentified species were observed off the Seychelles in 1980. [S5]

SHACKLE The wild shackle, called in Gaelic *buarach bhri*, was a river creature in which the Scots believed. It was believed to pull horsemen under the water until they drowned. The shackle must have been conceived as serpentine, for it would wind itself around the horse's legs, causing it to stumble. It sucked blood from its victims and this was said to ooze through nine holes in its back.   [F4]

SHAG A water monster supposed to have lived near Buckland (Surrey). The bloodstains of its victims are still pointed out on a rock. In ordinary usage, the name shag is sometimes applied to the green cormorant (*Phalacrocorax aristotelis).* [W3]

SHAGFOAL A bear-like animal, large and black with long hair, perhaps preternatural, reported from the region of Barnack (Northamptonshire). [146]

SHAGGY SHAPE This was over 6'/1.8m tall with no discernable facial features or limbs. It was encountered by a Mr and Mrs Singleton between York and Shipley. [141]

SHAMANU A subspecies of wolf (*Canis lupus hodophila*) which supposedly became extinct in its Japanese home in 1905. However, occasional reports indicate it may still exist. A possible specimen was photographed on Kyushu in 2000. [#1]

SHAMIR A strange creature in Hebrew lore. It was the size of a barleycorn and could be used as a cutting implement, being able to cut even diamonds. It was used for cutting into shape stones employed in the building of Solomon's Temple. When the Temple had been destroyed, the shamir was seen no more. [G4]

SHAMPE Shampes are gigantic humanoids in the lore of the Choctaw Indians. They live in a huge cave (or caves) and will not venture out in daylight. Some of them are hairy, some hairless. [147]

SHANGUI Alternative name for the yeren. It means 'mountain devil'. [D5]

SHANG YANG A bird of Chinese legend, the shang yang boasts a single leg. It drinks up river water, which it discharges as rain.

SHANNON MONSTER A monster with a small head, shining eyes and a neck about 12'/3.6m long was espied on this Irish river by many people on its banks and a ship's crew in 1922. [C1]

SHAR KHORKHOI A strange animal said to live in underground lairs in the Gobi Desert. [#8]

SHARPFIGHT MEADOW BEASTS Sharpfight Meadow lies on the banks of the River Stour in England. Two huge monsters, one reddish with spots, the other black, are said to have had a ferocious fight there in 1449. The black beast was triumphant and the combat gave its name to the location. The beasts were regarded as dragons. [#1]

SHEEP MUTILATORS Simian beings in the lore of the Navaho Indians. They left 5" footprints. [R7]

SHERMAN CREATURE A teenager from Sherman (NY) informed John Keel that, in the 1960s, creatures from a nearby swamp were observed by a number of persons. They sometimes walked on four feet, sometimes two (the creatures, that is, not the witnesses). When standing upright, they were 12-18'/3-5.5m tall. They also had long tails, 6-8'/1.8-2.44m. The creatures were covered in white hair.   [K1]

SHERWOOD FOREST THING A hominoid creature is part of the lore of Sherwood Forest. Four men searching for it one night saw glowing eyes about 8'/2.44m above the ground and made out a dark shape.   [31]

SHIASHIA-YAWA A large cat, smaller than a jaguar, white-furred and covered thickly with solid black spots, reported from Ecuador.   [30]

SHILLINGSTONE CASTLE CAT A large apparently preternatural cat reported from this earthwork in Dorset. Its tail was luminous.   [#6]

SHING MUNG TIGER A tiger reported in Hong Kong in 1965. Subsequently, it was alleged that the animal barked.   [S7]

SHINKE-CHO CREATURE This creature was observed by D. Nardiella in Shinke-cho (Osaka), Japan, in May, 2003. It had a face like a white snake's. a white neck, black eyes, catlike legs and paws, lizardlike body and batlike wings with which it flew off. [Sightings]

SHIRU These are hairy hominids reported from the Andes in Colombia and Ecuador. They do not tend to approach humans, though there is a report of one charging an Indian who tried to shoot him.   [S1]

SHOOPILTIE Alternative name for the noggle.

SHOOTER'S HILL ANIMAL An animal resembling a cheetah reported from the Woolwich area in 1963.   [S7]

SHORT GREY SNAKE Mystery animal in the lore of the Kalmyks of Russia. It is 20"/50cm long and seems to be no true snake, as it lacks bones. Strike it in the middle with a stick and it explodes. Apart from the standard variety, there is also supposed to be a shorter species. [#8]

SHOVELHEADED WHALE A kind of beaked whale reported from the Mexican coast.   [30]

SHTIYA Molala Indian term for a BHM. [H3]

SHUG MONKEY A shaggy, monkey-like creature, said to be seen from time to time in the vicinity of Rendlesham (Suffolk).   [64]

SHUKPA Name for the yeti used in Sikkim.   [#4]

SHUNKA WARAK'IN An animal in the tradition of the American Indians. The same signifies a beast that carries off dogs. It may be identical with the *ringdocus*, a mystery creature with wolflike characteristics killed in the 19th Century and subsequently exhibited. A photograph of this animal was taken. It combines features of wolf and hyena. Reports of a creature such as this have come in in modern times from various parts of the United States and Canada.   [C20]

SHUPCHERS Giants in the legends of the Wintun Indians of California. They lived in the region of Flume Creek, Shasta County. They did not bear weapons, but would squeeze people to death.   [W"]

SHUSWAP LAKE MONSTER A monstrous creature has been reported a number of times in this British Columbia lake.   [K4]

SIBBALD'S WHALE A sperm whale with a dorsal fin (which other sperm whales do not have) was observed by Robert Sibbald in 1692. Other reports of this creature have come in from the vicinity of the Shetland Islands.   [B6]

SICILIAN SEA SERPENT A creature with fins on its back and flippers observed from the yacht *Osborne* off Sicily in 1877.

SIEMEL'S CAT A mysterious felid shot in the early 20th Century by Sacha Siemel in the Matto Grasso (Brazil). It was fawn-coloured with brown spots and a dark stripe on the spine. It may have been some kind of hybrid.   [S7]

SIH-SIH Legendary Chinese fish which resembles a magpie with ten wings. [#11]

SILEN A creature in Greek mythology with a generally human form, but sporting a horse's ears, legs and tail. Silens were depicted as aged of aspect. Today the term silen is used for a species of monkey (*Innus silenus*).   [O]

SILWANE MANZI A bipedal creature with a turtle-like head and sharp ears or horns, said to live in watery habitats in KwaZulu (South Africa). That it is a sort of surviving dinosaur has been suggested.   [E]

SIL:QUEY These peculiar animals are aquatic, reported from lake and river in British Columbia. They are sometimes called "black alligators", but Canada is supposedly too cold for such creatures They are also known as horned water lizards. [30]

SIMURGH A huge bird of Persian legend. It was said to live for 1700 years, but it was not the only one of its kind – there was a population of simurghs. It had the head of a dog, a lion's claws and resesmbled a peacock. If you sought one, the Caucasus Mountains was a good place to begin. The Arabs called this bird *angka*, but seem to have confused it with the griffin. The simurgh appears to have evolved out of another legendary Persian bird, the senmurv.

SIN YOU Another name for the *kai tsi*.

SINACH In Irish mythology, a sea-monster killed in prehistoric times by Fergus MacLeide in Dundrum Bay. As Fergus is probably a god in origin, we may be dealing here with a purely mythical combat. [M4]

SINDAI Apparently another name for the orang pendek. [H9]

SINGA An animal in the legends of the Batak of Indonesia. It is often used as a motif in decoration which usually shows only the head, which can be variously shaped.

SIPANDJEE A sort of wildman with ghostly features reported from Gabon, where local people say it is aggressive. [#9]

SIRRUSH *see* **Mushush.**

SISEMITE According to the Quiche, a large hominid reported from Mount Kacharul (Guatemala). It has been said to be the same as bigfoot. Taller than any human, sisimites are said to eat men and to keep women prisoner. It is said by some that the sisemite yearns to make fire like a man and puts piles of twigs together, hoping to do so. There are also sisemites of diminutive size in Chorti and Pokoman belief. According to the Mopan, sisemites have neither backs nor joints. [S1 R7]

SISIUTL Kwakiutl name for the Sproat Lake Monster.

SISKIYOU WILD MAN A description of this humanoid was furnished in the 19th Century. It was 7'/2m tall, had a head reminiscent of a bulldog's, short ears, long head hair and a beard, but it was hairless elsewhere, apart from areas where pubic hair would grow on a human. This seems to single it out from the usual bigfoot type of creature. Its voice was like "a woman in great fear". [K1]

SISTER LAKES MONSTER A sturdy hominoid with hair in its eyes which was reported from Michigan in 1964. It scared off fruit pickers, was seen by farmers and young girls, was estimated at being 9'/2.74m tall and was described as looking like a cross between a bear and a gorilla. [C16]

SKAHA LAKE MONSTER Skaha Lake, Canada, is connected to Lake Okanagan of ogopogo fame. In 1988 a pilot flying over the lake saw three huge monsters swimming together away from the lakeside, possibly having emerged from caves. One was 30' long, the others not much smaller. [K4]

SKIFF LAKE MONSTER A 30'/9m serpentine monster has been reported from this lake in New Brunswick. [S10]

SKOOKUM   An alternative name for the sasquatch.   It comes from the Chinook language and its original meaning seems to have been merely "strong".   One particular skookum or group of skookums was supposed in times agone to have driven the Indians out of the Pe Ell Prairie in Washington state.   The term is also used for tentacled animals inhabiting lakes.   An example would be the two-tentacled animal with an orange body reported from a lake in Williamette Valley (Oregon). [C16 31]

SKREE   The Battle of Culloden (1746)   led to the defeat of the Stuarts by the Hanoverians.   On the night before it, this hideous leathery looking being was seen in the sky, shrieking over the opposing armies.   It is described as having red eyes. This is not the only occasion on which the skree has been reported. [C12]

SKRIMSL   An Icelandic monster said to inhabit the Lagerflot, a lake in the mountains. It has been reported since the Middle Ages.   An 18th Century sighting resulted in a report that it was long and had a hump.   In a 19th Century sighting onlookers discerned a seal-like bewhiskered head and two humps and estimated its length at 46'/13m.   A Dr Hjaltin examined flesh and bones – apparently in a somewhat amorphous mass – in the same century and could not identify them.   A photograph was supposedly taken of the beast in 1998.   The term skrimsl was also applied to a creature of the sea reported in Thorkafjord in the north of the country.   Tracks found in 1819 indicated that it had made a shore visit. The term has also been applied to other lake monsters.   Indeed, it was used by Icelandic settlers near Lake Winnipeg in Canada to designate a monster therein. [C25]

SKUNK APE   A humanoid creature reported over the years from Florida.   Some think it identical with bigfoot, some not.   Its aroma has bestowed its name.   In 1974 police Patrolman Robert Hollemayal fired a couple of rounds at one he found himself face to face with on a darkened road, which caused the creature to scream and run off speedily. In 1975 a man named Davis found a 9'/2.7m skunk ape in his yard.   He discharged his gun at it, but it didn't seem particularly perturbed and it retreated into the woods.   One story circulating was that the military had captured one, but it escaped.

Possible photographs of a skunk ape were taken in 2000.   They seem to have withstood examination well.   The creature shown in them looked like an orang-utan. Could skunk apes be a population of feral orang-utans?   Another opinion is that skunk apes are in fact of the same nature as napes.

According to C. Dobson the skunk ape is also to be found in Tennessee.

On 14th June, 2003, the first Everglades Skunk Ape Festival was held.   [F6 C16]

SKY BEAST   It has been argued by T.J. Constable that UFOs are actually living creatures, probably largely composed of energy with a very flimsy skin or carapace which would disintegrate if one fell to the ground.   This would presumably be what would happen should such a creature die.   Some doubt has been expressed as to whether creatures could survive at that altitude, but B. Sattler of Innsbruck University has demonstrated that bacteria at least can survive in clouds.

Constable is not the only one to suggest thst UFOs are animals.   J.P. Bessor did so in 1947.   E.E. Salpeter and Carl Sagan, speculating on what sort of life could thrive on

Jupiter, suggested animals there would be gas-filled sac-like creatures which would propel themselves by a sort of fart-power. Other scientists have suggested this kind of creature, which would conform to certain descriptions of UFOs, could exist on earth. [S8 D8]

SKY SERPENT Serpents making their way through the sky are by no means unknown. Thus one was observed in Devon in 1762. Described as 'twisting', it also seems too have generated light. In 1811 a fiery serpent, in the shape of a horseshoe, was espied in the skies over Geneva. In 1873 in Bonham, Texas, something "resembling" a yellow striped serpent the length of a telegraph pole was descried in the air by a farmer and others, while later in the year something similar was seen over Fort Scott, Kansas. About the year 1857, another of these creatures was seen over Missouri. It was said to be breathing fire and to have streaks of light along its sides. In 1935, a flying serpent was reported from Scandinavia. In 2000 a wayfarer in Spain in the El Encinar de Boadilla area claimed to have seen what looked like a snake coloured silvery white in the sky. [C17]

SKYFISH *see* **Rod.**

SLANE BEAST A mystery animal the size of a cat with a musteline face, four tusks (two going upwards, two downwards), a small mane and twelve toes or claws on each foot was captured in a rabbit trap at Slane, Ireland, about 1869.   [#1]

SLATKINA BEASTS A pair of doglike creatures seen drinking the blood of animals near Slatkina in the Balkans about 1995. The beasts were tailless, with short strong legs and a long snout.   [#11]

SLIMY SLIM *see* **Payette Lake Monster.**

SLUG-LIKE SNAKE A creature mentioned by Charles Craig in his autobiography *Black Jack's Spurs* (1954). This Paraguayan animal was described as having a dog's head, being as wide as a horse and having a stumpy tail with a spike in it. [#4]

SMAWY'IL Squanish Indian term for a BHM.

SMITHAM HILL BEAST A large apelike hominid, about 7'/2m tall, observed in this Somerset area in 1993. [31]

SNALLYGASTER Reported from 1909 (or maybe as early as 1902) from Frederick County (Maryland), it was said to have huge wings, a long beak, fierce claws and a single eye. It was also said to have killed and sucked the blood of a man named Gifferson, finally disappearing into the woods of Carroll County after a prolonged fracas with three men. It was supposed to have been seen again twenty-three years later and to have dropped into a vat of illicit alcohol and, overcome by the fumes, drowned. It is suspected that the snallygaster is largely – perhaps entirely – a journalistic hoax.

SNANAIK Bella Coola term for a BHM.

SNE NAH An Okanagan Indian name for a bigfoot-type creature, but, as it means 'owl woman', it is difficult to envisage what kind of beast it in fact betokens.

SNINIQ A hominoid in the lore of the Bella Coola Indians. Their hind legs are short. They can reverse their eyeballs so beams shoot out, knocking those on whom they are turned unconscious.   [M6]

SNOW SNAKE According to Native American lore, this white venomous creature is found in eastern North America. The whites also believed in its existence. [30]

SOAY BEAST A large reptilian beast descried off the island of Soay (Scotland) by Tex Geddes and James Gavin in 1959. It had protruding eyes and a red open, but apparently toothless, mouth. No nose was discernable. The head had scales and the back was serrated. It approached the witnesses so closely they could hear its breathing. [C/H]

SOESTERBERG DOGS Large dogs, said to be of a phantasmal character, have been reported from Soesterberg Air Force Base in the Netherlands and have been blamed for attacks on guards in the 1990s. They resembled Doberman-Pinschers.   [A]

SOGPA A name for the yeti in Sikkim. [H9]

SOLOMON HOMINOID This creature is said to be found on Guadalcanal and Lauderi in the Solomon Islands.   [31]

SOLOPENDRIA A fish of medieval lore. If it swallowed a hook, it threw up its innards until it was gone and then swallowed the innards once more.   [151]

SONGHUA LAKE MONSTER The lake concerned is in China's Jilin province. It is the locale of reports, which have been coming in since the 1950s, of a vaguely described monster, 7'/2m wide and 262-295'/80-90 metres long. The lake is man-made, but access may be from the Songhua River.   [#1]

SONGO Banziri name for the badigui. [H9]

SONORA CREATURE A creature observed by I. Ingram as he was driving through the Sonora Desert (Mexico) at night. It had a rabbit's face, a donkey's ears and a deer's body. Many, as one would expect, did not believe him when he told of this, but one friend of the family said it was a were-creature.   [C23]

SOUCOYANT A bat demon said to inhabit Trinidad.

SOUTH AFRICAN HOMINOID J.T. Robinson and C.K. Brain were reported to be collecting tales of a humanoid in South Africa, but little or nothing is known of their findings.   [K8/A]

SOUTH BEND BESSIE A lake monster reputed to live in Lake Erie, it takes its name from a nuclear power station. Sightings have been recorded since 1817, when it was beheld by two French Canadian brothers. There would seem to be more than one creature for the *New York Times* (22nd July, 1931) reported the capture of a serpent in the lake by two fishermen. A police captain was amongst those who saw the animal.

A cigar-shaped creature was seen in 1960. Witnesses in 1969 and 1981 spoke of it as being serpentine. Estimates of length put it in the 30'-35'/9-10m bracket. Video footage of the animal is not conclusive.   [16]

SOUTH CHINA TIGER This subspecies of tiger (*Panthera tigris amoyensis*) has been thought extinct, but some may linger in Jiangxi province. This province was in its former range and a man was apparently killed here by a tiger in 1999. Locals have reported tiger cries and a claw has been discovered.   [#3]

SOUTH GEORGIA PIG MAN A rather timid hominoid of the Okefenokee Swamp. It is said to look like a hairy ape with a piglike snout or nose. There have been no recent reports.   [46]

SOUTH SASKATCHEWAN RIVER MONSTER In this Alberta river, a monster was supposedly seen in 1949. It was given the name of *agopogo* by a journalist. [K4 C19]

SOUTH SHIELDS CRAB A species of crab, apparently unknown to science, found in the region of South Shields.   It may be a colour variation of a known species. [#1]

SO'YOKO Hopi Indian name for a BHM.

SPANISH REPTILE Unknown reptile reported from Spain, perhaps identical with the tatzelwurm.   [30]

SPANISH WILDMAN In 1968 a couple of sightings of wildmen occurred in Spain. In 1993 a couple of hairy wildmen were seen in the same country. An earlier specimen, which did not seem dangerous, was frolicking about the Pyrenees in 1774.   [31 B3]

SPECS A startling creature observed by diver Bob Wall in 1959. He had dived into the sea off Miami Beach (Florida). Noticing a cave, he peered in to see if it contained anything worth looking at. He saw a body 5'6"/1.68m long in the shape of a cylinder, supported on eight hairy legs, each 3'/1m long. It had a pointed head and large eyes on stalks. It advanced upon the human visitor, who beat a hasty retreat.   [S6]

SPIDER-SCORPION A strange insect 2-3"/5cm long, resembling a scorpion, white in colour, but depending from a web like a spider. This was seen by an Ontario family near the end of the 20th Century.   [2]

SPINIFEX MAN A kind of humanoid monster in which the Aborigines of Western Australia believe. It is thought to leave two-toed tracks in spinifex grass, but it has been suggested that these have been provided by feral ostriches. [S8/A]

SPITZBERGEN HOMINOID Such a beast, 7'/2m tall and covered in red-brown hair was spotted by Russian scientists in this remote location.   [#9]

SPLINTERCAT A term used for bigfoot or a similar creature in Clackamas River County (California).

SPLITTER A bizarre creature of Chinese legend. It looks like a coin, but, on the approach of man, it leaps up into the air and, when it comes down again, it splits into twelve pieces, each with a head capable of inflicting a deadly poisonous bite. If the creature is left alone, the pieces will reassemble.   [#11]

SPROAT LAKE MONSTER Indian tradition claims this British Columbia lake is inhabited by a serpentine creature and cryptozoologist J. Kirk reports seeing two dark shapes in it. [K4]

SQRAT The hybrid of a squirrel and a rat. There have been reports from time to time of such hybrids, but they have never been authenticated by science. The offspring of such an unlikely union would probably be infertile. [#9]

SQUARE SNAKE A legendary Chinese snake. It looks like a trunk. It squirts an inky fluid at people which kills them instantaneously.   [#11]

SQUATINUS A mud-dwelling fish of medieval lore, very difficult to pierce with weapons. Its skin could be used for sandpapering. [151]

SQUATTAM'S GROWLER A term used for a BHM in Dade County (Florida).

SQUEASEL This is supposed to be a pygmy variety of weasel. Although not recognised by science, it is widely believed in in parts of Britain. White coloured specimens are said to dwell on the island of Anglesey.   [D7]

SQUIRREL-LYNX HYBRID Such creatures cannot exist, yet they are believed by some to be the origin of a breed of domestic cat, the Norwegian Forest cat. [41]

SQUITTEN The supposed hybrid of a cat and a squirrel. This is regarded as scientifically impossible. The notion that such a creature could occur may come from observations of cats with radial hypoplesia. [45]

SRAHEEN'S LOUGH CREATURE Local folklore claimed that in this lough in Achill Island, Ireland, there dwelt a monster. A number of sightings were reported in the 1930s. In May, 1968, two witnesses saw a strange creature cross the road near the lough ahead of them. It was dark brown, ran on four legs, had a long neck and a head resembling a sheep's or a greyhound's. The tail was thick. It was 8-10'/2-3m long and 2'6"/70cm tall. The beast was seen by a cyclist shortly afterwards. He said it was bigger than a horse and jumped like a kangaroo. Gary Cunningham informs me there has been a more recent sighting.

STAR CHILD The term applied to a small skull, supposedly discovered in Mexico about 1950. The skull shows a number of peculiarities. It has been carbondated as 900 years old. It is now in the possession of Lloyd Pye, who feels it is the skull of an alien-human hybrid. However, Jonathan Downes has a rather different theory. He argues that the skull exhibits too many differences from the human norm to be merely a deformed human skull and argues that its owner was the hybrid of a human and some other primate. A mitochondrial DNA test on the skull proved inconclusive. [#9]

STAR CREATURE The Cherokee believed that stars were animals and that they had at some stage captured a couple. Their bodies were covered with downy feathers. Their heads stuck out like terrapins'. When the breeze eddied about their feathers, sparks issued from them. On the seventh night of their captivity, they escaped. The Cherokee were sure these strange animals were stars.   [105]

STELLER'S SEA COW This beast (*Rhytina stelleri*) takes its name from naturalist G.W. Steller, who accompanied a Russian ship to Alaska and described it in 1741. It was a huge, seal-like beast, 25'-30'/7.6-9m in length and it could weigh 3.5 tons. Its skin was wrinkly. These animals were vegetarian and coast-clinging. They were located on two islands, Copper Island and Bering Island. However, they were apparently wiped out by hunters in a very short time. Some have said the last one was killed in 1786.

However, the Russian ship *Buran* in 1962 saw a herd of unidentified animals that corresponded to the sea cow in many respects near Cape Navarin on the Siberian coast. Near the same case a carcass thought by those who found it to be a sea cow was discovered in 1976. It is therefore possible that this creature still exists. [S8 C5]

STELLER'S SEA MONKEY During the voyage of a ship from Siberia to Alaska in 1741, naturalist G.W. Steller noted a most peculiar creature swimming around the ship. It was about 5'/1.5m long. Its head was like a dog's and it had whiskers reminiscent of a Chinese mandarin's. The skin was grey at the back and a rufous or ruddy white at the front. There seem to have been no forelegs or fore-fins. The body ended in a tail with two fins, the upper being twice the size of the lower.

No similar animal was seen for many years and some thought the creature must surely be extinct. However, something very similar was sighted off the Aleutians in 1965. [S8]

STELLER'S SEA RAVEN An unknown bird described by the Steller expedition in the 18th Century. White in colour, it was seen on Bering Island. It may be that it is some bird since rediscovered that is now known by another name.   [S8/A]

STEWA RUTU In Bhutanese folklore, a ferocious aquatic animal with the stomach of a cow and tentacles. It is said to have supernatural powers. In one instance the dzongpon (i.e., the ruler of the local dzong, as my readers will doubtless know) put an elephant into the water. A titanic struggle ensued, but the elephant shambled ashore, the stewa rutu still clinging to it. The women poured hot sand on it and finished it off. This may not have been the only stewa rutu in Bhutanese belief. [C8]

STICK INDIAN A term used by the Stalo Indians of Washington state to designate a bigfoot-type creature. The Cowlitz Indians use this term for a hominoid closer to a human in size. The Cayuse Indians use the term for diminutive beings seen in the Blue Mountains of Oregon. [R7]

ST'IYAHA'MA Beings resembling apes in the beliefs of the Umatilla Indians of the north-western USA. [R7]

STOLLENWURM/STOLLWURM Alternative names for the tatzelwurm.

STONE GIANT The Iroquois believed in a race of Stone Giants. These may have been humanoids which rolled about in flinty material. The native name for them is *ge no sqwa*. The *strendu* of the Hurons may have done something similar. A Cherokee name for a BHM is *nun yunu wi* which signifies 'stone man'.

STOOR WORM A huge monster in the folklore of the Orkney Islands. It could coil itself around the whole world, but it met its end at the hand of Assiepattle, who managed to sail a boat into its monstrous jaws. Inside the creature he killed it by pouring hot peat into a hole he had cut in its liver. Its dead body became Iceland, some of its teeth became the Orkneys and some the Shetlands. Assiepattle, by the way, escaped. [W3]

STORE LEE MONSTER The lake of Store Lee is mainly in Sweden, with a small portion in Norway. A couple of persons have reported a creature reminiscent of a sea serpent in the lake. [126]

STORSJON MONSTER The earliest reference to a monster in this large Swedish lake occurs in a folkltale recorded in 1635, when we are told it was created by trolls. It must have already been well known and the discovery of an image of the Norse Midgard Serpent on a nearby runestone may not be a coincidence. Records of sightings of the creature date from 1820. It is said to be greenish-grey with black spots. Considerable variants occur in reports of its length, indicating a population of creatures, not merely some solitary monstrous Methuselah, a relict of primeval times. Sometimes elk, swimming in the lake, may be mistaken for the monster. In 1986 it became a legally protected species. An indistinct photograph of the creature was taken in 2002 by Asa Bengtsson-Ring. [C20 #1]

STREAMER The term "streamers" was used by the witness to describe flying eels or worms he saw over Houston (Texas) about 1952. [81]

STRENDU The Hurons believed in these giants covered, not with hair, but with flinty scales. Kind behaviour could lead to the temporary taming of a strendu. The flinty scales may in fact have been acquired due to rolling in stony ground. [M6]

225

STRIPED UNICORN In southern Africa these feature in cave paintings. They look like quaggas, but are of a yellowish colour, are fully striped and have a horn. One is reported to have been shot in modern times.   [31]

STUART RANGE CREATURE An unidentified giant reptile was reported by a miner in this area of South Australia in 1931.   [B9]

STUMP POND MONSTER A serpentine monster was reported from this Illinois lake in 1880. It was said to be dark green and as thick as a telegraph pole. Reports continued. All the lake's fish were electronically killed in 1964.   [H/C]

STURGEON BAY CREATURE An unidentified creature seen in the vicinity of Sturgeon Bay (Wisconsin) in 2003. Details have been difficult to make out. One witness said it was not a deer, dog or domestic cat. It was described as quite large with a head like a basket ball.   [Sightings]

STYMPHALIAN BIRDS Brass-winged birds killed by Hercules, as one of his twelve labours. It has been suggested they were an allegory for marsh gas or based on the waldropp (*Geronyius eremita*), a kind of ibis.   [S8/A]

SU/SUCCARATH An unknown beast of South America, described in 1558. It was possibly a ground sloth, if such creatures still existed at this time.   [S6]

SUCURUJU GIGANTE A huge boa in which the South American Indians believe. Support for this belief came from a Father Heinz who, in 1922, saw a snake he estimated at 80'/24m in the Amazon. He sighted another at the mouth of the Piaba in 1929. On the Jamunda one P. Tarvallo saw, in 1948, a snake he estimated at 150'/45m long. He was not happy when it followed his boat.. A beast allegedly killed by machine-gun fire in the same year and photographed was claimed to be 115'/35m long.   [H9]

SUDD GALLINULE A bird of uncertain species reported from Sudan. [#8]

SUEZ SEA SERPENT In 1879 an unusual sea serpent was espied in the Gulf of Suez from the ship *Philomel*. It was black on the upper parts, but the lower jaw was grey, giving way to salmon pink. It had a dorsal fin. The spread of its jaws was 20'/6m.

SUGAAR A dragon or snake in Basque lore. It is usually thought of as wingless, but it can nonetheless fly.   [4]

SUI RIU A species of Japanese dragon which produces red rain.   [J2]

SULA SEA SERPENT This was observed off the Norwegian coast in 2001. Two humps were visible, each 16-33'/5-10m long.   [126]

226

SULAWESI CROCODILE This animal, which have been rumoured to inhabit lakes on the island of Sulawesi (Celebes) in Indonesia, is thought to be an unknown species. [C1]

SUMATRAN HUMMINGBIRD Unclassified bird seen in 1957 and 1958. [E]

SUMSKE DEKLE *see* **VED**.

SUNDABARANS ANIMALS These have been noted at the mouth of the Ganges. They seem to be reptiles, perhaps monitor lizards (*Varanus*).   [C1]

SURREY PUMA One of the first British ABCs, this supposed animal came to prominence in 1964, although earlier sightings had been reported. It seemed to favour a farm named Bushlease. The farm managaer and his wife were among the witnesses. The puma tended to be seen after certain mysterious lights appeared. One of the 1966 witnesses was a policeman named Young. The puma was also reported in the neighbouring county of Hampshire. Although it ceased to be national news after 1967, reports of the animal continued. It has been suggested there was more than one beast. [B8]

SURUBIM-REI Alternative name for the minhocao.

SWAMFISK This peculiar sea creature is mentioned by Olaus Magnus. It has no real stomach, but what it eats becomes part of its main body. When enemies are about, it withdraws inside itself and feeds on its own flesh.   [C9]

SWAMPFOOT A humanoid giant reported because of its footprints, sounds and smell from Hannah's Swamp, Georgia. It is perhaps identical with the skunk ape.   [M8]

SWAN LAKE MONSTER A monster was reported in this Michigan lake in 1946. However, it may have been only a swimming cow.   [15]

SWEDISH WILDMAN A hominid reported from Sweden in 1985. Two swimming girls saw it and said it resembled a man more than an animal and gave off an horrendous stench. This beast or one like it approached the cabin of a couple named Gustavsson. It stood outside the cabin, howling in the moonlight. It also gave off a whistling sound. It thoughtfully left some excrement behind.   [31]

SWIMMING LION Sir Humphrey Gilbert (died 1583), the well-known English mariner, reported seeing at the Grand Banks off Newfoundland what appeared to be a lion with a "horrible voice" swimming in the water.   [C22]

SYRACUSE REPTILE Near Syracuse (*Siracusa*) in Sicily, a mystery reptile was killed by countryfolk in 1933. It had scales and was 11'/3.35m long.   [C1]

SYRIAN OSTRICH *see* **Arabian ostrich**.

SYSLADOBOSIS MONSTER A serpentine monster with a doglike head reported from this Maine lake.   [S10]

SZ A kind of unicorn, more bovine than equine, in Malaysian legend.   [26]

T

TABLE BAY SEA SERPENT A peculiar-looking creature which seemed to have a sort of head followed by a long string-like body, which was seen at this bay at Cape Town in 1857.

TABUYO DEL MONTE MONSTER A monster has been reported from the reservoir here in Leon, Spain. It is said to be 23'/7m long and will go on dry land. When rolled up, it has been thought to look like a tractor tyre.   [#15]

TAFF MONSTER A serpentine monster said to occupy a whirlpool in the River Taff at Cardiff.   [W3]

TAGAI LAKE MONSTER There was a creature 10'/3m long espied in this British Columbian lake, giving rise to belief in a monster which has been given the nickname Tag. J. Kirk suggests it is a sturgeon.   [K4]

TAHASH In Hebrew lore, a creature created specifically so that its skin could be used in the making of the Tabernacle. It seems to have survived this, but vanished when the tabernacle was finished. It had a horn in its forehead and was brightly coloured.   [G4]

TAILED LORIS An unidentified kind of loris, seen, photograophed and even captured in 1889 in the Lushai Hills, India. There have not been recent reports.   [S8/A]

TAILED MEN In days agone, even as late as the Tudor era, it was held in parts of Europe that Englishmen had tails, while in England itself, such appendages were ascribed in folklore to Kentishmen, Cornishmen and whatever you call people who live in Dorsetshire.

In ancient times Pliny had said there were tailed men in Taprobana (Sri Lanka). The Iznagin, a tailed race according to Peter Martyr, had stiff tails which required them to have holes in their chairs into which they could insert them.

A tailed man was supposedly encountered by a Dutch traveller named Struys on Taiwan. Though awaiting execution, this individual told Struys that all people on the southern part of the island had tails. His own exceeded a foot in length.

A tailed race called the Niam-niams was supposed to exist in Africa. Count de Castelnau in 1851 described a massacre of them by another race and said that, tails apart, they were no different from other blacks. His main source of information was African slaves in Brazil.

The Rev. A.R. Wright in Alaska in the early 1900s heard a legend of a race of men with tails who had lived in caves. When they killed an Indian, his fellow tribesmen stopped up the cave entrance with burning brands and brushwood. This apparently killed off the tailed men, whose caudal appendages were so long they used them as their chief means of locomotion.

The Orang Ekor of Malaysia are a legendary race of tailed men. There have also been reports of tailed men in the Philippine Islands, Borneo, the Nicobar Islands and in Kali off the island of New Britain. [H7 B11 #9]

TAILED SMALL MEN Arboreal creatures in the beliefs of the Kiowa Indians. [R7]

TALAHIANG A gigantic being with hair at once coarse and kinky (but this may be confined to his head). He is said to be twelve feet tall, his teeth are large and he lives in trees. He is scared off by noise. He is credited with shapeshifting ability. Belief in this creature is found in the Zamboanga region of the Philippines. [R1]

TAMANGO RIVER MONSTER A large unidentified animal's remains were found in or near this Argentine river by a man named Vaag in 1907. It was said he also found the tracks of another creature. [C1]

TANGIE An animal similar to the kelpie in the lore of the Orkney Islands. It is said to have originally been the steed of a freebooter named Black Eric. When now seen, it is believed to be covered with seaweed. [68]

TANNIWHA According to the Maoris, a huge lizard that once inhabited New Zealand. One legend says it took 340 warriors to kill one of these creatures. When the animal was cut open, many humans were found inside. [B2]

TANO GIANT A pithecoid creature of Ghana, its height is said to be greater than a man's, and it is white with black hair. It lacks thumbs. It will kill and probably eat children. It is said to carry some kind of animal skin, in which it will enwrap itself when chilly. [S1]

TANUKI A were-dog or were-badger in Japanese lore. It is also called a *minjina*. [122]

TARASQUE A monster of French legend. It had a leonine head, ursine claws and its skin was covered in spikes. Larger than twelve elephants, its father was Leviathan and its mother a giant snake called Onachus. It lived in the Rhone. It was captured by St Martha and brought to Arles, where it was killed. [F2]

TARMA A hominoid reported from Peru. [#4]

TASMANIAN BLOBSTER An unidentified creature washed ashore in Tasmania in 1998. It was 16'/5m long and 6'6"/2m wide. It was discovered on Four Mile Beach between Ahrberg Bay and Granville harbour. [78]

TASMANIAN DEVIL (MAINLAND) The Tasmanian devil (*Sarcophilus harrisii*) is supposed to exist only in Tasmania. However, they are occasionally captured on mainland Australia, where they have been thought extinct for 400 years. The captured ones may have been escapees or deliberate introductions rather than members of a relict population.   [S8/A]

TASMANIAN SEA MONSTER   In 1913 this sea monster was seen on the shore of Tasmania by O. Davies and W. Harris. The head was very small, it had neither tail nor fins, its length was 15'/4.5m, it had four legs and proceeded by bounding. It left footprints in its wake.   [B9]

TATZELWURM   A small creature reported from the Swiss Alps, whose existence is probable, but which is not yet recognised by science. It possibly exists in Poland also. It is described as being thick, generally around 3' in length and having short forelegs. It is said to be ferocious and capable of inflicting a poisonous bite. If one excludes the encounter by J. Tinner with a cat-headed lizard about 1711 (*which see*), the earliest sighting on record seems to be that of Hans Fuchs in 1779. One legend says a tatzelwurm that a farmer killed exuded green blood. A possible skeleton was found in 1924. It was 5' in length. There is doubt as to whether it is a reptile or an amphibian. In recent years there have been few reports of this creature.[H9 79]

TA-ZAM-A   A strange creature said to inhabit Lake Shuswap, California. The name means 'water-bear' and the animal is as large as a grown grizzly. The hair looks like that of a bear. One was killed by an Indian named Tomma San in 1904 and, when he skinned it, he found "concealed ears" beneath the skin. The head was like a bear's, but the face was elongated.   [C19]

TCETIN   These creatures in the lore of the Tanana Indians are simian entities, known in English as Tailed Old Men.   [R7]

TCIPITCKAAM   A one-horned water-dwelling monster in Native American lore. [M7]

TEGGIE   This monster is said to inhabit Bala Lake in northern Wales. In the Welsh language, this body of water is known as Llyn Tegid, thereby furnishing the monster with its name. It was seen by D. Bowen, retired lake warden, in 1975. He described it as looking like a crocodile with a hump. Persons sighting it in 1979 said it was 8' long, but did not seem in any way aggressive. In 1995 two boys were startled by what they thought was a tree trunk surfacing near their boat. Then it straightened up until it went 10'/3m into the air, a small head on a long neck.   [H5]

T EH-LMA   The smallest of the three kinds of yeti. They are said to live in the tropical valleys between the mountains, not on the mountains themselves. It has been suggested that they are related to the orang pendek.   [S1 C3*]

TEJU-JAGUA   The Guarani Indians of South America believed in this giant lizard which had seven dogs' heads.   [134]

TELESCOPE SNAKE A South American snake of which Percy Fawcett heard. About 3'/90cm long, it would telescope into itself before it struck. It was poisonous, but not all that poisonous. [C1]

TEMBLADERAS SERPENT A bizarre creature with seven heads and an appetite for cattle, reported from Peru.   [#12]

TENATCO Perhaps identical with bigfoot, this creature of Kaska Indian folklore was said to abduct humans and to sleep in holes in the ground.   [C16]

TENNESSEE MOTHMAN This creature was seen by J. Quintero and his cousin in a Tennessee forest at night. They saw a manlike creature, over 6'/1.8m tall with red eyes, which spread wings and flew off.   [2]

TESLIN LAKE MONSTER A mysterious, spotted creature has been reported from this lake in the Yukon, Canada.   [E]

TESSIE The name given to this monster of Lake Tahoe (California). It is known from Indian tradition and is reported to be over 60'/18m in length. A videorecording of the alleged monster has been made.   [101]

TEXAS FLIER In 1976 near san Benito (Texas) , two police officers were startled by something flying over their car. At first they thought it an aeroplane, but then they discovered it had a human-like body. Around the same time a nearby caravan-dweller beheld a creature outside his dwelling in the shadows with a monkey-like face, red eyes and folded wings. He estimated the creatures height at about 4'/1m. Some days later a man near Raymondsville was attacked by a creature from behind. This beast had a 10-12'/3-3.6m wingspan, was about 5'8"/1.7m tall and had slimy red eyes. It attacked with claws and his victim needed medical treatment for scratches. For other Raymondsville attacks, *see* **American Pterosaur.**   [R6]

TEXAS GARGOYLE A driver near Fort Worth (Texas) claimed to have seen an unidentified creature with short forelegs and long hind legs in April, 2003. It was bipedal and, although compared with a velociraptor, it was covered in hair. The animal's face seems to have led the motorist to liken it to a gargoyle.   [120]

TEYU-YAGUE This giant lizard of Argentine folklore has a head like a dog's or, according to another belief, has no less than seven doglike heads. It lives in deep water and a luncheon of human content is to its taste. Human sacrifice will ensure freedom from its unwelcome attentions.   [#15]

THAMES MONSTER A long-necked creature reported in the Thames Estuary in 1993. Seventy years earlier a sea monster was reported in the Black Deep area of the river by a Captain Hasselfoot.   [#1]

231

THETIS LAKE MONSTER Thetis Lake is in British Columbia. There have been a couple of sightings of a humanoid monster emerging from the lake. The creature had big ears and points sticking out of its head. Its body seemed to be coloured silver and to be bedecked with scales. It was about five feet tall. On 19th August, 1972, it chased two men from the beach, cutting one on the hand with the points on its head, which seemed very sharp. Two other witnesses saw the creature a few days later.   [C21]

THLOH MONG A creature known to the Lepchas, who say it dwells in Tibet. They aver it is but another name for the yeti. One Lepcha identified it with an orang-utan he had seen in a zoo, which would indicate that we have here a relict population of orang-utans. [N1]

THOES The hybrid of a panther and a wolf. Such a thing is not scientifically possible, but was believed to be so in the 17th Century. [H12]

THOMASTOWN BEAST A number of these animals were found in a cave near Thomastown, Ireland, in 1780 or 1781. They looked like boars, but, while no tusks are reported, they appear to have had spreading horns.   [#1]

THREE-EYED MAN On 28th July, 1962, a motor-cyclist was attacked near Bajada Granda in the vicinity of Parana, Argentina, by a three-eyed man with white hair and a round head.   [B9]

THREE-HEADED BEAST There is supposed to be a beast with three heads that guards treasure at Dobb Park Castle, Weston (Yorkshire).   [146]

THREE-HEADED MONSTER Aldrovandus speaks of this creature. Not alone did it have three heads, but they were of different creatures – fox, dragon and eagle.   [H12]

THUNDERBIRD A huge bird in the traditions of sundry North American Indian tribes. The frontiersman Daniel Boone (1734-1819) said he saw a child carried off by a thunderbird and the mountain man Jim Bridger (1804-1881) saw a giant bird attack a mule. White Bear (died 1905) was walking along with a deer tied to his back when he was carried off by a thunderbird, but managed to escape from its nest.

Thunder Bay (Ontario) was known as Thunderbird Bay (*Animike Wekwed*) by the Indians. Thunder Bay (Michigan) also seems to have been named after the bird and Thunder Lake (Wisconsin) undoubtedly was.

Native American nations with thunderbird traditions include the Arapaho, Sioux, Comanche, Cheyenne, Kiowa, Yakima and Kutenas. The Hoh, Quillette and Quinault on the west coast believe thunderbirds carry off whales. The Makahs of Vancouver Island thought a thunderbird actually lived on a mountain where whale bones were found. A Nootka Indian drum shows a picture of a thunderbird carrying off a whale: the whale does not look pleased.

While traditions of these mighty avians carrying off whales may be due to the discovery of carcases of stranded cetaceans, if these birds are capable of carrying off the other creatures mentioned in connection with them, they are unusual indeed. No known bird could carry such burdens. Condors, though large, do not have sufficiently strong claws and legs to carry off such beasts. The same is even true of eagles, which are much stronger. The supposedly extinct teratorns, which have been mentioned as possible originals for the thunderbird, could not do it either. Some thunderbird traditions may have arisen from sightings of birds which the onlooker could not identify. However, one cannot rule out the possibility that there exists or once existed a bird whose strength is unparalleled by any known species. Finally, it might be added that there have been regular thunderbird reports from Pennsylvania. On one occasion a thunderbird was seen to carry off a fawn. Even flocks of thunderbirds have been mentioned. *See also* **Big Bird.** [H]

THUNDER- HORSE The horse whose hoofbeats produce the thunder in the mythology of the Sioux. [S6]

THYLACINE An animal (*Thylacinus cynocephalus*) formerly found in Tasmania. It looked like the marsupial equivalent of a wolf with stripes and was variously called the Tasmanian wolf, Tasmanian tiger and zebra-wolf. What was thought to be the last existing thylacine died in 1936 at the Hobart Domain Zoo. Some experts, however, feel it still exists. For example, in 1968 V. Kelly said he had seen one. Three hunters asserted they had seen one in Mole Creek in 1980. J. Talbot averred he had seen one in 1982. A man named Porteous reported a sighting in 1986. H. Naarding, a zoologist, reported one in 1980 and a park ranger named C. Beasley made a similar report in the 1990s. Thylacines, it is claimed, are by no means infrequently found around Ferry Hill, Panama Road and Lone Stone Road.

There is also some evidence that the thylacine is to be found on mainland Australia. There is no trace of the creature in the lore of the Aborigines, but it is not impossible some were at one stage introduced from Tasmania. There have been sightings since the 1970s. Strangely, S. Slea claimed he had seen two dead thylacines, one stripeless and one black, in 1940 and 1943 respectively. Some evidence is also to be found for thylacine existence on New Guinea; *see* **Doglas.** [H6]

TIAMAT The chaos monster of Mesopotamia which, according to the Akkadian epic *Enuma elish*, was defeated by the god Marduk, though it seems that in an earlier version her opponent was Enlil, the deity of atmosphere. She is represented as a serpent with two small arms. A later depiction shows her with the foreparts of a lion, the back legs of an eagle and wings.

TIANCHI MONSTER A monster has been reported in China's Tianchi Lake for up to a hundred years. How it came there, if there it lurks in truth, is something of a mystery, as the lake is in the crater of a volcano, which was busily erupting 300 years ago. The monster, observed in 2002, has been variously described as looking like a kind of seal or having a horse's head and a turtle's body. In the case of a long-necked creature with a humped back, these details are not necessarily mutually exclusive. Videotape recordings of the beast are inconclusive. In July, 2003, several soldiers claimed to have seen the monster and asserted it had horns. It has been pointed out that the *Shanhaijing*, a collection of Chinese fairytales, features turtle-like creatures. [#1]

TICINO MONSTER A water monster seen at the mouth of the River Ticino, Italy, in 1934. [B9]

TIGELBOAT An extraordinary animal reported in 1975 as having been captured in Borneo. It did not long survive. It was said to combine features of tiger, elephant, goat, cow and lion. Karl Shuker argues that it was a juvenile Malay tapir (*Tapirus indicus*). This species is not officially to be found in Borneo, but there is evidence that it nonetheless exists there. [K5]

TIGER EAGLE A legendary Chinese bird with a 20'/6m wingspan. It is the size of an ox. [#11]

TIGER ROCKS SEA MONSTER This creature, estimated at over 60'/18m long, was seen a number of times off the east coast of South Africa in 1947. Its eyes looked like searchlights and it made a loud braying noise. [B9]

TIKBALANG In Filipino folklore, a creature combining features of horse and man. It has the face of a horse, with a brace of tusks in its lower jaw. Its hands boast three fingers and a thumb, covered with a hooflike carapace. The feet are hooves ending in talons. It exceeds 6'/1.8m in height. Tikbalangs are accompanied by a smell of burning hair. [4]

TIKIS RIVER CREATURE Five very large black creatures whose nature cannot be determined owing to the fact that their heads or tails are never seen have been causing alarm amongst the Aeta people living on the banks of the Tikis River in the Philippines. [12]

TIMIN A huge fish in Indian mythology. Even huger, and capable of swallowing this, is the *timin-gila*. Even larger, and capable of swallowing the latter, is the *timin gila-gila*. [D1]

TIN TIN A bat demon said to be found in Ecuador. It is not accompanied by a white dog called Milou or Snowy.

TINTINALUS In medieval lore, a fish smelling of thyme. [151]

TIONDO Kipringi name for the Gerit. [H7]

TIRICHUK Name of a monster said to be found in various rivers in Alaska. [C/H]

TIRUPATI LIZARD A monstrous lizard encountered by forest officials at Tirupati, India. Its length was estimated at 18'/5.4m. [#15]

TIZHERUK A kind of monster in Eskimo lore, quite fierce and capable of killing a hunter. It may occupy the same ecological niche in the Arctic as the sea-leopard (*Hydrurga leptonyx*) does in the Antarctic. It is also called the *Pal Rai Yuk*. [M2]

TLANUWA This was supposed to be a huge hawk, according to the Cherokee. It resembled a duck hawk or a peregrine falcon, but was much larger. It attacked both Indians and animals. [C20]

TOAD MAN In 1935 and subsequently, this large toad with human-like attributes was reported in Argentina.   [#12]

TODMORDEN CREATURE This was seen near Eagles Crag in Claviger Gorge (Yorkshire), a place noted for paranormal phenomena. The witness saw an upright creature with wide shoulders and a body that tapered down from these. It moved speedily. It reminded him of Taz, the Tasmanian devil in the Warner Bros cartoons. [85]

TOK A large hairy primate of China, perhaps identical with the gin-sung. It may also be identical with the dzu-teh, the biggest type of yeti. Ivan Sanderson had a correspondent who actually claimed to have wrestled with a tok which had entered his house by night. This occurred twice, so we are possibly dealing with two toks here. The animal made no resistance, but hastened away. Its hair was jet-black, its head small, its legs straight and the soles of its feet pale.   [S1]

TOKANDA In Madagascar they speak of this unknown animal, a quadruped that moves by jumping about.   [H9]

TOMBSTONE TOM A large white phantom cat reported from Yorkshire. [C4]

TOMPONDRANO A large striped sea-monster reported off the coast of Madagascar. [E]

TOMS RIVER MONSTER The town of Toms River (NJ) was founded by Indian Tom in 1737. He was supposedly dragged into the nearby river by a monster. The monster is said to have sunk a boat in the 1920s and sightings in the form of humps continue. [110]

TOO A black-furred animal reported from East Africa, of goat size and dangerous disposition. It is perhaps a ratel.   [H9]

TOONJUK Huge hominoids of Arctic Canada and Alaska. Their faces are humanlike and they have long hair. [30 129]

TOWNSVILLE SEA MONSTER A sea monster was seen off this area in Queensland a number of times in 1934. It was said to be covered with barnacles and scales. It had three humps. [B9]

TOYLONA Taos Indian name for a BHM.

TRAGELAPH A name given to the supposed hybrid of a goat and a deer.

TRAGOPAN This huge bird was supposed to live in Africa in classical times, being mentioned by both Pliny and Solinus. Its head was supposedly purple, its body brown and it was said to boast ram's horns.

TRANCO A hominoid reported from Colombia and Chile.   [#4]

TRANQUEBAR CREATURE A strange creature picked up by fishermen off south-eastern India, according to a newspaper report of 1973. It was about 3'/90cm long, it could move about easily on land, it was scaly and orange-coloured. What befell it is unknown. [S5]

TRANSCAUCASIAN BLACK CAT A cat found to the south of the Caucasus Mountains. C. Saturnin thought it a separate species, giving it the name *Felis daemon.* Other zoologists contend it is merely a feral domestic cat.   [S7]

TRAPPE PTEROSAUR *see* **Kongomato**.

TRATRATRATRA An animal in the lore of Madagascar, solitary of habit, which inspired much fear in the Malagasy. Its size was that of a calf of two summers, its head round, its face and ears like a man's, its feet like an ape's. It had a short tail and fuzzy hair. It might reflect the existence, later than is generally allowed, of the man-like lemur hadropithecus.   [H9]

TRAUNSEE MONSTER This lake in Austria is supposed to contain a spirit called the Lady of the Traunsee, who will drag men into the water. She has sometimes been seen riding on a monster.   [M7]

TRAVERSPINE GORILLA Name given to a creature, possibly a bigfoot, reported from Labrador in 1913. It had a white mane on its head. It was seen by a Mrs Michelin and some children, while others saw its tracks. These were two-toed, which is not generally consistent with bigfoot reports. One account said there were two beasts. [B8*]

TREE EATER Another name for the Forest Giant.

TRELQUEHUECUVE A creature like an octopus and therefore presumably tentacled in the lore of the Chilean Indians. Although a water creature, it can come onto the shore. [M7]

TRENTON CREATURE This animal was reported at night time outside Trenton (NJ) on 4th March, 2002. It was bipedal with a long tail and wings. Before appearing , it let out a horrifying scream. It turned and fled from the witnesses.   [145]

TRILOBITE Trilobites are not supposed to have existed for hundreds of millions of years; yet fresh tracks, reminiscent of those of trilobites, have been found on the ocean bed, indicating there may be trilobites still about. In case the reader is not on terms of back-slapping familiarity with trilobites, they were (and are?) creepy-crawly type creatures with segmented bodies. [B6]

TRIMBLE LIZARD A large lizard, black and white with orange spots, reported from Trimble County (Kentucky). [30]

TROY CREATURE Troy here is not the city of which Homer sang, but its namesake in New York state. If you visited the emporium of one Michael Griffa there about 1890, you would have seen, hanging on the wall, a peculiar creature which the proprietor claimed to have shot as it swam in the Hudson River. It was about two feet in length, its back covered in hair, its underside the colour of human flesh and it had wings, four legs, two fins and a tail, the latter porcine. Some persons described as "doctors" failed to identify it and who can blame them? [R6]

TRUE GIANT Term used by cryptozoologists to denote a kind of BHM which they regard as taller than bigfoot, sometimes attaining a height of 20'. Some of these are said to live in the same territory as bigfoot. [C20]

TRUNKO An unidentified sea-creature, covered in white fur, seen from the town of Margate, South Africa, in 1922. It was white and furry and fighting with two whales. The whales won. The animal was washed ashore. To the astonishment of those who saw it, it did not appear to have any head, but rather a trunk in its place. Creatures bearing some resemblance to this one have been reported off the coasts of Alaska, Australia and Gambia. [2]

TSAALO Bigfoot-type giants in the lore of the Quinault Indians.

TSEMAUS A fish in which the Indians of British Columbia believe. It inhabits the Skeena Estuary and its dorsal fin will cut a hapless swimmer in two. [M7]

TSE'NA'HALE A gigantic bird in Navaho lore, somewhat aquiline, but not to be confused with the thunderbird. [H]

TSERE-YAWA A small semi-aquatic felid that hunts in packs, said to inhabit Ecuador. [30]

TSHENKUTSHEN This animal is considered by some to be a kind of cat, but this may be an error. It is white with black spots, it has black, white, red and yellow stripes on its chest and paws on the end of its forelimbs to assist it in jumping about in the trees. In fact, it seems to combine elements of cat and monkey. In Ecuador, where it is said to live, it is regarded as more dangerous than any other forest animal. [30]

TSHINGOMBE Bantenbo name for the kikomba. [H7]

TSIATKO In the folklore of the Nisqually Indians of Washington state, a hairy giant, perhaps identical with the sasquatch.   [C16]

TSINQUAW A monstrous animal said to inhabit Cowichan Lake on Vancouver Island. On one occasion a fisherman was dragged around the lake for hours after something took his bait in 1959. An attempt to trap the creature proved unsuccessful.   [K4]

TSKHISS Georgian name for the wildman. (This Georgia is, of course, the one in the Caucasus).

TSOMGOMBY *see* **Kilopilopitsofy**.

TUA YEUA A bipedal humanoid reported from Thailand. A witness in the 1880s said he had seen one that was dark red and too tall to be merely a gibbon. In the same era a dead one was given to a Captain Bingham, but it was already decomposing, so he could save only the skeleton, which in due course became lost. It is possible the tua yeua might represent a relict population of orang-utans (*Pongo pygmaeus*) in Thailand.   [90]

TUNGU Term used for a wildman among the Nenets people of Siberia. Like other wildmen, the tungu is said to whistle. Some suppose he wears a blanket. Sightings were once quite frequent. [B3]

TUNNEL MONSTER In 1978 in Toronto, a witness encountered a three foot long monkey-like thing with grey fur and orange and red slanted eyes in a cave next to the building he lived in. The creature told him to go away in a hissing voice.   [18]

TUNTAPAN A sea-dwelling creature with a taste for crayfish and Aborigines reported from Port Philip (Victoria), Australia, in the 19th Century. It was said to have a horse's mane on an emu's head and neck. It was further supposed to have flippers and lay eggs. [C1]

TURTLE LAKE TERROR A monster of Turtle Lake, Saskatchewan. It is said to be long-necked with a head variously described. It has been reported since the 1920s and blamed for rending fishermen's nets.   [C22]

TURUL A huge hawk in Hungarian mythology.

TUSKED ELK Creature reported from the north-western USA. It is said to look like a wapiti (*Cervus canadensis*), but to be bigger and sturdier. [31]

TUTUATUIN A legendary being with tangled hair, perhaps a hominoid, in Eskimo lore. [M6]

TWIN LAKES MONSTER   A 25'/7m "water snake" was reported from this Massachussetts locale in 1890.   [S10]

238

TWO FACES A hairy giant in the lore of the Sioux Indians. It has large ears like an elephant and the two faces from which it takes its name, each with a lengthy nose. It has been said to use its ears to capture humans. Each ear can encompass a trio of adults. The captives are digested in the ears, which are endowed with appropriate fluids, and then absorbed through the same organs. Two Faces is capable of transforming victims into smaller replicas of itself.

Once when Two Faces was slain by Indians, he reconstituted himself some years later. One wonders if, behind this peculiar beast, lies a memory of the mammoth or mastodon, both of which frolicked in North America in days agone. [B7]

TWO-HEADED SNAKE The Arapesh of New Guinea believe in this animal. It is striped and lives in caves and pools. [J2]

TXALAALGORRI Preternatural red calf in Basque lore. [4]

TZALTECHUTLI In the legends of the Aztecs, a monster resembling a toad. [30]

TZARTUS-SAURUS A sea-monster with a horselike head reported from the coast of British Columbia. [E]

TZUCHINOKO A mystery snake reported from Japan and Korea. Unlike an ordinary snake, it is said to travel in a straight line or even to travel down declivities by rolling itself into a hoop. There have been reports of captured specimens, one being eaten by its owner. [6]

U

UAHTI Small but strong hairy manlike forest creatures in the lore of the Tukano Indians of South America. [R7]

UCLUELET SEA SERPENT A sea serpent observed from this location on Vancouver Island in 1947. The large size of its eyes was the subject of particular remark by the witness. [E]

UCUMAR A large hairy creature of Argentina, Bolivia and Peru, described as having features of both human and bear. The killing of one was recorded in 1549 and one was allegedly captured in 1917. It has been reported in Mexico where one was supposedly encountered by J. Santalay around 1957. Another encounter by B. Hoyos took place around 1974. There is reason to think it may have been at times confused with the spectacled bear. [#11 #12 C23]

UDINE SNAKE A mystery serpent was seen near Udine, Italy, in 1963. It was 12' long and whistled. [B9]

UFITI A term meaning 'ghost' applied to a simian captured in Malawi and sent to Chester Zoo, where she died shortly afterwards. Whether she was the only one of her kind is unclear: there had been reports of earlier sightings, so there might therefore be a population of these creatures in Malawi. She seemed to be a chimpanzee, but had characteristics which marked her out from known chimpanzee species. Moreover, there are not supposed to be any chimpanzees in Malawi. [C20]

UFUDU OLUKULU A large water-dwelling tortoise in Zulu tradition. It is said to be found in the River Umtshezi and to have an appetite for humans. [W2]

UILEBHEIST A sea-monster with a number of heads in the folklore of the Scottish Highlands. [S14]

UIRAPURU A small brown bird that can change itself into a boy in Brazilian legend. [122]

UKTENA A gigantic serpent in Cherokee lore, killed by Agan-unitsi, that he might procure the Ulunsu'ti, a blazing star embedded in its head. [111]

ULAK Amongst the Sumo Indians of Central America, a creature of perhaps human size that in other respects resembles an ape. The Rama Indians regard it as something of a wildman. Sometimes both peoples regard ulak as giants which will devour men. [R7]

ULAR TEDONG A monster supposed to inhabit Tasek Bera, a lake in Malaysia. No one claims to have seen this water dwelling creature in its entirety. The head looks like that of a snake with snail-like horns. When young, its scales have a slate-grey colour, but, as the years pass, they change to golden. It is said to be harmless insofar as humans are concerned. It is capable of giving the odd bellow. A similar beast has been reported from another Malaysian lake, Tasek Chini. [S6]

UNDERGROUND GIANT Writers on the periphery – or beyond the periphery – of science have contended that there are giants within the earth. A Dr Marlo argued the existence of giants called Terras, while Doreal contended underground caverns harboured a race of evil giants called Xians. How many followers of these authors believe in the existence of these creatures the present writer cannot guess. [K]

UNDERGROUND PUMA In Cherokee legend, pumas as intelligent as men live in a subterranean realm. [111]

UNHCEGILA According to the lore of the Lakota Indians, a draconic beast that lived on land. [R1]

UNICORN The unicorn or monoceros is well known, having the general shape of a horse sporting a single horn. However, what it looked like was not always so clear in the minds of those who wrote of it.

Ctesias gives perhaps our earliest description. As a physician at the court of the Persian king, he was in a position to glean information about Indian wildlife. He said the unicorn was a donkey of equine proportions, with a white body, a red head and a tricoloured horn. Aelian said its feet resmbled an elephant's and it had a black horn. Pliny informed his readers that it generally looked like a horse, but had a stag's head, an elephant's feet and a bopar's tail.

The unicorn appeared in the Physiologus and thence found its way into church art, making it familiar in Western Europe. It was also used to mistranslate the Hebrew *reem*, which occurs in the Bible. Unicorns' horns (in fact narwhal tusks) became quite widely available. It was said that, to catch a unicorn, you had to first send out a virgin, whom it would approach and leave unscathed, enabling hunters to trap it.

As to where unicorns might be found, though the ancients had placed them in India, a belief grew up that they were also to be found in Africa. Felix Fabri, on pilgrimage in 1485, claimed to have seen one near Jeb-el-Musa, in the Sinai Peninsula. Vartoman of Bologna claimed to have either seen or to know of a pair at Mecca, that had been brought thither from Ethiopia. Bermudez, visiting Ethiopia in 1535, averred unicorns were to be found in that country. This was supported by Marmolinus, who claimed they could be seen in the Mountains of the Moon. J. Lobo (1593-1678) also places them in Ethiopia, a country with which he was familiar, in the country of the Agaws. He describes them as looking like beautiful bay horses, with their manes hanging to the ground. A. Sparrmann in *Resa till Goda Hopps-Udden* (1783) said he had heard many reports of the unicorn in South Africa, nor was he the only one so to do. There have been rumours of unicorns in Tibet, but these seem to refer to the orongo (*Antholops hodgsoni*) which has two undoubted horns.

The Chinese had their own version of the unicorn called the *kilin*, of which *ki* is the male and *lin* the female. It was supposed to have a deer's body, an ox's tail and a solitary horn, the tip of which was fleshy. It was susceptible to domestication. The Japanese borrowed this animal, which they called the *kirin.*

In this context it is worth mentioning that in prehistoric times there existed an antelope called Protocamptoceras. Although this had a pair of horns, a single sheath would have covered them due to their proximity to each other. Surviving populations of this animal may well have given rise to unicorn legends, as may the memory of them passed down in human tradition. [C26 G5 S2/A].
See also **Drakensberg Unicorn, Patagonian Unicorn, Campchurch, King, Piao, Kai Tsi, Sin You, Kioh Twan** *and* **Striped Unicorn.**

UNKNOWN DEER Deer of unknown species have from time to time been reported in South America. [C3*]

UNKNOWN MONKEY A large monkey, pale yellowish in colour, with a brown stripe down its back and a sort of woolly coat, reported from Guyana in 2003. [#1]

UNKNOWN PORPOISE An unknown species of porpoise, brown on the back, white on the underparts, seen off the coast of Chile.   [30]

UNKNOWN RAIL It is possible an unknown species of rail exists on Malaita, Solomon Islands. It was photographed in 2002. It resembles Woodford's rail (*Nesoclopeus woodfordi*), but there are minor colour differences which may indicate it is a different species. [#9]

UPTON LAKE TURTLE A giant snapping turtle has been reported from this lake in New York state. It is known locally as "the big guy". [Sightings]

URAYULI A term used for a BHM amongst the Southwest Alaskan Eskimo. [1]

URCHOW A creature in the legends of the Tuchone Indians of Canada. It has large bottom teeth, with which it tears the bark off trees. From its description, it is something like a camel.   [#1]

URI LAKE MONSTER The monster of this Swiss lake is said to have been both seen and photographed.   [C1]

URSHANA According to Jewish legend, a creature on the Ark which did not pester Noah for food. Noah asked it if it did not wish to eat. The creature replied that he reckoned Noah was busy enough without having to feed him as well. Noah blessed it, asking God to keep it alive for ever.   [G4]

URUTURANGWE A fierce beast said to live in Rwanda. Its fur is believed to look like that of an hyena, but it generally resembles a leopard. It is said to suffocate people by placing its open mouth over their faces.   [S7]

USDADLI A kind of snake in Cherokee folklore. It had feet or suckers and could make a noise like a fawn.   [F10]

USHANT SEA SERPENT A snakelike beast seen off Ushant by those aboard the *Delta* in 1861. It had a fringe around the neck.

UTAH LAKE MONSTER In 1868 one H. Walker reported seeing a serpentine monster with a head like that of a greyhound in this lake. This was not the only early sighting. A more recent one occurred in 1921.   [101]

UVENGWA A white creature with a single eye and the ability to change shape reported from the African jungle.   [A]

UWTJVDA A legendary snake which proceeded by jerks in the folklore of the Cherokee.   [F10]

UYAN A brown, hirsute humanoid reported from Malaysia. [E]

V

242

VALHALLA SEA SERPENT The sighting of this creature was made by scientists and is consequently of particular note. The *Valhalla* was a yacht, sailing off the coast of Brazil in 1905. Aboard were E.G.B. Meade-Wadlow and M.J. Nicoll, Fellows of the Zoological Society of London. They described the animal they saw as having a head and neck followed by a frill, which in turn seemed to be followed by a considerable body. Head and neck were of an uniform thickness, about that of a slender human, and stood out of the water to an extent of 7-8'/2.2m. The head and neck were dark brown above and whitish below. The head and eye were reminiscent of a turtle's. Nicoll wrote three years subsequently that he felt the creature was a mammal rather than a reptile. [C9]

VAN MANAS A name applied in northern India to a kind of wildman. An incident investigated in 1950 by M. Behn led to her being told that a van manas which had abducted a woman had been hunted down and killed by herdsmen. In the 7th Century the Gupta king Harsha Vardhana (reigned 606-*ca.* 647) in northern Bengal received a present of one from the king of Assam. In the Himalayan region this creature is called the *ban manche.*   [T1 L1]

VANCOUVER ISLAND LIZARD A species of bipedal lizard which would probably put people in mind of dinosaurs, reported from Vancouver Island and Texada Island, British Columbia.   [30]

VARENGAN A magic bird, noted for its speed, in Persian mythology.

VASITRI About 1800 Alexander von Humboldt was told of vasitris, hairy men who lived in the woods. He was in the vicinity of the Upper Orinoco at this time. Vasitris were said to build huts, carry off women and eat men. It has been suggested that they are not really cryptids, but a tribe of Indians called the Yanomamo.   [H9 #12]

VASTROLLET A general Norwegian term for a lake monster.

VATEA A merbeing, half-human, half-dolphin, in Polynesian lore.

VEASTA [2 *syllables*] A sea-creature sighted off the Dorset coast, notably by Martin Ball in 1995. He described it as over 12'/3.6m high, looking like half a fish and half a giant sea-horse. He has found references to a peculiar creature rising from the sea in the same area in 1457 and 1757.   [D8]

VED A hairy, hominoid creature in the lore of Croatia. Sometimes a ved would help a human about the house. They were very tall. They lived in groups in the woods and had settlements. They wore ragged clothes. Skeletons of veds were found, sometimes in tree trunks. While veds were regarded as male, there were female hairy beings called *sumske dekle*, who possibly formed the female section of the race to which the veds belonged. Veds seem to have disappeared from human ken about halfway through the 19th Century. After World War II they were scarcely remembered.   [M6]

VEDETTE CREATURE   The Grimsby trawler *Vedette* brought up the skull of an unknown and possibly horned creature from the sea in 1930.   [C3*]

VELUE   A creature of medieval French lore, whose name signifies that it was hairy.   It had a snake's head and a round body.   Its fur was of green colour.   Like dragons, it was fire-breathing and it was the size of a bull.   If it dived into the waters of the River Huisne, whose vicinity it frequented, it caused floods.   Its fur was equipped with stings which wounded folk fatally.   It had a taste for children and maidens and the lover of one such maiden killed it by cutting its tail – its only vulnerable area – in two in revenge for the death of his innamorata.   [B10]

VENEZUELAN LIZARD   There have been a number of reports of a mystery lizard, perhaps a form of tegu or cayman, from Venezuela.   [E]

VENUS LAKE MONSTER   Venus Lake lies on the Italian island of Pontelleria.   Because noises were heard in the vicinity of the lake, a rumour grew up that it housed a monster.   [B9]

VEO   A creature reported from the small Indonesian island of Rintja.   It is the size of a horse, its sides are covered in scales and it has claws on its feet.   It comes to the coast at night to feed on crabs and shellfish.   K. Shuker suggests it may be some kind of pangolin.   [#9]

VERMONT ANIMAL   The same witness sighted this creature twice or else sighted two different creatures of the same kind.   He first discerned it in 2001.   It was a stocky animal, dark brown or black with claws or hands, sitting up like a meerkat and having a white marking like a moustache.   The second sighting seemed to be of an animal with a smaller moustache.   [2]

VIETNAMESE LUNGFISH   An undiscovered species of lungfish in Vietnamese folklore.   [S8/A]

VILUCO MONSTER *see* **Kangaroo-Legged Creature.**

VISHAP   A kind of dragon in Armenian belief, to be found in the vicinity of Mount Ararat.   If you happened on a dead one and dipped your arrows in its blood, they would become envenomed, dealing deadly wounds.

VOITA   A name for a wildman.   Its face is bare and its nose and ears protrude. [S1]

VOPNAFJORTHUR SEA MONSTER   In 1963 a sea monster was seen here in Iceland.   It was black and humped.   [B9]

VOSGES BEAST   A creature reported from Vosges, France, in 1977.   Although it was seen and even photographed, it could not be identified.   It was credited with killing at least 289 sheep and some other animals.   Some people felt that it was being deliberately set on livestock by an owner who controlled it with a high frequency whistle or some other device.   [#6]

VOUIVRE A serpent with bat-like wings which features in the folklore of Franche-Comte (France). It is said to have a carbuncle or diamond in its forehead. If it is washing or drinking, it removes the stone, but you try to steal it at your peril, for it exacts an awful vengeance. The belief about the stone seems allied to that of the South American carbuncle. The name of this creature is derived from Latin *vipera*, 'viper'. [56]

VUI Dark hominids said to have a tail and goats' feet in the legends of Vanuatu. [#4]

VUOKHO A huge disease-carrying bird in the legends of the Lapps/Saami. It spread plague and mosquitoes.

W

WAAKI Small hairy hominid of Australian Aboriginal lore.

WAKANDAGI In the lore of the Omaha Indians, a creature with some corvine characteristics which dwells in the water.   [M7]

WAITOREKE An otter-like animal reported from New Zealand. It has been described as having mammalian features which would generally exclude it from the fauna of this country. An exception to this rule, however, would be a monotreme of some sort, as they lived in the age of reptiles and would have had access to New Zealand. Waitorekes could also possibly be sea-otters which migrated from elsewhere in the Pacific. [H9]

WALCHENSEE MONSTER In the 19th Century this Bavarian lake was said to house some kind of monstrous animal, but details seem to have been vague.   [E]

WALDAGI A doglike animal with an unpleasant reputation in Australian lore. [S7]

WALKING FIR CONE In 1954 a police officer spoke of seeing a creature he described in these terms in Dumpton Perk, Ramsgate (Kent). Karl Shuker regards this as a good description of a pangolin. However, he then proffers plausible reasons why this is unlikely to be the animal concerned.   [S5]

WALLASEA ISLAND APE It is black, looks like an ape and its eyes glow yellow. You will find it, it is said, in the marshes of Wallasea Island (Essex). [31]

WALLENSEE MONSTER This Swiss lake is said to house a population of monsters which will devour those who drown there.   [M7]

WALLOWA LAKE CREATURE Do not confuse this with the monster in the article below. In this we seem to be dealing with a species of crustacean. They were said to be giant lobsters or crabs and to steal calves. One witness observed one locked in combat with a cow. Another one claimed the creature he saw had great flippers. They are no longer supposed to occupy the lake.   [#11]

WALLOWA LAKE MONSTER   This Oregon lake was the scene of a monster sighting by N. Cramer in 1982. He estimated its length at 50'/15m and said it had seven humps. There had been an Indian tradition of a monster in the lake.   [C1]

WA-MBILIKIMO   A diminutive hominoid – maybe even a human pygmy with long hair – reported from east Africa.   [H7]

WAMPUS CAT   A creature of American folklore. It was known to the Cherokee, who called it *ewah*. According to their tale, an Indian woman dressed in a puma skin to spy on her husband and for punishment was turned into a bipedal cat. After dying, she continued in this guise as a ghost.   A white origin story said that a witch, who had transformed herself into a cat, was unable to complete the spell to turn herself back and was doomed to live as a bipedal cat. The animal is known for its wailing and it is said an encounter with it can leave you insane. Slave owners used to discourage slaves from running away by telling them the wampus cat was about and would kill them should they undertake such an enterprise. Some slave owners would even go into the night and make wampus cat noises to terrify their unfortunate minions. The wampus cat seems to be an individual. It is to be found in the folklore of Tennessee, West Virginia, Kentucky and Pennsylvania.   Some say it lives in the mountains, some that it dwells underneath Knoxville.   [109]

WANAMBI   A creature in the beliefs of the Australian Aborigines. It supposedly inhabited northern Australia. It had a long neck, a large body, four legs, a tail and a mane on its back. The Aborigines depicted it in cave art. It seems to have been reptilian. [G3]

WANGUL Mystery creature of Western Australia, perhaps identical with the bunyip.

WANTAGE BEAST   A 7'/2m tall creature, hairy and bewhiskered, was reported from Wantage (New Jersey) in 1977. It made a screaming sound. It was chased away by men with firearms. The animal may have been a bear, though police said this was unlikely. They favoured a raccoon or wild dog, which strikes me as equally unlikely. [#2]

WARRACAIBA TIGER   A form of South American jaguar said to hunt in packs and to utter howls of an intimidating nature. Surprisingly, although these animals have been heard regularly, nobody seems to have actually seen one.   [S7]

WARREN COUNTY WOLFMAN   This creature had a head like a German shepherd/Alsatian and an hirsute but humanoid body. In 1985 it was observed in Warren County (New Jersey) carrying a dead deer.   [A1]

WARRIGAL In modern Australia the term *warrigal* is used to mean a dingo, a wild horse or, indeed, a person of yobbish habits. The name is more specifically employed, however, to denote a supposed unknown animal said to live in the Blue Mountains of

New South Wales. Early settlers gave these beasts the name of Blue Mountain lions. One of them was supposed to have killed a human in 1885. Aside from New South Wales, there have been reports of this creature from other states.

The Aborigines, R. Gilroy informs us, know of these creatures and aver they are 3'/1m tall and 6-7'/1.8-2m long. Their teeth are big and stick out from their jaws. The have manes, hence the term "lions" being applied to them, but witnesses feel they are not quite the same as lions. In 1945 four of the creatures were alleged to have been seen through binoculars. Hunters are said to have encountered one in 1977 in Mulgoa and to have chased it off with gunfire. Such localised unknown creatures as the Springden Lion and the Erskine Gap Monster sound like sightings of warrigals. We may have in this animal no true cat, but some catlike marsupial. [G3 S6]

WASGO In the Pacific northwest of America, this creature is a totem animal. It is long, like a snake, with a head like a dog's or crocodile's. The question arises as to whether it is based on a real animal.

WASHIPI In the folklore of the Toba Indians of South America, simian hairy creatures with long fingernails, 1-1.5'/30-45cm tall. [R7]

WATER BULL The water bull is to be found in the folklore of Scotland. It seems to be small, generally quiet and apparently earless. It will mate with ordinary cows, but the offspring produced will be of an inferior nature. It can prove fierce at times. [F4]

WATER CATTLE Unidentified creatures supposedly found in the Socho-nor Lake in Mongolia. [E]

WATER COW A creature in Scottish folklore. Water cows would emerge from the sea and seem to have been known on islands such as Harris and Skye. They were of tractable disposition and had red ears. They may have been thought of as preternatural – one story speaks of a water cow running into a cliff face and vanishing. [F4]

WATER DOG In the lore of the Indians, this is a spotted otter of large proportions, found in California. It drags its victims into the river and drowns them.

WATER ELEPHANT An elephantoid creature that dwells in the water, reported from the Congo (Brazzaville). Whether it is really a kind of elephant or just something that looks like one has not been established. [30]

WATER FOAL An animal that seems to be of the *each uisce* tribe, which was seen on shore by children and mistaken by them for a foal. It departed into Lough Ballynahinch (Ireland). [143]

WATER HORSE English version of *each uisce/uisge*, the Gaelic name applied to many lake monsters.

WATER LEAPER A legendary bat of Wales, said to attack fishermen. It is small in size. [124]

WATER WOLF A large animal in which the inhabitants of the Fens in England believed in the Middle Ages. If this was a real creature, what it was remains unknown. [C1]

WATERBOBBEJAN A mystery simian of South Africa, said to hang around farms to see what it might snatch.   [#9]

WATERLORD A water dwelling monster with seven heads in the legends of the Fulani of Nigeria. Its skin was scaly. It was slain at last by a hero who smote off all its heads. [K5]

WAYNESBORO APE Apparently a mystery simian whose footprints were discovered near Waynesboro (Pa.) in 2002, but they may have been planted there as a hoax. [53]

WEASEL-LIKE ANIMAL This strange beast was sighted in Brisbane, Australia. Its head looks like a fox's, its body like that of a weasel or mongoose. It was 4'/1m long. Its body was light brown and at least some of its underparts white.   [2]

WEB-FOOTED HORSE This animal is supposed to be found in Colorado, where its peculiar feet enable it to walk on sand dunes.   [E]

WEE-WA An unknown creature whose head was compared with a retriever's with long black hair seen in 1873 in a lagoon near Narrandera, Australia. It seems to be smaller than the similar bunyip.   [H9]

WEEWILMEKQ An antlered monster in the lore of the Pentagouet Indians. One of its antlers ends in two prongs, while the other is straight. It dwells in the water. It grows from a worm-sized original, perhaps assisted by human magic.   [M7]

WELSH WEREWOLF A creature which many believed responsible for the killing of two men in the Bickerton Hills in 1798. It was also blamed for slaughtering sheep and turning over coaches.   [S1*]

WELSH WILDMAN Accounts of wildmen are not unknown from Wales. Welsh wildmen have been reported from Denbighshire and near Llandudno. The latter was actually seen at Gloddaeth and was heavily covered in black hair. It had red eyes that glowed and was said to be twice the size of an adult male human.   [S1*]

WERE-EEL Lady Gregory was told of a woman in Ireland who could turn herself into an eel and, in that state, growl.   [G7*]

WEREFOX *see* **Kitsune.**

WEREHARE Certain women in Ireland were believed able to turn themselves into hares. [G7*]

WERELEOPARD This creature was believed to exist in Malaysia and Indonesia. [S17]

WERERAT In Pennsylvania folklore, a human capable of transforming himself into a rat. [206]

WERETIGER A creature of Chinese legend. It is also found in northerly parts of India and in Japan. [W* S17]

WEREWOLF The idea that man can transform himself into a wolf is widespread. It is possible that early hunters formed themselves into groups which identified with the wolf and perhaps wore wolf pelts and their memory is enshrined in the ubiquity of the werewolf figure. Herodotus mentions that there was a tribe called the Nueri, of whom it was rumoured that each member turned into a wolf for a few days each year, but he does not believe this tale. Pliny disbelieved in the werewolf. In some cases, there are actual accounts of men donning wolfskins and behaving like wolves, providing, perhaps, an analogy to the Leopard Men of Africa. The ritual they underwent involved an unguent, perhaps an hallucinogen. These groups were perhaps perpetuated in Norse society, where there were frenetic warriors dedicated to Odin who wore wolfskins. They were known as the Ulfhednar.

In Constantinople there was supposed to have been an outbreak of werewolfism in 1542, compelling Sultan Suliman II to lead an attack on them, killing 150.

In Italy belief in the werewolf (*lupo mannaro*) was once widespread. In Sicily the term *rucculu* or *ruzulo* was specifically used to mean the howl of the werewolf. The Sicilians believed that a child conceived at the new moon would become a werewolf. On the same island it was believed in Messina that you could cure a werewolf if you struck him with a key of a certain shape. Spain has very few traditions of werewolves. In Portugal the werewolf (*lobis-homen*) was often believed to be an unfortunate, enchanted by a spell. In southern Portugal the werewolf was regarded as being of a timid nature. The French werewolf (*loup garou*) was exported to Canada.

In Argentina it is believed the seventh son in a family (provided there are no intervening daughters) will turn into a werewolf (*lobison*). A somewhat similar belief obtains in Brazil, where the child becomes a werewolf (*lobisomem*) on his thirteenth birthday.

The bite or even scratch of a werewolf was deemed sufficient to pass on the condition. It is sometimes said that werewolves, when in human form, have bristles on their hands. Another tradition is that the werewolf will have a half moon or crescent moon on his thigh.

A silver bullet is supposed to be effective in killing a werewolf. So too is a silver club.

Lycanthropy, the condition whereby one believes one is an animal, is a recognised mental illness. The patient may not necessarily think the animal concerned is a wolf. I have heard of one sufferer who believes himself to be a gerbil. [S12 S17 S8/B]

WEST HAWK LAKE MONSTER C. Rutkowski mentions a monster in this Manitoba lake, but furnishes no further information. [R8]

WHANGDOODLE A creature seen in White County, Illinois, by a number of people around 1972. One Henry McDaniel found it scratching at his door and opened fire on it. It stood upright, but had no less than three legs. It was grey and hirsute and had bulging pink reflective eyes. McDaniel was not the only witness. Perhaps it was some kind of kangaroo whose tail was mistaken for a limb. Then again, what would a kangaroo have been doing in Illinois? But *see* **Devil Monkey.**

WHE-ATCHEE Name applied to a monster said to live in Lake Steilacoom in Washington state. [C/H]

WHEEL-SNAKE Wheel-snakes were reported from Sweden. They lived in Lakes Regneven and Alsjon and would travel from one to the other by forming themselves into a loop and rolling. They were regarded as very dangerous and would prey on children. They have not been reported for 200 years. [34]

WHISKERED SWIFT Unclassified swift reported from Africa and Asia. [E]

WHITE BOAR This seems to be, not merely a white-coloured boar, but a different species from the usual wild boar of Europe. It has been reported from Kosovo. [#11]

WHITE BROCKET DEER Reports of this unclassified species of deer were in circulation in Brazil in 2000. [E]

WHITE DOG Preternatural white dogs are sometimes reported from parts of Britain. A notable one is Galley Trot, reported from the north of England and Suffolk. [B8]

WHITE FROG A frog reported from Rwanda. Whether it constitutes a new species or is a mere colour variation has not been determined. [31]

WHITE HYENA An unusually coloured hyena seen by Dikembe Zgaur of Kenya. For further information *see* **Black Hyena.**

WHITE LAKE MONSTER This Argentine lake was said to contain a monster with a long neck which would surface at night. From sounds heard, it would seem it made nocturnal visits to the beach. Zoologist C. Onelli was informed of this in 1897. [C25]

WHITE MYSTERY CAT A mystery big cat, coloured pure white, has been reported recently from Scotland. Witnesses were John and Viola Smith and the former was able to take some video footage. [2]

WHITE RIVER MONSTER The White River in Arkansas is a tributary of the Mississippi. There have been a number of monster reports over the years. George Mann, fisherman, claimed he had seen it in 1915. Farmer Bramblett Bateman claimed to have seen a strange animal in the river in 1937 and Deputy Sheriff Z.B. Reid saw "something" which might have been a sturgeon or a catfish. Certainly, both fish can grow to huge proportions. In 1971, there were a number of reports. One commented on a lack of scales. A "spiny-backed" creature was seen near Jacksonport. Tracks were reported speaking of three clawed toes. R. Mackal thinks it was a sea-elephant, unrecognised for what it was by those who saw it, either *Mirounga leonina* or *Mirounga angustirostris.* It is certainly rather far north for the former.   [M2]

WHITE SEAL An unknown species observed in Birch Bay and other places off the coast of Washington state.   [31]

WHITE SERPENT A serpent in Swedish folklore. Witches were on the lookout for it, for consuming it would enhance their knowledge. Some said you might only see one once in a hundred years. If you did but lick the serpent, you would become a healer. [S7/A]

WHITE STAG A preternatural creature of the Pine Barrens of New Jersey. It is said to help endangered people.

WHITE VIPER A rare snake in Danish folklore, said to exist on the island of Mors in a fiord in Jutland. If you eat it, you will see hidden things and acquire great understanding. [S7/A]

WHITE-HAIRED MEN A strange race of humans which, Pliny informs us, were to be found in the region of the Caspian Sea. Every member of the race had white hair and green eyes.

WHITLEY BAY SEA-SERPENT   Some fishermen who had captured and killed a strange creature in Whitley Bay in the north of England, exhibited it locally and advertised it as "the great sea-serpent" in 1849. A correspondent of the *Zoologist* confessed himself unable to identify the creature.   [H5]

WHOWIE In the traditions of the Australian Aborigines, this awful beast was 20' in length and had a frog's head, six legs and a tail.   [134]

WIHWIN A   sea monster of Central American Indian lore, reported off the east coast.[E]

WILD MAN OF THE WOODS A creature with huge eyes and a scale-covered body. It was 6'5"/2m tall and, according to its exhibitor, had been captured in Tennessee in 1878. [K1]

WILD WOMAN OF NAVIDAD According to a Texas legend, a wild woman covered with short brown hair who would enter houses and pilfer food. Her tracks were discovered around 1837. Attempts to capture her failed. She seems to have had a male companion at first, but he died or disappeared. An escaped male slave who was captured was blamed for being the wild woman, but this is unconvincing. [90]

WILDMAN The term wildman has been used to designate hominoid creatures in European tradition. Jacob Grimm records that they were thought to be much the same as giants. They seem to have been well known amongst the early Germans amongst whom the terms *waltuoder* and *waltmann* are found designating them. The female was referred to as a *wild wip*. The Norse too spoke of wild women which they termed *ividjur* and *iarrvidjur*. They were portrayed in pageants and plays, the first such play being performed at Padua in 1208. Actual reports of sightings occur. In 1407 James Egelinus, a Scotsman shipwrecked on the Norwegian coast, saw wildmen and was told by the locals that they would raid human habitations at night and eat humans, unless driven off by dogs. In a forest in Saxony a humanoid couple were pursued by hunters. They killed the female, but captured the male, which was tamed. Another wildman was captured in 1531 in the forest of Salzburg, but would not eat and died of hunger. Wildmen were often depicted on inn-signs in the Low Countries. *For Basque traditions of wildmen, see* **Basa Juan;** *for modern European sightings, see* **Swedish Wildman, Spanish Wildman, Italian Wildman.** *For the English wildman, see* **Wodewose.** *For a possible Irish wildman, see* **Gruagach.**

WILTSHIRE WILDMAN A creature described as uncouth, he was reported in Wiltshire about 1877. He tried to abduct a farmer's wife, but dropped her when shot at. [W5*]

WINAMBOO Short hairy hominoid of Australian Aboriginal lore.

WINDIGO A fearsome giant in the folklore of the more eastern Native Americans. Different forms of the name exist and, if the Tete-de-Boule of Quebec are to be believed, it is identical with the *kokotsche* and *atshen*. The *chenoo* may be another name for the same creature. The windigo is said to rub himself against resinous trees and roll in the sand. This would eventually give the impression that he was covered in stone, which could have given rise to the Iroquoian belief in stone giants and the Huron legend of the *strendu*, said to be covered with flinty scales. Windigo voices are loud and thunderous, they are (or were) naked, but did not suffer from cold, they had no knowledge of the bow and they ate Indians. They are black and lipless. They may be identical with the creatures variously referred to as Eastern Bigfoot or Marked Hominids.
Windigos live in families and are occasionally supposed to marry humans. The windigo taste for human flesh is well known. Some say the windigo has a heart of ice, but whether they mean it literally or figuratively is another matter. Only by melting its heart can it be slain. There is a psychosis involving a craving for human flesh called after the windigo, which occurs in humans from time to time. [R3 R4]

WINGED CREATURE On July 23rd, 2003, Diego, a college student and two friends were visiting his grandfather's house in San Pedro, Chile. At 9 p.m. they were disturbed by the sound of scared dogs. At 9.15 something began knocking violently on the door, greatly affrighting those within. When they thought their visitor gone, they looked out and saw a creature 5'/1.5m tall with wings. Its skin was completely glossy and devoid of hair. Its beak was small, its wings batlike and its legs strong and clawed. It flew away.

It should perhaps be noted that Diego has also claimed to have encountered small entities to which he refers as imps, but they do not appear to fall into a cryptozoological framework. [28]

WINGED DEATH WORM Apart from the ordinary Mongolian death worm, there is supposed to be a winged variety, but this may be a discrete animal, perhaps a reptile, with legs resembling wings. [#8]

WINGED HUMANOID John Kuluk maintains he saw a grey, flying entity with a human-like face and no beak in Maryland in the 1970s. The creature had feathers all over, especially along its arms. [#7]

WINGED KANGAROO-LIKE CREATURE This animal was captured by a miner in Chile, according to the newspaper *Las Ultimas Noticias* in 2002, but it escaped again. It was seen later in a cave near the village of O'Higgins and was described as a giant bat. It was said to be 5'7"/1.7m tall.

WINGED RUNNING CREATURE Mauricio Sanchez of Santiago (Chile) was driving home one night when an unidentified creature with wings and of human size, ran past his car to disappear into the darkness ahead. [#9]

WINGED SERPENT Such creatures were to be found in Glamorgan, Wales, in the vicinity of Penllyn Castle. They seem to have been of many colours and looked beautiful, but they had a tendency to raid poultry. Local lore said they had a king and queen. An old woman told M. Trevelyan that she had seen the skin and feathers of one that had fallen in a fight with her grandfather and uncle.

Radnor Forest in the north of Wales was also a centre for these animals. They were apparently wiped out because of their farmyard raids. A piece in the magazine *Bye-Gones*, dated 1892, spoke of one supposed to have lived near a farm called Tan yr Allt.

Various ancient authors spoke of winged serpents. Thus, Herodotus averred they were to be found in Arabia, where they guarded frankincense trees. They were small and of various colours. He claimed to have seen the backbones and ribs of these creatures. Aristotle assures us you could find them in Ethiopia. Megasthenes placed such creatures in India and said they were nocturnal. [T3 G7]

WINNEBOZHO A creature which the Ho-Chuck Indians claim lives in Lake Michigan. It may be identical with the animal called Lenapizka by the Peoria. [R2]

WINNIPOGO A lake monster reported from Lakes Winnipeg and Winnipegosis (Manitoba). It has been estimated at more than 20'/6m in length. A large bone was found in the vicinity of the lake and then lost, but not before a wooden copy was made and this resembles the bone of a prehistoric whale, according to a University of Manitoba academic. [C20]

WINSTEAD WILDMAN   The story of this strange Connecticut creature surfaced in 1895. R. Smith was innocently picking blackberries, as you do, when he was astonished to find himself face to face with a naked man covered with black hair. This being then began cavorting wildly and making strange noises, before running off, his hair floating behind him. Ladies from New York who saw the creature felt it was an ape or a baboon. Chief of Police Steve Wheeler told of following a "gorilla man" into a swamp, but losing its trail. One view was that the Wildman was an escaped lunatic.

There was a supposition that the Wildman might have married the Witch of Winchester, thereby producing a later wildman, said to frequent such areas as the Bucket of Blood.

WITCH FISH   A fish supposed to live in Creve Coeur Lake in Illinois. According to legend, the daughter of an Indian chief had drowned herself here for love. The chief prayed to the god of the lake to imprison her soul as she had cherished a passion for one of the Spanish enemy. This he did and she now lurks there as the witch fish, dragging faithless lovers beneath the water.

From 1967 strange creatures, looking somewhat like alligators, have been discerned in the lake, but it is too far north for alligators to survive.   [#7]

WITCHIE WOLF   In Chippewa lore, a witchie wolf will guard a warrior's grave. There is supposed to be a population of these animals. Young people in cars have reported hearing their barking on the Omer Plains, near Omer (Michigan). Anyone who emerges from a car at such a time will be attacked by the invisible animals. [#12]

WOADD EL-UMA   A hominoid creature believed to live in the Nile in the Sudan. It is said to be covered with reddish-brown hair. A man named Kotschy found some possible tracks of this creature in the 19th Century. A local native filled in him and his companion Russegger with details of the animal. [H7]

WOBO   An animal of the cat variety known in Ethiopia, yellow/brown or grey/brown in colour, with black stripes. It has often been seen. It is said to have an almost human face. It is also known as the *mentilit.*   [S7]

WODEWOSE   The wildman of English legend. Pictures of it tend to emphasise its human attributes – there are no pithecoid features about it. However, it is unlikely any drawer of such pictures actually claimed to have seen a wodewose in the flesh. The wodewose does not always appear to have been regarded as evil. It was sometimes covered with moss rather than hair. A wild hairy man – a wodewose? – was reported at Sproughton (Suffolk) in the 16th Century.

WOG   In Britain this is a pejorative term for an oriental and in Australia it means a germ; but in Georgia (USA), it means a certain mystery animal which was to be found in the vicinity of Jug Tavern (now Winder) about 1800. Its head was like a bear's, it was nearly the size of a horse, it had black hair and its hind legs were shorter than its forelegs. Its mouth never seemed to close over its large white teeth, its tongue would flicker in and out. Its tail was large, of uniform width. There was a bunch of white hair on the end of it. When it walked it seemed to incline sideways, first to right, then to left. It would make a whizzing sound when it moved up and down and this it did all the time. It is said that domestic animals feared it. [M8]

WOKOLO *see* **Fating'ho.**

WOLF, THE No, this is not the familiar animal so-called, but rather a disease which was also an animal that looked like a lizard. It was the object of belief in 19th Century Wales. It would attack women only, lodging itself in the breast. It was supposed to enter a woman's system as a result of drinking contaminated water. A piece in the magazine *Bye-Gones* dated 1876 speaks of a man who claimed to have captured one of these creatures and who exhibited its supposed bottled remains at Oswestry.

WOLF POND MONSTER A monster like a giant snake has been reported from this body of water in Pennsylvania.   [C/H]

WOLF-CAT When the Spaniards reached the court of the Aztec emperor Montezuma II (reigned 1502-1520), they noticed in his zoo a mystery animal, which they referred to as a 'wolf-cat'. It may have been some form of hyena, possibly now extinct. [S7]

WOLF-LIKE ANIMAL A pure white creature resmbling a wolf said to be found in the Great Lakes area of North America.   [A]

WOLF-WOMAN 1 A creature reported from Mobile (Alabama) in 1971. Her top half was like a woman, her lower half like a wolf. The police were unable to find the creature.   [C10]
2 A creature blamed for the killing of a great number of poultry in Yucatan (Mexico). It was described as 4.9'/1.5m tall.   [1]

WOLLUNQUA A huge serpent in Aboriginal mythology, said to live in a water hole in the Murchison Range in Australia.   [B2]

WONTHAGGI MONSTER A term for an unknown animal that was killing sheep in Victoria, Australia, in 1955. A witness said it had canine features and stripes, which could mean it was a surviving thylacine.

WOOD DEVIL Hairy, grey-coloured creatures that were supposed to inhabit the woods of Cross County (New Hampshire) were known as wood devils. They had a shape somewhat like a human's, but their faces were very different.   [90]

WOOFIN NANNY A hairy catlike creature which killed animals near Greensboro (North Carolina) in 1966. It punctured the cadavers and bled them.

WOOLENEAG A black cat referred to as living in Maine in early times, much larger than a wildcat.   [C19]

WOOLLY BOOGER A term used in the southern United States for a BHM. [G7]

WOOLLY CHEETAH A kind of cheetah which differed from the norm in that its coat was woolly, darker and bore tawny spots. A specimen arrived at London Zoo from South Africa in 1877. It was larger than other cheetahs. Other specimens were recorded in South Africa. It now seems extinct and its classification remains a mystery. [S8]

WOOO-WOOO The name given by cryptozoologist Ivan T. Sanderson to a creature he heard, but did not see. All the wildlife round about him on his New Jersey farm whent silent when the sound *wooo-wooo* was heard. Eventually it receded, perhaps blending with a similar sound made by another creature. This incident occurred in 1965. Three other people reported having heard this sound. [H]

WORCESTERSHIRE MYSTERY ANIMAL According to the *Worcestershire Evening News* (1st August, 2003), a strange and unidentified creature walked onto the road near Knightwick. It had a long nose, was the size of a half-grown fox-cub, a brown and mottled skin, a long tail (not a fox's brush) and a hunched back.

WORM This term, sometimes spelled *wyrm*, is used to old records to designate a dragon. The Hiberno-English pronunciation *wurrum* is used to mean an Irish lake monster.

WORM MAN One of a species of worm which can, according to the Eskimo, take on the appearance of a man.   [B7]

WULASHA Simian creatures lacking tails with backward teeth and feet, about 5' tall in the folklore of the Chibchan-Paezan Indians of Latin America.   [R7]

WULVER A creature with the head of a wolf and a man's body covered in brown hair. He is said to live on Unst, one of the Shetland Islands. He would catch fish, leaving some as presents for the elderly.   [F4]

WYCHWOOD BEASTS Two creatures of unknown nature have been reported from this wood near Oxford. One looked somewhat like a bear and was seen by J. Blackwell in 1992. In 1993 the same witness heard shouts which became a howl and then he saw an animal resembling a bear chasing deer. Another beast, light silver in colour with a black dorsal stripe, about the size of a fox, with a bushy rail and catlike head was seen to rush into the woods. The three witnesses were sure it was not a fox.   [#1]

WYUNGARE'S MONSTER In Australian Aboriginal folklore, a great reptile that lived long ago. Fierce teeth filled its mouth. While its forelegs were too small to be useful, its hind legs were endowed with huge claws. Its head could be seen above the trees. It was killed by the hero Wyungare. [C19]

WYVERN A dragon with only one pair of legs. It is smaller than the normal dragon. The name seems to come from French *vouivre*, itself derived from Latin *vipera.*

According to Richard Freeman, it had a sting in its tail and was said to spread infection. One is said to be found in the environs of Cynhwch Lake in Wales. We may suspect that in this wyvern we have here an anglicisation of Welsh *gwiber*.   [#1 C1]

X

X A kind of man-beast, said to be found in Kenya. J. Roumegure, who gave it this name or, rather, this symbol, for it is not a name as such, claims there are four kinds of it. [5]

XIAO DE MAO REN A large hominoid reported from Manchuria (China). [77]

XI'LGO A bigfoot-type creature in the lore of the Nahelan-Tillanook Indians. It means 'wild woman' and may be the female form of the *yi'dyi'tay*, which is a similar creature whose name means 'wild man' in the lore of that nation.   [90]

XING-XING A mystery ape reported from China. It possibly represents a relict population of orang-utans, thought to be extinct in that country. According to the monumental dictionary of the Emperor K'ang Hsi (reigned 1661-1722), the xing-xing has a doglike face and emits cries like children's wails.   [#4 T1]

XIPE A hominoid creature of Nicaraguan folklore, hairy and of simian appearance. [#9]

XIUCOATL Serpents in which the Aztecs believed. They perhaps breathed fire and certainly had fiery associations.

XUEREN An alternative name for the yeren. It means 'snowman'. [D5]

XWOXWA:YA INSECT A species of insect said to occupy this pond (i.e. Xwoxwa:ya) in British Columbia. Its bite was said to be fatal and it could grow larger than a man's hand. [#11]

Y

YABALIK-ADAM A Central Asiatic wildman with yellowish hair. One was allegedly captured in 1912 and taken away by the Chinese authorities.   [E]

YABOY-ADAM Name used for a wildman in Xinjiang (China).

YACU-MAMA A huge serpent said to be found off the coast of South America and in the Amazon. [B13/A]

YAGIS A sea-monster in the lore of the Kwakiutl Indians. It has a taste for human flesh.   [134]

YAGMORT   The name given to a wildman by the Komi, who live to the west of the northern part of the Urals in Russia. Reports of encounters with yagmorts include one about 1983, one in 1985 and one in 1986.   [B3]

YAHO   A name for diminutive hairy beings in the folklore of Bermuda. The hair is dark or red-brown, the big toe is splayed. They have a generally simian aspect.   [R7]

YAKHETAN AMAI   A creature, perhaps preternatural, reported on a road which stretches from Pennsylvania to Georgia. It is 3'/1m tall with canine characteristics, but it is regarded as too tall to be a dog and insufficiently robust to be a wolf. The name given above is Cherokee. In English it is variously called the red dog fox and the fence rail dog.   [A]

YALE   This animal is described by Pliny, who says that it was the size of an hippopotamus and had two movable horns. When fighting, it could use one horn as a weapon and hold the other in reserve. It is possible to train the horns of cattle to go in different directions and the sight of such cattle may lie behind the legend of this beast. Its jaws resembled those of a wild boar. Its body was spotted. Its name may be derived from Hebrew *ya'el*, a wild goat.

YALI   A legendary creature of India, said to have an lion's body with an elephant's tusks and trunk.   [4]

YAMAMAYA   On Iriomote, one of the Ryuku Islands, the natives tell of this tigrine beast about the size of a sheepdog. This should not be confused with the animal known as the Iriomote cat (*Felis iriomotensis*). It may be a subspecies of clouded leopard (*Neofelis nebulosa*).   [S7]

YANA PUMA   Black mystery cat in the lore of the Incas.

YANAZH   In the legends of the Circassians, a kind of one-eyed giant. [H3]

YANGSHOU DRAGON   Apparently two "dragons" were driven to the ground in stormy weather in this remote village in Anhui Province in November, 2002. They were locked in a barn. While one was subsequently released, the other, when last heard of, was still in captivity.   [88]

YAPUT CHAKIANAK   The Athabascan Indians of Alaska believe in these cyclopean giants. They can be mistaken for rocks. They fight amongst themselves.   [A]

YAQUARU   A catlike animal supposed to live in South America. Thomas Falkner, S.J., said he had seen one diving into the Parana in 1774. In the same book he gave a description supplied by the Indians – it looked like an otter or 'river wolf', was the size of a donkey, was endowed with tusks and dwelt in the depths of the river or in whirlpools at the confluences of streams.   [S7]

YARA-MA-YHA-HO An Australian aboriginal mystery animal, a toothless creature that resembles a frog-like man with suckers on its hands. It is supposed to suck the "substance" out of children on whom it drops.   Heuvelmans argues that these characteristics, apart from the last one, coincide with those of the spectral tarsier, but then points out that this animal has never been known in Australia. The ancestors of the Aborigines are supposed to have reached Australia 50,000 years ago and could hardly have retained a memory of this creature which is found to the north in Indonesia. Heuvelmans argues for some migrations being much later, perhaps not long before the whites arrived.   [H9]

YARD-PIG *see* **Earth Hound**.

YAROMA Variant name for the yowie. [M17]

YAVO-KHAL'G Name used for a wildman in Xinjiang (China). One of these which was killed was reported to have yellow hair.   [T1]

YEAHOH A name for a BHM in Harlan County (Kentucky).

YEHO A hairy creature the size of a man in the folklore of the Bahamas. [R7]

YEHWE ZOGBANU In the beliefs of Benin (formerly Dahomey), a giant with thirty horns. It fights with hunters.   [4]

YE'IITSOH Navaho Indian name for a BHM.

YENOSU'RIYE A short-sized kind of hominoid in Catawba Indian folklore.   [R7]

YENRISH A creature in Huron lore, said to inhabit Lake Erie. [M7]

YEREN A wild man of Chinese lore, often referred to simply as the Chinese wildman. Wildmen are often mentioned in Chinese literature and the term *yeren* is the word most frequently used to designate this creature. Strangely enough, the yeren seems to be sometimes associated with laughter, though it is averred that it has no language. Yerens are said to be capable of eating humans, to have long hair and to have the ability to maintain an upright stance.   The colour of their hair is grey/brown, red, black or occasionally white.   Wang Zrlin, a biologist, saw a dead yeren in the 1940s. Fan Jinquan, a geologist, encountered a couple of living ones, a mother and young, in the 1950s. The testimony of these scientifically trained individuals cannot be taken lightly.

A considerable number of sightings have occurred in the provinces of Hubei (particularly Fang County) and Yunnan.

In 1957 an alleged yeren attacking a young girl was itself attacked and killed by village women hastening to her aid. However, when scientists examined the hands and feet of this animal twenty years later, they pronounced them to be those of a stump-tailed macaque, which shows this monkey can be mistaken for the yeren.

Chinese scientist Zhou Guoxing, collating data available, concludes the height of the animal varies from 4-8'/1.2-2.5m and that it drops on all fours when running or climbing. It is mainly vegetarian and insectivorous.   [D5]

YETI The creature which many regard as synonymous with the Abominable Snowman. Actually, there may be several animals for which this is used as an umbrella term:-

[a] the *meh-teh*, which is about the size of a human; generally described as being brown (older specimens greying) with a conical head, a thick neck, broad feet and a jaw that sticks out somewhat;

[b] the *dzu-teh*, which is very large and is reported from Tibet and Xingiang and which may be identical with the gin-sung, tok and kung-lu;

[c] the diminutive *teh-lma*, which attains a height of 4-5'/1.5m, said to have thick red fur and a slight mane..

Of course, Sherpas and other locals have been almost on terms of back-slapping familiarity with yetis, but European knowledge of the beasts seems to date from the 19th Century (with the possible exception of one classical allusion). L.A. Waddell reported its tracks in Sikkim in 1887. Tracks were also reported by J.R.O. Gent in 1915; by an unnamed hunter in 1922; and by E. Bentley Beaumont in 1931. As regards sightings, H.J. Elwes claimed to have seen one in 1906; C.K. Howard-Bury saw a group of them in 1921; one was discerned by members of the Everest expedition in 1922; and A.M. Tombazi beheld a specimen in 1925. Writers on cryptozoology have also claimed sightings: John Keel in 1956, Peter Byrne in 1957.

Yetis are said to venture above the snowline from the forest to obtain saline moss. It may be that they are also looking for lichens, a good source of Vitamin E. They make a whistling noise (the same has been said of bigfoot) and are omnivorous. They are supposed to be ferocious and capable of killing a man.

Y. Takahashi claimed to have come upon a yeti cave in 1994. Unfortunately, his camera froze before he could photograph the yetis within. He is currently (2003) making a further attempt to find a photograph the creature. M. Nabuka has recently contended that the yeti is nothing more than a brown bear, known locally as *meti*. Nepalis argued that the yeti cannot be explained away by the mere confusion of near homophones and point out that *meti* does not mean a bear exclusively, but can also be applied to a supernatural creature.

Regarding whether yetis are friendly or hostile, there are conflicting reports – perhaps because this varies from yeti to yeti. Thus Captain d'Auvergne claimed he was aided by a 9'/2.7m tall hominoid when injured in the Himalayas in 1939, yet in 1957 Tom Slick heard of yetis battering people to death.

The yeti has been a protected species in Nepal since 1958. [C21 S7 H9]

YI'DYI'TAY *see* **Xi'lgo**.

YING LONG In Chinese dragon lore, a dragon with wings. [J2]

YOFUNE-NUSHI A sea-serpent of Japanese legend. Maidens were sacrificed to this beast until one of them, more enterprising than her sisters, took a knife with her and killed it.   [K7]

YOKYN A mysterious animal with doglike characteristics reported from Australia. It is known to both Aborigines and whites. It sometimes has stripes.   [S7]

YOSER An alternative name or nickname for the yowie. I am grateful to Tim the Yowie Man for clarifying this matter for me.

YOWIE This is the name currently given to a mystery ape-like or hominid creature rumoured to exist in Australia. However, it has come into use only recently; before that it was referred to as the *yahoo*. This was the name used for bestial humans in Swift's *Gulliver's Travels* (1726) and it is possible that the name for the Australian creature came from this source.

The yowie seems to have been well known to the Aborigines, who harboured a tradition that they largely replaced the yowie race. The word itself may come from Wiradjuri *youree* and there may be some relationship to Yuawaalaraay *yuwi* (dream spirit). J. Holman in *Travels* (1835) regarded the "devil or yahoo" as a masked man. Mrs Charles Meredith, in a book published in 1844, claimed the yahoo was a mythical evil spirit. Not everyone would have concurred. In the *Quenbeyan Observer* in 1903 one Harry Williams claimed to have seen Aborigines killing a creature of this sort, which itself looked like an Aborigine covered with grey hair.

Earlier, in 1881, a creature said to look like a large monkey was reported in the *Goulbourn Herald.* A "wild man or gorilla" was reported by a boy in 1894. One Charles Harper, writing in the *Sydney Sun* in 1912, said he had met reliable men who claimed to have seen the yowie and asserted that he himself had seen it once, at night time by firelight, when it approached his camp. About 5'9"/1.7m in height, he claimed it had brownish-red hair on its body and limbs and possibly black hair (though the light here may have been deceptive) on its shoulders and back. It had long protruding canine teeth. The stomach hung over the thighs like a sack. A drawing in the paper does not seem to conform entirely to this description. A drawing by witnesses who claimed a sighting in 1962 shows a much stockier, gorilla-like creature, with the face somewhat obscured by a tree branch. There have been various other sightings reported over the years.

Yowies are described as neckless creatures. Two boys who claimed they had seen a pair of yowies in 1981 said their legs were straight, not bowed like a gorilla's, and their hair was brown. Reports of yowies tend to come from the south-eastern parts of the country. Official science treats the subject of the yowie with considerable caution.

YUHO A name used amongst the Rama Indians of Central America and the Creoles for the wulasha.   [R7]

YUKON CREATURE This Yukon is not the Canadian territory so called, but Yukon in Canada County, Oklahoma. In 1988 two witnesses claimed to have seen a strange creature in the woods. It had a head like a horse or a camel, a body like a Great Dane and small wings. At first it proceeded on all fours, but then stood up and walked on its hind legs.   [R6]

YUURI Little hairy manlike creatures of Australian Aboriginal folklore. One wonders if there is any linguistic connection between their name and that of the yowie.   [H6]

Z

ZABAIRO A primate the size of a tree in the folklore of the Cote d'Ivoire. It goes about carrying a torch in each hand. Heuvelmans considers it to be inspired by reports of the gorilla, which does not dwell that far west.   [H7]

ZALUZUGU Waraga name for the kikomba.   [H7]

ZAMBA ZARAA This animal is said to live in Mongolia and looks like a hedgehog. It is said to be able to inflate itself to the size of a yurt or Mongolian tent. [#8]

ZARATAN A marine creature in oriental lore, which, it was said, sailors would mistake for an island. It was supposed the zaratan had woods and clefts on its back, but, when seamen having disembarked lit a fire, it would awaken the beast, which would start to submerge.   [B10]

ZEBRO This animal is mentioned in medieval and renaissance Spanish works. It looked like an ass, was grey, had a dark muzzle and there was a black stripe on its back. A recent theory is that it may represent a population of *Equus hydruntis*, a creature hitherto thought to have died out 12,000 years ago. The word *zebra* may be derived from this, rather than being a native African word.   [#1]

ZEMLEMER A word meaning a land surveyor, applied to hominoids in Siberia. [C3]

ZEZENGORRI In Basque lore, a preternatural bull, red in colour, which lived underground. [4]

ZIKTA In Jewish legend, a small creature on the Ark. Noah did not know what to feed it until he made the happy discovery that it ate worms.   [G4]

ZIPHIUS A huge fish with an owl's head, it figured in medieval bestiaries. Its beak was the shape of a wedge, its mouth was the size of a pit. It frequented the northerly seas, inspiring sailors with dread.   [H2]

ZIZ A giant bird in Hebrew lore, it dominated all the fowls of the air. It was created especially to frighten the birds of prey, so that they would not destroy the other birds. Its wings when spread out would hide the sun from view. They also shielded the earth against the ravaging winds from the south. If it stood in the midst of the ocean, the waves would but lap about its ankles. There is also a female ziz. She lays a single egg at one time and it is of vast proportions. The fledgling ziz breaks its way out of the egg and does not need the mother to hatch it.   [G4]

ZU The bird of storm in Sumerian mythology. It had the head of a lion.

ZUGERSEE GIANT FISH A huge fish reported in this Swiss lake in 1509. [E]

ZUIYO-MARU MONSTER A supposed sea monster fished out of the sea by a Japanese vessel in 1977. It was in fact a rotting basking-shark.

Bibliography and Sources

Early Writers

Aelian (3rd Century AD) A Roman author, in full *Claudius Aelianus.* He is the first person on record to mention fly-fishing.

Aldrovandus, Ulysses (1522-1607) Prominent Italian naturalist.

Ctesias (about 400 BC) Greek physician at the Persian court.

Gesner, Conrad (1516-1565) Extremely important naturalist of his time.

Herodotus (5th Century BC) Greek historian who wrote a large historical work and who did his best to be reliable. He was sceptical of some of the material he reported.

Kircher, Athanasius (1602-1680) Jesuit polymath. He was much interested in dragons and also wrote a work on Noah's ark, which included the names of many supposed hybrids. Additionally, he suggested that disease might be carried by small or microscopic organisms and he invented the magic lantern.

Linnaeus, Carolus (1707-1778) Swedish naturalist who invented the original taxonomic classification for biology.

Olaus Magnus (1490-1558) Archbishop of Uppsala (Sweden). Writer on geography noted for his *Carta marina* (1539) and his *Historia de gentibus septentrionalibus* (1555).

Physiologus The prototype of the medieval bestiaries, which contained much animal lore.

Pliny (23-79 AD) In full, *Gaius Plinius Secundus;* noted Roman natural historian. He died because he went up the slopes of Vesuvius to glean information about volcanoes, only to be overcome by fumes.

Pontoppidan, Erik (1698-1764) Bishop of Bergen (Norway) and notable academic, he wrote on sea creatures.

Solinus (3rd Century AD) Writer on natural history and other subjects.

Ssuma Ch'ien (2nd Century BC) Prominent Chinese historian.

Topsell, Edward (17th Century) Author of two notable volumes, *The History of Four-Footed Beasts* (1607) and *The History of Serpents* (1608).

Books

A   Arnold, N. *Clandestine Creatures* n.p.: 2003.
A1   Arnold, N. *Odd-Bodies* n.p.: 2003.
A2   Ashton, F. *Curious Creatures in Zoology* n.p.: n.d.
A3   Austin, S. *The Sand Whales of Mars* Findon: n.d.
B1   Baring-Gould, S. *Curious Myths of the Middle Ages* London: 1866.
B2   Barrett, C. *The Bunyip* Melbourne: 1946.
B2/A   Bartrum, P. *Welsh Classical Dictionary* Aberystwyth: 1993.
B3   Bayanov, D. *In the Steps of the Russian Snowman* Moscow: 1996
B4   Beer, T. *The Beast of Exmoor* Barnstaple: n.d.
B5   Benwell, G./Waugh, A.A. *Sea Enchantress* London: 1961
B6   Bille, M. *Rumors of Existence* Surrey (B.C.): 1995.
B7   Blackman, W.H. *Field Guide to North American Monsters* New York: 1998
B8   Bord, J. and C. *Alien Animals* St Albans: 1980.
B8*   Bord, J. and C. *The Bigfoot Casebook* London: 1982.
B9   Bord, J. and C. *Modern Mysteries of the World* London: 1985.
B10   Borges, J.L. *Book of Imaginary Beings* New York: 1969
B11   Brandon, J. *Weird America* New York: 1978.
B12   Bradley, M. *More Than a Myth* Willowdale: 1989.
B13   Brewer, E.C. *The Reader's Handbook* London: 1919.
B13/A Brewer, E.C. *Dictionary of Phrase and Fable* Philadelphia: 1898.
B14   Brierley, N. *They Stalk by Night* Bishops Nympton: 1989.
B15   Bright, H. *Giants in the Sea* London: 1989.
B16   Brown, C.E. *Sea-Serpents; Wisconsin occurrences of these weird water creatures*
          Madison: 1942.
B17   Butler, H. *Ten Thousand Saints* Kilkenny: 1972.
C1   *CFZ Yearbook 1998* Exeter: 1998.
C2   *CFZ Yearbook 2002* Exeter: 2002.
C3   *CFZ Yearbook 2003* Exeter: 2003.
C3*   *CFZ Yearbook 2004* Exeter: 2004.
C4   Campbell, M. *Strange World of the Brontes* Wilmslow: 2001.
C5   Carrington, R. *Mermaids and Mastodons*   London: 1957.
C6   Childress, D.H. *Lost Cities and Ancient Mysteries of South America* Stelle: 1986.
C6/A   Childress, D.H./Shaver, R. *Lost Continents and the Hollow Earth.* Kempton:
          1999.
C7   Choden, K. *Bhutanese Tales of the Yeti* Bangkok: 1997.
C8   Choden, K. *Folk Tales of Bhutan* Bangkok: 1994.
C8/A   Citro, J.A. *Green Mountains, Dark Tales* Hanover (NH): 1999.
C9   Clair, C. *Unnatural History* London: 1967.
C10   Clark, J. *Unexplained!* Detroit: 1998.
C11   Clark, J./Coleman, L. *Creatures of the Outer Edge* New York: 1978
C11*   Clarke, D. *Supernatural Peak District* London: 2000.
C12   Coghlan, R. *Handbook of Fairies* Chievely: 1998.
C13   Cohen, D. *Encyclopaedia of Monsters* London: 1989.
C14   Cohen, D. *Modern Look at Monsters* New York: 1970.

C15   Cohen, D. *Monsters, Giants and Little Men from Mars* New York: 1975.
C16   Coleman, L. *Bigfoot* New York: 2003.
C17   Coleman, L. *Curious Encounters* Boston: 1985.
C18   Coleman, L. *Mothman* New York: 2002.
C19   Coleman, L. *Mysterious America* New York: 2002.
C20   Coleman, L./Clark, J. *A-Z of Cryptozoology* New York: 1999.
C21   Coleman, L./Huyghe, P. *Field Guide to Bigfoot* New York: 1999.
C21/A Collins, A. *The Brentford Griffin* Wickford: 1985.
C22   Colombo, J.R. *Mysterious Canada* Toronto: 1988.
C23   Corrales, S. *Chupacabras* Murfreesboro: 1997.
C24   Corrales, S. *High Strangeness in Puerto Rico* Maulden: 1998.
C25   Costello, P. *In Search of Lake Monsters* London: 1974.
C26   Costello, P. *The Magic Zoo* London: 1979.
C/H   Coleman, L./Huyge, P. *The Field Guide to Lake Monsters, Sea Serpents and Other Denizens of the Deep* New York: 2003.
D1   Dowson, C. *A Classical Dictionary of Hindu Mythology and Religion* Calcutta: 1982.
D2   de Camp, L.S./Ley, W. *Lands Beyond* New York: 1952.
D3   de Faoite, D. *Paranormal Ireland* Ashbourne: 2002.
D4   Dixon-Kennedy, M. *Encyclopedia of Russian and Slavic Myth and Legend* Santa Barbara: 1998.
D5   Dong, P. *Four Mysteries of Mainland China* Englewood Cliffs: 1984.
D6   Downes, J. *Only Fools and Goatsuckers* Exeter: 1999.
D7   Downes, J. *Smaller Mystery Carnivores of the West Country* Exeter: 1996.
D7/A Downes, J. *The Owlman and Others* Exeter: 2001.
D8   Downes, J./Wright N. *The Rising of the Moon* Corby: 1999.
D9   Duplantier, G. *Subterranean Worlds of Planet Earth* Willowdale: n.d.
E   Eberhart, G.M. *Mysterious Creatures* Santa Barbara: 2002.
E1   Ellis, R. *Monsters of the Sea* New York: 1994.
F1   Fanthorpe, L. *World's Greatest Unsolved Mysteries* Willowdale: 1996.
F2   Farmer, H. *Oxford Dictionary of Saints* Oxford: 1982.
F3   Ferrell, E. *Strange Stories of Alaska and the Yukon* Fairbanks: n.d.
F4   Fleming, M. *Not of This World* Edinburgh: 2002.
F5   Floyd, E.R. *Great Southern Mysteries* Little Rock: 1989.
F6   Floyd, E.R. *More Great Southern Mysteries* Little Rock: 1994.
F7   Fort, C. *Complete Books* New York: 1974.
F8   Francis, D. *Beast of Exmoor* London: 1993.
F9   Francis, D. *Cat Country* Newton Abbot: 1983.
F10   Franklin, A. *Cherokee Folk Zoology* New York: 1990.
F11   Fritze, R. *Legend and Lore of the Americas Before Columbus* Santa Barbara: 1993.
G1   Gaal, A. *In Search of Ogopogo* Surrey (BC): 2001.
G2*   Garner, B. *Canada's Monsters* Hamilton: 1976.
G2   Garner, B. *Monster! Monster!* Blaine: 1995.
G3   Gilroy, R. *Mysterious Australia* Mapleton: 1995.
G4   Ginzberg, L. *Legends of the Jews* Philadelphia: 1913-1938.

G5   Gould, C. *Mythical Monsters* London: 1886.

G6   Gray, A. *The Big Grey Man of Ben MacDhui* Aberdeen: 1970.

G7   Green, J. *Sasquatch; the Apes Among Us* Saanichton: 1978.

G7* Gregory, A. *Visions and Beliefs in the West of Ireland* London: 1920.

G8   Griffiths, B. *Meet the Dragon* Loughborough: 1996.

G9   Grimm, J. *Teutonic Mythology* London: 1880.

H   Hall, M. *Thunderbirds* Minneapolis: 1988.

H1   Halliday, R. *McX: Scotland's X-Files* Edinburgh: 1997.

H2   Hargreaves, J. *Hargreaves' New Illustrated Bestiary* Glastonbury: 1990.

H3   Halpin, H./Ames, M. (ed.) *Manlike Monsters on Trial* Vancouver: 1980.

H4   Harrison, P. *Encyclopaedia of the Loch Ness Monster* London: 1999.

H5   Harrison, P. *Sea Serpent Legends of the British Isles* London: 2000.

H6   Healy, T./Cropper, P. *Out of the Shadows* Chippendale:1994.

H7   Heuvelmans, B. *Les betes humaines d'Afrique* Paris: 1980.

H8   Heuvelmans, B. *In the Wake of the Sea Serpent* London: 1968.

H9   Heuvelmans, B. *On the Track of Unknown Animals* New York: 1959.

H10 Hichens *African Mystery Beasts* (essay in *Discovery*, December, 1937).

H11 Holiday, F. *The Dragon and the Disc* London: 1973.

H11* Holland, R. *Supernatural Clwyd* Llanrwst: 1989.

H12* Hough, Peter *Supernatural Britain* London: 1995.

H12 Hulme, F. *Natural History Lore and Legend* London: 1895.

H13 Hughes, M./Evans, W. *Rumours and Oddities of North Wales* Llanrwst: 1986.

H14 Hunt, G. *Bizarre America* New York: 1988.

I   Izzard, R. *The Hunt for the Buru* London: 1951.

J1   Jones, A. *Dictionary of World Folklore* Edinburgh: 1995.

J2   Jones, D. *An Instinct for Dragons* New York: 2000.

K   Kafton-Minkel, B. *Subterranean Worlds* Port Townsend: 1989.

K1   Keel, J. *The Mothman Prophecies* Lilburn: 1991.

K2   Keel, J. *Complete Guide to Mysterious Beings* New York: 1994.

K4   Kirk, J. *In Search of Lake Monsters* Toronto: 1998.

K5   Knappert, J. *African Mythology* London: 1990.

K6   Knappert, J. *Indian Mythology* London: 1991.

K7   Knappert, J. *Pacific Mythology* London: 1992.

K8   Kossy, D. *Strange Creations* Los Angeles: 2001.

K8/A Krantz, G. *Bigfoot Sasquatch Evidence* Surrey (BC): 1999.

K9   Kutz, J. *Mysteries and Miracles of Arizona* Corrales: 1992.

L1   Lall, K. *Lore and Legend of the Yeti* Delhi: 1988.

L*   Leblond, P.H./Bousfield, E.L. *Cadborosaurus; survivor from the deep.* Victoria (BC): 1995.

L1/A Ley, W. *Exotic Zoology* New York: 1966.

L2   Linahan, L. *More Pit Ghosts, Padfeet and Poltergeists* Rotherham: 1996.

L3   Linahan, L. *Pit Ghosts, Padfeet and Poltergeists* Rotherham: 1994.

L4   Lum, P. *Fabulous Beasts* London: n.d.

M   McBeath, A. *Sky Dragons and Celestial Spirits* London: 1988.

M1   Mackal, R. *A Living Dinosaur?* Leiden: 1987.

M2   Mackal, R. *Searching for Hidden Animals* London: 1983.

M3 McCloy, J./Miller, R. *The Jersey Devil* Wallingford: 1976.

M4 McKillop, J. *Oxford Dictionary of Celtic Mythology* New York: 1998.

M5 Marinacci, M. *Mysterious California* Los Angeles: 1988.

M6 Markotic, V. (ed.) *Sasquatch* Calgary: 1984.

M7 Meurger, M. *Lake Monster Traditions* London: 1988.

M8 Miles, J. *Weird Georgia* Nashville: 2000.

M9 Montgomery-Campbell, E. *In Search of Morag* New York: 1973.

M10 Munro-Hay, S. *Aksum* Edinburgh: 1990.

N1 Napier, J. *Bigfoot* New York: 1973.

N2 Nigg, J. *Wonder Beasts* Englewood: n.d.

O *Oxford Classical Dictionary* Oxford: 2000.

P1 Pennick, N. *Dragons of the West* Chievely: 1997.

P2 Potts, M. *The Myth of the Mermaid and her Kin* Chievely: 2000.

R1 Ramos, M. *Creatures of Midnight* Quezon City: 1990.

R2 Rath, J. *The I-Files* Madison: 1999.

R3 Rath, J. *The M-Files* Madison: 1998.

R4 Rath, J. *The W-Files* Black Earth: 1997.

R4* Redfern, N. *Three Men Seeking Monsters* New York: 2004.

R5 Reed, A.W. *Treasury of Maori Folklore* Wellington: 1963.

R6 Rife, P.L. *America's Nightmare Monsters* San Jose: 2001.

R6/A Riggs, R. *In the Big Thicket* New York: 2001.

R7 Roth, J. *American Elves* Jefferson: 1997.

R8 Rutkowski, C. *Unnatural History* Winnipeg: 1993.

S1 Sanderson, I. *Abominable Snowmen: Legend Come to Life* Philadelphia: 1961.

S1* Saunders, C. *Into the Dragon's Lair* Llanrwst: 2003.

S2 Sergent, D./Wamsley, J. *Mothman; the facts behind the legend* Point Pleasant: 2002.

S2/A Shepard, O. *The Lore of the Unicorn* London: 1930.

S3 Shuker, K. *Dragons* London: 1995.

S4 Shuker, K. *Extraordinary Animals Worldwide* London: 1991.

S5 Shuker, K. *From Flying Toads to Snakes with Wings* St Paul: 1997.

S6 Shuker, K. *In Search of Prehistoric Survivors* London: 1995.

S7 Shuker, K. *Mystery Cats of the World* London: 1989.

S8 Shuker, K. *Mysteries of Planet Earth* London: 1999.

S8/A Shuker, K. *The Beasts That Hide from Man* New York: 2003.

S8/B Simek, R. *Dictionary of Northern Mythology* Cambridge: 1993.

S9 Simpson, J./Roud, S. *Oxford Dictionary of English Folklore* Oxford: 2000.

S10 Skinner, C.M. *Myths and Legends of our own Land* Philadelphia: 1896.

S11 Smith, M. *Bigfoots and Bunyips* Alexandria (NSW): 1993.

S12 South, M. (ed.) *Mythical and Fabulous Creatures* New York: 1987.

S13 Spaeth, F. (ed.) *Mysteries of the Deep* St Paul: 1998.

S14 Spence, L. *The Minor Traditions of British Mythology* London: 1948.

S15 Steiger, B. *Out of the Dark* New York: 2001.

S16 Story, R. (ed.) *The Encyclopedia of Extraterrestrial Encounters* New York: 2001.

S17 Summers, M. *The Werewolf* London: 1933.

S18 Sunlin, M. *Water Dragons* London: 1997.

T1   Tchernine, O. *The Yeti* London: 1970.

T2   Thorpe, B. *Northern Mythology* London: 1851.

T2/A Thompson, C.J.S. *The Mystery and Lore of Monsters* New York: 1970.

T3   Trevelyan, M. *Folklore and Folk Stories of Wales* London:1909.

T4   Trubshaw, B. *Dragon-Slaying Myths* Loughborough: 1993.

W*   Walters, D. *Chinese Mythology* London: 1992.

W"   Walton, B. (ed.) *Mount Shasta; Home of the Ancients* Mokrlumne Hill: 1985.

W   Wasson, B. *Sasquatch Apparitions* Bend: 1979.

W1   Wales, T. *Sussex Customs, Curiosities and Country Lore* Southampton: 1990.

W2   Werner, A. *Myths and Legends of the Bantu* London: 1933.

W4   Wildman, S. *Black Horsemen* London: 1971.

W5   Wilkins, H. *Secret Cities of South America* London: 1950.

W5*   Williams, M. *Supernatural Investigation* Bodmin: 1993.

W6   Wilson, R. *Everything is Under Control* London: 1999.

Y   Young, R. and J.D. *Ozark Ghost Stories* Little Rock: 1995.

Z1   Zarzynski, J. *Champ: Beyond the Legend* Wilton: 1988.

Z2   Zarynski, J. *Monster Wrecks of Loch Ness and Lake Champlain* Wilton: 1986.

Periodicals

#1   *Animals and Men*

#2   *Crypto Chronicle*

#3   *CryptoDominion*

#4   *Cryptozoology*

#5   *Dead of Night*

#6   *Folklore*

#7   *Fate*

#8   *Fortean Studies*

#9   *Fortean Times*

#10   *INFO*

#11   *North American Bio-Fortean Review*

#12   *Strange Magazine*

#13   *Witness*

#14   *Journal of American Folklore*

#15   *Bilk*

#16   *Encounters*

#17   *Lincoln Journal*

#18   *Athena*

Internet chatroom

Sightings

Websites

In listing these websites, usually either the title of the website or its address is given, rarely both; but a search engine will readily provide the address of the website if only the title is provided.

1   Centre for Fortean Zoology [www.cfz.org.uk]
2   www.cryptozoology.com
3   pibburns
4   Encyclopedia Mythica
5   Occultopedia
6   Cryptozoologix
7   Serene Dragon
8   Crypto Chronicle
9   Loren Coleman
10   Crypto
11   www.dudeman.net
12   FarShores
13   Friends of Bigfoot
14   Franko's Universe
15   CryptozooArchives
16   www.monstertracks.com
17   Weird Wisconsin
18   Paranormal Researchers of Ontario
19   www.cryptoz.freeserves.com
20   anomalyinfo
21   www.beastwatch.co.uk
22   Ben Roesch
23   www.messybeasts.com
24   homins
25   Cryptozoological Realms
26   Gareth Long's Encyclopedia of Monsters
27   Maria-brazil.org/myths.htm
28   www.paranormalnews.com
29   Kentucky Cryptids
30   Cryprodominion
31   British Hominid Research
32   Online Lake Cryptid Directory
33   Arkansas Monsters
34   GUST
35   Cryptozoology by Region
36   Ohio Cryptids
37   Gryttie homepage
38   Legend of One-Eye
39   www.hidges.com
40   www.meta-religions.com
41   Virtual Institute of Cryptozoology
42   www.beastwatch.com

43 www.skygaze.com
44 www.dragonsunlimited.tripod.com
45 www.messybeast.com
46 Okefenokee X-Files
47 Ron Schaffner
48 www.forteanfieldguide.com
49 BJ's Crypro Chronicle
50 Cryptozoology by Charles Carlta
51 Matthew Bille
52 Rich La Monica's Northeastern Ohio's Researchable Cryptids
53 Dave's Mythological Creatures
54 Paranormal and Crypto
55 www.urbanlegendsabout.com
56 Franche-Comte Website
57 www.pantheon.com
58 Cryptozoo
59 Page of Shadow
60 www.ukbigcats.co.uk
61 www.felinomania.com
62 www.ueuarios.lycos.co/cryptozoo
63 www.pers.wanadoo.fr/danuc/western.htm
64 www.linoln.org
65 Crypto Web
66 www.geocities.com/bigfootrus/monkeyman.html
67 www.red4.co.uk
68 www.skell.org/SKELL/mythhim.htm
69 www.unexplained-mysteries.com
70 www.creatureventures.com
71 www.forestry.sarawak.gov.mg
72 www.npr.org
73 www.uspto.gov
74 Strangeark
75 Draconopedia
76 Cryptokeeper
77 www.pers.wanadoo.crypto
78 Mystery Magazine
79 Shadowlands
80 X-Project Paranormal Magazine
81 www.cryptozoo.com
82 Cryptozoologia
83 www.strangenation.com.au
84 Australian Yowie Research
85 Fortean Times
86 www.mysteries.pwp.blueyonder.co.uk
87 www.pterodactyl.tv
88 www.cryptozoology.sl

89 Ohio Bigfoot Research and Study Group
90 www.rain.org/campinternet/bigfoot/bigfoot-folklore.html
91 Internet Virtual Bigfoot Conference
92 www.wesclark.com
93 Hairy Hominid Archive
94 www.n2.net/prey/bigfoot/creature.htm
95 www.monsterinthelake.com
96 Crypto Cumbria
97 www.marsearthconnection.com
98 www.bubernet/Basque/Folklore/folk.html
99 www.paranormal.miningco.com
100 Blather
101 www.shadowlands.net
102 Dragons of York
103 www.paranormality.com
104 Natural History Museum
105 Monsters You Never Heard Of
106 www.mysteriousbritain.co.uk
107 www.mysterymag.com
108 www.ksks:essortment/com/wampuscat_rnvr.htm
109 www.johnsrealmsonline.com/paranormal/wampus-cat/index.html
110 Weird New Jersey
111 Native American Myth
112 Bigfoot Encounters
113 www.pucabob@aol.com
114 camp internet
115 Creature Chronicles
116 www.geocities.com/Area5/Hdlw/1776/PARKEK.HTM
117 www.virtualask.cnn/current_issue/fish_get_not_talking.html
118 Cryptoquest
119 www.megaraptors.com
120 www.american_monsters.com
121 www.trueauthority.com/crytozoology
122 www.werewolfpage.com
123 www.strange.info
124 www.cryptozoo.monstrous.com
125 www.web.raex.com/~obsidian
126 www.expressandstar.com
127 www.fortunecity.com
128 Beastwatch UK
129 www.burlington-news.net
130 www.folklore.bc.ca
131 www.indigenouspeople.net
132 Norka
133 www.mjoesormen.nw
134 www.probertencyclopaedia.com

135 Bestiarium
136 www.floridasmart.com
137 Flood Stories from Around the World
138 www.mythome.org
139 www.unsolvedmysteries.com
140 www.angelfire.com/realm/eubyfilesO/hauntedoregonbigfoot.html
141 www.thisisbradford.co.uk
142 the.honoluladvertiser.com
143 Irish Lake Monsters
144 Ohio Cryptids - Winged Things
145 www.worldofthestrange.com
146 www.paranormaldatabase.com
147 Bigfoot Encounters
148 expage.com/alabamaapeman
149 Weird Wiltshire
150 www.mothmanlives.com
151 Fantastic Fish of the Middle Ages

Additional Material Consulted

Aineamneacha Planda agus Ainmhithe Dublin: 1978.
Philips, C.H. *Handbook of Oriental History* London: 1951.

Printed in the United States
131736LV00002B/2/A